DOING DIGITAL METHODS

Sara Miller McCune founded SAGE Publishing in 1965 to support the dissemination of usable knowledge and educate a global community. SAGE publishes more than 1000 journals and over 800 new books each year, spanning a wide range of subject areas. Our growing selection of library products includes archives, data, case studies and video. SAGE remains majority owned by our founder and after her lifetime will become owned by a charitable trust that secures the company's continued independence.

Los Angeles | London | New Delhi | Singapore | Washington DC | Melbourne

DOING
DIGITAL
METHODS

RICHARD ROGERS

Los Angeles | London | New Delhi
Singapore | Washington DC | Melbourne

Los Angeles | London | New Delhi
Singapore | Washington DC | Melbourne

SAGE Publications Ltd
1 Oliver's Yard
55 City Road
London EC1Y 1SP

SAGE Publications Inc.
2455 Teller Road
Thousand Oaks, California 91320

SAGE Publications India Pvt Ltd
B 1/I 1 Mohan Cooperative Industrial Area
Mathura Road
New Delhi 110 044

SAGE Publications Asia-Pacific Pte Ltd
3 Church Street
#10-04 Samsung Hub
Singapore 049483

Editor: Mila Steele
Production editor: Ian Antcliff
Copyeditor: Richard Leigh
Proofreader: Neil Dowden
Indexer: Martin Hargreaves
Marketing manager: Ben Griffin-Sherwood
Cover design: Shaun Mercier
Typeset by: C&M Digitals (P) Ltd, Chennai, India
Printed in the UK by Bell & Bain Ltd, Glasgow

Library of Congress Control Number: 2018953682

British Library Cataloguing in Publication data

A catalogue record for this book is available from the British Library

ISBN 978-1-5264-4471-4
ISBN 978-1-5264-4472-1 (pbk)
ISBN 978-1-5264-8799-5 (pbk & interactive ebk)

At SAGE we take sustainability seriously. Most of our products are printed in the UK using responsibly sourced papers and boards. When we print overseas we ensure sustainable papers are used as measured by the PREPS grading system. We undertake an annual audit to monitor our sustainability.

CONTENTS

ACKNOWLEDGEMENTS

The New Media Research Methods course, upon which this book is based, has had a particular working model and rhythm. The model and rhythm are akin to a 'sprint', where participants undertake a research project (encapsulated in each chapter of this book) in a single, pressure-packed week. In a flipped classroom approach, the initial tool training is video tutorial homework. Students are required to watch the video tutorials which are software walk-throughs, a common video genre on the web, and itself a digital method (Light, 2017). Subsequent hands-on training takes place through actual project work in a lab setting, with moveable tables and own laptops rather than in a 'computer room' or a tiered lecture hall.

Having read the chapter and viewed the tutorial, to kick off the lab session, groups of students pitch project ideas, in the form of five slides — introduction to subject matter, research questions, methods, expected outcomes and 'why is it interesting?' The groups of students (no more than four) work at the same table, and teachers are on hand during the sessions where data are being collected and analysed, and nitty-gritty questions may be posed, such as 'what does this setting do?'

Students write research reports weekly (or bi-weekly if one would like to dedicate a week to discussing related academic literature). After they have handed in their research report, they are given the next chapter for the following week's assignment. The course finishes with a week-long data sprint, where there is a theme (e.g., migration crisis) and the students apply whichever methods they have learned that best fit the research questions they pose.

Issue or subject matter experts are often brought in to the sprints and asked to (1) explain the state of art of their field, (2) their current analytical needs and (3) what web or social media data may add. These subject matter expert pitches form the basis for sprint projects from which participants may choose.

The city government of Amsterdam made inquiries about Airbnb which led to a project on the hotelization of private apartments, as was found through Airbnb image analysis. Greenpeace International were interested in how their campaigns resonated during a UN climate summit, which resulted in a critique of issue celebrities and their symbolic power (Couldry, 2001), given the attention to the appearances of Leonardo DiCaprio and Emma Watson at the summit, rather than to NGO campaigns. These are only two Amsterdam-based prompts that led to compelling projects, but the model has been applied across digital methods and sprint-oriented courses elsewhere, too (Laursen, 2017; Venturini et al., 2018). It also explains in part the issue-oriented focus found throughout the cases and sample projects in the book (see also Rogers et al., 2015).

The projects described in this book have been the product of these sprints, undertaken together with students, the local Digital Methods Initiative staff members as well as international participants. The Issuecrawler mapping of the 'old guard' and the 'new right' benefited from the source list-building technique, termed associative query snowballing, developed with Natalia Sánchez Querubín. The overall mapping of some 20 countries, supported by the Open Society Foundations and published as 'Right-wing formations in Europe and their counter-measures: An online mapping', had a multitude of co-authors: Jan Bajec, Federica Bardelli, Lisa Bergenfelz, Sharon Brehm, Alessandro Brunetti, Gabriele Colombo, Giulia De Amicis, Carlo De Gaetano, Orsolya Gulyas, Eelke Hermens, Catalina Iorga, Saskia Kok, Juliana Paiva, Olga Paraskevopoulou, Simeona Petkova, Radmila Radojevic, Tommaso Ranzana, Ea Ryberg Due, Natalia Sanchez, Catherine Somzé and Lonneke van der Velden. The Issuecrawler software itself, supported by the Open Society Institute, was developed with Noortje Marres, David Heath, Suzi Wells, Marieke van Dijk, Auke Touwslager, Erik Borra, Koen Martens and Andrei Mogoutov. An earlier version of the chapter was published in 2018 as 'Issuecrawling: Building lists of URLs and mapping website networks', in Celia Lury, Patricia T. Clough, Una Chung, Rachel Fensham, Sybille Lammes, Angela Last, Mike Michael and Emma Uprichard (eds.), *Routledge Handbook of Interdisciplinary Research Methods*, London: Routledge, 169-175.

The techniques described in the Internet Censorship chapter were first developed in a project with the Open Net Initiative at the University of Toronto and the Berkman Center at Harvard, together with Ron Diebert and Rafal Rohozinski. Erik Borra developed the software that fetches the URLs through proxies. Jidi Guo's project on the effectiveness of Chinese Internet censorship is described in some detail.

Making a screencast documentary of an archived webpage was inspired by Jon Udell's 'heavy metal umlaut' video on the coming into being of a Wikipedia article. 'Google and the Politics of Tabs' was the first one of its kind that colleagues and I made, with production by Menno Endt and Theun Hendrikx and research by Laura van der Vlies, Kim de Groot, Esther Weltevrede and Erik Borra, who developed the software to extract links from the Wayback Machine and array them in order to play back the history of a webpage in the style of time-lapse photography. Emile den Tex created the screenshot generator. Two compelling examples of video projects are discussed: the evolution of the *New York Times* online (nytimes.com) by Eelke Hermens, and that of theknot.com by Maya Livio, Jules Mataly and Mathias Schuh, where changes over the years to the wedding planner website show the commercialization of the web (and marriage). A previous edition of the chapter appeared in 2017 as 'Doing Web history with the Internet Archive: screencast documentaries', *Internet Histories: Digital Technology, Culture and Society*, 1(1/2), 1–13.

The search as research chapter, originally co-written with Esther Weltevrede, benefits from the work undertaken on the Google Scraper and later the Lippmannian Device, developed during the MACOSPOL project, Mapping Controversies on Science for Politics, led by Bruno Latour. The Scraper itself, together with the DMI Firefox plug-in that allowed the scraping to be off-loaded to the individual user's browser, was developed by Erik Borra and Koen Martins. The revamped Search Engine Scraper that includes multiple engines was the work of Stijn Peeters. The 'source distance' method that is built into the Google Scraper was developed at the first Digital Methods Summer School, where the project with Anne Helmond, Sabine Niederer, Bram Nijhof, Laura van der Vlies and Esther Weltevrede concerned how close to the top of the web are the climate change sceptics as well as which animals are most prominent in the climate change issue space. The 'Rights Types' project, undertaken with Vera Bekema, Liliana Bounegru, Andrea Fiore, Anne Helmond, Simon Marschall, Sabine Niederer, Bram Nijhof and Elena Tiis, makes use of an ambiguous query ("rights") in multiple languages in order to perform cross-cultural comparison. The triangulation tool for list comparison, developed by Erik Borra, received impetus from a project by Natalia Sánchez Querubín that compares the country origins of sources returned for the query, "Amazonia". The Craig Venter example derives from a workshop at Lancaster University with Adrian MacKenzie, and the technique of mapping the issue agenda of a movement or network (such as that of the global human rights network) benefited from collaboration with Charli Carpenter at the University of Massachusetts Amherst.

The observation that Wikipedia articles on the 'same' subject matter in different languages have 'cultural points of view' may be traced to the project comparing Srebrenica articles in Bosnian, Serbian and Dutch (among other languages), undertaken by Emina Sendijarevic. The tools for article comparison (such as the Wikipedia Cross-Lingual Image Analysis) were developed by Erik Borra. The Wikipedia categories scraper, which may be used for cross-lingual event analysis, was developed during the Digital Methods Summer School project comparing Brexit articles, with analysis by Viola Bernacchi, Carlo De Gaetano, Simon Gottschalk, Sabine Niederer, Warren Pearce and Mariasilvia Poltronieri. The comparison of Auschwitz articles (in German, Polish and Portuguese) was performed by students at the University of Mannheim, Nathalie Bielka, Helena Buhl and Monica dos Santos. They found that only the Polish article discussed the controversy surrounding the notion of 'Polish death camps'.

The proposition of debanalizing Twitter and turning it into a story-telling machine that recounts events on the ground and in social media is rooted in the #iranelection RT project conducted with Erik Borra, Marieke van Dijk, Sabine Niederer, Michael Stevenson and Esther Weltevrede, and shown at Arts Santa Mònica in Barcelona, together with the IP Browser, in the Cultures of Change exhibition curated by Josep Perelló and Pau Alsina. Arraying the top three retweeted tweets by day, in chronological order, is among the many modules built into DMI-TCAT, the Twitter Capture and Analysis Toolset, developed by Erik Borra, Bernhard Rieder and Emile den Tex.

The Facebook analysis relies in part on Netvizz, the Facebook data extraction software by Bernhard Rieder. The most engaged-with content analysis technique was developed during the counter-jihadism winter school, 'What does the Internet add? Studying extremism and counter-jihadism online', a collaboration with the London-based NGO, Hope not Hate.

The analysis of the Facebook page, 'Stop Islamization of the World', was conducted by Ana Crisostomo, Juliana Marques, Joe Mier and Despoina Mountanea. The exercises on studying memes were aided by discussions with Marc Tuters.

The Cross-Platform analysis techniques, where Instagram and Tumblr tools make an appearance, benefits from a teaching unit created by Bernhard Rieder, who also was behind many of the techniques discussed in the YouTube chapter. The sample projects comparing content across platforms about Aylan Kurdi and the Cologne New Year's incidents were led by Marloes Geboers. An earlier rendition of the chapter appeared in 2018 as 'Digital Methods for Cross-Platform Analysis', in Jean Burgess, Alice Marwick and Thomas Poell (eds), *SAGE Handbook of Social Media*, London: Sage, pp. 91-110.

The data journalism chapter has been inspired by exchanges with Liliana Bounegru and Jonathan Gray, who together with Tommaso Venturini and Michele Mauri, compiled the 'Field Guide to Fake News', where we also studied Russian disinformation campaigning. Mischa Szpirt was instrumental in refining the Google Analytics ID network discovery technique. The EXIF camera data extraction technique was aided by software reworked by Emile den Tex in the Gezi Park (Istanbul) research project, a collaboration with Greenpeace International and Soenke Lorenzen. The painstaking work of identifying the cameras taking the iconic 'Lady in Red' and other pictures and looking up the cameras' retail prices was undertaken by Giulia De Amicis, Federica Bardelli, Carlo De Gaetano, Saskia Kok, Sandrine Roginsky, Saya Saulière and Thijs Waardenburg.

The more conceptual chapters on positioning digital methods as well as query design had their forerunners. The positioning piece in an earlier form appeared in 2015 as 'Digital Methods for Web Research', in Robert A. Scott and Stephen M. Kosslyn (eds), *Emerging Trends in the Behavioral and Social Sciences*, Hoboken, NJ: Wiley. A previous version of the query design chapter appeared in 2017 as 'Foundations of digital methods: Query design', in Mirko Schaefer and Karin van Es (eds), *The Datafied Society: Studying Culture through Data*, Amsterdam: Amsterdam University Press, pp. 75–94.

The book was made possible by the students, participants, designers, programmers, teachers and staff taking part in the New Media Research Methods course as well as the Digital Methods Winter and Summer Schools at the University of Amsterdam. The information designers from Density Design, Milan, have been pivotal in the development and rendering of the research: Elena Aversa, Matteo Azzi, Federica Bardelli, Andrea Benedetti, Agata Brilli, Angeles Briones, Gabriele Colombo, Giulia Corona, Giulia De Amicis, Carlo De Gaetano, Alessandra Del Nero, Serena Del Nero, Tommaso Elli, Giacomo Flaim, Beatrice Gobbo, Stefania Guerra, Michele Invernizzi, Irina Kasatkina, Michele Mauri, Marco Mezzadra, Claudia Pazzaglia, Chiara Piva, Mariasilvia Poltronieri, Tommaso Renzini, Donato Ricci, Chiara Riente and Ginevra Terenghi. Special thanks for the dedication on the part of the Digital Methods teachers as well as the organizers of multiple Summer and Winter Schools: Erik Borra, Liliana Bounegru, Jonathan Gray, Saskia Kok, Sabine Niederer, Bernhard Rieder, Natalia Sánchez Querubín, Fernando van der Vlist and Esther Weltevrede.

BEFORE BEGINNING DIGITAL METHODS

Digital methods and methodologies

This book is an elaboration on the practice of collecting data online and undertaking contemporary research with digital methods. The digital methods described hereafter are often built into tools and are thus 'programmed methods' (Borra and Rieder, 2014). They evolve with the medium, meaning that they are updated when a web service changes or deprecated when it is discontinued. In between these states, there may be workarounds or manual alternatives. While digital methods may often make use of certain software tools, they do not solely depend on them, and thus also should be considered digital methodologies. These are more generalized ways and means of performing online research, often just with a browser.

These generalized ways of performing online research include building URL lists out of search engine results in order to map networks on the web and perform internet censorship research. There is also a foundational, keyword list-building technique, used for 'query design' and doing 'search as research' with a repurposed Google for term resonance analysis and the study of bias. Other methods include compiling historical screenshots from the Internet Archive and narrating screencast documentaries about web history. This book introduces techniques for comparing the images, references and tables of contents of the 'same' Wikipedia article across different language versions, posing questions about cross-cultural comparison and the politics of memory. There are how-to's on performing single-platform and cross-platform analysis (with Twitter, Facebook, Instagram and others) in order to research dominant voice, concern, commitment and other 'critical analytics', or to undertake 'remote event analysis'. There are procedures to locate the content on Facebook that has elicited the most engagement, inquiring at the same time into the formats that circulate well (such as memes) and the groups animated by them (such as the alt-right). Finally, there are recipes for detecting trackers and other third-party elements on websites in order to show (for example) the reliance by radical groups on Silicon Valley technology. One may also identify the owners – be they individuals or media groups – of websites purveying junk news or undertaking disinformation campaigns. Digital methods thereby enter the realm of data journalism research.

Foundations of digital methods

The early chapters introduce two core skills – building keyword and source lists. Keywords may be part of programmes or anti-programmes, such as 'blood diamonds' and 'conflict minerals', and building lists of them (be they the words themselves or hashtags) enables one to design a query that answers research questions about the uptake and circulation of one campaign or initiative over another. Using search engines in creative ways (such as the so-called 'associative query snowball' technique) results in source lists that can be used in internet censorship research, where one checks whether or not a website is blocked in a particular country. One can also deploy such lists in mapping networks on the web, such as those of the right-wing extremists and the new right, in order to discover and interpret links between them. Subsequently, these keyword and source building skills are applied when doing 'search as research', 'single-platform studies' (such as Twitter and Facebook) as well as 'cross-platform analysis' that also includes Instagram (and in passing Tumblr as well as YouTube), as touched on above. They are also useful for building lists of junk news, disinformation or other thematically poignant sites and pages in order to discover who is behind them as well as what is linked to them, and ultimately make journalistic accounts.

The foundations of digital methods are the spine of the book, and throughout its pages the recurring themes are how to formulate a research question as well as how to tell a story of the findings or outcomes. The starting point for the formulation of a research question is to invert a current claim, be it from the academic literature or the intellectual or tech press, where many conceptual innovations in new media and digital culture originate (e.g., crowdsourcing and 'filter bubble') or claims arise (e.g., continuous partial attention). Making findings and creating accounts of them are detailed initially in network story-telling techniques (in the web network mapping chapter), but also in narrating a screencast documentary of the history of a web page. Formulating research questions and telling stories with findings are also emphasized throughout the internet censorship, search engines, Wikipedia, and the three social media chapters, especially in the sample projects inquiring into the Falun Gong, climate change sceptics, Srebrenica, Auschwitz, #iranelection, Aylan Kurdi, Russian influence campaigning and others.

Doing digital methods: Stepping behind the scenes

For those expecting otherwise, digital methods are not single-click operations in the immaculate conception of 'finished' work with stunning graphics, but rather often manual and deliberate proceedings, with the occasional do-over. For example, for studying web history with the Internet Archive, the researcher is asked to choose a webpage and compile historical screenshots using a so-called Wayback Machine link ripper as well as a screenshot generator. In the research protocol – for capturing the changes to a webpage and making a movie of them – one step reads, 'Go to bed and check your results in the morning', followed by 'see if all went well' in the auto-capturing of the historical screenshots that occurred overnight. The advice not only gives a sense of the social life surrounding the research practice, but also the occasions when the tool may turn up the unexpected, including gaps in the historical collection.

Where in one case one may allow the machine to run overnight, in another active monitoring is required. When running a scraper, one might overhear a researcher asking another, 'Did you just close your laptop?' 'Yes, why?' 'That means that the scraper stopped working. You'll have to relaunch it.' Such exchanges point up some normalcies of collecting web data, even since the advent of the social media API, and its supplanting of scraping. Facebook's API for one has changed repeatedly over the years (through versioning), on each occasion narrowing the scope of what is available to the researcher. In the wake of the Cambridge Analytica scandal, when some 80 million Facebook users unknowingly had their profiles and likes harvested, changes have been more abrupt than phased, pointing up another potential obstacle faced by the researcher – the prospects of sudden lock-out, and the need for a workaround or a manual procedure. By way of prefacing the book, I would like to step behind the scenes, and provide a series of insights about doing digital methods, including some admonitions as well as bright spots per methods chapter.

Mapping networks on the web

The issuecrawling chapter, on how and why to undertake hyperlink analysis and network mapping, illustrates how an expert practitioner learns how a medium has changed. That is, over the past number of years, and perhaps moving forward, the web has become 'dated' by social media. Websites as well as blogs are only occasionally edited, lie fallow or have been taken over by a domain reseller. Link lists, a staple of the early web's information culture, have disappeared, or are not up to date. Such a state of affairs, which its co-inventor Tim Berners-Lee warned of on the web's 25th anniversary, also leads to research opportunities. Which parts of the web are still fresh and engaged (perhaps the governmental), and which ones have embraced social media at the expense of the open web (perhaps the non-governmental), since that is where the people are, so to speak. Indeed, one can research the state of the open web with hyperlink analysis and be faced with the result that the links lead to social media platforms, meaning that platform studies inevitably are the next phase in the research. Some skip directly to studying social media, which in a sense reinforces the trend of the drying up of the open web.

Internet censorship research

The internet censorship chapter, introducing heuristics for source list building, discusses how to study (through documentation) the banning of web materials in such countries as China and Iran. It also provides an elaboration of the most significant research questions in the area, given that at the outset it seems censorship research consists of the answer to the deceptively simple question of whether or not a website is blocked. We have taught these materials with students and researchers from the countries under study, but the main issue nowadays is the extent to which state regimes are able to learn they are under observation, and care to act on that knowledge. Given the rise of state surveillance online (including the revelations concerning the work in authoritarian countries by the Italian company, the Hacking Team, and doubtless others), we no longer teach this module with a large group of students and suggest internet censorship research is undertaken in well-supervised, less experimental settings.

Screencast documentaries with the Internet Archive

The web history chapter employs screen-capturing software that utilizes the output of a scraper of Wayback Machine URLs to compile them into a movie, ready for recording a voiceover narrative. Rereading that sentence, you will note there are a few steps to creating a screencast documentary of the history of one webpage. Indeed, once one is able to compile and playback the screenshots, in a movie, a couple of days of work may have been expended, only for the researcher to realize that creating and recording a voiceover narrative with a compelling storyline requires yet more time investment. Indeed, that project may be the most arduous, and oftentimes the most rewarding for its creative output.

Repurposing Google

'Search as research' (with the Google Scraper) breaks Google's terms of service, for one is not allowed, in its so-called 'browse wrap' contract, to query Google outside of its search bar, save results, or create a derivative work from them. It would be worthwhile to work with alternative engines that do not have such restrictions or are less diligent in blocking non-standard uses, but given Google's dominance, both its study ('Google studies') as well as social research with Google are considered important enough to ask the engine (and company) for its forbearance. At issue, however, is the practicality of batch-querying Google, for it continues to block such practices by occasionally or frequently issuing a 'captcha' or other human-user verification checks which the researcher has to overcome, in order for the work to continue. Thus, it is very much a semi-automated, small-scale data collection technique. The newer Search Engine Scraper tool (accessing and studying a longer list of engines) provides a workaround and offers the capacity for cross-engine studies.

Comparing Wikipedia language versions

Unlike commercial engines and platforms that block research and break tools with their 'updates', Wikipedia is remarkably stable and research-friendly. Both the platform as well as the tools built upon it have a higher likelihood than others of remaining in place. The method described in the chapter – and the sample project on Srebrenica, also detailed in my previous *Digital Methods* book (Rogers, 2013b) – relies on a remarkable finding that upon reflection seems mundane: the 'same' articles in the various language versions of Wikipedia may have telling differences, worthy of study. Writing an account of these differences has proven to be one of the most compelling modules, however much by this point some may wish to lighten the subject matter, away from the Srebrenica massacre or the subtle differences between how the Polish and German Wikipedia language versions discuss 'Auschwitz', which are the sample project examples.

Twitter as story-telling machine

Twitter studies are often taught with DMI-TCAT, the Twitter Capture and Analysis Tool, which requires central installation on a server at the university where the students or researchers are located. While 'easy' to install, given the instructions on the GitHub page, it is a technical and administrative threshold. It also requires resources, such as a fast server, lest the users wait and watch progress bars. Once installed, it could or should be populated with data sets that are of contemporary interest, such as tweet collections of Donald Trump and Hillary Clinton supporters (from the 2016 US presidential elections), or a #metoo collection on the movement to address sexual harassment. As tweet collections become sizeable, one also can boast of them (millions of tweets at our disposal!), though there are growing pains. Tweet collections (unless stopped) would accumulate from the date they are started, and over time additional servers may be necessary. Thus, data collections move forward in time from when they are launched, rather than backwards. Twitter has paid services for historical tweets, through their own API (Gnip). Resellers such as Texifter once provided an interface to allow the researcher to obtain a cost estimate for a tweet collection, which is in itself of relevance for research. What would a robust historical tweet collection concerning climate change actually cost? The answer can be concretely applied to data commodification critiques. Alternatively, one could import another research group's historical tweet collections by asking for a set of tweet IDs, and then recapturing them from the Twitter API that TCAT uses. In the recompilation data from any deleted tweets or accounts would no longer be part of the tweet collection. Inasmuch as that importation is possible, it is another technical hurdle requiring expertise and resources.

Identifying engaging content on Facebook

Facebook allows for historical data collection, so one is able to collect the data from a Facebook page, or a curated set of pages, from their inception, unless it has been deactivated or deleted. There are three methods for Facebook studies discussed: one that compiles the highlights of a Facebook page over time and plays them back, another that performs inter-liked page network analysis, and a third that outputs the 'most engaged-with' content of a set of pages for a particular period of time. The third technique is most often used, and the first least often, at least as we have employed them. Earlier Facebook studies of friend networks and profile interests, or 'tastes and ties' work, are now improbable, given changes to Facebook's API in early 2015. Postdemographics research, the notion I put forth in the *Digital Methods* book, is the comparative study of a set of friends' interests, such as the interests of Hillary Clinton's and Donald Trump's Facebook friends, in order to make an inquiry into the culture wars or other questions about the politics of media and preference. The work would have to be performed manually these days.

Co-linked, inter-liked and cross-hashtagged content

Cross-platform analysis, such as querying the 'same' hashtag on Twitter as well as Instagram (e.g., #selfie), is less straightforward than it sounds, given distinctive platform cultures or vernaculars, and the differences in what the counts may mean. On Instagram there are more hashtags used per post than on Twitter. The chapter on cross-platform studies provides examples of using the same digital object in two or more platforms and comparing their use across each platform, making findings on how to characterize a platform's relationship with news, for example. Apart from the specificity of platform cultures and the types of research questions one may pose, cross-platform studies are reliant on each of the single platform's APIs, unless manual work is performed. Instagram, for one, often pulls the plug on researcher use of its API. Online token generators or other access strategies (software scripts) for an Instagram Scraper may provide a workaround.

Tracker analysis

Finally, the detection work behind tracker analysis and Google Analytics ID owner searches brings an investigative journalism spirit to digital methods training that engages researchers, though there is a risk that the sleuthing and 'open source intelligence' gathering does not turn up anything 'juicy', so to speak. It also may be the case that both analytics companies and website owners implement new masking or cloaking techniques to conceal owner identities, thereby rendering certain fingerprinting and reverse look-up services less useful. The chapter also describes procedures to study the history of tracking per website or website type, employing the Tracker Tracker software (built atop Ghostery), and loading it with historical versions of webpages from the Wayback Machine of the Internet Archive. In comparison to the ever-evolving masking strategies of website owners, such an approach to the study of the history of surveillance is likely to abide.

YouTube teardown

Finally, there is a series of methods put forward to 'tear down' YouTube, an exercise in platform studies where privileging mechanisms may be laid bare. YouTube recommends videos in at least three manners: when watching, there are videos in the carousel that are 'up next'. Lists are returned when one searches. Channels subscribe to other channels and feature other ones; additionally, there are related channels. Through capturing the outputs of each mode of watching, one can strive to break down how these recommendation systems work, and for whom. For which subject matters and queries are the native YouTubers (with high subscription counts), (junk) news channels or more establishment voices granted the authority and privilege to be viewed?

Doing digital methods in the contemporary situation

Behind the making of this book is a decade-long exploration of how to undertake research *with* the web, rather than just about it. The general digital methods approach may be historicized, for it shares an outlook and practice from a web whose data may be scraped, mashed up, and outputted in visualizations that can make findings, tell a story or otherwise describe a current state of affairs. They are very much webby methods and techniques, built on and for the open web. With the rise of social media, and especially the API taking over from the scraper as main data source, data collection has become in part API critique. Is there researcher access? How generous are the data limits? How does the API shape what may be researched? How does it obstruct research? How to undertake research when the API is shut down?

The rise of the social web over the info-web (or social media over the open web) also has brought with it human subjects. Of course, human subjects were always present on the web, but in the info-web period one was apt to research organizational and issue networks rather than personal and social ones. Upon its arrival, social media heralded the prospect for social network analysis, and at the same time brought with it a palpable site not only for a heightened awareness of the ethics of internet research but also for its ethical study. The distinction, elaborated upon below, is between an ethical research practice and the study of the ethics of existing (and proposed) internet research.

Data ethics

Taking up the latter (to begin with), critical studies on data ethics address two assumptions that often underlie research with social media data: first, that online data is already public, and therefore its collection for research purposes is not a delicate ethical matter; and second, that since the social media user agreed to the terms of service, the researcher can fall back on those terms and use them as cover. Although online data is already public, and the terms have been agreed to, a social media user does not necessarily expect that her data will be used outside of the context in which it was originally posted, despite terms of service (on Twitter, for example) clearly stating that the data may be employed for academic research (as well as marketing purposes and in-house software improvement). Taking as a starting point the user's so-called contextual privacy is crucial in the study of the ethics of existing (and proposed) internet research (Nissenbaum, 2011).

The social media platforms themselves have developed privacy settings as well as rules and guidelines that are oriented towards users and are of interest to ethics researchers. Since 2015, Facebook, for one, has only allowed the harvesting of 'pages', rather than personal profiles and friend networks. Thus, as mentioned, social network styles of analysis ('tastes and ties') are no longer supported by the application programming interface (API), so to speak. The platforms also routinely block scrapers that may try to collect such data. The newly typical research practised with Facebook pages consists of inter-liked page network analysis as well as most engaged-with content (variously weighted sums of likes, reactions, shares and comments), where the individual user generally is not identified, though a particularly popular post will be. In social issue-oriented work, the engaged-with posts are often from the press, governmental or non-governmental sources, but also may be from individuals or aliases readily identifiable with some online discovery technique, beginning with search and extending to reverse look-ups of available usernames, where one takes note of the use of an alias on other platforms, and hunts for real names or other identifiable material. Another, related issue is whether to cite these individuals and aliases as authors. They are not authors in the sense of those who have rendered a cultural product through the sweat of the brow, though an act of creation may be wrought in a mere few words. Does a high level of engagement constitute evidence of creative expression, making the 'data' into a quotable phrase? A single tweet someone has written could be found (through sentiment analysis, for example) to be the angriest or most joyful of all election-related tweets. Is it thus deserving of authorship, and cited, or should it be anonymized? Does it matter if it is posted by a readily identifiable individual who is not a public figure?

Indeed, if following guidelines that invite one to be 'ethics compliant', here it would be necessary to examine the analytical outputs for individual user traces, and consider redacting the user upon publication, not to mention in any aggregated data set that would be made published or held for research use. Here a good compliance practice is to seek to redact individuals including aliases, while retaining public figures as well as organization names.

If one decides that online users posting content are not authors, one may seek a form of 'informed consent', which for small data sets could be undertaken through direct messaging. On a medium-sized data set, more elaborately, one also could consider using a research bot that would inform Twitter account holders that their user accounts (and selected tweets) would be in the analytical output. Having given a description of those outputs and the accompanying research project, the researcher would invite the subject to opt out. An opt-in bot, or manual procedure, also could be developed at the outset of a project.

PART I

BEGINNING

DIGITAL

METHODS

ONE

POSITIONING DIGITAL METHODS

Digital methods are research strategies
for dealing with the ephemeral and
unstable nature of online data

Digital methods for internet-related research

Digital methods are techniques for the study of societal change and cultural condition with online data. They make use of available digital objects such as the hyperlink, tag, time-stamp, like, share, and retweet, and seek to learn from how the objects are treated by the methods built into the dominant devices online, such as Google Web Search. They endeavour to repurpose the online methods and services with a social research outlook. Ultimately the question is the location of the baseline, and whether the findings made may be grounded online.

Digital methods as a research practice are part of the computational turn in the humanities and social sciences, and as such may be positioned alongside other recent approaches, such as cultural analytics, culturomics, webometrics and altmetrics, where distinctions may be made about the types of data employed (natively digital or digitized) as well as method (written for the medium or migrated to it). The limitations of digital methods are also treated. Digital methods recognize the problems with web data, such as the impermanence of web services, and the instability of data streams, where for example APIs are reconfigured or discontinued. They also grapple with the quality of web data, and the challenges of longitudinal study, where for instance Twitter accounts and Facebook pages are deleted just as researchers are beginning to study the reach of Russian disinformation campaigning during the US presidential election (Albright, 2017).

When one raises the question of the web as a site for the study of social and cultural phenomena, a series of concerns arises. Web data are problematic. They have historical reputational issues, owing to the web's representation and study as a medium of self-publication as well as one of dubious repute, inhabited by pornographers and conspiracy theorists (Dean, 1998). This was the cyberspace period, with an anything-goes web, where it often was treated analytically as a separate realm, even a 'virtual society' (Woolgar, 2003).

Later, the web came to be known as an amateur production space for user-generated content (Jenkins, 2006). Nowadays the web is becoming a space for more than the study of online culture. Rather it has become a site to study a range of cultural and social issues, charting for example 'concerns of the electorate' from the 'searches they conduct', and 'the spread of arguments ... about political and other issues', among other questions concerning society at large (Lazer et al., 2009: 722; Watts, 2007). Of course, it also remains a site to study online culture and undertake medium research. Digital methods are approaches to studying both, a point I return to when taking up the question of whether one can remove medium artefacts (such as manipulated search engine results or bots) and have a purified subject of study.

Scrutinizing web data

As indicated, however, the web has had the general difficulty of meeting the standards of good data (Borgman, 2009). As such, web data are also candidates for a shift, however slight, in methodological outlook. If web data are often considered messy and poor, where could their value lie? The question could be turned around. Where and how are web data handled routinely and deftly? Digital methods seek to learn from the so-called methods of the medium, that is, how online devices treat web data (Rogers, 2009). Thus, digital methods are, first, the study of the methods embedded in the devices treating online data (Rieder, 2012). How do search engines (such as Google) treat hyperlinks, clicks, timestamps and other digital objects? How do platforms (such as Facebook) treat profile interests as well as user interactions such as liking, sharing, commenting and liking comments?

Digital methods, however, seek to introduce a social research outlook to the study of online devices. 'Nowcasting' (however newfangled the term for real-time forecasting) is a good example and serves as a case of how search engine queries may be employed to study social change (Ginsberg et al., 2009). The location and intensity of flu and flu-related queries have been used to chart the rising and falling incidence of flu in specific places. The 'places of flu' is an imaginative use of web data for social research, extending the range of 'trend' research that engines have been known for to date under such names as Google Trends, Google Insights for Search, Yahoo Buzz Log, Yahoo Clues, Bing Webmaster Keyword Research, AOL Search Trends, YouTube Keyword Tool, YouTube Trends, and the Google AdWords Keyword Tool (Raehsler, 2012; US Centers for Disease Control and Prevention, 2014). It is also a case where the baseline is not web data or the web, but rather the (triangulated) findings from traditional flu surveillance techniques used by the Centers for Disease Control and Prevention in the United States and its equivalents in other countries. Search engine query data are checked against the offline baseline of data from hospitals, clinics, laboratories, state agencies, and others. The offline becomes the check against which the quality of the online is measured.

For those seeking to employ web data to study social phenomena, the webometrician, Mike Thelwall, has suggested precisely such a course of action: ground the findings offline. Given the messiness of web data as well as the (historical) scepticism that accompanies its use in social research (as mentioned above), Thelwall et al. (2005: 81) relate the overall rationale for a research strategy that calls for offline correlation:

> One issue is the messiness of Web data and the need for data cleansing heuristics. The uncontrolled Web creates numerous problems in the interpretation of results ... Indeed a sceptical researcher could claim the obstacles are so great that all Web analyses lack value. One response to this is to demonstrate that Web data correlate significantly with some non-Web data in order to prove that the Web data are not wholly random.

Online groundedness

Digital methods raise the question of the prospects of online groundedness. When and under what conditions may findings be grounded with web data? One of the earlier cases that pointed up the prospects of web data as having a 'say' in the findings is journalistic and experimental. In the long-form journalism in the *NRC Handelsblad*, the Dutch quality newspaper, the journalist asked the question whether Dutch culture was hardening, given the murders and the backlash to them of the populist politician, Pim Fortuyn, and the cultural critic, Theo van Gogh in the mid-2000s (Dohmen, 2007). By the 'hardening of culture' is meant becoming less tolerant of others, with even a growing segment of radicalizing and more extremist individuals in society. The method employed is of interest to those considering web data as of some value. Instead of embedding oneself (e.g., among hooligans), studying pamphlets and other hard-copy ephemera, and surveying experts, the research turned to the web. Lists of right-wing and extremist websites were curated, and the language on the two types of sites was compared over time, with the aid of the Wayback Machine of the Internet Archive. It was found that over time the language on the right-wing sites increasingly approximated that on the extremist sites. While journalistic, the work provides a social research practice: charting change in language over time on the web, in order to study social change. The article also was accompanied by the data set, which is unusual for newspapers, and heralded the rise of data journalism. The journalist read the websites, in a close reading approach; one could imagine querying the sources as well in the distant reading approach which has come to be affiliated with the computational turn and big data studies more generally (Moretti, 2005; boyd and Crawford, 2012).

Another project that is demonstrative of digital methods is the cartogram visualization of recipe queries, which appeared in the *New York Times* (Ericson and Cox, 2009). All the recipes (on allrecipes.com) queried the day before Thanksgiving, the American holiday and feast, were geolocated, showing the locations whence the search queries came. For each recipe, the map is shaded according to frequency of queries by state (and is statistically normalized), where one notes differences in recipe queries, and perhaps food preference, across the United States. It presents, more broadly, a geography of taste. Here the question becomes how to ground the findings. Does one move offline with surveys or regional cookbooks, or seek more online data, such as food photos, tagged by location and timestamped? Would Flickr or Instagram provide more grounding? Here the web becomes a candidate grounding site.

Online data have been employed to study regional differences. One case in point is the classic discussion of language variation in the use of the terms 'soda', 'pop' and 'coke' in the United States. Geotagged tweets with the words 'soda', 'pop' or 'coke' are captured and plotted on a map, displaying a geography of word usage (see Figure 1.1). In the project the findings are compared to those made by another web data collection technique, a survey method migrated online, also known as a 'virtual method', discussed below. A webpage serves as an online data collection vessel, where people are asked to choose their preferred term (soda, pop, coke, or other) and fill in their hometown, including state and zip code (see Figure 1.2). The resulting map shows starker regional differentiation than the Twitter analysis. Chen, while not confirming the earlier findings, reports 'similar patterns', with pop being a midwestern term, coke southern and soda northeastern (2012; Shelton, 2011).

The natively digital and the digitized

Digital methods may be situated as somewhat distinctive from other contemporary approaches within the computational turn in the social sciences and the digital humanities (see Table 1.1). First, like other contemporary approaches in the study of digital data, they employ methods based on queries and have as a research practice what may be called search as research. They differ, however, from other approaches in that they rely largely on natively digital data and online methods as opposed to digitized data and migrated methods.

Two approaches in the digital humanities that may be compared to digital methods are culturomics and cultural analytics. While digital methods study web or natively digital data, culturomics and cultural analytics have as their corpuses what one could call digitized materials, which then are searched for either words (in culturomics) or formal material properties (in cultural analytics). Culturomics queries Google Books and performs longitudinal studies concerning the changes in use of language from the written word, inferring broader cultural trends. For example, American spelling is gradually supplanting British spelling, and celebrity or fame is increasingly more quickly gained and shorter-lived (Michel et al., 2011). Cultural analytics is a research practice that also queries, but at a lower level in a computing sense; it queries and seeks patterns and changes not to words but to formal properties of media, such as the hue, brightness and saturation in images.

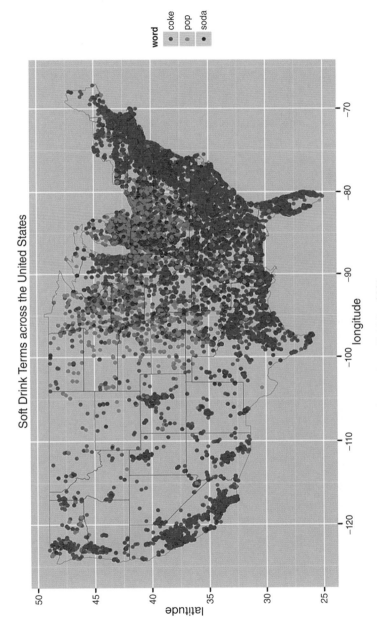

Figure 1.1 US map of self-reported usage of terms for soft drinks, 2003.

Source: Campbell, 2003.

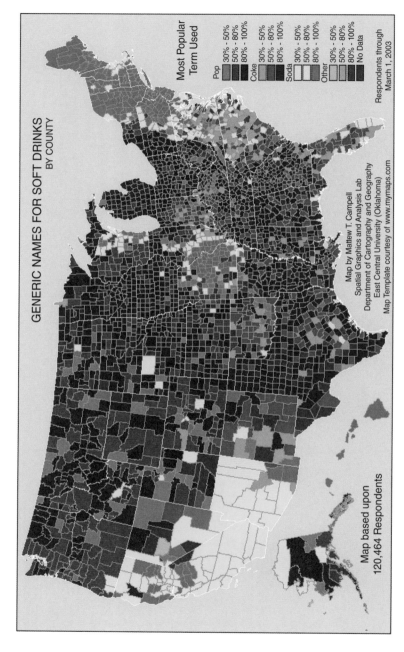

Figure 1.2 US map showing distribution of usage of terms (in geotagged tweets in Twitter) for soft drinks, 2012.

Source: Chen, 2012.

Table 1.1   Situating digital methods among other approaches in the computational turn in the humanities and social sciences, according to their use of natively digital or digitized data and methods.

		METHOD	
		DIGITIZED	**NATIVELY DIGITAL**
DATA	**DIGITIZED**	▶ Culturomics* ▶ Cultural Analytics*	
	NATIVELY DIGITAL	▶ Webmetrics ▶ Altmetrics	▶ Digital Methods

*Uses 'search as research'
Source: Adapted from Rogers, 2014.

Digitized data are often considered better than web data, as mentioned. Both culturomics and cultural analytics have to their advantage the study of what has been described as 'good data'. For culturomics the queries are made in a large collection of historical books, which the researchers describe as the study of millions of books, or approximately '4% of all books ever printed' (Michel et al., 2011: 176). For cultural analytics, the preferred corpus is the complete oeuvre of an artist (such as Mark Rothko) or the complete set of covers of a magazine (such as *Time*). In those cases, the data are good because they exist or have been captured from the beginning, cover long periods of time, and are complete, or rather so. One knows the percentage of missing data. With the web much of the data is from a recent past, covers a short period of time and is incomplete, where there is often a difficulty in grasping what complete data would be.

Two approaches in the e-social sciences also may be compared to digital methods: webometrics and altmetrics. Both are scientometric or bibliometric approaches of studying reputation or impact, applied to web data. As such they migrate citation analysis to the web, albeit in distinct ways. Webometrics studies hyperlinks (much like the Issuecrawler as discussed in Chapter 3) and derives site reputation or impact from the quantity and quality of links received. It uses natively digital objects (hyperlinks) and digitized method (bibliometrics). Altmetrics is similar, employing social media metrics (natively digital activities such as retweeting) to assign an 'attention' score to a published academic article (digitized method). The score increases depending on the quantity of mentions across online sources. Mentions in the news and in blog postings weigh more heavily than on Reddit, for example.

Virtual and digital methods compared

Indeed, the difficulties of moving methods and collecting data online are the subject of a social science approach, in the computational turn, called virtual methods. While digital methods seek to make use of the methods of the medium, virtual methods migrate the social science *instrumentarium* online, such as online surveys. The transition of the methods online varies in smoothness. Online, net or virtual ethnography has been able to define communities, enter them and observe and participate (Hine, 2005). For other techniques virtual methods seek to overcome some difficulties inherent in the web as a site of study and data collection realm. When surveying, the question is how to find the respondents, and whether one knows a response rate. For sampling, similarly, there are questions about whether one can estimate the population of websites or Facebook pages on a given topic. The migration of method online could be said to raise questions about the fit between the method and the medium.

Digital methods, contrariwise, strive to make use not only of born-digital data but also the methods that are native to the medium. 'Native' is meant not in an ethnographic or anthropological sense. Rather it is applied in the computing sense of that which is written for a particular processor or operating system, rather than simulated or emulated. Native here is that written for the online medium, rather than migrated to it.

Recently a third type of digital object has been introduced, beyond the natively digital and the digitized. The reborn digital object is that which was once born in the medium, archived and 'reborn' as an archived object in a digital library (Brügger, 2012). Thus, the study of web archives would be the study not only of the natively digital materials, but also of the effects of the archiving as well as the archive as institution or regime. For example, the Library of Congress's Twitter collection, when it is eventually made accessible to researchers, begins with Jack Dorsey's first tweet in March 2006, but has certain gaps (such as user profiles only from September 2011), and researchers likely will have to take account of the fact that Twitter's terms of service changed a number of times (Osterberg, 2013). There are also certain Twitter policies about the user's intent that the archive would be expected to follow (such as not allowing access to deleted or suspended tweets, even if available). The completeness of the collection is finite, for beginning in 2018 the Library of Congress will only create special tweet collections. Making tweet collections, and to what research ends, is also a subject of this book.

Digital methods have a general research strategy, or set of moves, that have certain affinities with an online software project, mash-up, or chain methodology. First, stock is taken of the available digital objects, such as hyperlinks, tags, retweets, shortened URLs, Wikipedia edits, anonymous user IP addresses, timestamps, likes, shares, comments and others. Subsequently it is asked how the devices online handle these objects. How may we learn from online methods? Here the social research outlook enters the purview. How to repurpose the online methods and the devices so as to study not online culture or the virtual society, but cultural condition and societal change? At that point, the question of triangulation and benchmarking arises. How to ground the findings made with online data? Must we step offline to do so, may we combine online and offline data and methods, or can the findings be grounded in the online?

Digital methods as a research practice

Given certain devices or platforms (e.g., Internet Archive, Google Web Search, Wikipedia, Facebook, Twitter, and others), how may they be studied for social research purposes? It should be said at the outset that digital methods are often experimental and situational, because they develop in tandem with the medium conditions, and occasionally are built on top of other devices. They may be short-lived, as certain services are discontinued. They may fall victim to changes made by a platform, such as when a service is discontinued, advanced search in social media is removed, or if an API is discontinued. When there are such changes research may be affected or perhaps discontinued; longitudinal studies are affected. Here, adding to Thelwall above, the researcher sceptical of the value of web data becomes wary of the instability of the infrastructure that provides it. Critique, especially of commercial search engines and social media platforms, arises. Search engines and social media platforms may deny legitimate research use of engine results or other post data, for it may not be part of a business model to serve researchers at least as a distinctive user group.

In the following the Internet Archive, Google Web Search, Wikipedia, Facebook, and Twitter are each taken in turn for the opportunities afforded for social research purposes, *à la* digital methods. For each the question is what digital objects are available, how are they handled by the device, and how can one learn from medium method, and repurpose it for social research.

Internet Archive

The interface on the Internet Archive, the Wayback Machine, has as its main input a single URL. One is returned the stored pages of that URL since as far back as 1996. One also may have uniques returned. One research practice that has been developed follows from the Wayback Machine's single-site focus, parlaying it into single-site histories. Changes to the interface of a homepage are captured, screengrabbed, placed in chronological order, and played back, in the style of time-lapse photography. A voiceover track is added, where the suggested approaches (among others) concern how the history of a single website can tell the history of the web, the collision between old and new media (such as the history of an online newspaper), or the history of an institution (such as whitehouse.gov). Making a single-site history as a movie builds on particular, well-known screencast documentaries, especially the seminal 'Heavy Metal Umlaut', on the evolution of the Wikipedia article of that same name, in a sense telling the story of Wikipedia's editing culture (Udell, 2005).

Here one tells the story of a platform or crowdsourcing through the history of a single Wikipedia article. The first example of a single-site history screencast documentary, made from screenshots taken from the Wayback Machine of the Internet Archive, is 'Google and the Politics of Tabs' (Rogers and Govcom.org, 2008). By examining the changes to the search services privileged (as well as relegated) by google.com on its interface over time, the story is told of the demise of the human editors of the web (and the web directory), and the rise of the algorithm and the back-end taking over from the librarians.

Google Web Search

Google Web Search has become so familiar that it requires some distancing efforts to consider its potential as a social research tool over its everyday value as a consumer information appliance. Google treats such digital objects as hyperlinks, clicks, and datestamps (freshness). It is a ranking and also status-authoring machine for sources per keyword, based on algorithmic notions of relevance. Relevance increasingly relies on users' clicks and the page's freshness over how sites are linked, as in the past. Thus one could view the results of the query "climate change" as a list of websites, mainly organizations, ranked according to relevance. Once one has a list of the 'top sources' for climate change, one could query each source for the names of climate change sceptics, noting how close to the top of engine returns each appears (and with what frequency). 'Source distance' is the name given to this two-step method which seeks to measure distance from the top of the web for a given name or sub-issue, in a larger issue space (Rogers, 2013b). It is the web equivalent of studying the top of the news (see Figure 1.3).

Figure 1.3   Source cloud. Presence of a climate change sceptic in the top Google results for the query ["climate change"], July 2007. Output by the Lippmannian Device, Digital Methods Initiative, Amsterdam.

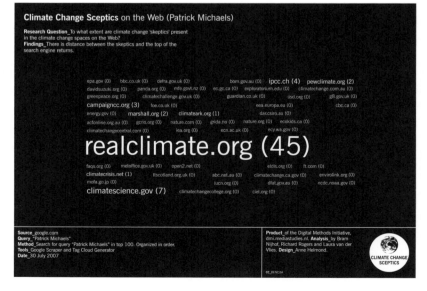

Apart from a ranking machine, Google is also a massive indexing machine, meaning, for the user, that the contents of websites may be queried, not only for single terms but also multiple ones, so as to gain a sense of which words appear more frequently than others. One may make use of such single-site indexing to study an organization's concerns. For example, Greenpeace.org is queried for all its campaigns, individually, to gain a sense of which campaigns have greater internal resonance than others, at least according to the number of mentions on its website (see Figure 1.4). Given Google's presentism, it would deliver recent concern, though with date range queries one could begin to gain a sense of changes in concern, or what could be called commitment. One may also query multiple websites for single terms, or for numerous terms. For example, one could query human rights websites for different sorts of terms – such as campaigns and sub-issues – to gain a sense of the significance of each across the range of organizations. One could imagine seeking to begin the study of the agendas of the global human rights network in such a manner. This is precisely the purpose of the Lippmannian Device (another use case of the Google Scraper described above in the source distance work). The Device allows the user to create source clouds (which sources mention which issues) and issue clouds (which issues are mentioned by the given sources).

Wikipedia

Wikipedia, the online encyclopedia, has a series of principles which its editors follow in order to have its articles achieve and retain 'encyclopedia-ness', namely, neutral point of view, no original research, and source verifiability. It is also routinely returned in the top results of Google for substantive queries (compared to navigational and transactional

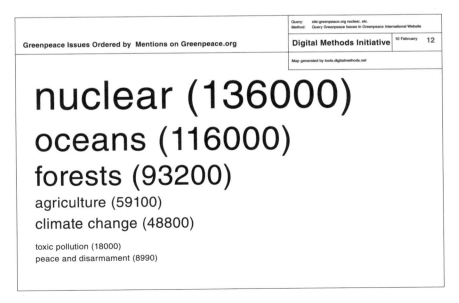

Figure 1.4 Issue cloud. Greenpeace campaigns mentioned on Greenpeace.org's website, February 2012. Output by the Lippmannian Device, Digital Methods Initiative, Amsterdam.

Greenpeace Issues Ordered by Mentions on Greenpeace.org

Query: site:greenpeace.org nuclear, etc.
Method: Query Greenpeace Issues in Greenpeace International Website
Digital Methods Initiative 10 February 12
Map generated by tools.digitalmethods.net

nuclear (136000)
oceans (116000)
forests (93200)
agriculture (59100)
climate change (48800)
toxic pollution (18000)
peace and disarmament (8990)

ones), making it a highly visible source of reference for its users. How would a digital methods researcher approach it? When examining its affordances, Wikipedia also has language versions, and each article has links to its other language versions ('interwiki links'), so that the researcher can view the collection of articles on the one subject across language Wikipedias. If the articles are not (recently) translated, then they are available for cross-cultural (or cross-linguistic) analysis. What may be compared? Each article has a series of digital objects such as anonymous edits with the IP address of those editors, whose location can be looked up. Thus, one can study the places of edits. It also has a revision history and a discussion history (talk pages), so one can study the intensity of editing as well as of debate. Furthermore, there are the article's title, editors (including bots), table of contents, images and references. All may be compared. Projects such as Manypedia and Omnipedia have automated means of comparison of Wikipedia articles across language versions, which the former calls LPOV, or language points of view. Instead of a reference work, Wikipedia becomes the source of study for cultural reference, or even national or cultural point of view. One case in point is the Srebrenica massacre, which is how it is titled in the Serbian version, the Srebrenica genocide (Bosnian), and the Fall of Srebrenica (Dutch). This is a comparison of three significant parties to the events of July 1995, when some 6000–8000 (Serbian version), 8000 (Bosnian), or 7000–8000 (Dutch) Bosnians were killed (Rogers and Sendijarevic, 2012). The Bosnian entry has distinctly different images, including a 13-year-old boy's grave, which, given that he was not of fighting age, would be evidence of genocide (see Figure 1.5). The Dutch version emphasizes the military side of the story, and the Serbian, once similar in that respect to the Dutch, is alone in providing a section on the events according to the Republika Srpska, the part of Bosnia and Herzegovina where the town of Srebrenica is located. The articles also do not share references, or editors. The differences between the articles, not to mention the differences in locations of the edits as well as the activities of the editors, provide materials for the study of cultural memory as well as controversiality, which has prompted scholars to encourage home-grown articles over translations from the English-language Wikipedia (Callahan and Herring, 2011).

Figure 1.5   Wikipedia as the study of cultural point of view. Comparison of images present on the Srebrenica article in the Dutch, English, Bosnian, Croatian, Serbian and Serbo-Croatian Wikipedia language versions, 20 December 2010. Output by the Cross-Lingual Image Analysis Tool, Digital Methods Initiative, Amsterdam.

Facebook

The digital objects much studied on Facebook were once ties (friends) and tastes (profiles) (Lewis et al., 2008a, 2008b). Using its API and the application Netvizz, for example, one could perform ego network research, pulling in the available data from yourself and your friends. Facebook's other digital objects include the profile, which provide the opportunity to study what I refer to as postdemographics – the media preferences and tastes of sets of social media users. In experimental work employing the advanced search of MySpace, compatibility comparisons were made of the interests of John McCain's friends and those of Barack Obama, prior to the 2008 US presidential elections where the two faced off (see Figure 1.6). Here the profiles are repurposed to inquire into the so-called culture wars, considering the extent of the polarization between red (Republican) and blue (Democratic) supporters.

el**friendo** BETA

FAQ | ABOUT

PROFILE BASED ON OBAMA		COMPATIBILITY	PROFILE BASED ON MCCAIN	
General	, barack obama, reading, music, writing, history, politics, movies, traveling, friends, bob marley, peace, family guy, chicago, books, democrats, photography, harry potter, as a u, running, the producers, jon stewart, the daily show, art, senator, macs, napoleon dynamite, conan o'brien, sleeping, guinness, italy, the beatles, psychology, cats, dancing, shopping, summer, poetry, democracy, voting, gay rights, obama, mythology, coffee, borat, concerts, george orwell, david sedaris, icons, buddhism, ingrid chavez, pink floyd, piano	17%	General	yes, sometimes, edwin mccain, friends, reading, music, swimming, concerts, piercings, shopping, com, movies, metal, get paid to take surveys!, create your own!, (8), death metal, art, what?, soemtimes, laguna beach, jj mccain, john mccain, the beach, fugazi, freya, from autumn to ashes, full blown chaos, from first to last
Music	radiohead, belle and sebastian, the beatles, the roots, pearl jam, sufjan stevens, bob dylan, swervedriver, the smiths, cat power, nina simone, amy winehouse	0%	Music	the shins, com, the bravery, coldplay, evanescence, guster, blink 182, dido, green day, taking back sunday, the used
Movies	little miss sunshine, american beauty, goodfellas, alice in wonderland, amelie, a clockwork orange, archangel, secretary, memento, magnolia, lost in translation, rushmore	0%	Movies	love actually, old school, garden state, kill bill, pirates of the caribbean, napoleon dynamite, shawshank redemption, big fish, princess bride
Television	the office, arrested development, weeds, the daily show, lost, heroes	16%	Television	family guy, project runway, top chef, america's next top model, csi, desperate housewives, lost
Books	atlas shrugged, books, alice in wonderland, gone with the wind, harry potter, 1984, america: the book, catch-22, josef mengele, gravity's rainbow, the baroque cycle (quicksilver, being written before obama decied on a political career it offers an honest introspective look that few other politicians could ever have offered:	0%	Books	to kill a mockingbird, com, me talk pretty one day, "sneaking into the flying circus, it's just enough to get the blood pumping!
Heroes	my mom, , johnny cash	0%	Heroes	haha, kat von d, john lennon, barry goldwater

Figure 1.6 Aggregated profiles of the interests of the top 100 friends of Barack Obama and John McCain, MySpace.com, September 2008. Analysis and output by Elfriendo.com, Govcom.org Foundation and Digital Methods, Initiative, Amsterdam.

Since the 'ethics turn' in social media research, arguably prompted by Michael Zimmer's deanonymizing the students (from Harvard College) who were the subject of the tastes and ties research discussed above, Facebook changed its API, no longer allowing the study of friends and profiles (Zimmer, 2010a; Rieder, 2015a). Only Facebook pages (and groups) were available to the researcher, using the API. (Later closed groups, even when joined, were no longer open to data analysis.) Thus, on Facebook the operative digital objects for analysis became the page and the open group, together with what a user may do there: like, react, share and comment. Pages can like other pages. In a digital methods technique developed and built into Netvizz, an 'inter-liked page network' can be produced (with one or two degrees of separation). It may be analysed through a network story-telling approach and/or by examining 'most engaged-with content', techniques described below. A researcher also could curate a set of pages related to a particular subject matter, such as right-wing extremists, and study the content that most animates the users of those pages. On Facebook one has access to the data set of post engagement per page, also longitudinally. One is able to determine which content (and which content types) has elicited engagement (including which types of engagement). What is engaging to those who like, comment, and share on Stop Islamization of the World (see Figure 1.7)? One also may join a group and, in doing so, gain access to its data. The researcher would create a 'research profile', self-identifying and pointing to the project, in the form of a Facebook post, blog entry or webpage where the subject matter, questions, methods and expected outcomes are described. Inquiring into sensitive or underground matters may require other approaches. In a pioneering technique, researchers put up ads in right-wing groups, inviting members to participate in a project, thereby being transparent as well as gaining consent (Bartlett et al., 2011). Justification for undertaking monitoring work (without self-identifying) may be found in its public interest value.

Figure 1.7   Most engaged-with content, according to quantities of likes, comments and shares, on the Facebook page, Stop Islamization of the World, January, 2013.

Twitter

In its early study tweets from Twitter were categorized as banal or having pass-along value, which eventually would be codified by its users as RT (retweets), or those tweets of such interest that they should be tweeted again (Rogers, 2013a). The retweet was joined by other digital objects fashioned by its users, especially the hashtag, which would group content by subject, such as an event. Retweeted tweets per hashtag became a means of studying significant tweets of the day, such as the Iran elections and their aftermath in June 2009. How to repurpose the stream? In an effort to 'debanalize' Twitter, one digital methods approach has been to invert the reverse chronological order of Twitter and place the most significant retweets per hashtag in chronological order, so as to tell the story of an event from Twitter (see Figure 1.8). Here the key question remains the relationship between what is happening on the ground and in social media – a debate that has been led by Evgeny Morozov, who quotes Al Jazeera's head of new media as saying that during the Iran election crisis there were perhaps six Twitter users tweeting from the ground in Tehran (Morozov, 2011).

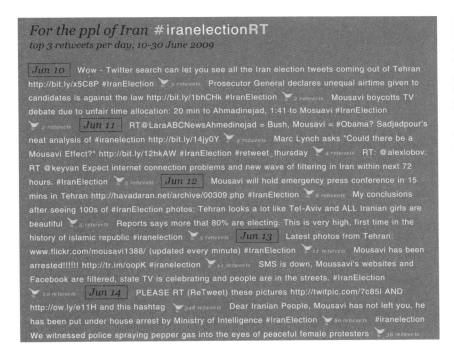

Figure 1.8 Top three RTs per day with #iranelection hashtag, 10–30 June 2009, in chronological order, telling the story of the Iran election crisis from Twitter. Data collection at rettiwt.net. Digital Methods Initiative, Amsterdam, 2009.

Twitter, the company, began to recognize, as its co-founder Jack Dorsey related, that it does 'well at natural disasters, man-made disasters, events, conferences, presidential elections' (Sarno, 2009b). It changed its slogan in 2009 from 'What are you doing?' to 'What's happening?,' indicating a shift from Twitter as a friend-following tool (for ambient or remote intimacy) to a news medium for following events, especially elections and disasters. Here

Twitter becomes a data set not only of commercial but also historical value, indicated by the significance of Library of Congress's embracing Twitter as a digital archival project. Routines to build tweet collections and to output them as event chronologies for 'remote event analysis' are among the scholarly uses and the specific digital methods developed and discussed below. One also may make a tweet collection of an 'issue space', such as global health and development or human rights. Once demarcated, the space of actors posting campaigns, event announcements, resources, story links and other formats to do the issue (so to speak) may be studied with a variety of techniques, including 'critical analytics'. These are engagement metrics that seek to research dominant voice, matters of concern, commitment, positionality, and alignment. They are critical in two senses. First, they provide an alternative to 'vanity metrics', or brute follower counts often boosted by paying for better numbers, which allows one to show off. Second, they demonstrate whether the space marginalizes certain participants and issues, at the same time scrutinizing the dominant actors for issue trend-following and other commitment critiques.

YouTube

The earliest archived YouTube page shows a dating site from which to 'broadcast yourself', but the platform quickly became associated with amateur content, and more generally the user-generated content and creativity implied in the notion of participatory culture. While critique arose about the 'cult of the amateur' and the value of such material as 'Charlie bit my finger', lament followed with the platform's commercialization, witnessed by the overtaking of user-created videos by commercial content (e.g., music) on the most viewed lists. A more recent period of YouTube studies has concentrated on the labour put in to become a YouTuber, or native micro-celebrity, in a wide range of subject areas, including those where the utterance of extreme speech is prevalent. The digital methods approaches are critical diagnostics of the workings of the recommendation systems and device or ranking cultures. Is it the amateur, the commercial video or the YouTuber who is recommended 'up next' and in search results? In an approach borrowed from Swedish researchers investigating Spotify, the 'tear down' of YouTube critically examines the output of its various recommendation systems, investigating how it ranks, and who benefits.

Beyond single-platform studies

Single-platform studies have come into being largely owing to API-driven (and accompanying tool-driven) research. Rather than being researcher led, the social media company also dictates the data available, and the terms of accessibility. 'Transmedia' and cross-media scholars often lament the focus on the single platform, both conceptually and empirically, as I relate below. The story of an event or issue space (including campaigns and their effectiveness) may unfold across multiple platforms, and actors readily employ more than a single platform to do their issue work. Link analysis software (such as the Issuecrawler or Hyphe) could provide insights into the key platforms (as well as websites) of relevance to a subject matter, and also point to which platforms may be worthy of study. Each could be studied in isolation, but, as I elaborate, strategies for undertaking cross-platform analysis benefit from a comparison of the data points of each platform (e.g., likes on Facebook and Twitter, hashtags on Twitter and Instagram, web links on most platforms). Also of importance is an appreciation of how the platforms differ (e.g., hashtag inflation on Instagram compared to Twitter). Performing cross-platform analysis thus is also the study of distinctive platform use cultures or 'platform vernaculars'.

Digital methods' repurposing outlook

Digital methods begin with an observation concerning the ontological distinction between objects born in the medium and those migrated to it. The observation is extended subsequently to methods. There are those methods that could be described as 'of the medium' and those that have been ported onto it. While not absolute (or absolutist), the differentiation between the natively digital and the digitized (in terms of both content and method) prompts reflection on how to approach the medium for research purposes. Rather than lament data ephemerality and medium instability and conclude that web data are not good data, could one learn from the methods built in, and repurpose them for research?

'Repurposing' in digital methods shares a lineage or outlook with such approaches as reverse engineering and unobtrusive measures. It also draws most readily from new media practice with the open web.

With reverse engineering one develops an understanding of a system (and specs it out, so as to imitate or emulate it) 'without the original drawings' (Chikofsky et al., 1990). In a similar manner, without knowing the contents of the proverbial black box, one learns from the medium and redeploys that knowledge. How do the engines and platforms recommend content, and how could one learn from such workings? With engines one reads the trade press (including the search engine optimization (SEO) literature) and saves engine results; with platforms one also examines the API and the (changing) data fields available to the researcher. 'Reversing' is also part of other techniques put to use. Above, mention was made of reverse look-up software, for example, when identifying the multiple websites associated with a single Google Analytics or AdSense ID. 'Reverse image search' is another case in point, where one looks up which websites contain a particular image facsimile or approximation.

The repurposing approach also has affinities with the study of residuals, otherwise known as unobtrusive measures. With such an approach one obtains data through 'non-reactive' means, eschewing the survey and questionnaire for a focus on traces (Webb et al., 1966). What may be observed and learned from the traces left by users online? For example, 'shares' in social media not only are means of post placement and boosting (as we learn from platform methods), but also could be said to be indicators of the content that animate groups. Perhaps traces are no longer the preferred term, for one is often conducting research with logged (rather than left) activities on the basis of what once was called 'registrational interactivity'.

Digital methods, finally, should be viewed as a webby project of 'putting things on top of other things', as the net artist Heath Bunting once described new media. Web cartographers also describe the early mash-ups (or 'web application hybrids') as such (Woodruff, 2011). 'Repurposing' also speaks to other new media 're-' words, such as remixing (in the creative output sense used by Lawrence Lessig (2004)). Practically speaking, one takes stock of the digital cultural landscape for the objects on hand, asks how they are treated by online devices, and considers how that stock-taking and device-learning could be put to a productive research use. Hyperlinks connect webpages but can be indications of reputational value; retweets are content sharing gestures but can be viewed as content valuations; and likes are social bonding as well as animation indicators. More specifically, shared Google Analytics and AdSense IDs show common ownership, but when mapped could also make visible influence networks or media group strategies. Indeed, throughout this book one takes note of how online objects and methods may be recombined and reused.

TWO

STARTING WITH QUERY DESIGN

On formulating research questions as queries

Digital methods and online groundedness

Broadly speaking, digital methods may be considered the deployment of online tools and data for the purposes of social and medium research. More specifically, they derive from online methods, or methods of the medium, which are reimagined and repurposed for research. The methods to be repurposed are often built into dominant devices for recommending sources or drawing attention to oneself or one's posts. For an example of how to reimagine the inputs and outputs of one such dominant device, consider the difference between studying search engine results to understand in some manner Google's algorithms, or treating them as indications of societal concerns. Here, there is a shift from studying the medium to using engine data to study the societal. That is, akin to the digital methods outlook generally, anticipatory instruments use online social signals to measure trends not so much in the online realm but rather 'in the wild'.

Once the findings are made the question becomes how to ground them, that is, with conventional offline methods and techniques (mixed methods), or through additional, online methods and sources. In digital methods research, online groundedness, as it may be termed, asks whether and when it is appropriate to shift the site of 'ground-truthing', to use a geographer's expression referring to the appropriate place to calibrate instruments. Can findings be grounded in other online data and methods? As a case in point, when verifying knowledge claims, Wikipedians check prior art through Google searches, thereby grounding claims in online sources via the search engine.

Digital methods thereby rethink conditions of proof, first by considering the online as a site of grounding, but also in a second sense. One makes social research findings online, and, rather than leaving the medium to harden them, one subsequently inquires into the extent to which the medium is affecting the findings. Medium research thus serves a purpose that is distinct from the study of online culture alone. As I relate, when reading and interpreting social signals online, the question concerns whether the medium, or media dynamics, is overdetermining the outcomes.

Making use of 'socialized' and semantic data

As noted, digital methods make use of online methods, by which I refer to an array of techniques from the computational and information sciences – crawling, scraping, ranking and so forth – that have been applied to and redeveloped for the web. Online methods also may refer to algorithms that determine relevance and authority and thereby recommend information sources as in Google's famed PageRank, but also boost all manner of items, from songs and 'friends' to potential 'followers'.

Many of the algorithms are referred to as 'social', meaning that they make use of user choices and activity (purposive clicks such as liking), and may be contrasted with the 'semantic', meaning that which is categorized and matched, as in a library's book classification, Wikipedia's category portals or Google's knowledge graph. Digital methods seek to take particular advantage of socially derived rankings, that is, users making their preferences known for particular sources, often unobtrusively. Secondarily, the semantic, or sources that have been pre-matched or sorted into a taxonomy, are also of value, for example when Wikipedia furnishes a curated seed list of sources ('climate change sceptics', as a case in point), which have been derived manually by information experts or the proverbial crowd guided by the protocols of the online encyclopedic community.

The distinction between social and semantic is mentioned so as to emphasize web-epistemological 'crowdfindings' (as implied by the 'social'), as distinct from 'results' from information retrieval. Thus, with digital methods, as I relate below, one seeks to query in order to make findings from socialized web data (so to speak) rather than query in order to find pre-sorted information or sources, however well annotated or enriched with metadata.

Google as epistemological machine

Over the course of the past decade or more, Google arguably has transformed itself from an epistemological machine, outputting reputational source hierarchies, to a consumer information appliance providing user-tailored results. Here I would like to take up the question of how and to what ends one might still employ Google as an epistemological machine.

There are largely two research purposes for querying Google: medium and social research. With medium research, one studies (often critically) how and for whom Google works. To what degree does the engine serve a handful of dominant websites such as Google properties themselves in a 'preferred placement' critique, or websites receiving the most attention through links and clicks? One would seek to lay bare the persistence of so-called 'googlearchies' that boost certain websites and bury others in the results, as Matthew Hindman's (2008) classic critique of Google's outputs would imply. Here the work being done is an engine results critique, where the question revolves around the extent to which the change in 2009 in Google's algorithmic philosophy, captured in the opening chapter of Eli Pariser's (2011) *Filter Bubble*, from universal to personalized outputs, dislodges or upholds the pole positions of dominant sites on the web. Indeed, another critical inroad in engine results critique is the so-called filter bubble itself, where one would examine the effects of personalization, investigating Pariser's claim that Google furnishes increasingly personalized and localized results. In this inquiry, one may reinvigorate Nicholas Negroponte's (1995) 'Daily Me' argument in favour of a fully personalized morning newspaper and Cass Sunstein's (2001) response concerning the undesirable effects of homophily, polarization, and the end of the shared public exposure to media which leaves societies without common frames of reference. In this line of reasoning, personalization leads to social atomization and severe niching, otherwise known as 'markets of one', as described by Joseph Turow in *Niche Envy* (2006). It also would imply the demise of the mass media audience.

In the second research strategy, there is a mode switch in how one views the work of the search engine (and for whom it could work). Google's queries, together with its outputted site rankings, are considered as indicators of societal trends. That is, instead of beginning from the democratizing and socializing potential of the web and subsequently critiquing Google for its reintroduction of hierarchies, one focuses on how examining engine queries and results allows for the study of social sorting, or how users collectively determine which results belong to which queries. How to study the subsequent source hierarchies Google offers? Which terms have been queried most significantly (at what time and from which location)? Do places have preferred searches? May we geolocate temporal pockets of anxiety? The capacity to indicate general and localizable trends makes Google results of interest to the social researcher.

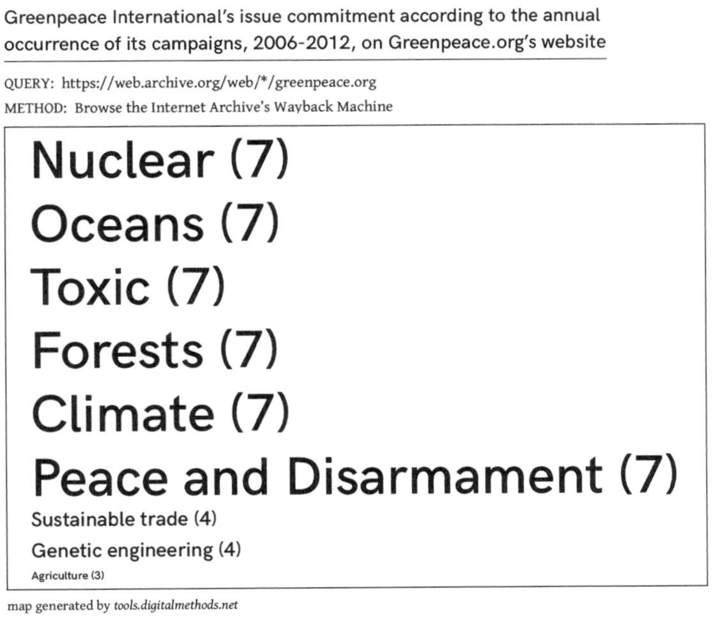

Greenpeace International's issue commitment according to the annual occurrence of its campaigns, 2006-2012, on Greenpeace.org's website

QUERY: https://web.archive.org/web/*/greenpeace.org
METHOD: Browse the Internet Archive's Wayback Machine

Nuclear (7)
Oceans (7)
Toxic (7)
Forests (7)
Climate (7)
Peace and Disarmament (7)
Sustainable trade (4)
Genetic engineering (4)
Agriculture (3)

map generated by *tools.digitalmethods.net*

Figure 2.1 Greenpeace International's commitment according to the annual occurrence of its campaigns, 2006–2012, ranked and arrayed as word cloud according to frequency of appearances on the Greenpeace.org front page.

Source: Data from the Internet Archive, archive.org. Analysis by Anne Laurine Stadermann.

Figure 2.2 Greenpeace campaigns mentioned on Greenpeace.org as ranked word cloud, 2012, indicating a distribution of concern.

Source: Data from Greenpeace.org gathered by the Lippmannian Device, Digital Methods Initiative. Analysis by Anne Laurine Stadermann.

Greenpeace International's distribution of concern according to campaign word count, 2012, on Greenpeace.org

QUERY: site:http://www.greenpeace.org Nuclear, "Climate change", etc.

METHOD: Query Google Scraper / Lippmannian Device

Nuclear (11300)
Climate change (9860)
Oceans (9390)
Forests (9370)
Agriculture (8790)

Peace & Disarmament (8720)

Toxic pollution (8540)

map generated by *tools.digitalmethods.net*

From studying trends to dominant voice

Apart from trends one may also study dominant voice, commitment and concern. One may ask, in the first instance, when and for which keywords certain actors appear high on the list and others marginal. Which actors are given the opportunity to dominate and drive the meaning of terms and their discussion and debate? Here the engine is considered as serving social epistemologies for any keyword (or social issue) by virtue of what is collectively queried and returned.

The engine also can be employed for the study of commitment in terms of the continued use of keywords by individual actors, be they governments, non-governmental organizations (NGOs), radical group formations or persons. Here the researcher takes advantage not of the hierarchies inputted and outputted (socio-epistemological sorting) but of the massive and recent indexing of individual websites. For example, the NGO Greenpeace has had the dual agenda of environmentalism and disarmament (hence the fusion of 'green' and 'peace'). Querying Greenpeace websites lately for issue keywords would show that their commitment to campaigning for peace, while consistent over the years, has waned in comparison to that for environmental causes, for green words resonate more than disarmament ones. Here one scrutinizes commitment (year-on-year campaigning) by counting incidences of keywords on web pages (see Figures 2.1 and 2.2).

One also may query sets of actors for keywords in order to have an indication of the levels of concern for an issue. For example, querying a representative environmental group and a species group (respectively) for "Fukushima" would show that the environmental group is highly active in the issue space while the species NGO is largely absent, showing a lack of concern for the matter (see Figure 2.3).

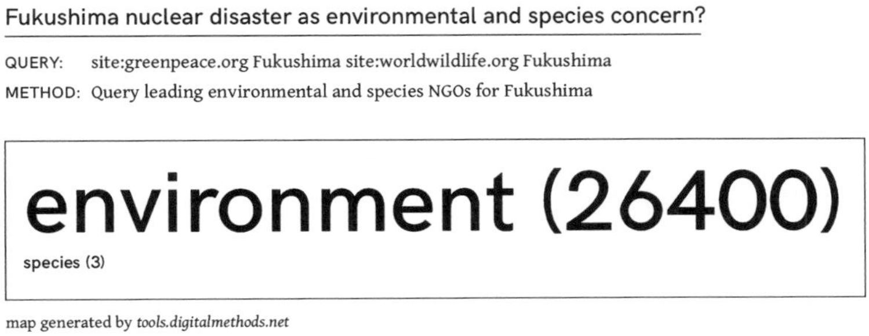

Fukushima nuclear disaster as environmental and species concern?

QUERY: site:greenpeace.org Fukushima site:worldwildlife.org Fukushima
METHOD: Query leading environmental and species NGOs for Fukushima

environment (26400)

species (3)

map generated by *tools.digitalmethods.net*

Figure 2.3 Mentions of "Fukushima" by Greenpeace and World Wildlife Fund, November 2016, indicating to which NGO Fukushima is a matter of concern.

Source: Data and visualisation by the Lippmannian Device, Digital Methods Initiative. Analysis by author.

In all, for the social researcher, Google is of interest for its capacity to rank actors (websites) per social issue (keyword), thereby providing source hierarchies, and allowing for the study of dominant voice. Who has been authorized by the engine to furnish information at the top of the results? It is also pertinent for its ability to count the (recent) incidence of issue words per actor or sets of actors, thereby allowing for the study of commitment through continued use of keywords.

Societal and medium research entangled

One might distinguish between the two research types above by viewing one as primarily doing media studies and the other social research. Yet in practice, the two are entangled with one another. As mentioned above, the entanglement assumes a particular form. Medium research is in service of social research in the sense of concentrating on the extent to which the findings made have been overdetermined by media effects.

It is important to stress from the outset that it not assumed that engine effects can be removed in total, thus enabling a researcher to study 'organic' results, the industry term for editorial content untouched by advertising or preferred placement. Rather there should be awareness of a variety of types of routinely befouling artefacts ('media effects') that nevertheless are returned by the engine. Google properties (e.g., YouTube videos), Google user aids (e.g., 'equivalent results' for queried terms), and SEO'd products (whether through white or black hat techniques) are all considered media effects, and in principle could be removed, or footnoted. There are software settings in some tools to do so (e.g., remove Google properties from results, in the Harvester, which extracts URLs from text, source code or search engine results). There is also query design (use quotation marks for exact matches) to remove equivalent results, and strategies for detecting at least obviously SEO'd results (stuffed with repeated keywords).

The more problematic issue arises with any desired detection of the effects of personalization. The point here is that users now co-author engine results. The search engine thereby produces artefacts that are of the user's making. The search engine, once critiqued for its Matthew effect in the results, leans towards inculpability, since users have set preferences (and have preferences set for them) and some results are affected. There is the question of detecting how many and which results are personalized in one form or another, according to one's location (country as well as locality), language, personal search history as well as adult and violent content filter.

Certain queries would likely have no organic results in the top ten, thus making any content cleaning exercise into an artificial act of removal, given that most users (a) click the top results, (b) have the results set to the default of ten, and (c) do not venture beyond one page of results. There are also special cases to consider for removal, such as Wikipedia, which is delivered in the top results for nearly all substantive queries, making it appear to be at once an authoritative source (for its persistent presence) and an engine artefact (for its uncannily persistent presence). Wikipedia's supra-presence, so to speak, provides a conundrum for the researcher who may wish to clean content of Google artefacts and media effects, and is perhaps the best case for retaining them at least in the first instance.

One way forward would be to remove the user, so speak, and strive to have the engine work as unaffected as possible. Removing the user is a means of reconjuring the pre-2009 distinction between universal results (served to all) and personalized results (served to an individual user). A research browser would be set up, where one is logged out of Google, and no cookies are set. Advanced settings are used to return results tailored to a set geographical location, rather than the default city. I return to the matter of advanced settings when discussing setting up the research browser in more detail.

Studying media effects or the societal 'in the wild'

The question whether Google merely outputs Google artefacts and medium effects or reveals societal trends has been raised in connection with the flagship big data project, Google Flu Trends (Lazer et al., 2014). As mentioned at the outset, the project, which was run by Google's non-profit google.org, monitored user queries for flu and flu-related symptoms, geolocated their incidence and outputted the timing and locations of heightened flu query activity; it is a tool for tracking where the virus is most prevalent. Yet does the increased incidence of queries for flu and flu-related symptoms indicate a rise in the number of influenza cases 'in the wild', or does it mean that TV and other news of the coming flu season prompt heightened query activity? TV viewers may be using a 'second screen' and fact-checking or enhancing their knowledge through search engine queries. Given that Flu Trends was overreporting for a period of time, compared to its baseline at the Centers for Disease Control and Prevention (and its equivalents internationally), the project seemed to be overly imbued with media effects.

Thus, one may seek research strategies to study medium effects, formulating queries that in a sense put on display or amplify the effects. For which types of queries do more Google properties appear? How can Google be made to output user aids that are telling? How to detect egregiously SEO'd results?

When using Google as a social research machine, the task at hand, however, is to reduce Google effects, albeit without the pretension of completely removing them. This is the main preparatory work, conceptually as well as practically, prior to query design.

When words are keywords

The question of what constitutes a keyword is the starting point for query design, for that is what makes querying and query design practically a part of a research strategy. When formulating a query, one often begins with keywords so as to ascertain who is using them, in which contexts and with what spread or distribution over time. In the following a particular keyword query strategy or design is put forward, whereby one queries competing keywords, asking whether a particular term is winning favour and among whom.

The keyword has its origins in the notion of a 'hint' or 'clue'. The *New Oxford American Dictionary* calls it 'a word which acts as the key to a cipher or code'. In this rendering, keywords have not so much hidden but rather purposive meaning so as to enable an unlocking or an opening up. Relatedly, Raymond Williams, in his book *Keywords*, discusses them in at least two senses: 'the available and developing meanings of known words' and 'the explicit but as often implicit connections which people are making' (Williams, 1976: 13). Therefore, behind keywords are both well-known words (elucidated by Williams's elaborations on the changing meaning of 'culture' over longer periods of time, beyond the high/low distinction) or neologistic phrases such as recent concerns surrounding 'blood minerals' or the more defused 'conflict minerals' mined and built into mobile phones. The one has readily available yet developing meanings and the other are new phraseologies that position. For the query design I am proposing, the purposive meaning of keywords is captured by Williams most readily in his second type (the new language). The first type may apply as well, as in the case of a new use or mobilization of a phrase, such as 'new economic order' or 'land reform'. The question then becomes what is meant by it this time.

Query design with the 'programme' and 'anti-programme' approach

Concerning how deploying a keyword implies a side-taking politics, I refer to the work of Madeleine Akrich and Bruno Latour (1992) and others, who have discussed the idea that, far from having stable meanings (as Williams also related), keywords can be parts of programmes or anti-programmes. The term 'programme' refers to efforts made at putting forward and promoting a particular proposal, campaign or project. Conversely, anti-programmes oppose these efforts or projects through keywords. Following this reading, keywords can be thought of as furthering a programme or an anti-programme. There is, however, also a third type of keyword I would like to add, which refers to efforts made at being neutral. These are specific undertakings made not to join a programme or an anti-programme. News outlets such as the BBC, the *New York Times* and the *Guardian* often have dedicated style guides that advise their reporters to employ particular language and avoid other. For example, the BBC instructs reporters to use generic wording for the obstacle separating Israel and the Palestinian Territories:

> The BBC uses the term 'barrier', 'separation barrier' or 'West Bank barrier' as an acceptable generic description to avoid the political connotations of 'security fence' (preferred by the Israeli government) or 'apartheid wall' (preferred by the Palestinians). (BBC Academy, 2013)

When formulating queries, it is pertinent to consider keywords as being parts of programmes, anti-programmes or efforts at neutrality, as this outlook allows the researcher to study trends, commitments and alignments between actors. To this end (and in contrast to discourse analysis), one does not wish to have equivalents or substitutes for the specific issue language being employed by the programmes, anti-programmes and the neutral programmes. For example, there is a difference between using the term 'blood minerals' or the term 'conflict minerals', or using 'blood diamonds' or 'conflict diamonds', because the terms are employed (and repeated) by particular actors to issuefy, or to make into a social issue forced and often brutal mining practices that fuel war (blood diamonds or minerals) or to have industry recognize a sensitive issue and their corporate social responsibility (conflict diamonds or minerals). Therefore, they should not be treated as equivalent and grouped together. Here it is useful to return to the point that one should use quotation marks around keywords when querying, because without quotation marks and thus specific keyword queries, Google returns equivalents. Mobile phone and cell phone are examples of equivalents. Indeed, one should treat 'conflict minerals' and 'blood minerals' as separate because, as parts of specific programmes, they show distinctive commitments and can help to draw alignments. If someone (often a journalist) begins using a third term, such as 'conflict resources', it probably constitutes a conscious effort at being neutral and not joining the programmes using the other terms. Those who then enter the fray and knowledgeably employ what have become keywords (in Williams's second sense) can be said to be taking up a position or a side or avoiding one.

A programme and an anti-programme on display

To demonstrate the notion of programmes, anti-programmes and efforts at neutrality further, the Palestinian–Israeli conflict, alluded to above, presents a compelling case for studying positioning as well as (temporary) alignment. There are two famous recorded exchanges that took place at the US White House: firstly, between President George W. Bush and the leader of the Palestinian Authority, Mahmoud Abbas; and, secondly, between President Bush and the Prime Minister of Israel, Ariel Sharon (see Figure 2.4). These exchanges, from the time when the barrier was under construction, show the kinds of positioning efforts that are made through the use of particular terms and thus the kind of specific terminology that one should be aware of when formulating queries. They also reveal temporary alignments that put diplomacy on display, with the US President using the Palestinian and then the Israeli preferred terminology in the company of the respective leaders, but only partly, thereby never fully taking sides.

"When words are keywords"

U.S.-Palestinian Exchange, 25 July 2003

PRESIDENT BUSH: Israel will consider ways to reduce the impact of the security fence on the lives of the Palestinian people.?(…)

PRIME MINISTER ABBAS: [T]he construction of the so-called separation wall on confiscated Palestinian land continues (…).

[T]he wall must come down.?(…)
[JOURNALIST] QUESTION: Would you like to see Israel (…) stop building this barrier wall??

PRESIDENT BUSH: Let me talk about the wall. I think the wall is a problem, and I discussed this with Ariel Sharon. It is very difficult to develop confidence between the Palestinians and the Israel – Israel – with a wall snaking through the West Bank.

U.S.-Israeli Exchange, 29 July 2003

PRIME MINISTER SHARON: [A] number of issues came up: the security fence, which we are forced to construct in order to defend our citizens against terror activities (…). The security fence will continue to be built, with every effort to minimize the infringement on the daily life of the Palestinian population.?

[JOURNALIST] QUESTION: Mr. President, what do you expect Israel to do in practical terms in regarding the separation fence that you call the wall? Due to the fact that this is one of the most effective measures against terrorism, can you clarify what do you oppose – the concept of the separation fence, or only its roots??

PRESIDENT BUSH: I would hope, in the long-term a fence would be irrelevant. But, look, the fence is a sensitive issue, I understand. (…) [W]e'll continue to discuss and to dialogue how best to make sure that the fence sends the right signal that not only is security important, but the ability for the Palestinians to live a normal life is important, as well..

Exchanges between US. President G.W. Bush and the Palestinian and Israeli leaders, Rose Garden, White House, 2003. Source: "The Divide," Exhibition, Gallery Centralis, Budapest, Hungary, 2004.

Figure 2.4 The use of keywords by US, Palestinian and Israeli leaders, showing (temporary) terminological alignments and diplomacy. Exchanges between the leaders at the Rose Garden, US White House, 2003.

The first exchange between President Bush and the Palestinian leader, Abbas, begins with a discussion in which Bush refers to the barrier as a 'security fence', which is the official Israeli term. Abbas then makes an attempt to correct this keyword by replying with the term 'separation wall', thereby using a very different adjective – separation instead of security – to allude to the interpretation of the purpose of the barrier as separating peoples and not securing Israel, as well as a poignant noun, wall. The word 'fence', as in the Israeli 'security fence', connotes a lightweight, neighbourly fence. By calling it a 'wall', however, Abbas connotes the Berlin Wall. The third person in this exchange, the journalist, then steps in with the term 'barrier wall' in an effort not to take sides, though at the moment 'wall' actually gives the Palestinian position some weight. Following this exchange, Bush, being diplomatic, realizes when talking to Abbas that the word 'wall' is being used, so he switches terms and concludes by using, albeit without an adjective, the term 'wall', which would validate Abbas and clash with the official Israeli term.

Four days later, the Israeli Prime Minister, Sharon, visits the White House to talk to President Bush, and he begins by using 'security fence', the official Israeli term. A journalist steps in and seems not to have read any newspaper style guides on the matter, because he first says, 'separation fence' and then 'wall'. The journalist, moreover, does not use 'security fence' and, therefore, the question he poses, while critical, also seems one-sided for it was preceded by quite some Palestinian language (separation, wall). Bush concludes by being diplomatic once again to both parties involved: he is tactful to Sharon by using the word 'fence', but he does not use any adjective so as to be wary of Abbas, his recent visitor.

Wall and fence talk in the Middle East, of course, is very specific conflict terminology, but it does highlight a particular programme ('security fence'), an anti-programme ('separation wall') as well as an effort at being neutral ('barrier wall'). It also shows how temporary alignments, often only partial ones, are made with great tact, providing something of a performative definition of diplomacy.

Issue spaces can be analysed with this sort of keyword specificity in mind. A related example in this regard concerns the United Nations Security Council's debates on the barrier between Israel and the Palestinian Territories, which took place in 2003 and 2005 when it was first being constructed (Rogers and Ben-David, 2010). The terms used by each country participating in the debates were lifted directly from the Security Council transcripts. The resultant issue maps, or bipartite graphs, contain nodes that represent countries, clustered by the term(s) that each country uses when referring to the barrier (see Figures 2.5 and 2.6). The network clearly demonstrates the specificity of the terminology put into play by the respective countries at the table as well as the terminological alignments that emerge. When countries utter the same term, groupings or blocs form, to speak in the language of international relations. For example, the largest surrounds 'separation wall', and mention of other terms ('expansionist wall', 'racist wall', 'security wall', 'the barrier', 'the fence', 'the wall', 'the structure', 'separation barrier', and so forth) make for smaller groupings or even isolation.

In 2003 a majority of countries come to terms around 'separation wall' or 'the wall', both Palestinian side-taking keywords, and there is a smattering of more extreme terms, such as 'racist wall'. On the other side of the divide, the term 'security fence', the official Israeli nomenclature, is only spoken by Israel and Germany, showing terminological alignment between the two countries. Two years later, in 2005, the next UN Security Council debate on the barrier took place, and a similar pattern of terminology use emerged, albeit with two distinct differences. Neutral language has found its way into the debate, with 'the barrier'

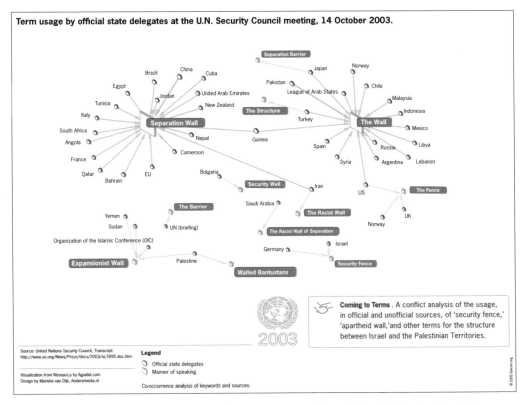

Figure 2.5 Cluster graph showing co-occurring country uses of terminology for the structure between Israel and the Palestinian Territories, UN Security Council meeting, 2003. Visualization by ReseauLu and Marieke van Dijk.

Source: Rogers and Ben-David, 2010.

enjoying support. And this time, Israel is alone in using the term 'security fence' and is thereby isolated.

Countries are 'linked' or isolated by terminology. They settle into positionings by subscribing to programmes, anti-programmes and efforts at neutrality, together with light gestures towards the one side or another (e.g., by using just 'wall' or 'fence'). In some cases, there are evident language blocs. Each bloc shows alignment in that countries (over time) come to terms with other countries by means of using the same language. It is precisely this alignment of actors to programmes, anti-programmes, or efforts of neutrality that one seeks to build into query design from the outset.

Designing ambiguous and unambiguous queries

If one peruses the search engine literature, there are mentions of navigational queries, transactional queries and informational queries, among other types. Yet, on a meta level,

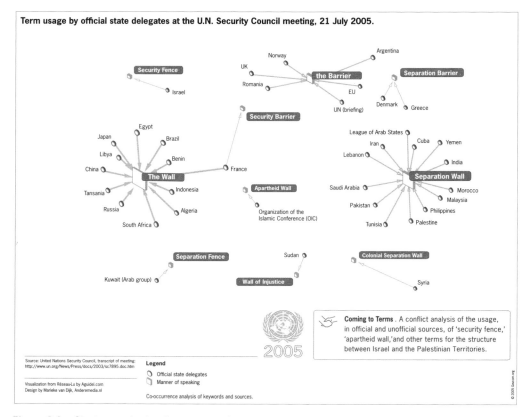

Figure 2.6 Cluster graph showing co-occurring country uses of terminology for the structure between Israel and the Palestinian Territories, UN Security Council meeting, 2005. Visualization by ReseauLu and Marieke van Dijk.
Source: Rogers and Ben-David, 2010.

we can broadly speak of two kinds of queries: unambiguous and ambiguous. The original strength of Google and its PageRank algorithms lay in how it dealt with an ambiguous query that matches more than one potential result and thereby is in need of some form of 'disambiguation'. An example that was often used in the early search engine literature is the query "Harvard". It could refer to the university, a city (in Illinois, USA) or perhaps businesses near the university or in the city. It also could refer to the man who gave the university its name. By looking at which sites receive the most links from the most influential sites, PageRank would return Harvard University as the top result because it would presumably receive more links from reputable sources than a dry-cleaning business near the university, for example, called Harvard Cleaners. The outputs depend on a disambiguating mechanism (Google's PageRank) that places Harvard University at the top. The ability to disambiguate is also thereby socio-epistemological or one that reveals and stabilizes social hierarchies. Harvard University is at the top because it has been placed there through establishment linking practices.

More recently, the inlink has been supplemented as an authority marker by other so-called signals such as user clicks and freshness, as discussed in the search as research chapter.

Suffice it to say, the social researcher may take advantage of how the search engine treats ambiguous queries. As a case in point, the ambiguous keyword 'rights' is queried in a variety of local domain Googles (e.g., google.co.jp, google.co.uk), in order to create hierarchies of concerns (rights types) per country (or Google country), thereby employing Google as a socio-epistemological machine.

Contrariwise, an unambiguous query is one in which it is clear which results one is after (e.g., "Harvard University"). If we return to the cluster maps of countries using particular terms for the barrier between Israel and the Palestinian Territories, recall that precise terms are used. By putting these terms in quotation marks and querying them, Google would return an ordered list of sources that use those specific terms. If one forgoes the use of quotation marks in the query, Google, as mentioned, 'helpfully' provides the engine user with synonyms or equivalents of sorts.

It is instructive to point out a particular form of annotation when writing about queries. When noting down the specific query used, Google's own recommendation is to use square brackets as markers (Cutts, 2005). Therefore, a query for "apartheid wall" with exact match quotation marks included would be written, ["apartheid wall"]. Oftentimes, when a query is mentioned in the literature, it will have only quotation marks without the square brackets. A reader is often left wondering whether the query was in fact made with quotation marks or whether the quotation marks are used in the text merely to distinguish the term as a query. To solve this problem, the square brackets annotation is employed. If one's query does not have quotation marks they are dropped but the square brackets remain.

Research browser

There are two preparatory steps to take prior to doing search as research. The first is to install a research browser. This means installing a separate instance of one's browser, such as Firefox, or creating a new profile in which you have cleaned the cookies and otherwise disentangled yourself from Google. The second is to take a moment to set up one's Google result settings. If saving results for further scrutiny later (including manual interpretation as in the Rights Types project discussed below), set the results from the default 10 to 20, 50 or 100. If one is interested in researching a societal concern, one should set geography in Google to the national level – that is, to the country-level 'regional' setting and not to the default city setting. If one is interested in universal results only, consider obfuscating one's location. In all cases one is not logged into Google.

One example of research conducted using unambiguous queries concerns the Google image results of the query for two different terms for the same barrier: ["apartheid wall"], which is the official Palestinian term for the Israeli–Palestinian barrier mentioned previously, versus the Israeli term, ["security fence"] (see Figure 2.7). The results from these two queries present images of objects distinct from one another. The image results for ["apartheid wall"] contain graffitied, wall-like structures, barbed wire, protests, and people being somehow excluded, whereas with ["security fence"] there is another narrative, one derived through lightweight, high-tech structures. Furthermore, there is a series of images of bomb attacks in Israel, presented as justification for the building of the wall. There are also information graphics, presenting such figures as the number of attempted bombings and the number of bombings that met their targets before and after the building of the wall. In the image results we are thus presented with the argumentation behind the building of the fence. The two narratives resulting from the two separate queries are evidently at odds, and these are the sorts of findings one is able to tease out with a query design in the programme/anti-programme vein. Adding neutral terminology to the query design would enrich the findings by showing, for example, which side's images (so to speak) have become the neutral ones. Studying the politics of neutral or generic images also may be undertaken with Getty Images, the stock image company, where for example the number one image sold for [woman] has

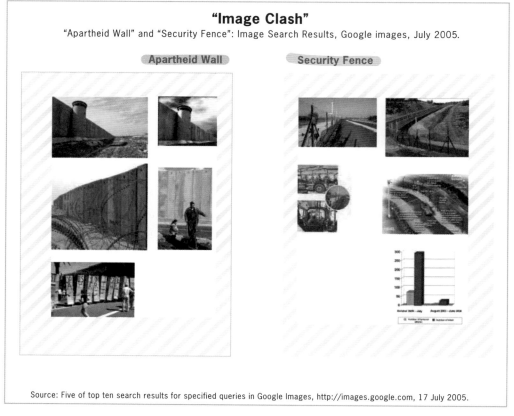

Figure 2.7 Contrasting images for ["Apartheid Wall"] and ["Security Fence"] in Google Images query results, July 2005.

changed over time from one lightly clad in bed to mountain hiker, or 'from sex object to gritty woman', as the *New York Times* phrased it (Miller, 2017).

Search engine artefacts

When doing search as research as above, the question is often raised whether and under what circumstances to remove Google artefacts and Google properties in the results. Wikipedia, towards the top of the results for substantive queries, is ranked highly in the results for the query ["apartheid wall"] yet has as the title of its article in the English-language version an effort at neutrality in 'West Bank barrier'. (The article, as one may expect, includes a discussion of the various names given to the barrier.) While a Google artefact, Wikipedia's efforts at neutrality should be highlighted as such rather than removed. A more difficult case relates to a Google artefact in the results for an underspecified query [rights] in google.com, discussed in more detail below. At the time of the analysis, the non-governmental organization R.I.G.H.T.S. (rightsforartists.com) was returned highly in the results, owing more to its name than to its significance in the rights issue space. Here again the result was retained, and footnoted (or highlighted) as a Google artefact, which in a sense answers questions regarding the extent or breadth of artefacts in the findings. Here the research strategy is chosen to highlight rather than remove an artefact, so as to anticipate critique and make known media effects.

The last example is a project using an ambiguous query that takes advantage of Google's social sorting. In this case we undertook a project about rights, conducted by a large group of researchers who spoke some 30 languages among them. Using this abundance of diverse language skill, we set about determining what sorts of rights are held dear to particular cultures relative to others. In the local languages we formulated the query for [rights], and we ran the query in all the various local domain Googles per language spoken, interpreting the results from google.se as Swedish concerns, .fi for Finnish, .ee for Estonian, .lv for Latvian, .co.uk for British, and so forth. With the results pages saved as HTML (for others to check), the researchers were instructed to work with an editorial process where they manually extract the first ten unique rights from the search results of each local domain Google. Information designers visualized the results by creating an icon for each rights type and a colour scheme whereby unique rights and shared rights across the languages (or local domain Googles) are differentiated. The resultant infographic graphically shows rights hierarchies per country as well as those rights that are unique to a country and those shared among two or more countries. One example of a unique right is the case of Finland, in which the 'freedom to roam' is high on the list (see Figure 2.8). Far from being a trivial issue, this right implies that one can walk through someone's backyard, whereas in other countries (e.g., the UK) ramblers make great effort lobbying for the right to ramble and walk the ancient pathways. Another example is in Latvia, where pension rights for non-citizens are of particular importance.

Figure 2.8　Rights types in particular countries, ranked from Google results of the query [rights] in the local languages and local domain name Googles (google.se, google.fi, google.ee and google.lt), July 2009. Black indicates a unique right (on the graphic).

Source: Rogers, 2013b.

Conclusions: Query design for search as research

Digital methods have been developed as a distinctive strategy for internet-related research where the web is considered both unstable and an object of study for more than digital culture only. As a part of the computational turn in social research, digital methods may be considered as a counterpart to virtual methods, or the importation of the social scientific instrumentarium onto the web, such as online surveys (Rogers, 2009a). Digital methods, as an alternative, strive to employ the methods of the medium, imagining the research affordances of engines and platforms, and repurposing their methods and outputs for social (and medium) research.

The above is foundational is the sense of outlining certain premises of digital methods but also the nitty-gritty of doing online analysis. In conclusion, I would like to return to the premises of doing digital methods with Google Web Search in particular as well as to the finer points of query design, which underpins 'search as research' as an approach distinctive to other analytical traditions, such as discourse analysis.

First, in the digital method of search as research, Google is repurposed from its increasing use as a consumer information appliance, with personalized results that evermore seek to anticipate consumer information needs (such as with autosuggest or the erstwhile service, Google Instant, which populated the results page as one typed a query). Rather, with digital methods, Google is relied upon as an epistemological machine, yielding source hierarchies and dominant voice studies (through its ranked results for a keyword query) as well as individual actor commitment (through its quantitative counts for a single or multiple site query). Transforming Google back into a research machine (as its founders asserted in the early papers on its algorithms) these days requires disentangling oneself from the engine through the installation of a clean research browser and logging out. Once in use, the research browser is not expected to remove all Google artefacts from the output (e.g., Google properties, SEO'd results); rather they become less obfuscated and an object of further scrutiny (medium research), together with the social research one is undertaking with repurposed online methods.

Query design is the practice behind search as research. One formulates queries whose results will allow for the study of trends, dominant voice, positioning, commitment, concern and alignment. The technique is sensitive to keywords, which are understood as the connections people are currently making of a word or phrase, whether established or neologistic, leaning on Raymond Williams's second definition of a keyword. Indeed, in the query design put forward above, the keywords used could be said to take sides, and are furthermore conceptualized as forming part of a programme or anti-programme, as developed by Madeleine Akrich and Bruno Latour. I have added a third means by which keywords are put into play. Journalists, and others conspicuously not taking sides, develop and employ terms as efforts at neutrality. 'West Bank barrier' is one term preferred by BBC journalists (and the English-language Wikipedia) over 'security fence' (Israeli) or 'apartheid wall' (Palestinian). Querying a set of sources (e.g., speeches at the UN Security Council debates) for each of the terms and noting use as well as common use (co-occurrence) would show positioning and alignment, respectively.

For digital methods practice, I would like to emphasize that for query design in the conceptual framework of programme/anti-programme/efforts at neutrality, one retains the specific language (instead of grouping terms together), because the exact matches are likely to show alignment and non-alignment. Furthermore, language may also change over time. Therefore, if one conducts an analysis over time, one can determine whether or not certain actors have, for example, left a certain programme and joined an anti-programme by changing the language and terms they use. Some countries may have become neutral, as was noted when contrasting term use in the 2003 and 2005 Security Council debates on the barrier. As another example, one could ask whether there has been an alignment shift signified through actors leaving the 'blood minerals' programme and joining the 'conflict minerals' programme.

While the discussion has focused mainly on unambiguous queries, search as research also may take advantage of ambiguous ones. As has been noted, if we are interested in researching dominant voice and commitment as well as showing alignment and non-alignment, an unambiguous query is in order. Through an ambiguous query, such as [rights], one can tease out differences and distinct hierarchies of societal concerns across cultures. Here a cross-cultural approach is taken which for search as research with Google implies a comparison of the results of the same query (albeit in each of the native languages) of local domain Google results.

Finally, query design may be viewed as an alternative to forms of discourse analysis (and topic modelling), which may have labelled category bins with keywords (and associated items) tossed into them. Google's helpful 'equivalents' would fall into this category. In query design, however, specificity of the language matters for it differentiates rather than groups. Moreover, it allows one to cast an eye onto the entire data set, making as a part of the analysis so-called long tail entities that previously might not have made the threshold to qualify as a label. One studies it all without categorizing and without sampling, which (following Akrich and Latour), allows not only for the actors to speak for themselves and for the purposes of their programme, anti-programme or efforts at neutrality, but – following Lev Manovich's (2007) cultural analytics – provides opportunities for new interpretive strategies. That there arise new computational hermeneutics which combine close and distant reading could also be seen as the work ahead for the analytical approach.

Query design

1   General rationales for query design

- Measure success or 'impact' (e.g., buzz of a brand or mentions of leader's name in the news). For example, the European Commission (Directorate-General for Communication) has a daily query set up for its president so as to monitor mentions in the news.
- Measure circulation, resonance or salience of a claim (e.g., climate change is human-induced).
- Measure competition between 'programme' and 'anti-programme' as well as 'efforts at neutrality'. For example, the structure between Israel and the Palestinian Territories is a 'fence' or a 'wall'. It is for 'security' or 'apartheid'. An effort at neutrality could be 'barrier'.
- Show keyword diplomacy and slighting. In an act of diplomacy, leaders may use 'wall' when in the presence of Palestinian leaders, but not wish to use both the official adjective and noun ('apartheid wall') so as to appear to endorse positioning or policy. A diplomatic slight would be to use 'fence' or even 'security fence' in their presence. How are keywords deployed in specific settings?
- Document keyword avoidance and resistance. Employees may have been instructed not to use particular language, such as 'evidence-based' (in the case of the Department of Health's Centers for Disease Control and Prevention during the Trump administration). Has the Centers for Disease Control's website been cleansed of keywords? Has such cleansing spread to other agencies and even larger departments? May one document resistance to the keyword policing?

2   Guidelines for keyword list building and querying demarcated source sets

- Identify and retain specific 'issue language' per actor.
- The collection of terms is inclusive, so as to include all actors' issue language (multiple terms for programme, anti-programme, neutrality efforts).
- Design queries (with quotation marks) so as to study resonance of each actor's or each programme's specific issue language.
- Consider actors' terminological innovation (repositioning).
- Note which issue language is successful (and less successful) with particular actors through greater (and lesser) resonance over time.
- Watch actors adopting or distancing themselves from old and new programmes through analysis over time.

PART II

DOING

DIGITAL

METHODS

ISSUECRAWLING
Mapping networks on the web

Building a website list (with the associative query snowballing technique) is the first step in mapping networks on the web

Mapping web networks

This chapter is dedicated to locating networks on the web, an exercise that can be undertaken with link analysis software such as the Issuecrawler or Hyphe. The Issuecrawler and Hyphe are web network mapping software tools, where one enters a list of URLs and the software crawls them and finds links between them and to other websites. Issuecrawler is more automated and includes off-topic links in the network (unless excluded in advance), and Hyphe is semi-manual and more labour-intensive where the goal is corpus-building through the inclusion of only on-topic links in the network, editing out others (Ooghe-Tabanou et al., 2018).

How to build a list of websites to be crawled in order to explore a claim and seek to answer a research question? In the following the associative query snowballing technique is detailed; it is a method, or heuristic, to build a list of URLs using a search engine. Subsequently, in an exemplary case study, the Issuecrawler mapping software is introduced through a case study with a research question. Right-wing populist and extremist websites in a series of European countries are crawled and mapped in order to inquire into whether the 'new right' is overtaking the 'old guard', as has been claimed (Bartlett et al., 2011). The 'new right' distinguishes itself from its older counterpart through employing issue language of the left such as globalization critique. In the event, certain technical characteristics show a more interlinked, responsive and fresher 'new right' web than the old guard's; they also appear to exchange 'blood and soil' rhetoric for identitarian, anti-Islam as well as other distinctive issue language, albeit with geographical differences where northern Europe contains more anti-Islam material than southern. Thus, the interpretation of the network has both quantitative as well as qualitative dimensions, mixing so-called computational hermeneutics with close reading.

Making URL lists of right-wing populist and extremist groupings

Making lists of sources is the initial step in numerous analytical undertakings. In the 'how to' research protocol that follows the aim is to build lists of URLs so as to seed link crawling software and ultimately make link maps of 'new right' populism and right-wing extremism in particular European countries. The maps show links between websites, or online networks of websites that may be analysed according to a series of technical characteristics (size, responsiveness and freshness), but here a substantive analysis is also undertaken to examine claims made in the popular press and by a prominent, London-based think tank concerning the rise of the new right supplanting the (fascist or neo-Nazi) old guard in a series of European countries, with an orientation distinctive from the 'blood and soil' pathos of old (Van Gilder Cooke, 2011). According to the study by Demos, the think tank, the new right is 'defined by [its] opposition to immigration and concern for protecting national and European culture, sometimes using the language of human rights and freedom' (Bartlett et al., 2011: 15). How to examine these claims empirically through an online, interdisciplinary approach that combines crawling techniques from web science and close reading of websites from the humanities? It is a quanti-quali (so-called) method that may be situated alongside reading party manifestos and favoured literature, going native by embedding oneself in the groups, interviewing imprisoned or former group members, and other qualitative techniques to distil significant content. The online mapping method could be considered either as an exploratory step that provides leads for further in-depth analysis, or as a means to create country reports with a broad stroke.

The exercise commences with the collection of the URLs of populist right-wing and right-wing extremist websites in a series of countries named in the popular press article as well as the Demos study: Austria, Belgium, Bulgaria, Denmark, France, Germany, Greece, Hungary, Italy, the Netherlands, Norway, Portugal, Romania, Serbia and Spain. The lists of websites are made by following a particular heuristic, referred to as the associative query snowballing technique. (See below for a step-by-step elaboration.) Queries are formulated and made via the advanced 'region' setting in the countries in question, in the respective local languages, largely in these styles: [populist right parties] as well as [right-wing extremist groups]. When the names of parties, groups or other related entities (e.g., a webshop selling right-wing T-shirts, music and literature) are found, they are entered as lists (each in quotation marks) into the search boxes of the respective local domain Googles, and the results are read to identify new group names. This process is repeated until no new names are found. That is, lists of populist right and extremist groups are slowly built up from the query results.

Once the lists gathered from the web search engines are finished, they are compared to expert lists. To find expert lists, queries are made in Google Scholar, first in the home language, and subsequently in English (or another language deemed relevant for the relevant scientific literature). The queries made are similar to those entered in the local domain Googles, in the first round of list building from the web. Any new groups found on the expert lists in the scholarly literature are searched for online, and if they have a web presence, they are added. Thus, the expert lists add to the web lists (which may be counter-intuitive at first, but is ultimately more productive, at least in this exercise). For each group, actor or entity on the list there should be an accompanying URL or multiple URLs.

The work of locating URLs may be arduous for the right's web presence may be 'on the move', dodging authorities, as is the case in many countries such as Germany where website owners regularly change URLs (and hosts to outside the country) and also migrate to social media such as Facebook, so as to attract a larger, more active following and make it more burdensome for the authorities to take down what it may construe, nationally, as 'illegal content' (Prodhan and Lauer, 2016).

Quanti-quali analysis of European right-wing formations online

The URLs of the populist right, the extreme right and the populist and extreme right together are crawled, per country, in three, separate analytical procedures, using the Issuecrawler. For both the extreme right as well as right-wing populist networks, of interest are their comparative sizes as well as other indicators of activity such as responsiveness and freshness. By 'responsiveness' is meant whether the sites are online and return a response code (or http status code) of 200, when loaded in a browser. Freshness concerns their last update, and their recent consistency in updating (last updated date or post freshness).

The two seed sets are crawled together, in order to compare them and gauge their interconnectedness. Do they form one cluster, or are they (largely) separate? Thereby one is able to begin to examine the claims that the populist right is distinctive (clustered separately) and overtaking the old guard (more populous and more active), at least according to online network analysis. For the analysis, one asks whether the new right has larger, denser clusters and more active and fresher websites than those of the old guard? In most countries under study the answers are in the affirmative, thus largely confirming the popular press and think tank claims (see Figure 3.1).

In terms of the method, for each set of populist, extreme right and combination of URLs, automated co-link analysis is performed, with 'privileged starting points' (a special setting), keeping the seeds on the map, if linked to, whereby those websites receiving at least one link from the seeds are retained in the network. 'Newly discovered' sites would require receiving two links to be in the network (standard 'co-links'). The 'privilege starting points' feature gives the seeds an increased chance of remaining in the network.

Each of the networks is visualized as a cluster graph (according to measures of inlink centrality), and the findings are described. First, are there other (heretofore) undiscovered groups found through the link analysis? Co-link mapping is a procedure that discovers

Figure 3.1   Danish right-wing networks combined, showing the ascendancy of the 'new right' counter-jihadists and their links to the American alt-right (and extremist) movements. Issuecrawler co-link map, 20 March 2013, redesigned and labelled.

related URLs through interlinking. In the event we found Facebook to be a large node in many countries, which not only is in keeping with the impression of groups 'on the move' to social media but also prompts the question of its (separate) analysis, for Facebook cannot be crawled as above. (Thus, only links to Facebook are on the map, not outlinks from Facebook.) Second, which sites are responsive and fresh? Are they mainly the populist ones? Indeed, the old guard's web in a variety of European countries such as Belgium is often stale, indicating either a decline in the movement or in its use of the web (or both). The question is also which part of the right has moved to social media, and which part has simply declined online.

When locating the right online, it also may be of interest to inquire into where the websites are registered and by whom (using 'whois' services). Are they registered under aliases and hosted outside the country? Or are they registered in country, under one's own names? In certain countries these are signs that groups are in hiding or operating in plain sight, so to speak. In Germany the groups often mask themselves, while in Austria they may operate out in the open (and 'whois' records are available).

Apart from the 'technical' characteristics of the websites in the networks (network size as well as site responsiveness, freshness, georegistration and use of alias) the qualitative analysis concerns the groups' orientation as well as activities, especially in their outreach, forms of communication as well as youth recruitment. Is there an active music scene? Are there forums or other online means to become acquainted (and even radicalized)? Where does one go in order to participate in person in populist and extreme right-wing culture? Generally, the substantive characteristics of the right-wing formations online specific to the country may be understood by spending significant analytical time reading the websites on the (clickable) Issuecrawler or Hyphe map of each of the national right-wing scenes in question, picking out significant themes. One may also perform close reading with a ranked list of the sites in the network, and write thick, albeit brief, descriptions of the cultural activities as described on the top sites, ranked by inlink count.

Right-wing outreach and potential counter-measures

The findings, initially, are of use to answering the question concerning the ascendancy of the populist 'new right' over the old guard, but they also may lead to questions concerning the counter-measures being undertaken in the countries, and whether they ultimately 'match' the activities of the right. In Hungary the supposed Mongolian language roots have been appropriated by the right (old and new), and recruitment and outreach are performed at yurt camping outings as well as heritage festivals. Are there activities to try to take back the yurt? These would be the 'counter-measures' under study, and in the event there do not seem to be counter-counter-festivals, so to speak. Unlike in Bulgaria (and Spain), where the old guard still thrives (online), in Serbia there is a new, right-wing civil society, with think tanks, which seek to shape the discussion on the future of Serbia around the questions of land and Kosovo. What is the state of the left-wing civil society and think tank culture? France, witnessing the rise of identitarian (youth) groups and ethno-differentialism, is a dividing line between northern and southern Europe in the sense that counter-jihadism (also referred to as anti-Islam and Islamophobia) is present but a less dominant theme compared to Scandanavia. In Denmark, Norway and to an extent the Netherlands, counter-jihadism (the self-description for anti-Islam) increasingly organizes the new right (see Figure 3.1). In terms of counter-measures, the Netherlands is experiencing a weakening of progressive groups monitoring hate, as was found. Especially in northern Europe and Scandinavia, we find some of the language of the new right the London think tank described. The claim that the new right employs a vocabulary of immigration opposition borrowed from 'rights talk' is difficult to pinpoint, but anti-globalization (and anti-Europe) expressions are prominent. In Austria, contrariwise, the populist right's critique is anti-capitalist (against lavish

Viennese balls, and the storage of Austrian gold abroad). In Germany there is (still) a preponderance of 'brown culture', with demonstrations (and anti-fascist counter-demonstrations). Apart from graffitied walls and symbolic dress, the right's style also is one of info-sharing, providing legal advice as well as internet counter-surveillance tips.

While mentioned in passing above, in a larger, separate exercise, it may be asked whether there are counter-networks in place with counter-measures that address the outreach, recruitment and styles of the new right or whether a (perhaps misplaced) confrontation is still taking place with the (weakened) old guard. A similar exercise may be undertaken, where one sources URLs concerning the counter-movement(s), perhaps distinguishing between anti-fascist and anti-hate groups, which could be construed as old guard and new guard counter-movements or counter-networks, respectively. Here one builds lists of URLs, using the associative query snowballing technique (described in detail again below), crawls the anti-fascist and anti-hate lists of sites separately as well as together, and performs close reading of their activities. Do they match and address the old or the new right's outreach?

In conclusion the list-building technique is elaborated in more detail, prior to a reflection on the types of lists that may be authored with the aid of search engines these days, now that the editorial practice of creating web directories has waned. Thereafter there is a discussion of hyperlink network analysis, including the kinds of stories often told with networks by interpreting clusters, single nodes as well as chains of nodes.

Conclusions: List building and issuecrawling

List building in preparation for seeding the Issuecrawler or other link crawling software such as Hyphe (and VOSON) often relies on 'link lists' as seeds (Jacomy et al., 2016; Ackland et al., 2006; Ackland, 2013). In the past preferred starting points were those lists maintained by Dmoz.org, the open directory project, and Yahoo!, the original web 'directory' which categorized URLs. Both projects are defunct. In a sense, directories of all kinds on the web have been supplanted by search engines, which also author lists, albeit of query results rather than list of websites categorized by human editors. Intergovernmental organizations as well as NGOs also have been keepers of expert lists, but their curation practices have been in abeyance for years. Wikipedia continues to be one of the few human-edited list-makers; given their encyclopedic quality, they may require paring.

The list-making, and query-building, technique introduced above is designed for a post-directory web. It strives to build lists anew, with the aid of search engines, first by locating lists of mentions of groups, actors or entities (in this case of the right wing), and subsequently by sourcing their URLs, again via search. It is a digital method dubbed 'associative query snowballing' because each of the actors or entities found has been acquired by association to other actors through iterations of query results.

Once the seed lists are compiled, the issuecrawling commences, whereby one maps networks on the web, ultimately seeking the extent to which the new right and old right are conjoined or separate, and whether the one or the other is larger, denser, more responsive and fresher. Telling the story of the network may start with close readings on the top nodes, together with where they are registered and whether they operate in the open or use aliases. Additionally, how do they recruit, and what kinds of activities do they undertake for the purposes of group formation? Finally, are these activities countered or 'matched' by initiatives that seek to mitigate the rise of the (new) right? In a second network mapping exercise, the research focuses on locating the counter-networks and counter-measures, inquiring into the extent to which they address the (new) right's recruitment measures and outreach activities.

URL list-making with the associative query snowballing technique

The objective is to assemble three URL lists per country under study: extreme right, populist right and a combined list. 'Extreme right' and 'populist right' are broad terms not categorized in advance, but instead the authors of online lists classify them as such.

Below are the step-by-step instructions on how to make a list through what is termed associative query snowballing. The example of list building is for the 'extreme right' in Spain; however, much of the process is the same for any country. The third list is made eventually by merging the first two. Thereafter there are instructions of use for the Issuecrawler.

Building a URL list using a search engine query technique

1   Open in the browser the local domain Google search engine for the country in question (e.g., google.es) or use the appropriate 'region' setting in Google's interface. Design a broad query that will output extreme right groups in Spain. For example, use [Grupos de extrema derecha en España] (translation: 'Extreme right groups in Spain').

2   After performing the query, the user is returned a set of results, some of which are lists. 'List' is meant in a broad sense. For example, a news article that reviews the most influential extreme right-wing groups usually will name a number of them across the article. One might find that the article refers to parties or groups not only from the country in question but also to other international groupings. From the pages and articles extract the names of the groups that correspond to the country in question, and also find the URLs and include them in a spreadsheet. Suppose in this first step two main groups have been found: España 2000 and Plataforma per Catalunya.

3   Return to the Spanish Google. Enter the names of the groups found in the previous search results as a query using quotation marks: ["España 2000" "Plataforma Catalunya"]. The fresh set of results returned contain ideally not the two groups used in the query but also new ones that will be associated with them (associative snowballing). Comb through the results, select the names of the new groups and add them to the spreadsheet. For example, the first result contains the new name, 'Democracia Nacional'.

4   Enter the two initial groups (España 2000 and Plataforma per Catalunya) together with the new group (Democracia Nacional) in the search box, using quotation marks around each group. Again, one will receive results in which the three groups may be associated with other groups. Add the new ones, including their URLs, to the spreadsheet.

5   Repeat until either the same results continue to be returned or no new groups are found. For the purposes of robustness, one may wish to make queries that contain new combinations of fewer groups.

6   As a note, the last groups to make the lists could be thought of as marginal or historical. It is advisable, as a last step, to query the marginal groups separately, which ideally will return a new set of even more marginal groups, though these also could be from other countries. Repeat until no new country-specific results are found.

Finding expert lists, compiling them, adding them to the web list, and making the final list

1   Search for academic literature that mentions the extreme right in Spain. Academic articles and grey literature case studies usually have their own collections of names. One may use Google Scholar to query in the original language or in English, again employing broad search terms: [extreme right-wing Spain]. From the results explore and choose approximately three or more articles that you have detected containing lists. Recall that lists do not always look like lists.

2   Extract the names of the groups, and search for the groups' URLs, if (as is often the case) they are not included. Make a list of all groups and URLs. This is the expert list.

3   Compare the web list (from the associative query snowballing technique) with the expert list. There is a list comparison tool, 'triangulation', at https://tools.digitalmethods.net/beta/triangulate/. It shows the URLs unique to each list as well as those that are common.

4   Take note of the groups or other entities that are unique to the expert list or to the web list. Query the unique groups' names in the search engine and ascertain whether it has one or more URLs. Retain those groups on the expert lists that have a web presence, that is, one or more associated URLs claiming to represent or give significant voice to the group.

5   Concatenate the URLs from the web list and the expert list.

Finally, one may take note of what the web yields in comparison to the expert. One may compare epistemologies (how lists are made) as well as ontologies (types of lists). Expert lists (including Wikipedia's) are often exhaustive and alphabetical, and include historical actors, while web lists outputted by search engines are in the main hierarchical and fresh.

Issuecrawler 'how to' guide, including allied tools

The Issuecrawler is web network and visualization software that works in a browser. It consists of crawlers, databases, analysis engines, and visualization modules and works in the spirit of the Dartmouth time-sharing system, where users can queue their (crawl) request and the system will start crawling whenever there is capacity on the system. The software and the project documentation are written in English, and certain power users have created French, Italian and Korean language instruction guides. It is language-independent in the sense that it does not rely on keyword entries, but rather webpages or hyperlinks, and is thus applicable across languages. Non-Roman character URLs are also supported.

Enter a set of URLs and the software returns the network the URLs disclose through how pages or sites link. The software relies on co-link analysis, a scientometric sampling or network demarcation technique based on citation analysis. The set of URLs entered into the software are crawled, the outlinks are captured and the co-links retained, in one, two or three iterations of the procedure, as selected by the user. There are also inter-actor and snowball crawling methods built into the software; inter-actor methods find the links between the seed URLs entered in one iteration, and snowball methods find the outward links of the seeds in up to two or even three iterations. The results are analysed for centrality measures and visualized in a directed graph, showing site interlinkings (nodes and lines with arrows). The file format of the graph is a scalable vector graphic (SVG), which also may be saved in a variety of other file formats, including PNG and PDF. There is a GEXF file for importing into Gephi, the network analysis and visualization software, where more formal network measures are also available. The online SVG graphic loads in the browser, and is interactive, whereby the user can click the URLs behind the nodes and may turn on and off links as well as domains. The purpose of the interactivity is to provide a single, graphical space for users to explore specific interlinkings between sites (who links to whom, and who does not?) as well as to spend time reading the content of the pages in the network. The default setting of the crawler is 'by page' analysis, meaning that the most significant pages in the network are retained. Returned 'deep pages' (i.e., non-front pages) are indicative of the most significant content or items collectively referenced by the network (a document, petition, database, etc.). Thus, content analysis of the issue network may begin with deep page analysis. Through the links (and missing links) between websites, one may study associations, and derive a politics of association between the actors, such that (in one example) Armenian NGOs link to each other and (aspirationally) to intergovernmental organizations. Intergovernmental organizations link to each other, but not to the Armenian groups, in a sense ignoring their outreach (see Figure 3.2).

Apart from the cluster map generator, there is a geographical mapping module, the Issue Geographer, built into the Issuecrawler, which plots the actors' registered (whois) location, if available, on a geographical map, where one critical question concerns the geographical distance between the central actors on an issue and the location of the issues on the ground (Marres and Rogers, 2008). Are the (local) issues redefined by international actors? For such a project one would note how the local actors discuss the issue compared to the international ones.

Objective of the Issuecrawler

The objective of the Issuecrawler project is to give users the capacity to map networks on the web; it has been conceived and designed to map what is termed 'issue networks', though it also may be employed for 'dynamic link sampling' or finding URLs related to the seeds entered (Rogers, 2010; see Chapter 4 below). The original notion of the issue network was developed in the mid-1970s by a writer from the conservative think tank, the American Enterprise Institute (AEI), as a means of describing and also admonishing against the rise in influence of clutches of (left-of-centre) NGOs, funders, think tanks and academics, developing powerful streams of thought as well as policy prior to the proper legislative procedure (Heclo, 1978). Heclo considered issue networks a threat to democracy through their lack of legibility and accountability. Indeed, much of the 'mapping' of networks – from the classic Medici family marriage network (Padgett and Ansell, 1993) to social network analysis of the George W. Bush diagrams of power in the artistic work of Mark Lombardi (Hobbs, 2003) and the 9/11 terror network in the applied network analysis work of Valdis Krebs (2005) – concerns making structures of social relations visible. Hyperlink mapping, as performed by the Issuecrawler, has as an additional purpose, to put on display the normal 'politics of association' in evidence through public displays of connection (links) on the Web. With the software it is less the historical, 'deep structures' of connection that are of interest, however much

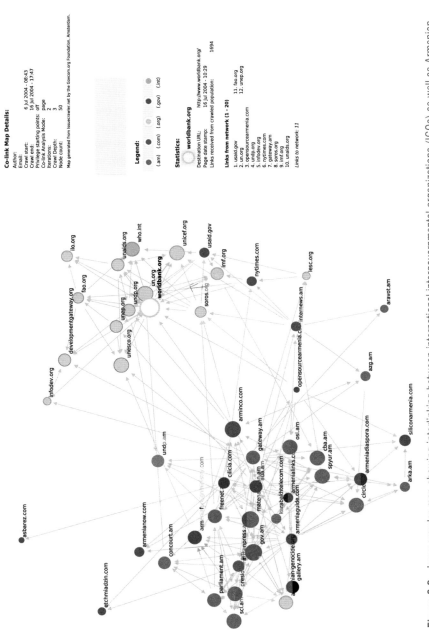

EGovernment and Armenia

Co-link Map Details:

Author:
Crawl start: 6 Jul 2004 - 08:43
Crawl end: 16 Jul 2004 - 17:47
Privilege starting points: off
Co-link Analysis Mode: page
Iterations: 2
Crawl Depth: 3
Node count: 50

Map generated from Issuecrawler.net by the Govcom.org Foundation, Amsterdam.

Legend:

(.am)   (.com)   (.org)   (.gov)   (.int)

Statistics:

⊙ **worldbank.org**

Destination URL: http://www.worldbank.org/
Page date stamp: 16 Jul 2004 - 10:29
Links received from crawled population: 1694

Links from network (1 - 20)

1. usaid.gov   11. fao.org
2. un.org   12. unep.org
3. opensourcearmenia.com
4. undp.org
5. infodev.org
6. nytimes.com
7. gateway.am
8. soros.org
9. imf.org
10. unaids.org

Links to network: 11

Figure 3.2 Issuecrawler map showing interlinking between international intergovernmental organizations (IGOs) as well as Armenian NGOs. In a form of aspirational linking (and the politics of association), note that the Armenian NGOs link to the IGOs, but the IGOs do not link back. The one exception is that imf.org (International Monetary Fund) links to cba.am (the Armenian Central Bank), which can be seen at a glance by clicking on imf.org (and noting its outlinks).

such work could be undertaken through time-series analysis (with the Issuecrawler scheduler). Rather, the effort has been to create a tool that performs a form of 'live social science' (Rogers, 2002). Each crawl result returns current, existing linkages.

Getting started (including with the allied tools)

To prepare a crawl, one first considers a research question (e.g., is the new right supplanting the old right?), and builds one or more URL lists (e.g., of new right and old right groups, using the associative query snowballing technique or other means). In sourcing germane URLs, one may come upon a link list or a series of URLs mentioned inline on a webpage (such as at the University of Minnesota's Human Rights Library (http://hrlibrary.umn.edu), where there is a list of human rights organizations, discussed paragraph by paragraph, with a link to each). In order to capture that list, one may wish to use the simple 'link ripper' tool, which strips hyperlinks from a webpage. (It also strips URLs from multiple pages entered into the software.) As the name indicates, the tool, with the option 'outlinks' selected, rips links from a webpage, creating a tidy list in order to enter them into the Issuecrawler as seed URLs (or onto a spreadsheet as one forages further). One can also rip internal links from a page, for example, to other pages on the same site, where there may be more outlinks to be captured than on the original page.

In discussing the preparation of inputs into the Issuecrawler and list building more generally, it is crucial to mention here that one must input crawlable URLs. These are webpages that do not block crawlers of all kinds by default. Search engine results URLs are not crawlable, but one can extract the URLs from that page by entering that URL (e.g., Google's results page) into the link ripper. Social media URLs (such as a Facebook page) are not crawlable, but the results of a Facebook search query, which includes not just Facebook profiles, pages and groups but also web links, could be extracted. All in all, some work is required to craft a list of seed URLs. The Issuecrawler takes as its input not only web links that are crawlable, but preferably those that contain links. Finally, one also should check the URLs entered into the Issuecrawler and ascertain whether they are responsive as well as whether they resolve or are redirected elsewhere. Use the URLs that ultimately load in the browser as the seeds to crawl.

Once a crawl has completed, one may render the crawl result as a graph, and explore it for clusters, top nodes, top deep pages (non-homepages) and linking patterns. Which nodes have received the most links? Here one can begin to describe the overall network. Which nodes dominate the clusters? Here one moves to describe the clusters. More delicately, who links to whom, and which links are missing? Are there filter bubbles, or links between the like-minded or substantively oriented, rather than across ideological divides? Does one encounter aspirational linking, and a politics of association, as in the Armenian case above (see Figure 3.2)? If a network has been found of some analytical interest, one may consider scheduling it to run at regular intervals (e.g., monthly), and track the changes in the network (rankings per node, and per node type) over time.

One may export the Issuecrawler result (GEXF file) to Gephi, the network analysis and exploration tool. Once in Gephi, there are preferred analytical regimes, whereby one is first and foremost striving to create clusters and label them. In Gephi, choose an algorithm (often ForceAtlas2), which pulls nodes together and pushes them apart according to attraction and repulsion measures, thereby producing clusters. Those nodes that are most attractive (through strength of connection) come together, and most repulsive (through weakness of connection) are pushed away (Jacomy et al., 2014). Through adjusting scaling and gravity (and occasionally resorting to the LinLog mode and to the modularity algorithm), one is able to produce clusters, which are then labelled. (While adjusting the settings, one strives to maintain the structure of the network.) A discussion of the labelled clusters' comparative size, density and positionality is typically the beginning of the 'story of the network', though one may add sub-stories concerning individual nodes as well as the distance between both clusters as well as nodes (see Table 3.1). As discussed above, two clusters in the right-wing network (the old right and new right) would indicate a separation between the two right-wing formations; other (webby rather than network) measures provide additional story-telling elements, such as their websites' responsiveness as well as their freshness, where the new right may be found to be more active than the old guard.

Table 3.1 Network story-telling routines (often utilized for Gephi-related work)

1	Entire network
(a)	the groups or themes (clusters and holes)
(b)	their (im)balance (size and density)
2	Single nodes (with specific positioning)
(a)	authorities and hubs (centrality)
(b)	bridges and brokers (betweenness)
3	Routes (linked node chains)
(a)	grand tour (diameter/perimeter) – 'Eulerian walk'
(b)	short cuts (shortest paths)

Source: adapted from Venturini et al., 2017.

Indeed, adding web elements to the story-telling routines may enable more to be told. Beyond the cluster labels (often derived by browsing the content of the main nodes in the clusters), there is of course the deep content for both distant as well as close reading. For a media analysis, one may strive to locate the (most referenced) videos, images, news stories, memes and other content types. Are there certain media formats that dominate the network? For a content analysis (from more of a distant reading perspective), one may build a list of keywords (e.g., around counter-jihadism and anti-Islam), and query the URLs (in the entire network, or in each of the clusters) with the Google Scraper (a.k.a. Lippmannian Device), which allows one to input a list of sites that are outputted from the Issuecrawler and query those sites for keywords and phrases. Is the specificity of the 'new right' in their use of particular counter-jihadist or other language, and does the old guard continue to use another vocabulary? A more systematic approach to building a keyword list would be to visit each website, make or extract a list of issues or poignant terms used per site, and create a word cloud from them, thereby gaining a sense of the prevalence of terms through their resizing in the 'clouding' technique. One also would query the terms in each of the sites (using the Lippmannian Device), deriving in a sense the agenda or orientation of the network, as well as the individual clusters. The results of the analyses could be construed as long-form labelling.

Compiling a set of right-wing sites in Greece

'The sourcing of the starting points proceeded through a search [in Google] for extreme right groups in Greece, where *Golden Dawn* and *Laos* ("the people" in Greek) were returned. Combining these two search terms produced a third group, *Mavroskrinos* (black lily). Searching for the three groups returned two further ones, *Metopo* (front) and *Ellinokratein* (Patriotic Hellenic Association).

'Visits to the five websites turned up related sites, e.g., the youth and the law students groups of *Laos* ("the people"). The final list (which added three regional sites, *Group21* for Macedonia, *Rethimno* for Crete, and the *Greek Resistance Movement* in Cyprus) was completed after surfing the sites mentioned above' (Rogers, 2013c: 21).

VIDEO 1 Mapping
networks on the web

PROJECT 1

Map the relationship between right-wing populists and extremists

RESEARCH GOAL To explore and characterize the relationships between the alt-right and alt-lite in the United States, and between right-wing extremists and right-wing populists in European countries.

1   Curate lists of alt-right and alt-lite actors, respectively. The alt-right is often considered more extremist (and white supremacist) in their language and outlook than the alt-lite which is transgressive and against political correctness. Alternatively, in the countries of one's choosing, curate lists of right-wing populists (who claim to represent 'the people' against a corrupt or out-of-touch establishment) and right-wing extremists, respectively.

2   Crawl the lists separately and together, using co-link analysis. In the separate crawls, ascertain the relative size and density of each network, and also whether the one group pulls in the other. In the total crawl, inquire into the extent to which each clusters separately, or overlaps into a unified group formation.

3   Consider the freshness of the websites, and their activity levels.

4   Through close reading of the top websites per cluster, inquire into substantive similarities and differences. Even if they do not cluster together, they may share the same language. Are the extremists (or alt-right) and the populists (or alt-lite) substantively coherent, in the sense they constitute a united whole in terms of the language they use? Do they use language of the old right (blood and soil) or the new right (anti-globalization, anti-political correctness).

5   Study, too, how the groups communicate, and recruit through a close reading of the top populist and extremist websites. Which outreach and retention activities do they organize? Are the populists and extremists similar in how they attract and keep adherents?

PROJECT 2

Map right-wing online formations and counter measures taken against them

RESEARCH GOAL To investigate networks of both populist and extremist right-wing groups and map the measures taken to counter their rise in a chosen country.

1   Create a single, overlapping network of right-wing extremists and right-wing populists as described in project 1. Examining the top nodes, locate descriptions of their outreach activities.
2   Subsequently, using the query snowballing technique described above, curate a list of the group names of anti-fascist, anti-hate and other initiatives (whether more activist, non-governmental organizations or funders) formed to combat the rise and spread of right-wing populism and extremism.
3   Crawl and create a network of the sites.
4   Through a close reading of the top websites, answer the following questions. Do these counter-measure activities match those of the extremists and populists? Are they addressing the right's (outreach) activities, or are they missing the mark? What sorts of recommendations may be made to the groups seeking to counter the rise of right-wing populism and extremism?

Video tutorial

- 'Harvester – Extracting URLs from a Web Page' (1' 24"), https://www.youtube.com/watch?v=kzaq9DXfO_g

Watch the tutorial to learn how to extract URLs from a webpage, and operate the Harvester, a tool that creates a ready-made list of URLs for inputting into the Issuecrawler.

Tools

- Harvester, digitalmethods.net. Available at https://wiki.digitalmethods.net/Dmi/ToolHarvester.
- Hyphe, medialab.sciences-po.fr. Available at http://hyphe.medialab.sciences-po.fr.
- Issuecrawler, issuecrawler.net. Available at https://www.issuecrawler.net (request login).
- Link Ripper, digitalmethods.net. Available at https://tools.digitalmethods.net/beta/linkRipper/.

URL FETCHING
Internet censorship research

*Treating the deceptively simple question of
whether a website is blocked or not*

This chapter is dedicated to rationales and research techniques to investigate state internet censorship at a juncture when the rationales remain clear, but the techniques may be ethically objectionable, owing to surveillance regimes in place in the countries under study. How to carry on with the important work on censorship detection and monitoring without putting the researchers and/or the computer users in the countries in question in harm's way? In the following, research questions for censorship inquiries are laid out, such as its discovery, unintended consequences, effectiveness, circumvention, censor duping, Western complicity, censored content effects as well as the effects of being watched (self-censorship). Additionally, techniques are put forward for drawing up URL (and keyword) lists to be studied, as well as for fetching URLs in the countries in question to check for blockage. Short (historical) case studies concerning Chinese and Iranian internet censorship illustrate certain lines of inquiry and as well as techniques, including current ethical issues. The chapter concludes with considerations about practising and contributing to internet censorship research when its ethical and technical study are at a crossroads.

The evolution of state internet censorship and its study

Generally speaking, internet censorship research rests on sourcing claims about existing blocking practices for the country or countries under study, building URL or website lists, and checking the websites in the countries for censorship. When a website is censored by the state (such as in Iran), a so-called block page appears, with an official message alerting the user to the illegality of accessing the content (see Figure 4.1). With the block page or a less overt technical indication in countries that do not use them (such as in China where the connection times out), the website is confirmed as censored. Censorship practices online subsequently may be indexed, reported and interpreted.

Over the past few years, however, internet censorship has become more involved, and with it its study. Not just websites as such are blocked, in the way a book or film in the past was banned (Darnton, 2014). Keywords may be targeted, such as those appearing in URLs, search engine queries or content typed into messaging services. One case in point occurs in Weibo and WeChat in China, where a long list of words relating to a particular government crackdown returns no results in the one, and messages containing the words remain undelivered in the other (Ruan et al., 2017).

There is a certain technicity to how content is censored on the internet. Websites may be blocked temporarily or only in certain cities like the capital during elections or a street protest; such spatial and temporal blocking is distinctive from national content bans for all citizens and has been dubbed second-generation internet censorship. Internet connection speeds may be slowed, or ground to a halt, as took place in Iran in June 2009 during the election crisis. Websites loading in the browser may time out or be pointed to the wrong address. When users are not only blocked from particular websites (through covert means, without a block page appearing) but also their requests are monitored, censorship may be coupled with surveillance and user logging, or what researchers have called third-generation internet censorship (Deibert and Rohozinski, 2010).

How to capture and study the phenomenon? Are there also techniques to capture these first, second as well as third generations of internet censorship? Are there other forms that do not fit the categories? For countries that block URLs (and perhaps put up censorship notices), simple techniques of URL fetching in a browser on location, or remotely through proxies or virtual private networks (VPNs), allow the researcher to gain a sense of the kind of content being censored. Repeated requests would show the persistence of censorship, and likely content policies. But for the so-called next-generation types of censorship (which do not necessarily follow chronologically from one another and may occur simultaneously), updated censorship detection tools and research practices are required. Temporary and/or regional blocking demands geographically and temporally distributed monitoring and takes more time and resources. It becomes necessary to use multiple researchers, volunteers, proxies and VPNs with known locations using IP-to-geo look-up services to pinpoint the server coordinates. It also may become important to run more voluminous URL requests through the servers in the countries in question, given that blocking may be done 'just in time'. One could imagine that as the volume of queries increases the prospect of those being flagged by system administrators as unusual behaviour (possibly to be reported) may increase.

Figure 4.1 Block page in Iran redirects to a directory of acceptable national websites.
Source: Lee, 2013.

The ethical stakes

Discussing internet censorship research that relies on third parties (without their consent or without proper discussion of potential repercussions), be they friendly volunteers who have agreed to run some URLs, or the owners of proxy servers, one researcher writes that 'a user innocently aiding a researcher in mapping their national filter, resulting in their computer suddenly attempting to connect to all forms of banned content, may find themselves under very unwelcome scrutiny' (Wright et al., 2011: 5). In a later article, a similar point is made less equivocally: 'Deliberate misuse of a network service for the purposes of detecting internet filtering may be illegal in many jurisdictions, and such misuse without the consent of users or system operators is clearly unethical' (Wright, 2014: 128). Raising the ethical stakes for researchers performing remote internet censorship research (and repurposing devices in order to do so) also coincide with the awareness of the mass state surveillance reported by Edward Snowden (beginning in June 2013), and the spreading of third-generation censorship practices to more countries through Western companies such as the Hacking Team, based in Milan. Concerns about the state watching internet censorship research raise questions. How to monitor and record internet censorship when the means to do so are (potentially) illegal in the country in question? Would such research that uses a third party – without their knowing it – put that person at risk? How to mitigate, or eliminate, the risks?

Figure 4.2   Global internet filtering map by the Open Net Initiative, last updated December 2014, indicating that countries have pervasive, substantial, selective, suspected or no evidence of blocking websites.
Source: http://map.opennet.net/filtering-pol.html.

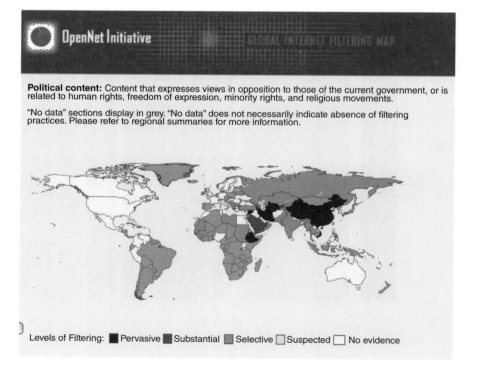

As stated at the outset, it is of importance to be informed of the censorship practices in the country under question. Are they known to practise next-generation monitoring and surveillance? If so, what kinds of censorship research practices would still be considered responsible? Joss Wright developed a technique to test URLs for filtering that did not involve third parties in China; it relies on a particular censorship practice (DNS hijacking/poisoning/tampering) and thus is well suited to China but less so to the countries using other techniques such as filtering software purchased from Western companies. Other researchers engage informed volunteers and/or employ stealth DIY research practices, running URLs through servers inside the countries in question and securely exporting the data. (This research protocol was performed for nearly a decade in the pioneering work at the Open Net Initiative.) Papers are published with pseudonyms, detailing how the investigative work was done in-country, without tipping off the authorities (Aryan at al., 2013). Still others use proxies and VPNs, with or perhaps without some grasp of the origins of these services and the people behind them.

Here the focus is on the kinds of rationales put forward for testing for blocking, generally, given the sensitivity of (repeatedly) requesting banned websites in some countries. Additionally, there is the question of which internet censorship detection technique may be used for different types of content under scrutiny. As a case in point, majority Muslim countries are known to block alcohol-related websites, so sporadic and minimal testing could be performed to confirm that finding (if deemed worthy of research), rather than systematic and voluminous checks (Noman, 2011). Thus, here I concentrate on ways in which to avoid having research experience a chilling effect by its object of study. The emphasis is on the capacity for observing and monitoring internet filtering and the manner in which to do so responsibly.

Doing internet censorship research with research questions

In describing techniques for building URL lists, the aim is also to formulate compelling research questions about internet censorship, beginning with the ethical ones (as above) but also with respect to its discovery, unintended consequences, effectiveness, circumvention, censor duping and effects on the content being censored or its authors being watched (self-censorship). There is also detective work in tracing the filtering software used by censoring countries to its Western manufacturer. Did a US (or Canadian, British, German, French or Italian) company really sell censorship software to those authoritarian countries? How much credence can be lent to the claim that the companies are following the laws of the country to which they sell the software (Reporters without Borders, 2017)? Also described are tools for the use of proxies and VPNs, together with guidelines concerning how to decide when and how intensively to use them.

At the outset it may be instructive to mention early claims (in the 1990s) about the internet being immune to censorship, and contrast those with the general observations made two decades later by the most significant internet censorship research, the Open Net Initiative (Elmer-Dewitt, 1993; Rogers, 2009c). The 'civil libertarian's dream' built into the architecture of the internet that would treat censorship as a 'multifunction and route around it' has been supplanted by 'extensive [national] filtering practices' (Boyle, 1997; Open Net Initiative, 2014). By the time it suspended its research at the end of 2014, the Open Net Initiative's decade-long programme sought evidence of online censorship in some 60 countries (see Figure 4.2).

How to carry on with the work? This chapter provides some (modest) means to undertake internet censorship research by investigating URLs blocked by the state, where the examples are drawn from the more studied countries (such as China and Iran) that block or interrupt websites for their sensitive content (see Figure 4.3). URLs containing particularly troubling keywords may be filtered, as are some search results. Connections are also slowed or timed out.

Seemingly straightforward – in that content is or is not blocked – internet censorship research is actually rather technical, and the terminology used suffused with computational lingo, especially in the web science literature. For example, Iran is known to employ the following censorship techniques: 'HTTP host-based blocking, keyword filtering, DNS hijacking, and protocol-based throttling' (Aryan et al., 2013: 1). The first term refers to website blocking, and the second to the same (when a particular keyword appears in the

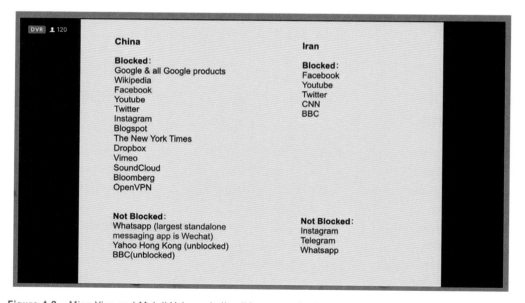

Figure 4.3   Miao Ying and Mehdi Yahyanejad's slide concerning leading websites blocked in China and Iran at Rhizome's Seven on Seven conference, New Museum, New York City, 22 April 2017.
Source: Ying and Yahyanejad, 2017.

URL) (Warzel, 2013). Protocol-based throttling means slowing the connection speed, for example, to 'https' connections (secure protocol) because certain internet circumvention software employs it, among other reasons. 'DNS hijacking' describes how the web user (e.g., typing in "Facebook.com") is sent to the wrong web location (i.e., to a numerical IP address other than Facebook's).

Countries make large projects out of internet censorship, and NGOs and researchers monitor them, issuing reports and white papers that make (researchable) claims and provide justification for more work to be done to study censorship's technicity and effects.

China and Iran

China is known to have a proverbial 'Great Firewall', known as the 'Golden Shield Project' (Dong, 2012). Chinese state filtering, however, is not often overt; neither a block page appears, nor a directory with a list of acceptable websites, as in the case of Iran (see Figure 4.1). As mentioned, banned websites (such as Facebook since 2009) time out, meaning that after attempting to load there is an unexpected disconnection. That tampering (rather than outright blocking) has a series of implications for internet users and researchers, the most crucial one of which is thought to be the possible logging of those requesting unacceptable websites. As one researcher has put it: 'there is evidence that DNS requests for blocked services may be logged in the case of China' (Wright, 2014: 128). 'Blocked in China', the website that performs live second-generation censorship research (returning filtering results from Beijing, Shenzhen, Inner Mongolia, Heilongjiang Province and Yunnan Province) treats the concern on an FAQ page about how to circumvent censorship:

> VPNs are not strictly illegal in China. There's no precedent we know of in which someone has been arrested for using one. The goal of authorities is to censor, not punish. That being said, using a VPN to break Chinese laws or publish anti-Communist rants could still get you in trouble. (blockedinchina.net, 2017)

The extent to which VPN access is maintained in future is in question, however (Haas, 2017).

In Iran there was a time when it was widely reported that the state was building its own 'halal internet' (a term used by an Iranian official, Ali Aghamohammadi), which would be equivalent to a white list of websites that users could access, with the rest of the World Wide Web (or 'haram internet') blocked (Farivar, 2011; Rhoads and Fassihi, 2011). The makings of such an internet have been visible since at least the Iran election crisis of 2009 when the block page would redirect to a directory listing of approved national sites. After the Stuxnet virus disrupted nuclear progress in 2011, the official rationale for the national internet project was put this way: 'Isolation of the clean Internet from the unclean portion will make it impossible to use the Internet for unethical and dirty businesses' (Article 19, 2016). In the event, the phased roll-out of the national internet has been supplemented by the 'intelligent filtering' project which updates techniques of state censorship. While more research is called for, it is being monitored by NGOs and others, which have detailed the coincidental blocking of websites including ones that reported city government corruption in Tehran (Reporters without Borders, 2016b; Small Media, 2017). As is its mandate, Article 19, the advocacy group, has been vocal about (recent) Iranian filtering, providing also a compelling reason overall to study internet censorship:

> If [the national internet is] fully implemented, there is no doubt that it would fly in the face of international standards on freedom of expression. In particular, Article 19 of the ICCPR [signed by Iran] provides that the right to freedom of expression includes the individual's freedom to seek, receive and impart information and ideas of all kinds, regardless of frontiers and through any other media of his choice. (Article 19, 2016)

State internet censorship is often couched as a rights issue, prompting but also justifying its study, even if illegal. Other rationales for its study include unintended consequences such as over-blocking or the so-called 'Streisand effect' which stipulates that blocking content brings more attention to it, and prompts its further spread (Masnick, 2015). From the perspective of awareness-raising (among the NGO activities discussed here), it would be of normative value to point to blocked sites so as to highlight their contents, as Amnesty International's Irrepressible Info anniversary project (mentioned below) once did. There is also a circulationist thesis to be explored; does blocked content become leaked and spread like samizdat, or through other means such as content aggregation? Here the question concerns the very effectiveness or even *raison d'être* of blocking.

Research questions also may treat the effects of censorship on content and voice. Does censorship kill content? In a study conducted on Iran it was found that despite being censored, Iranian bloggers continued to write postings and keep their websites fresh, providing circumstantial evidence to the idea that there is active censorship circumvention, as well as readerships outside of Iran in the diaspora and elsewhere (Rogers et al., 2012; Alimardani, 2014).

Table 4.1   Categories in the pioneering 'Global URL List' for state internet censorship research by the Open Net Initiative, 2006.

Alcohol	Major events
Anonymizers	Medical
Blogging domains	Miscellaneous
Drugs	News Outlets
Dating	P2P
Email	Porn
Encryption	Provocative attire

Entertainment	Religion (fanatical)
Environment	Religion (normal)
Famous bloggers	Religious conversion
Filtering sites	Search engines
Free webspace	Sexual education
Gambling	Translation sites
Gay/lesbian/bisexual/transgender/queer	Terrorism
Government	Universities
Hacking	Weapons/violence
Hate speech	Women's rights
Human rights	VOIP
Humour	

In other countries such as Saudi Arabia and Bahrain, filtering software is installed by the state, and populated with URL blacklists, whitelists and/or keywords (Reporters without Borders, 2014). Internet censorship research has been directed at detecting which filtering software is used so as to out (and shame) the purveyor, which may be based in the USA or Canada. As Open Net Initiative researchers found, for example, SmartFilter and WebSense (both USA-based) and NetSweeper (Canada) have been deployed in countries that censor the Internet (Babcock and Freivogel, 2015). (SmartFilter, now owned by McAfee, denied selling it to Iran.) European firms later stepped into the market, too, prompting Reporters without Borders (2013) to call this the 'era of digital mercenaries'. Here the research is of interest to investigative journalism and corporate social responsibility (among other discourses) where the question concerns the ethics and business of selling software to authoritarian regimes to censor critical content. The Milan-based firm, Hacking Team, is perhaps the most egregious (and recent) case of unethical selling, where their software is used by a variety of authoritarian regimes to track down dissidents. Internal email exchanges between company employees, themselves available through a hack, reveal the story of a company concerned with Italian export regulations and the recipient countries' own laws, rather than the ethics of putting people in harm's way (Currier and Marquis-Boire, 2015).

Internet censorship research techniques: From URL list building to checking URLs

Once one has looked into the claims concerning internet censorship in certain countries, and considered the research questions to pose, the work commences to build URL lists and check them. To start, five general approaches to building URL lists are sketched: editorial, crowdsourcing, search engine work, device studies and dynamic URL sampling. URL list-building approaches also may be combined (and lists merged or concatenated). The approaches have been used by censorship researchers as well as NGOs seeking to raise awareness of the issue, as is detailed. Subsequently, means by which to check URLs in the countries under study are treated.

Editorial list building

Conventionally website directories have been used to build URL lists, such as those of Yahoo!, Dmoz.org or national ones such as startpagina.nl for the Netherlands. For more than a decade now, however, the search engine has replaced the human-edited directory as the main content organization device of the web. Manually edited expert lists for websites, with global categories, are gradually becoming extinct, as are 'link lists' on websites. Yahoo!'s seminal directory became defunct in December 2014, and Dmoz's lasted until March 2017. Amnesty International no longer has a link list of human rights organizations. Choike, the Global South NGO portal, does not appear to have updated its directory of NGOs per category for some years now. The United Nations maintains lists of accredited NGOs per category, however much certain of the lists appear as PDFs without links to the websites, prompting manual work (extracting NGO names from the PDF, looking up URLs and perhaps making decisions concerning an organization's main website given subsites with different languages).

For research into a single country, or cross-country comparison research, often a steady, so-called global list of URLs is built. This list contains URLs organized into categories that would be run for all countries under investigation, so as to be able to make comparisons in the form of types of sites blocked. This is the original method employed by the Open Net Initiative. The research began in the mid-2000s with an internet censorship monitoring programme that relied on a global list of URLs culled from Web directories such as Yahoo!'s and dmoz.org's, with some 37 categories of website types, as well as on country-specific lists, put together by country and subject matter experts (see Table 4.1).

Where may one start to build an editorial list these days? With respect to borrowing URL lists from institutions that expertly categorize websites, the Webby Awards may be considered. In its promotional literature to express the weightiness of its award, the International Academy of Digital Arts and Sciences states that in 2017 there were 1,029,615,402 websites and 387 Webby Award winners, thus giving an indication of the number of categories they consider (which has increased greatly since its founding in 1996). One may also take up specific categories (such as 'activism'), and plumb earlier winners, making a longer list of significant websites for each category.

Since the classic directories and link-list makers have discontinued their web librarian work, Wikipedia is increasingly becoming the rare, manual alternative for link lists. It is an editorial source providing lists and list-building opportunities, especially with its directory-like articles such as 'List of human rights organizations' (https://en.wikipedia.org/wiki/

List_of_human_rights_organizations). Language versions of Wikipedia also should be considered; the list of human rights organizations in the German Wikipedia is distinctive from that in the English-language one. Wikipedia even has a list of 'websites blocked in China' (with, as discussed below, Greatfire.org as its source) as well as a series of other countries. At the other end of the spectrum from the Webby awards, Wikipedia's editorial style tends to be exhaustive as opposed to selective, leading to lengthy lists that the researcher may wish to cull by creating a significance threshold.

Wikipedia is also a source for keywords through the names of its articles or by other means. In one internet censorship research project, which one could call a baseline censorship 'discovery' project, the researchers collected all article titles from the Chinese language Wikipedia and searched for them on Weibo. Those queries returning the Weibo-service message saying 'based on Chinese laws and regulations, search results are not shown' were retained. Eventually the project compiled 'Blocked on Weibo', a list of words that are on Chinese censors' blacklist. Here Wikipedia is used as a source, but querying the terms in Weibo reduces the otherwise long list.

Crowdsourcing blocked sites

A second technique for building URL lists is crowdsourcing. Through this approach, a list of websites is sourced from the outside by asking others, for example, to fill in online forms or install an extension. To that end, the expertise is also outsourced. It is a technique that has particular rationales for being undertaken, such as the sheer scale of the work to be done or the challenge of foreign languages. Seminal cases of crowdsourcing, borrowed from earlier resource sharing projects such as SETI at home, have included reCaptcha and Google Image Labeller, where the former has users help to transform scanned text into machine-readable material and the latter with tagging images or checking whether machine techniques are working.

Crowdsourcing has been applied to internet censorship awareness-raising as well as research. One of the earliest cases of awareness-raising is greatfirewallofchina.org, which asked the user to input his or her own website (or whichever one the user chooses), whereupon it would test it for blocking in China, thereby gradually building up a database with a history of discovered or confirmed blocks. In its earliest version, if the website were blocked, it became a kind of brick in a visual display of a great wall of China. One also could download and display a banner on one's website, indicating that it has been tested. Another project with a similar name (greatfire.org) is less artistic and awareness oriented, and more service-minded with research capacities. Greatfire.org provides means to circumvent censorship, while also monitoring multiple online platforms for the state of Chinese censorship more generally (see Figure 4.4). One also may test websites as well as keywords. While one may test sites for blocking, greatfire.org has what I would call a 'device studies' approach (using multiple online platforms) rather than primarily a crowdsourced one (multiple users), as is discussed below.

Figure 4.4   Greatfirewallofchina.org, launched in January 2007, once provided a 'wall' comprised of websites blocked in China, together a means to query live blockages (as depicted).

Another early example of crowdsourcing was irrepressible.info, built for Amnesty International's 45th anniversary in 2006. It showed content from websites that were blocked, making it a blocked content collection website, with show-and-tell capacities, so to speak. It thereby also took a circulationist approach to censorship circumvention in so far as one could place content from blocked websites on irrepressible.info, and thereby make it available (and thus 'irrepressible'), though of course irrepressible.info itself could be blocked. Herdict.org (the verdict of the herd in contrast to the wisdom of the crowd), the project by the Berkman Center at Harvard University, also asks the crowd for URLs (Palfrey and Zittrain, 2011). One becomes a user of Herdict by downloading the Firefox add-on and providing one's location. Then, when blocked websites are encountered, they can be reported to Herdict, together with one's location. Individual URLs also can be entered in order to find out the status of those particular URLs per user location. In this way, the herd is meant to visit more websites (than any individual could) and ultimately compile a much larger reporting on the state of internet censorship. Perhaps more to the point, one may also use Herdict's lists of blocked websites so as to confirm or otherwise chart a change of course in censorship.

Figure 4.5 Comparison of Google Images search results from google.com.cn and google.com for the query, [Tiananmen].
Source: Open Net Initiative, 2007.

Finally, with regard to crowdsourcing, one should mention the China Digital Times, the University of California at Berkeley project that has crowdsourced URLs and sensitive keywords (Meng, 2011). A well-known story of the use of a sensitive keyword concerns the Chinese term, 'grass-mud horse'. In Mandarin, this invented term sounds similar to a curse word, and became something of a meme, launching a movement of using terms that are just slightly different from the originals (Yang, 2016). A copious lexicon of these terms was subsequently created, and the China Digital Times project collected them in order to determine the extent to which they are effective in circumventing internet censorship (or 'censor duping') in China. Therefore, while the original words or phrases that these terms are similar to may be blocked the question is whether the new 'grass-mud horse' sorts of terms are also being blocked. The question leads to further inquiries into the general effectiveness of internet censorship per country and in particular in China – a question formulation discussed below in the case of the effectiveness of Chinese censorship of Falun Gong related websites.

When it comes to researching awareness-raising concerning internet censorship, especially in China, google.com.cn's redirect to google.com.hk (in 2010) is probably the most significant, having taken place after the public scrutiny in the USA and beyond of Google, Yahoo! and Microsoft for complying with censorship law in China – and also supplying, either voluntarily or through being hacked, information about dissidents to the Chinese

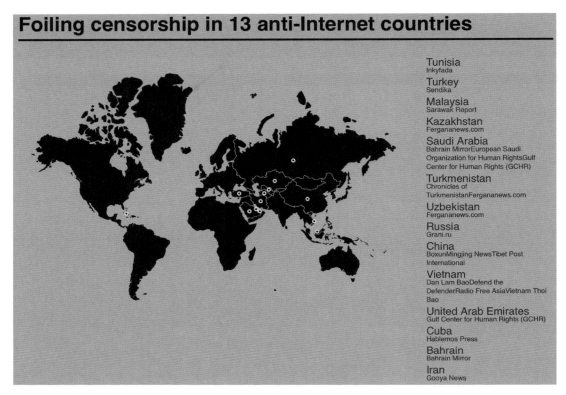

Figure 4.6   The 'unblocking' of critical news websites in countries known for internet censorship, on the 'World Day against Cyber Censorship', 2016.
Source: Reporters without Borders, 2016a.

authorities (see also Figure 4.5). Non-governmental monitoring projects include the ones by Reporters without Borders and Freedom House (with such titles as 'Enemies of the Internet' and 'Internet Freedom') (Reporters without Borders, 2013). Reporters without Borders, together with Amnesty International, have also performed calendar work and created additional formats to draw attention to the issue. The 'World Day against Cyber Censorship' falls annually on 12 March, although it has not recently been as well observed as in the early years after its founding in 2008 (see Figure 4.6). The China Channel Firefox add-on, while no longer functioning, is still worth mentioning when creating a genealogy of internet censorship awareness projects, especially software projects to that end. The extension can still be found, though one probably needs to install a retrograde version of Firefox to use it. The add-on automatically turns on a Chinese proxy in Firefox and gives the user the experience of visiting websites in China. For users outside China it was one of the initial ways to experience Chinese internet censorship (and DNS tampering), whereby the connection one is trying to make to a (forbidden) website times out. Chinese censorship makes it appear that one's internet service is poor. It also whitewashed the Tiananmen Square massacre, awareness-raising campaigns about which likely contributed to Google's decision to move domains. The Open Net Initiative created a side-by-side browser window experience, with ready-made queries, showing results from the same query in google.com.cn and google.com (Figure 4.5).

Search engine work

The use of search engines to source URLs and make lists seems obvious, and one could consider employing the associational snowball query technique (described in the chapter on issuecrawling) for making a list of a type of website, such as right-wing populist and extremist sites in Germany or critical Iranian bloggers inside and outside Iran. The research question would revolve around whether these websites persist, given their targeting by authorities. Another question would concern whether censorship (or banning) kills content, as remarked above. That is, do the Iranian bloggers or other critical voices continue to blog, even though they are censored in Iran and voided of an audience?

Search engines also may be used to build a country-specific or local list, using advanced search settings, such as setting to Persian, and querying controversial terminology. Here the list of URLs retained would be checked for censorship, with the question concerning the extent to which censors are active in following the use of controversial terminology and blocking sites that use the terms. How active is censorship? Here one relies on Google's algorithm to return significant or relevant sites per language, particularly fresh ones, allowing for some understanding of how quickly censors are on the scene.

Another outcome of search engine work is a national list. A query is formulated in a local domain Google, using a search operator, [site:], and a top-level country domain [site:.uk], and subsequently second-level country domains [site:co.uk]. With the United Kingdom as an example, one builds a list of UK websites by using google.co.uk and the advanced setting, 'return sites from the UK'. One can query google.co.uk for [site:.uk] as well as a generic keyword, in order to output a list of 1000 websites, or the maximum number of sites returned by Google. One could subsequently lengthen the list of UK websites by querying Google for second-level country domains; rather than querying .uk, one would use .co.uk, .ac.uk, .org.uk and so forth. By following this procedure, one can build a decent list of ranked British URLs, and also subdivide them into lists of companies (.co.uk), universities (.ac.uk), NGOs (.org.uk), and so forth. To build such lists, more generally, a directory of second-level country domains is needed; Wikipedia and Internet registrars are sources for lists of this kind. (The Norwegian internet registrar at norid.no has been known for having one of the more accessible and orderly lists of top-level and second-level country domains.) It is also helpful to know that some countries only have top-level but no second-level country domains, such as the Netherlands (.nl) and Germany (.de). Conversely, France has a wide range of second-level domains, but some are seldom used. Therefore, when conducting preparatory work, one should familiarize oneself not only with which countries have second-level domains but also the national use culture.

Another means of compiling lists of relevant websites per country is the use of Alexa's top sites by country feature, which is derived from the surfing behaviour of Alexa toolbar users and the postcode they entered when downloading and installing the software. (SimilarWeb also has top 50 country lists.) Here, with Google and Alexa, one is making lists of relevant sites as opposed to lists of categories of sites, in the first instance. 'Top sites' from Alexa would be checked for filtering as opposed to category-specific sites such as file-sharing, famous blogger or provocative attire websites, in the site category approach. When one combines the lists from Google site search, the Alexa top sites per country and other devices claiming to output a country or language list of top URLs, the approach could be called (national and language) 'device studies'.

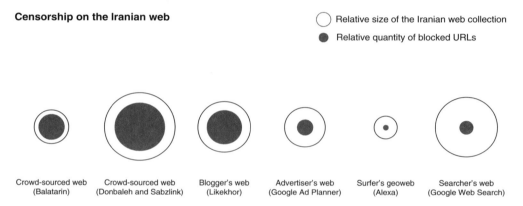

Censorship on the Iranian web

○ Relative size of the Iranian web collection

● Relative quantity of blocked URLs

| Crowd-sourced web (Balatarin) | Crowd-sourced web (Donbaleh and Sabzlink) | Blogger's web (Likekhor) | Advertiser's web (Google Ad Planner) | Surfer's geoweb (Alexa) | Searcher's web (Google Web Search) |

Figure 4.7   Iranian URL collections, with relative quantities of blockages.
Source: Rogers et al., 2012.

Device studies

The fourth technique for building lists is device studies, which largely entails outsourcing the work of list-making to multiple online devices or platforms. In the proof-of-concept project, a study of websites significant to Iranians, to Alexa's top sites in Iran and Google's web search results for Iranian websites were added other outputs of devices including blog aggregators, advertising tools as well as social news aggregators and web content rating sites (Rogers et al., 2012). One could consider each distinctive entry point to the web (the searcher's, the blogger's, the advertiser's, etc.), and indeed each outputs relatively distinctive lists of websites (see Figure 4.7). There is a list of sites frequently visited by those based in Iran (Alexa's list). There is a list of sites in Persian and/or published in Iran which is available in Google's 'region' drop-down menu in the advanced search settings. (There is no google.co.ir, or for that matter local domain Googles for Cuba, North Korea, Sudan or Syria, because of sanctions imposed by the United States Office of Foreign Assets Control that also restrict the use of Google Ads. There is a google.ps for Palestine.) A third kind of device are advertisers' tools such as Google Display Planner, Adwords or those by other companies that provide lists of URLs, such as top URLs per country or per language. These are lists of links that are attractive to advertisers for they receive higher amounts of traffic. Blog aggregators are another type of useful device for building lists of URLs. In certain countries, bloggers are considered influential voices (and some are themselves aggregated on 'global voices', the Berkman Center project). There may be lists of top bloggers or blogs. In the research on Iran, the bloggers were the most significant targets of the censors, more readily blocked than other types of websites (see Figure 7). Social news aggregators (such as Balatarin in Iran or Reddit) may be used to harvest significant URLs to gain an indication of blogosphere censorship compared to other types (or spheres) of websites (such as top news stories 'uprated' by the Iranian crowdsourced aggregator, Balatarin).

As mentioned above, greatfire.org takes a device studies approach, having created lists of websites as well as keywords relevant to China and Chinese users, and charting their block-age (see Figure 4.5). It is an awareness-raising (and transparency) project (mentioned above) that takes a device studies approach, using URL lists sourced from different devices, includ-ing Wikipedia, Weibo and Alexa's list of the top URLs in China, showing levels of censorship per list (see Figure 4.8).

Creating a country-specific URL list with Twitter is possible, though topic-specific lists are more readily prepared from a tweet collection made with multiple keywords and hash-tags, whereby the URLs in that collection are extracted. While laborious, for country-specific URL lists one could strive to create a national tweet collection and harvest (and unshorten) referenced URLs, such as in the work on mapping the Australian twitter-sphere (Bruns et al., 2014).

Figure 4.8 Greatfire.org's 'device studies' approach showing collections of URLs culled from various engines and platforms, and percentages of them blocked.
Source: Greatfire.org.

Dynamic URL sampling (list lengthening)

With the list-building approaches sketched above, sometimes the size of the list of URLs is rather limited. With what is termed 'dynamic URL sampling' the lists may be lengthened by crawling websites and capturing outlinks. The crawling technique could be co-link or snowball analysis, and each iteration of the method (one degree, two degrees or three degrees of separation from the seed list) would lengthen the original list. Thus, one may wish to launch multiple crawls, concatenate the lists and remove duplicates, using the triangulation tool. In the sample project the dynamic URL sampling technique is utilized to study the effectiveness of state Chinese censorship of Falun Gong websites.

Measuring the effectiveness of the censorship of the Falun Gong in China

How effective is Chinese state censorship of Falun Gong websites? How 'well' does the state censor those websites? Have some slipped through? This project was carried out with proxies, but given the potential in China for next-generation censorship (logging users), it is important to consider using known VPNs or services that monitor Chinese state censorship.

Having curated a list of Falun Gong websites using the techniques discussed above (editorial approach as well as search engine work), and lengthened the list (with the Issuecrawler), one fetches the URLs through the Censorship Explorer, checking for blockage (see Figure 4.9). As mentioned, one should become familiar with the blocking techniques in the country in question through a brief review of the claims (Bamman et al., 2012). In China, note again that the censorship techniques often result in no response code, or a time-out, for the TCP connection may be reset for consecutive requests because (for example) a keyword from a blacklist is in the URL or the site itself is blacklisted. The same effect may be observed if a proxy or VPN is not working. To ensure, first, that the proxy server or VPN is functional, enter a non-censored website and check the response code.

How to be certain, or reasonably so, that a URL is blocked by the state in a certain country (including China)? For national blocking, triangulation or checking multiple ISPs in the country in question is advised, where one seeks agreement between ISP results, while also ensuring that the website is up and running (response code 200) in the Netherlands, for example, which is where the Censorship Explorer tool is based. For selective blocking (second-generation internet censorship), as mentioned above, ISPs from one city (say, the capital or a separatist region) may be targeted rather than those from other locations in the same country. One may consider travelling to a country in question or engaging and informing on-the-ground researchers; however, such work requires knowing the risks. When using the remote analysis approach – fetching URLs through a proxy, VPN or censorship monitoring service – it is advisable to ascertain information about the services in question, especially concerning whether the server may be traced to an unwitting individual

issuecrawler

| the Lobby | Issue Crawler | Network Manager | Archive |

Monday, March 14, 2011

@550.I

Harvester

Type or paste
text and URLs
into the
Harvester

The text will be
stripped to create
starting points for
the Issue Crawler

http://theepochtimes.com/
http://www.ntdtv.com/
http://soundofhope.org/
http://clpfg.org/
http://faluninfo.net/
http://falundafa.org/
http://zhuichaguoji.org/
http://clearwisdom.net/
http://pureinsight.org/
http://fofg.org/
http://www.fighrwg.net/
http://falunau.org/
http://www.clearharmony.net/
http://www.facts.org.cn/
http://dcfalundafa.org/
http://www.falunaz.net/

Next step »
Fine tune and
Launch Crawl

Harvest

Current and Queued Crawls

4 Mar 2011	BBB11_Snow_Blogs_8
4 Mar 2011	Mexican News Sites vs International News Sites
14 Mar 2011	Aljazeera English Africa1
4 Mar 2011	Lab IA 3 11-03-04
6 Mar 2011	110306_parliamentary election_2011_Denmark_parties_snowball
6 Mar 2011	110306_parliamentary election_2011_Denmark_parties_inter_actor
6 Mar 2011	Groep WNF - Herkansing - Snowball
7 Mar 2011	110307_parliamentary election_2011_Denmark_google_issue_snowball
7 Mar 2011	110307_parliamentary election_2011_Denmark_google_establishment_snowball
7 Mar 2011	KSA_3 months later
8 Mar 2011	Egypt_Twitter "Revolution"
9 Mar 2011	NovaTrotters
10 Mar 2011	energy & environment 2
10 Mar 2011	junkscience snowball
10 Mar 2011	junkscience interactor
10 Mar 2011	junksci/mom snowball
10 Mar 2011	junksci/mom interactor
10 Mar 2011	Main Mythbusters co-linkedinter-actor take 2
10 Mar 2011	All Mythbusters inter-actor take 2

(Continued)

Figure 4.9 (Continued)

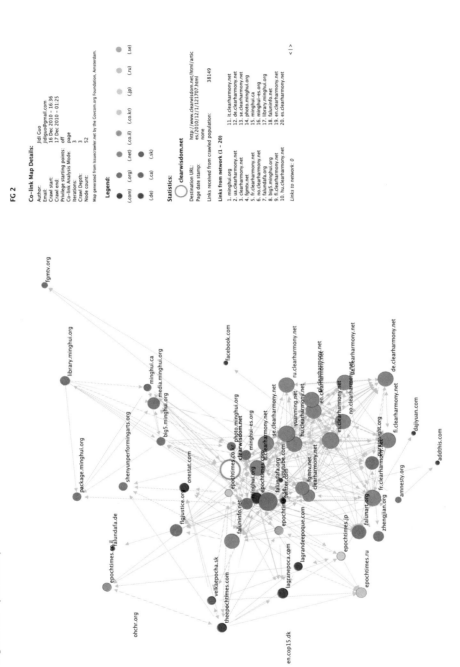

FG 2

Co–link Map Details:

Author: Jidi Guo
Email: jidiguo@gmail.com
Crawl start: 16 Dec 2010 – 16:36
Crawl end: 17 Dec 2010 – 01:25
Privilege starting points: off
Co–link Analysis Mode: page
Iterations: 3
Crawl Depth: 3
Node count: 52

Map generated from Issuecrawler.net by the Govcom.org Foundation, Amsterdam.

Legend:

(.com)   (.org)   (.net)   (.co.il)   (.co.kr)   (.jp)   (.ru)   (.se)

(.de)   (.ca)   (.sk)

Statistics:

clearwisdom.net

Destination URL: http://www.clearwisdom.net/html/artic
Page date stamp: es/2010/12/1/121707.html
none

Links received from crawled population: 38149

Links from network (1 – 20)

1. minghui.org
2. ua.clearharmony.net
3. clearharmony.net
4. fgmtv.net
5. fr.clearharmony.net
6. no.clearharmony.net
7. falundafa.org
8. big5.minghui.org
9. fi.clearharmony.net
10. hu.clearharmony.net

11. it.clearharmony.net
12. de.clearharmony.net
13. se.clearharmony.net
14. photo.minghui.org
15. minghui.ca
16. minghui-es.org
17. library.minghui.org
18. faluninfo.net
19. en.clearharmony.net
20. es.clearharmony.net

Links to network: 0   < 1 >

Figure 4.9 Issuecrawler input and output. Falun Gong websites inputted into the Issuecrawler, with the resulting map. Use 'retrieve starting points and network URLs' for a list of the outputs.

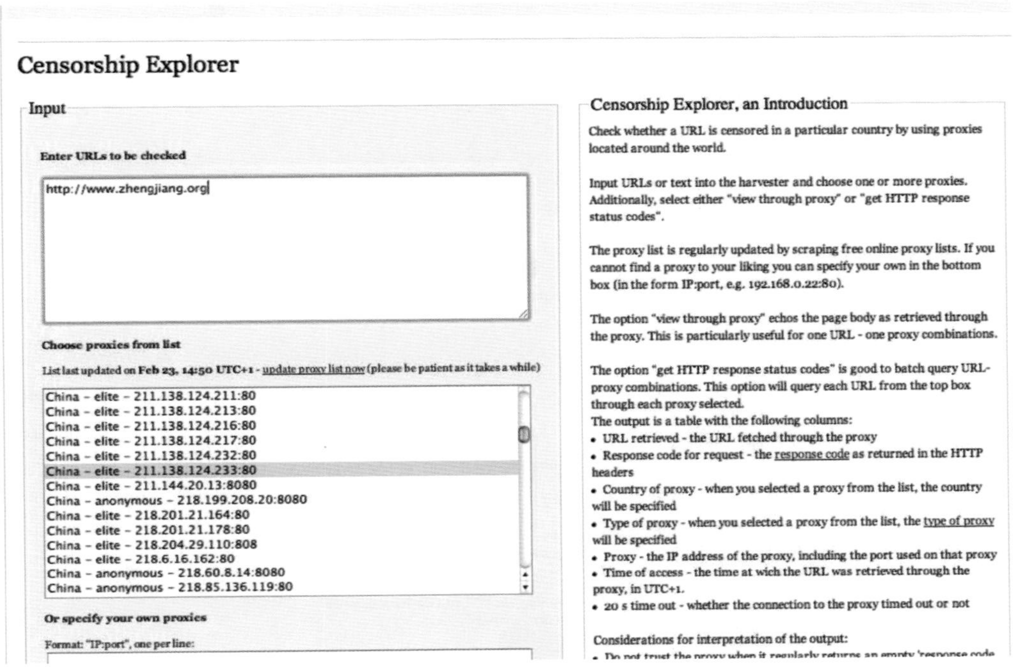

Censorship Explorer

Figure 4.10 Censorship Explorer tool.

(see Figure 4.10). Censorship monitoring services or VPNs designed to deliver sensitive content are preferred, but proxies may be considered in countries not known for logging or expected to log user activity.

In the event, across multiple locations in China, Falun Gong websites are blocked by timing out. The pages do not load after considerable waiting time, making it appear as if they are down, rather than blocked. The censorship is effective across all of the sites checked (see Figure 4.11). It is also effective in sites in both Mandarin as well as English, raising the question of the extent to which blocking is undertaken of sites in even more languages.

Discovering previously unknown censored websites in Iran, and confirming blocking

Around the time of the Iran election crisis (June 2009), considerable efforts were made to study Iranian internet censorship, including the throttling of the connection speeds, the blocking of particular sites as well as (temporary) network outages. In two related projects, researchers and I sought to discover (previously unknown) blocked websites as well as confirm those reported to be blocked. For the confirmation work, a group of regional journalists and I collected press reports of blocked websites in Iran, compiled a list, added to the list URLs from Alexa's top 20 websites in Iran, and checked them for blocking, thereby both

Figure 4.11   Recoded map of the Falun Gong co-link network, showing nearly all sites blocked in China.

confirming but also expanding the list of known blocked sites (Caucasian Causes, 2009). So that others could confirm the findings (or at least know whence they came), we also published the proxy IP addresses. At this stage one did not consider whether the research use of another computer user's proxy, whether it was made available purposively or unknowingly, could put him or her (or the organization) in harm's way.

For the blocked website discovery, the technique entailed using an expert list of 'sensitive sites', crawling them for links to other (related) sites, and fetching the URLs of the newly discovered sites (from the network analysis) in Iran (using proxy servers). Among the findings were that certain newly discovered sensitive websites were still accessible in Iran and that the country also practised page-level (rather than only site-level) blocking as in the case of bbc.co.uk/Persian (Rogers, 2009c). Apart from the proxy issue, here one is confronted with the question of how (and whether) to publish the results (see Figure 4.12). One 'map'

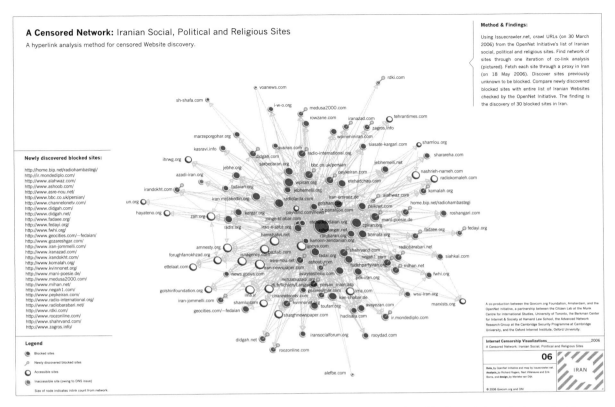

Figure 4.12 Colour-coded network map of Iranian social, political and religious sites. The hyperlink analysis method for internet censorship research in this case resulted in the discovery of 30 previously unknown blocked sites in Iran. The map, made at the Digital Methods Initiative, appeared in *Le Monde* on 23 May 2009 (http://www.lemonde.fr/proche-orient/article/2009/05/23/facebook-interdit-d-acces-en-iran-avant-la-presidentielle_1197253_3218.html). It also appeared on the website of the American National Public Radio.

was published in *Le Monde* (23 May 2009) as well as on the website of the American National Public Radio (NPR), whereupon discussions ensued regarding how the maps are double-edged. The findings are of interest to the censors, too. Future outcomes of such work, including in the subsequent national web study of Iran, would be data-embargoed, and the maps would remain unpublished, or only made available to bona fide researchers in the area of internet censorship research (Rogers et al., 2012).

Conclusions: Contributing to internet censorship research, post Snowden

How to make a contribution to internet censorship research, while considering whether it is conceivable that the researcher and/or the computer users in the country in question will be placed in harm's way? Covert research continues but, given the risks, it is challenging to repeat and scale. Remote research still may be practised, but much caution should be taken. Since the Snowden revelations of widespread state surveillance, and the publication of techniques via WikiLeaks, research has concentrated on detecting whether Western filtering and monitoring software is in use in authoritarian countries. In-country software, however, may have been developed to monitor and filter, too.

The notions of 'network authoritarianism' and third-generation internet censorship have been put forward to capture how states achieve censorship through monitoring in the first place, and secondarily through filtering (MacKinnon, 2011). That is, while there is blocking, a state follows the online chatter, and intervenes in the content spaces with correctives as well as noise. Following the corrective information, disinformation, 'fake news' and other content interventions become a means to study not so much censorship but rather content control, reach and spread. The effects of network authoritarianism become the objects of study rather than the logging and interpretation of blocked URLs and keywords.

Among the work to be done is the development of techniques to discover networks of content interventions and their effects (see Chapter 11 on tracking for network discovery and content interpretation techniques). The research questions developed for internet censorship are still of relevance. Slightly rephrased, they may be put to use to study such questions as content network discovery, unintended consequences, effectiveness, circumvention, monitor duping, Western complicity and monitored content effects.

PROJECT 3

VIDEO 2 Internet censorship research

Investigate the effectiveness of state internet censorship in China

RESEARCH GOAL To determine the effectiveness of Chinese state internet censorship by building and analysing a list of websites the authorities are known to block.

1   Build a list of Falun Gong websites through an editorial approach or associative query snowballing (search engine work).
2   Optional. Crawl and expand the list (of related sites) with the Issuecrawler (dynamic URL sampling). Extract the expanded list of websites from the Issuecrawler (using 'retrieve starting points and network URLs' feature). Remove off-topic URLs.
3   Run the list of URLs (at least hosts) through the Censorship Explorer software, choosing a variety of ISPs, or by other means, considering the ethical issues discussed above. One could consider using ISPs that are geographically dispersed in order to check for regional differences in filtering (such as in Macau and Hong Kong). One also may wish to spot-check using the Blocked in China website (blockedinchina.net or the test URL feature at greatfire.org).
4   If using the Issuecrawler, colour-code (or greyscale-code) the map (manually), using Adobe Illustrator or similar, indicating blocked and unblocked sites.
5   Note the effectiveness of the censorship across the landscape of Falun Gong sites.
6   As an additional undertaking, consider curating lists of Falun Gong sites (or of other sensitive subject matters) in additional languages, and checking for blockages, in order to ascertain the reach of the effectiveness of state internet censorship.

PROJECT 4

Investigate state internet censorship in Iran through a discovery technique

RESEARCH GOAL To discover previously unknown censored websites in Iran using the Censorship Explorer and the Issuecrawler.

1   Obtain or build a list of websites known to be blocked in Iran. As discussed above, non-governmental organizations and Wikipedia articles have descriptions of the (types of) sites blocked or lists thereof. One may also wish to compile lists from news reports and other sources.
2   Optional crawl and expand the list (of related sites) with the Issuecrawler (dynamic URL sampling or another hyperlink analysis tool).

3   Check the (expanded) URL list for blocking, through the Censorship Explorer or another means, considering the ethical issues discussed above.

4   Colour-code the map, or annotate a list (after removing off-topic URLs), with three types of nodes: blocked, unblocked and newly discovered blocked.

5   Are there newly discovered blocked websites on the map (or on the list)? Consider adding them to the record of known blocked websites (on Wikipedia or elsewhere). Are there sensitive websites on the map (or on the list) that are not (yet) blocked? Consider how to report this information yet embargo the details.

PROJECT 5

Conduct internet censorship research in one or more countries

RESEARCH GOAL To discover or confirm and report on online content blocking in a country or countries of choice.

1   Choose one or more countries, and build a list of websites to be checked for blocking.

- The amount of internet censorship research available on that country. What is known, and what is claimed? For internet censorship research per country and region as well as for claims, see (among other sources) http://www.opennet.net/, http://www.freedomhouse.org/ and http://www.rsf.org/.

- General contribution to make. Where are the overall gaps in knowledge about censorship? Are there urgent analytical needs, such as new claims about censorship or current events which could give rise to blocking, including upcoming elections or planned protests?

- Research questions to be posed. Does the research concern discovery, unintended consequences, effectiveness, circumvention, censor duping and effects on the content being censored or its authors being watched (self-censorship)? Is it striving to do detective work about the filtering software being used (and who supplies it, such as Western software firms)?

- URL list-building. Consider techniques such as editorial, search engine work and so forth as well as types of websites to be checked, such as categories of sites (OpenNet-style or other), top sites per country (e.g., Alexa, Google queries), platforms (e.g., social networking sites), event-based (e.g., elections) and so forth. Consider also the lengthiness of the list of (types of) sites suspected of being blocked in order to make general claims. Shorter lists may be as powerful as longer ones, if they are the 'top sites'. Make a case for your list-making technique that is a reasoned consideration of whether your list allows you to test claims.

2   Check for blocking: consider VPNs, proxies and verification strategies. If in existence in the country in question, consider using an existing censorship monitoring service such as greatfire.org for China.

- The Censorship Explorer allows you to check URLs for blocking via VPN or proxies.

- If using a VPN, install the DMI browser toolbar, https://wiki.digitalmethods.net/Dmi/FirefoxToolBar. The Censorship Explorer opens the URL via the DMI toolbar in the browser and sends the result to the Censorship Explorer. If using a VPN on your computer, the URL is retrieved via your VPN.

- The Censorship Explorer provides a list of open HTTP proxies, often scraped from other sites. You can also add other proxies (e.g., found by searching for [free proxy lists]). Although all proxies listed in the Censorship Explorer are publicly available on the web, they might not all be made accessible intentionally. Open proxies can mistakenly be left open and found by sites scanning for open proxies. Consider the political situation in the country of the proxy you are using in relation to the types of URLs you wish to fetch through the proxy. URL blocking is mostly intentional and web traffic from a proxy to a blocked site may have consequences for the owner of the proxy. For ethical reasons, use VPNs (check their terms of service to see whether you can request certain types of content via their service) or institutional proxies (such as from universities) so as not to put individuals in harm's way. Avoid having friends or acquaintances check URLs on site in the countries where censorship is practised.

- How to build trust in the results returned by the VPN or proxy? For open proxies it is often challenging to infer the owner, its location and its representativeness for a country, region or city. Before checking for URL blocking, endeavour to find out who owns the VPN or proxy and where it is located. Thereafter test the VPN or proxies with two unblocked URLs to ensure they are working. Use proxies that produce consistent and reliable results.

- How do you know that a URL is blocked? The Censorship Explorer automatically also queries each URL from a Dutch IP address, in order to verify VPN or proxy results with control results from a country that does not censor. Blocking can transpire in different ways. Do the response codes differ when accessed through the VPN or proxy versus when accessed through the control server? That is, does the control server produce consistent 200 OK HTTP status codes, and the VPN or proxy output different results? Does the connection time out? Is there a redirect to an unexpected page?

- What is the type of blocking? Is it transparent (e.g., does it provide a block page)?

- What type of proxy was used? Does that influence the results? Note that transparent proxies do not modify the request or response beyond what is required for proxy authentication and identification, and non-transparent proxies modify the request or response in order to provide some added service to the user agent, such as anonymity filtering.

- Where is the VPN or proxy located? On which network (ISP) does the proxy reside? Do you receive different results for different proxies in the same country? To obtain answers to these questions you can use tools such as http://whatismyipaddress.com/ip-lookup or http://www.whatismyip.com/tools/ip-address-lookup.asp.

3 Document findings.

- Make a list of the tests in a spreadsheet. For each URL tested and each proxy used, the list should at least contain the IP address and port of the proxy, date and time of the test, response code returned, type of proxy used, the network (ISP) on which the proxy resides and the geographical location of the proxy.

4 Discuss implications.

- Discussion of the findings, and contribution to internet censorship research, in light of the literature and current state of the field. How does the research contribute to discovery, unintended consequences, effectiveness, circumvention, censor duping, effects on the content being censored, self-censorship, or (Western) filtering software detection?

- Is the contribution newsworthy?
- Consider introducing both the limitations of the work as well as the needs for future research, be it conceptual or methodological.

Tools

- Censorship Explorer, digitalmethods.net. Available at https://wiki.digitalmethods.net/Dmi/Tool CensorshipExplorer.
- Harvester, digitalmethods.net. Available at https://wiki.digitalmethods.net/Dmi/ToolHarvester.
- Issuecrawler, issuecrawler.net. Available at https://www.issuecrawler.net.
- Triangulation, digitalmethods.net. Available at https://wiki.digitalmethods.net/Dmi/ToolTriangulation.
- What Is My IP Address, whatismyipaddress.com. Available at http://whatismyipaddress.com/ip-lookup.
- IP Address Lookup, whatismyip.com. https://www.whatismyip.com/ip-address-lookup/.
- Test if a site is blocked in China, https://www.comparitech.com/privacy-security-tools/blockedinchina/

Resources by list-building approach
Editorial approach

- Open Net Initiative, http://opennet.net/
- Reporters without Borders, http://www.rsf.org/
- Blocked on Weibo, http://blockedonweibo.tumblr.com/

Crowdsourcing

- Harvard's Berkman Center Herdict project, http://www.herdict.org/
- Amnesty International's anniversary project, http://irrepressible.info/ (look up in the Wayback Machine at archive.org)
- Great Firewall of China, GreatFire.org, https://greatfire.org/

Search engine work

- Google search operators, https://support.google.com/websearch/answer/2466433

Device studies

- Online censorship in China, GreatFire.org, https://greatfire.org/
- Alexa, Top 500 sites by country, http://www.alexa.com/topsites/countries
- SimilarWeb, Top 50 sites by country, https://www.similarweb.com/top-websites

Dynamic URL sampling

- Issuecrawler instructions, http://www.govcom.org/Issuecrawler_instructions.htm
- Issuecrawler scenarios of use, http://www.govcom.org/scenarios_use.htm
- Issuecrawler FAQ, https://wiki.issuecrawler.net/Issuecrawler/FAQ

WEBSITE HISTORY
Screencast documentaries with the Internet Archive

*Doing web history with new media
methods and techniques*

Web history, media history and digital history

The chapter is dedicated to investigating the history of the web, or history with the web, as may be undertaken using the platform that organizes it most palpably to date, the Wayback Machine of the Internet Archive. Among the research opportunities afforded by the Wayback Machine is the capacity to capture and 'play back' the history of a webpage, most notably a website's homepage. Created with special techniques and software tools, these playbacks assume the form of screencast documentaries, or narrated histories of websites. While the technique remains stable – screencapturing archived webpages, loading them into a deck and playing them back in the style of time-lapse photography – there are at least three kinds of histories that may unfold: 'web history', 'media history' and 'digital history', the last one referring to recounting the past with (mainly) digital sources (Cohen and Rosenzweig, 2006). In other words, the researcher may recast the evolution of the web (as seen through a decade of changes to Google's homepage, for example), the history of media (as seen through the online transformations of the *New York Times* or the *Guardian*), or the history of an institution (from the substantive edits to the homepage of the US White House, especially during the transition from one president to the next). More generally, the screencast documentary is one technique to unlock the archive, and brighten it with uses, which is a concern for the digital humanities as more and more materials are digitized or, as is the case with the archived web, 'digitally reborn' (Brügger, 2012).

In the following, common use cases for web archives are put forward from legal, bibliographical and historiographical discourses. In those deliberations, there emerges digital source criticism of web archives. Are archived webpages to be considered accurate duplicates as well as valid and referenceable sources? Did the archived website ever appear in the wild in the same form and substance as it now does in the archive? Has the archive added to or subtracted material from the website?

Thereafter I discuss web historiography, and a number of approaches to archiving and accessing the web of the past, with the Internet Archive's Wayback Machine being only one manner of doing archiving. Alongside the biographical (or single-site histories) from the Wayback Machine, there are also event-based, national and autobiographical traditions. Each is built into collection and access routines (or the absence thereof) and shapes the histories that may be written.

The particular approach introduced in this chapter, the single-site history, is rendered practicable with a technique called the screencast documentary. It builds upon Jon Udell's pioneering screencapturing work retelling the edit history of a Wikipedia page (discussed below). It also rests on the digital method of the 'walkthrough' (Light, 2017). Screencapturing and narrating the use of software (as a means to provide instructions of use), video and computer game 'cheating' (showing how to level up) and even unboxing videos on YouTube of how to put together and play with toys are all common forms of online walkthroughs (Kücklich, 2007; Marsh, 2016). In employing the screen capture and playback technique that walks us through the history of a webpage, I also discuss overarching strategies for narrating histories of the web as seen through the changes to a single page, in order to undertake web history, media history or digital history (or some combination).

The value of web archives

The Internet Archive as well as the web archives of national libraries are increasingly thought of as sources for 'digital history', which refers to history-writing with digital materials (Rosenzweig, 2003; Cohen and Rosenzweig, 2006; Brügger, 2012). The creation and maintenance of web archives often are justified for digital history purposes, considering the wealth of online materials not only compared to other media but also because they encompass them. The argument for the specificity of web archives thus lies in the growth of 'born-digital' materials, in contrast to digitized ones of media archives. It also rests especially upon their use by future historians, when they come to write the history of particular periods, such as the 1990s. The value of the archived web is thus often thought to lie in its special contents that are otherwise unavailable elsewhere and in its future use by historians, as Milligan (2016: 80) notes: 'Imagine a history of the late 1990s or early 2000s that draws primarily on print newspapers, ignoring the [internet] technology that fundamentally affected how people share, interact, and leave historical traces behind.'

Web history, on the other hand, may be distinguished from digital history, as it concerns employing the web to tell its own story, in the tradition of medium history (Hay and Couldry, 2011). While there are exceptions, web archives are not as often justified as sources for specific web or media histories (Ben-David, 2016; Stevenson, 2016; Goggin and McLelland, 2017). Moreover, broader internet histories may be written largely without them

(Abbate, 2000; Ryan, 2011). Indeed, be it for digital, media or web history, actual historian use of web archives remains limited (Brock, 2005; Dougherty et al. 2010; Hockx-Yu, 2014).

How to reconsider and further accrue value to web archives? The point of departure here is to build upon 'website history', a term put forward as an alternative use of web archives other than digital history (Brügger, 2008). That is, the screencast documentary approach, discussed below, is both an approach to studying website histories and a means to provide researcher use for web archives, which itself is understudied (Dougherty et al. 2010). It takes advantage of the organization of the Internet Archive, and especially the interface and query machine built on top of it to access its contents: the Wayback Machine.

While it recently has added a keyword search, for over a decade now the Wayback Machine has had as its primary (and default) input field a single URL. Using digital methods, or tool-based methods to extract and analyse web data and objects for social and cultural research, the screencast documentary approach put forward here captures the outputs of the Wayback Machine (list of archived pages with dates), screenshots the unique ones, and arrays them in chronological order so as to play back the history of the website in the style of time-lapse photography (Rogers, 2013b).

Narrations or particular goals for telling the history of a website are put forward. They offer means to study the history of the web (as seen through a single website or webpage like Google Web Search), the history of the web as media (such as how a newspaper has grappled with the new medium) as well as the history of a particular institution (such as marriage, as seen through a leading wedding website). Arguably, the first is a form of web (or medium) history, the second media history, and the third digital history, however much each also blends the approaches and blurs the distinctions.

It should be pointed out that the Wayback Machine of the Internet Archive is itself a web-historical object. In a sense it also tells the story of the web, or at least a particular period of it, through the manner in which it primarily grants access to websites. By the default means by which it is queried and also how archived webpages are interlinked, the Wayback Machine of the Internet Archive has organized a surfer's web *circa* 1990s rather than a searcher's web of the 2000s or a scroller's of the 2010s (with a smartphone).

Here it is argued that the Wayback Machine also lends itself to a particular historiography that is embedded in the screencast documentary approach, namely a single-site or site-biographical method of recounting history. Having developed that argument in brief, the chapter concludes with how to put to use the Wayback Machine of the Internet Archive to tell single-site histories with screencast documentaries.

The Wayback Machine: Surf the web as it was, or use the Internet Archive as source

The Wayback Machine of the Internet Archive, with its original slogan 'surf the Web as it was', was conceived and presented in part as a solution to the 404 problem, the response code signifying that the file or webpage is not found. With the Alexa toolbar installed in a browser (in the late 1990s; see Figure 5.1), the web user confronted by a 404 error message would receive a flashing WayBack icon on the toolbar that indicates that the missing page is in the Internet Archive. If the button did not flash, there was no archived version, and the page had been lost. In return for Alexa's solution to the 404 problem as well as the content at the Internet Archive, the user would aid in populating the archive. That is, when downloading the toolbar, permission would be given to have his or her browsing activity logged, and webpages or sites that a user visited would be sent to Alexa. If a site was not yet in the archive, a crawler would visit it. Thus grew the Internet Archive. Later, high-traffic and other significant sites would be earmarked for regular archiving.

Figure 5.1   Alexa toolbar, with WayBack icon to access the Internet Archive, December 2004.

The Wayback Machine's architecture, designed in the mid-1990s, aimed to furnish an ideal surfer's experience, frictionless and without dead ends. Once onto a website in the archive, clicking links takes the surfer to the page closest in time, and, if unavailable, to the page on the live web. The surfer jumps through time as if in an atemporal hyperspace, one of the earliest web metaphors or structuring devices for a document universe without directories or search engines. The Wayback Machine thus sacrifices temporal matching for smooth navigation, and as such embeds a period in web history, in an experience that could be described as more living museum of a surfer's space than historian's meticulous archive.

Apart from the 'way it was' experience, the Wayback Machine is also suggestive of particular research practices and ultimately historiographical approaches. With respect to the research practices there are largely two afforded by the interface. At archive.org the input field invites a single page URL so as to summon its history. At the outset, in other words, one is asked to submit a URL and pursue its history through two outputs, one of which shows minute changes to the contents of the pages in the archive (additions and deletions), and another that suggests the exploration of a fuller arc, where one can click backward and forward arrows through larger chunks of the page's history, month by month.

In the original results page, asterisks next to datestamps indicate changed content on the webpage. One may thus peruse a webpage's history to spot the crucial, detailed change (or 'diff' in computational language). As a research output one perhaps would wish to put two or more pages side to side, highlighting the specific, telling diff, such as an infringement of one's intellectual property, which is a common use case of the Wayback Machine in the legal arena, discussed in more detail below.

[I]n *Telewizja Polska USA, Inc. v. Echostar Satellite Corp.*, the plaintiff alleged that the defendant was using the plaintiff's trademark name in violation of its intellectual property rights. In response, the defendant introduced the print-out of the defendant's archived webpage dated before the plaintiff received the trademark of its brand. (Gazaryan, 2013: 221)

The form of output navigation for exploring the fuller arc of history is the timeline (see Figure 5.2). Instead of pouring over the detailed changes, with the timeline, one makes a sweep through the interface and content of a webpage over the years with an eye towards the broader themes, such as the introduction and subsequent locking down or removal of comment spaces and other interactive features on websites that once made new media new.

Figure 5.2 Wayback Machine banner accompanying the archived webpage loaded in a browser. The example is Myspace.com, indicating the date it changed from a social networking to a music-oriented social entertainment site.

Source: http://web.archive.org/web/20101116021305/http://www.myspace.com/.

The interface to the Internet Archive thus creates at once a surfer's experience from a particular period in web history while also affording modes of historical work that privilege focusing on the minute as well as the sweeping change to a single page.

Digital source criticism

Seen from the perspective of digital history (history-writing with web materials), the Wayback Machine also could be said to invite the user to seek a specific source and scrutinize it for its veracity because it is a web source. Here, with the Wayback Machine, one brings the web, and its pages, into the evidentiary arena of source criticism. There are at least three sets of questions or aspirations for the 'digitally reborn' sources online now that they appear as web.archive.org URLs rather than in their original name space state (Brügger, 2012). Once captured and put back online, the archived webpages face tests, from a series of overlapping scholarly discourses, before they may be employed as proper sources. In legal studies do they count as duplicated sources, in the social sciences (and elsewhere) as valid and in history as sufficient substitutes for missing materials? From the start one of the more popular use cases for the Internet Archive, apart from the 404 error while surfing, has been as evidence (Howell, 2006). One could go back in time to a website for evidentiary purposes, checking for trademark and intellectual property infringements, as was the case with its first-time deployment in US courts in 2003 when printouts from the Wayback Machine were introduced as exhibits (Eltgroth, 2009). Here the questions concern the extent to which one can treat the archived page as a duplicate of the original no longer online, or in a lesser test, at least warrant through testimony that it represents accurately the material the site owner put online. In the event, the archived website need not be a duplicate in code and data to be admissible; rather it need only be an accurate representation. It also need not have archived all of the page. As a US court wrote in 2016: '[T]he fact that the Wayback Machine does not capture everything that was on those sites does not bear on whether the things that were captured were in fact on those sites. There is no suggestion or evidence … that the Wayback Machine ever adds material to sites' (Bychowski, 2016). Here accuracy is defined in part as the absence of addition.

Apart from its authenticity in legal arenas, a webpage faces scrutiny as a source for scholarly referencing purposes, in order to anchor an account of events, for example. In the very first place, the challenge put to the web as source may rest upon its overall (historical) reputation problem, as a medium of pirates, pornographers, conspiracy theorists and self-publishers (Dean, 1998). As the fake news scandals surrounding the US presidential campaigns of 2016 pointed to anew, it is a space with and without professional editors, and has been subject to the question of its quality, even as the web further domesticated, in its nearly 30 years of use (Thelwall et al., 2005; Marres, 2018).

More to the point is the question whether (presumably unstable) URLs should be referenced at all as sources, and if offline, whether a Wayback URL could stand in sturdily. Apart from the reputation problem, it is often argued that the web's ephemerality, or perhaps its uneven maintenance, disproves its worthiness as source. Referenced URLs break, as links rot (Veronin, 2002; Klein et al. 2014). In this context the Wayback Machine may be viewed as a set of well-tethered (rather than broken) source links. The Internet Archive thus becomes an early attempt at providing permanence to ephemeral web sources, in a lineage of such attempts from both the tradition of hypertext (permalinks in blogs and edit history retention in wikis) to that of library science (DOI numbers). Once accepted as not only references but referenceable, web sources that break and are reborn in the Internet Archive face further tests. Are the archived ones 'valid'? Such a determination relies, among other things, on whether the datestamps of archived webpages, including new archived versions, match the dates of the webpages when online, an issue studied by a series of authors (Murphy et al., 2007; Dougherty et al., 2010; Dougherty and Meyer, 2014). In the event, the Internet Archive has met validation challenges concerning webpage (and thus content) age, despite the atemporal surfing experience it affords.

For referencing, a Wayback URL supplements rather than replaces an original URL. According to the Modern Language Association (MLA) style guide, even (original) broken URLs should be referenced, with access date, for the reader may be able to 'evaluate the credibility of the site that published the source or locate the source under a new URL' (Gibson, 2016). In all the MLA recommends adding the Wayback URL to the reference after the broken URL, rather than pruning the citation through the use of the archived URL only (Internet Archive, 2016).

For historians, a further test concerns whether a reborn website in the archive was ever online as such in the first place (Brügger, 2012). Websites reconstituted by the archiving appear to be damning critiques of their value as historical sources (Russell and Kane, 2008). Newspapers especially, as proverbial first drafts of history, are susceptible to hotchpotch archival reconstructions, where certain plugged-in content is saved at another time than the front page of the newspaper, and when one recombines it in the archive the 'digitally reborn source' becomes a novel artefact of its archiving process. Even given the missing original, the question steps beyond whether the incomplete, archived source is acceptable, in the spirit of save what one can. When writing digital history, or using the web as historical source, being a scholar of the history of the web (and dynamic websites) together with the history of its archiving (and the treatment of dynamic websites) becomes crucial.

Web historiographies in brief

As discussed above, the architecture of the Wayback Machine of the Internet Archive invites website or webpage histories, given that one fetches the history of a URL through the interface, and peruses it looking for minor changes with the aid of the asterisks in the classic interface, or with a broad sweep, forward clicking month by month, examining the larger thematic changes to the life and times of the site.

Before introducing examples of website histories, in the style of Jon Udell's pioneering recounting of the edit history of the 'heavy metal' Wikipedia article, it is instructive to mention that the biographical (in which a website history would fall) is among at least four dominant traditions of web archive collection, access as well as usage. The second tradition is of a special collection, where typically elections, disasters and changes of power or transitions are archived, such as US presidential elections and the installation of a new pope (Schneider and Foot, 2004). Here the approach to web historiography is event-based. In the archiving there is an attention cycle to consider, both the run-up to an election and transition as well as its aftermath. Archiving agility (especially for a sudden disaster) is also called for.

A third type of web historiographical approach is embodied in the efforts by national libraries to demarcate and save 'national' webs, beginning with the preservation of the official public record and continuing often with a carefully considered definition of a website of relevance to national heritage (Jacobsen, 2008; Rogers et al., 2013). For example, the Danish national librarians, pioneers in web archiving, define a relevant national website as having at least one of four properties: in the top-level country .dk domain, written in Danish, about a Danish subject matter (e.g., the author Hans Christian Andersen) or material of relevance to the Danish or Denmark, the last type of which expands the material to such an extent that it becomes a matter of editorial selection, bringing the librarians back into web content curation (after the demise of the online directories and the rise of the algorithm and the automated back-end).

A fourth, the autobiographical, is the most recent, and concerns web properties that are essentially no longer considered websites, at least as we have known them to be as accessible without a password and residing for the most part on an open web. Whether they are social media platforms or smartphone apps, they are difficult to collect and preserve, and

Figure 5.3 'Amalia Ulman: Excellences & Perfections', @amaliaulman, Instagram art work in the autobiographical tradition, 2014. See Rhizome, 2014.

improbable to make accessible at any scale, owing to the fact that they are personal, behind user logins, or have other novel social and technical constraints. Facebook pages of public figures, organizations and events may be stored. For example, Archive-It, the Internet Archive service, has a default user on Facebook (Charlie Archivist, without friends or a profile) who is logged in and captures sets of pages that a web archivist enters into the software interface. For social media and the mobile web, there are additional approaches, such as capturing just the data rather than the HTML (e.g., through an API or by individuals requesting personal data dumps from Facebook) or by videorecording a user interacting with her mobile phone. The collections become social media data sets, or a user video together eventually with the smartphone itself. Relatedly, at Rhizome, the digital arts collective, the 'webenact' technique, put online as webrecorder.io, has been developed to capture or record a social media user's pages so as to re-enact them or play them back. The work was developed on the heels of the critically acclaimed performance piece of the Instagram user, Amalia Ulman (Figure 5.3; see Rhizome, 2014).

Web history, media history, digital history

From the standpoint of web historiography, a website history or single-site biography may be understood as the unfolding of the history of the website, and with it a variety of stories may be told. First, the history of a website could be seen to encapsulate the larger story of the history of the web. In one example discussed in detail below, the history of the changes to the front page of google.com (in particular the tabs or menu items) may be read as the history of the demise of the human editors of the web, and the rise of the back-end, of the algorithm, taking over from the librarians. From the history of a website, secondly, one also may tell the story of the history of media, such as how a newspaper, a radio station, or a television channel grappled with the web, over time (Bødker and Brügger, 2017). Has the old media form, so called, embraced new media features, only to settle back into a digitized version of its original self? How have newspapers domesticated the blog, or tamped down the comment space where readers can talk back to the institution referred to historically as gatekeepers?

In a screencast documentary of the history of nytimes.com, the newspaper has experimented repeatedly with new media forms, beginning as a separate entity from the print version, without any reference to the print version or to subscriptions (Hermens, 2011). It was directed at a web-only audience with such features as 'cybertimes' and forums. Often these special new media forms would be jettisoned, though some have remained such as a curated comment space as well as novel newspaper navigation through 'most emailed', 'most viewed' and 'recommended for you'.

A third strategy is telling the history of an idea, individual, organization, institution or other entity to which a website has been dedicated, also known as digital history (or history-telling with digital sources). Examining the evolution of the contents of the 'issues' tab at whitehouse.gov shows at a glance how the priorities of the US presidential administration have changed, sometimes abruptly; after the 9/11 attacks on the World Trade Center and the Pentagon in 2001, almost all issues on whitehouse.gov included the word 'security', only gradually to broaden their scope in the years to come (Rogers, 2013b). In another case, examining the history of theknot.com over a ten-year period, researchers found how a simple advice and registry site became a complex wedding planner, multiplying expenses and product placements, concluding that nowadays for weddings 'no expense should be spared' (Livio et al., 2012). Thus one view on the evolution of the institution of marriage, reconstructed through a single-site history, is its commercialization (together with the company's expanding efforts at monetizing its web offerings).

Techniques for making screencast documentaries of the history of a webpage

There are practical aspects to creating a screencast documentary of the history of a webpage. At the Digital Methods Initiative, colleagues and I have created tools and techniques to compile the archived versions of a webpage and assemble them chronologically as a movie. There are four steps: make a list of the archived pages, capture or download them, load them in a moviemaker and record a voiceover. In the first step, to make a list of the archived pages, one may use the Internet Archive Wayback Machine Link Ripper. One enters the URL to be captured from the Wayback Machine (e.g., http://www.google.com), and the tool creates a list of links of its archived pages, removing duplicates by default, and providing options concerning the capture interval (e.g., daily or monthly). To study minute changes to the webpage over time, one chooses daily snapshots, and for a fuller arc of history, monthly. Other selection strategies of 'halving' and 'zooming' are mentioned below. In the second step the Wayback Machine URL list (a text file) is subsequently inputted into a screenshot generator (such as a browser extension or a dedicated digital methods tool). Screenshots are made of each archived webpage. The pages need to load in the browser for the screenshot to be made, so it is advisable to fine-tune the amount of time between screenshots so as to make sure the pages have arrived before the screenshots are taken. The third step is to load the screenshots into an image viewer such as iPhoto and make a project in movie-making software such as iMovie. Finally, the voiceover is recorded, and the movie is ready for playback.

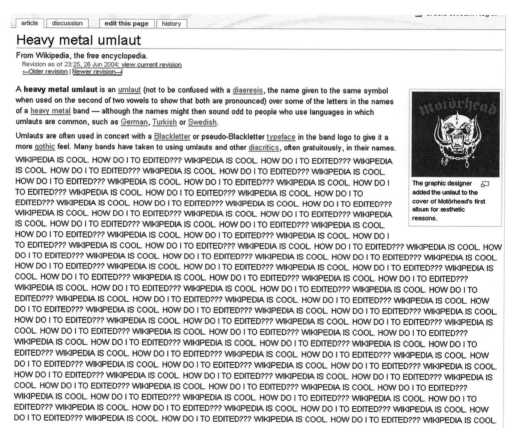

Figure 5.4   Screenshot from Jon Udell's 'Heavy Metal Umlaut,' screencast documentary, 2005, discussion of graffiti defacing a Wikipedia article.

For the voiceover consideration should be made of the narrative strategy. In 'Heavy Metal Umlaut' Jon Udell (2005) establishes the literary and social value of the (webpage) screencast documentary, previously known for software instructions of use and video game walkthroughs. In the screencast, Udell deploys a simple narrative strategy that could be employed as a starting point. He opens with an overview of his subject matter, the revision history of the Wikipedia article on the heavy metal umlaut. Through a 'quick flight' of the changelog (speeding up the chronological loading of the pages) he shows the growth and occasional vandalism of the article, speaking with awe about Wikipedians' vigilance (see Figure 5.4). Subsequently he introduces four themes and treats them one by one. The Spinal Tap theme concerns the typographical as well as factual question of the n-umlaut (or heavy metal umlaut). In the vandalism piece, he is impressed by the dedication shown by the Wikipedians, cleaning the graffiti and reverting other offensive edits only minutes after they have been made. He spends time talking about the organization of the article, and how the table of contents matures over time. (The focus on the changes to the table of contents led us to build a tool, the Wikipedia TOC scraper, that captures a Wikipedia article's table of contents, and with the use of the slider, shows its changes over time.) Finally, Udell mentions issues of cultural sensitivity, and in particular how the look of the font and the n-umlaut is no longer associated with Nazism (as it was initially in the article), but rather is described as Germanic. Without summarizing the four themes, Udell concludes the screencast documentary by returning to the first edit and jumping to the last, making mention of the achievement of a 'loose federation of volunteers', in this new type of content creation, otherwise known as the wisdom of the crowd (Surowiecki, 2004). In the edit revision history of a single Wikipedia article, it is as if web history was made. The screencast captures the birth of user-generated content.

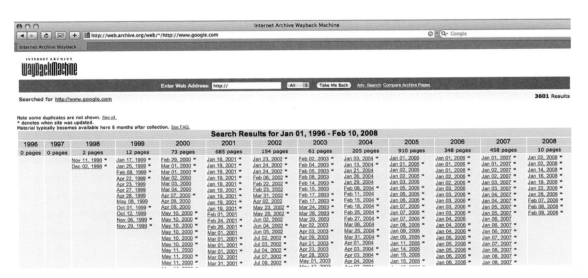

Figure 5.5 Original output of Wayback Machine for the query, http://www.google.com, August 2008, with asterisks indicating unique pages, compiled for screencast documentary, 'Google and the Politics of Tabs'. See R. Rogers and Govcom.org, 2008.

'Google and the Politics of Tabs' is the first single-site history made that follows in Udell's footsteps, and also tells a history of the web through the changes made to one page. It is the history of Google seen through its interface from 1998 until early 2008, and through seemingly tiny changes to the tabs above the search box it tells a larger story about the history of the web (Rogers and Govcom.org, 2008). It makes use of all the available, updated Google front pages in the Internet Archive, captured and played back, in the style of time-lapse photography (see Figure 5.5). 'Google and the Politics of Tabs' chronicles the subtle changes to the Google front-page real estate, showing the services that have risen to the interface, achieving tab status, and the others that have been relegated to the 'more' and 'even more' buttons. As its main theme, it tells the story of the demise of the directory (particularly Dmoz.org's), and how the back-end algorithm has taken over the organization of web information at the expense of the human editors and librarians.

Conclusions: The value of capturing website histories

Archived websites may be re-rendered for web, media and digital history. In terms of those to be told in the voiceover narrative of a webpage history, one could be of loss; something of value has been taken or replaced. In 'Google and the Politics of Tabs', which details a decade's worth of subtle changes to the google.com interface, ultimately the algorithm has taken over from the librarian on the web. Another is about transformation, or even continuity. Despite massive change around it, the object or subject has remained remarkably the same (or nearly so). In another variation, despite transformation, it has returned to its original form. As discussed above, the enthusiastic embrace of new media or its stubborn resistance is made the subject of the screencast by scrutinizing how a newspaper website has evolved. Has the old media form, so called, radically embraced cyberspace and new media features, only to settle back (largely) into a digitized form of its original self, as in the case of nytimes.com? How have newspapers domesticated the blog, or tamed the comment space where readers once could talk back to the institution referred to historically as gatekeepers? Here the story concerns incorporating new media into established practices. In each case one is considering the overall narrative of change, concentrating on a limited number of storylines, and leaving out the rest. A third strategy is to allow the history of an idea, individual, organization, institution or other entity to unfold in the changes to a website. The wedding as institution could be simple, or it can be industrialized, as a website, theknot.com, and the web is further monetized with the rise of e-commerce. One can thus build in the recipe of a great novel. Capture the times through the changes occurring in the life of an institution – on its leading website.

Table 5.1   Top issues at whitehouse.gov before and after the transition from President Obama to President Trump.

19 January 2017

Civil Rights
Climate Change
Economy

| Education |
| Foreign Policy |
| Health Care |
| Immigration |
| Iran Deal |
| 20 January 2017 |
| America First Energy Plan |
| America First Foreign Policy |
| Bringing Back Jobs And Growth |
| Making Our Military Strong Again |
| Standing Up For Our Law Enforcement Community |
| Trade Deals That Work For All Americans |

Source: Wayback Machine of the Internet Archive (archive.org).

On 20 January 2017, with the incoming presidential administration, whitehouse.gov changed dramatically. A story in the *New York Times* opened: 'Within moments of the inauguration of President Trump, the official White House website on Friday deleted nearly all mentions of climate change. … The purge … came as part of the full digital turnover of whitehouse.gov, including taking down and archiving all the Obama administration's personal and policy pages' (Davenport, 2017). Capturing 'transitions' such as the Papal in 2005 by the Library of Congress is an event-based web historiography, pioneered in the websphere technique that curates a collection of thematically related and interlinked sites over a period of some months. One also may capture such transitions through website histories, where changed front pages are made into screenshots (or otherwise captured) and played back as a screencast documentary or even as an animated gif. Here the display of content removal tells the story of changes in political (and policy) priorities. One may also focus on additional sections or pages on the website, such as the changes under the 'issues' tab, where after 20 January 2017 whitehouse.gov had such issues as 'America First Energy Plan' and 'America First Foreign Policy', which are distinctive in (sloganeering) style and substance to those on 19 January 2017 prior to the administration turnover (see Table 5.1).

The Internet Archive (and web archives generally) are commonly thought of as sources for 'digital history', however much actual historian use of web archives appears to be limited (and is understudied). With such use digital source criticism becomes a focal point with concerns about how in the archiving a 'digitally reborn' source may be reconstituted in a form that never existed in the first place. Here is a particular case where digital history may draw from web history, and its study of different forms of ephemerality (Chun, 2013). Indeed, web archives have not necessarily been justified for the purposes of telling web history (or media history), however much active use may be made of them by researchers in that field. Above I reintroduced the notion of 'website history' and put forward a particular approach to it (screencast documentary) that allows one to pursue a variety of histories: web, media as well as digital history.

The screencast documentary approach derives from digital methods, or the use of tool-based methods for web data extraction and analysis. The research affordances of the Wayback Machine are the point of departure, for it provides a list of stored pages (and an indication of which ones have new content, a.k.a. the 'diffs') that can be captured and played back in the style of time-lapse photography. The website history, it is argued, could be seen in the web historiographical tradition of website biography, which is distinctive from event, national or autobiographical styles of collection and curation. Once captured, the website history may be narrated; in the examples given the stories revolved around loss, continuity and transformation. They concern how the history of a single website may encapsulate the history of the web, how so-called old media perpetuates itself in the new media, and how the transformation of an institution may be captured.

PROJECT 6

Produce a screencast documentary on the history of a website

VIDEO 3 Web history with screencast documentaries

RESEARCH GOAL To capture past versions of a website via the Wayback Machine of the Internet Archive, and narrate website history in a screencast documentary.

1   Consider the type of website history to tell: web history, media history or digital history.

   a   Web history. The history of some websites may be seen as encapsulating a larger story of the history of the web. See 'Google and the Politics of Tabs', where it is put forward that with the demise of the directory in Google, ultimately the algorithm took over from the librarian on the web.

   b   Media history. The relationship between old and new media forms can be scrutinized by examining how a newspaper, a radio station, or a television channel has 'webbified' itself over time. Has the old media form translated its features and ported them onto the web, or embraced 'new' media, transforming itself along the way? Has it experimented only to revert to its original self, with perhaps a smattering of online cultural forms retained? Newspapers are intriguing candidates for a study of the collision between the web and print, for the web promised to do away with gatekeeping through debate and comment spaces, and also introduce citizen journalists, with content sourced from the crowd.

   c   Digital history. A third strategy is to recount the history of an institution or other entity to which a website has been dedicated. A typical example would be the analysis of the issue lists of the US White House over time. One can view the changing times and priorities through the changes to a webpage. Counter-intuitive stories are of particular interest; one could find stability despite outward, massive change.

2   Choose a website to study and obtain the list of archived versions of its URL from the Internet Archive Wayback Machine.

3   Type the URL into the Internet Archive Wayback Machine Link Ripper. Choose to exclude duplicates and multiple page versions per day to show broad changes over time, and a longer arc of history. There are scenarios where one may be interested in multiple page versions per day. In a micro-temporal project, one could consider a 'developing' story over short periods of time, such as the changing headlines of a newspaper on election night.

4   Once the tool has completed its task, choose the tool's output menu and save the list of URLs of the archived versions as a text file.

5   Make a selection of the archived versions. Consider using a threshold technique (halving or zooming) in order to remove archived versions less relevant to your narrative. In your screenshot collection, select an image from the middle of the list, and compare it to an earlier and later screenshot; if the one in the middle is the same as the earlier screenshot, all in between are probably the same as well. Consider an 'even' history by choosing archived versions at stable intervals or an 'uneven' history by using only archived versions from key dates.

6   Use a screenshot generator to produce the snapshots of the archived versions.

    a   Insert URL list.

    b   Screenshot generator is set to 1024x768.

    c   Time to wait is 20 seconds between screenshots to allow Wayback Machine URLs to load. You may wish to conduct a test to determine whether the time to wait should be adjusted.

    d   Wait until all screenshots have been captured. This may take a couple of hours, depending on the number of archived pages in your selection.

    e   Check if all went well by looking at the screenshots. Sometimes the archive returns an error. Note the URLs of the erred screenshots in a new text file and use screenshot generator to capture them anew.

7   Prepare your narration. Here are some considerations based on Jon Udell's 'Heavy Metal Umlaut' screencast on the evolution of eponymous Wikipedia article. Below is also the narrative of the seminal screencast documentary, 'Google and the Politics of Tabs'.

    a   Jon Udell's narrative strategy provides an overview of the story at the beginning ('quick flight'), and then delves into a set number of sub-elements or aspects in detail, closing with a larger point. As in a presentation of a network visualization, first is the overview, then zoom in to a few clusters, and zoom back out so as to conclude.

    b   Consider the overall narrative of change. The story to be told may be one of loss; something of value has been lost or replaced. It may have returned but the environment has changed. Another is about transformation, or perhaps continuity. Despite massive change around it, the object or subject has remained remarkably the same. Despite transformation, it has returned to its original form.

    c   Concentrate on discrete storyline(s) and cut the less relevant. Resist exhaustiveness. Select a small number of key aspects to focus on rather than narrating every minute detail.

    d   Consider web attention span, and the YouTube style. Compile the images into a video with narration that is maximum 10 minutes in length (an early YouTube cut-off), but preferably half that amount of time.

8   Load screenshots into an image viewer. Consider annotating the screenshots to highlight specific narrative elements.

9   Make project in a movie maker. Sort by name, which keeps the pages in chronological order. Record narrative. Alternatively, use http://screencast-o-matic.com and record your narrated slideshow through this web service. There is also a built-in screen-recording feature in QuickTime.

Screencast documentary example:
'Google and the Politics of Tabs'

Narrative voice-over. This is the history of Google as seen through its Interface. From the beginning, sometime in November 1998 all the way up until late 2007. These are screenshots of Google Interface taken from the Wayback Machine of the Internet Archive. The history of the Google is important. For some people, Google is the Internet. And for many, it's the first point of access. And Google, as the face of the Internet, has remained virtually the same over the past ten years. But there have been some subtle changes to the Interface. So let's go back and look at this in a little bit more detail.

You see initially Google with a standard Web search button and its intriguing 'I'm feeling lucky' button have been your only options. Then the Directory gets introduced with some front-page fanfare. It's the Open Directory Project, Dmoz.org, that Google's built an engine on top of. Then come the Tabs on top of the Search box with the Web search being privileged at the far left, followed by Images, Groups (that's searching Usenet), and the Directory makes it to the front page. News, the Google news service, the news aggregator was next. Froogle is introduced; that was that cost comparison e-commerce service. And that stayed on the front page for a while, then was dropped. Followed by Local, which later became Google Maps. You can see that the services are becoming more and more present; there are now five or six at the top bar. Then they add a 'More' button. What we're interested in is which services remain on the front page and which get relegated to 'More' or 'Even More'. But let's look at this in some more detail.

Let's look at the fate of the Directory over time. It's a story of the demise of the librarian, of the demise of the human editors of the Web, and the rise of the back end, of the algorithm taking over from the editors. Now you see that it's introduced with great fanfare in 2000. The Web is organized by human editors. It remains on the front page. It achieves the Tabs status that we talked about previously. Fourth Tab here. And keeps its place on the front page even as other services are introduced. However, in 2004 something happened: it got placed under the 'More' button. You had to click 'More' to find the Directory. And in 2006, if you clicked 'More', the Directory wasn't there; you had to click 'Even More' and there you would find the Directory. As it loses its standing, it also loses recognition. Lots of people don't really remember that there is a Directory just like other services that have left the front-page real estate. Also of interest are the services that climb from being 'Even More' to 'More' and all the way to the front page. But with the Directory, it's a sadder story. As the interface of Google moves upper left, and you click 'More', you see that there's no Directory any longer. And you also see that there is no 'Even More'. So nowadays you have to search Google for its Directory to find the Google Directory.

'Google and the Politics of Tabs' by R. Rogers and Govcom.org, Amsterdam, 2008.

Quicktime movie, 5'00", https://movies.digitalmethods.net/google.html.

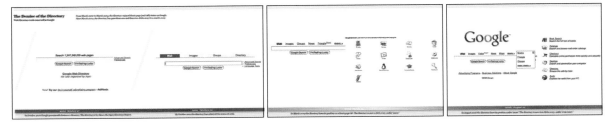

Figure 5.6   Google's Directory on Google's front page in 2000 and receiving tab status in October of 2001 (left), before being relegated to under the 'more' (middle) and finally the 'even more' buttons (right). Excerpt from Digital Methods Initiative and Kim de Groot, 'The Demise of the Directory: Web librarian work removed in Google', Information Graphic, 2008, http://www.govcom.org/publications/drafts/GCO_directoryfall.pdf

PROJECT 7

Recount the history of an event via Facebook

RESEARCH GOAL To recount (or replay) an event using the 'most engaged-with content' on its associated Facebook pages, with posts placed in chronological order.

Between 2010 and late 2018 Facebook had been among those that inserted a robots.txt exclusion file in the code of its website, thereby requesting (the Wayback Machine and others) not to index its site. As a result both facebook.com as well as thefacebook.com were inaccessible via the Wayback Machine, which prompted scholars to seek alternative means of writing Facebook history such as using descriptions of historical features available in the trade press and newspapers, or screenshots of them found via Google Images (Brügger, 2015). After a long hiatus, facebook.com and thefacebook.com have reappeared in the Wayback Machine of the Internet Archive, enabling anew histories of its 'about' pages, user privacy policies of Facebook and its early history, more generally. (As would be expected, nothing behind the logins is accessible in the archive.)

Studying digital history via Facebook, on the other hand, may be accomplished perhaps more readily using 'pages' (not personal accounts) on Facebook, for example, the We Are Khaled Said page, which could be said to chronicle the Egyptian revolution of 2011 (Rieder et al., 2015). One means of providing an account of such events would be to capture the 'most engaged-with content' of a page, using Netvizz, and arraying the content in chronological order, so as to re-enact or play back the events, where the content has been filtered according to interest (or quantity of engagement). (The following describes a procedure using Netvizz, the Facebook data extraction tool, but it also may be performed with Facepager manually.)

1   Choose Facebook page.
2   Look up Facebook page ID, for example, https://findmyfbid.com.
3   Insert Facebook page ID in Netvizz, and open .tsv file as spreadsheet.
4   Sort spreadsheet by engagement score. Choose threshold of engagement. Those pages above the threshold should be pasted in another spreadsheet (or sheet in the same spreadsheet file).
5   Sort by date.
6   Use screenshot generator for each page post.
7   Make movie project, and replay the event, by page chronology, narrating it according to most engaged-with content on Facebook.

Video tutorials

For Project 6 view these two tutorials on how to operate the Wayback Machine:

- 'Research with the Internet Archive's Wayback Machine' (7' 02"), https://www.youtube.com/watch?v=mShvg718JN8
- 'The Internet Archive Wayback Machine Link Ripper' (2' 04"), https://www.youtube.com/watch?v=DVa2TBhp4a4

For Project 7 view this tutorial on how to generate screenshots from a list of URLs extracted with Netvizz:

- 'Generating Screenshots from a List of URLs Extracted with Netvizz' (8' 06"), https://www.youtube.com/watch?v=nO16lEzeaFk

Tools

- Internet Archive Wayback Machine Link Ripper, https://tools.digitalmethods.net/beta/internetArchiveWaybackMachineLinkRipper/
- Screenshot Generator, https://tools.digitalmethods.net/beta/screenshotGenerator/
- Find your Facebook ID, https://findmyfbid.com
- Netvizz, https://apps.facebook.com/107036545989762/

SEARCH AS RESEARCH
Repurposing Google

*Transforming the consumer information
appliance into a research machine*

Search engine results for repurposing: Google studies and societal search

The chapter is dedicated to the question of search as research, and in particular how Google, the dominant web search engine, may be repurposed as a research machine both for medium as well as social research. After considering the extent to which one is only studying Google when perusing search engine results, ultimately, the goal is to consider how to perform social research with Google, or what, in short, may be termed 'societal search'. Here one would employ Google, in separate exercises elaborated below, for the study of local or national concern as well as the study of partisanship.

Since the mid-2000s Google has offered so-called local domain Googles, where one performs searches at google.nl (in the Netherlands), google.fr (in France), google.de (in Germany), and so forth (see Figure 6.1); they are also called 'regions' and are accessible via the advanced settings if one is not located in the country corresponding to the local domain Google (Kao, 2017). In other words, the engine user is directed by default to the local domain Google on the basis of user's location, read from the IP address or set location preference. After an engine query is made, the results are returned in the local language, as are the advertisements. Google's 'local' also serves its business model, and the results are delivered within national legal jurisdictions, such as European countries where users have the right to oblivion, or certain results removed (Floridi et al., 2015).

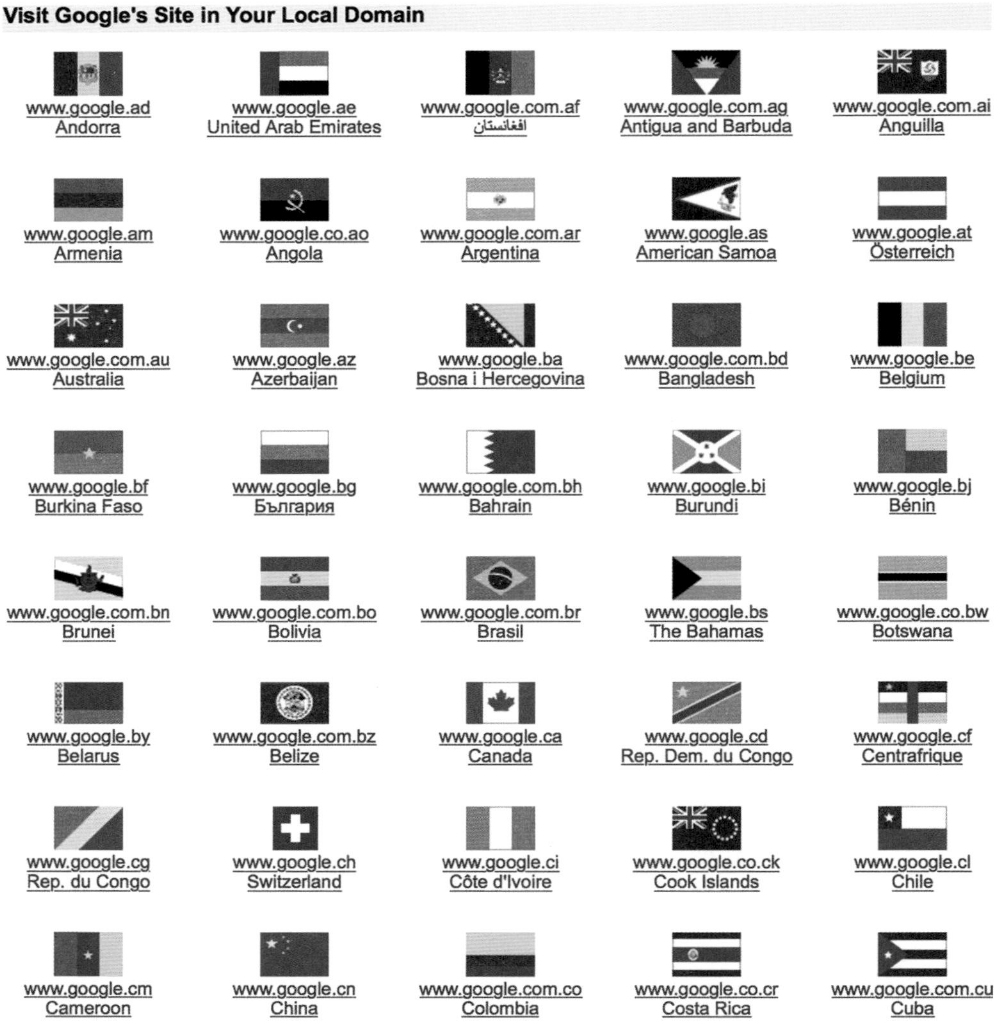

Visit Google's Site in Your Local Domain

www.google.ad Andorra	www.google.ae United Arab Emirates	www.google.com.af افغانستان	www.google.com.ag Antigua and Barbuda	www.google.com.ai Anguilla
www.google.am Armenia	www.google.co.ao Angola	www.google.com.ar Argentina	www.google.as American Samoa	www.google.at Österreich
www.google.com.au Australia	www.google.az Azerbaijan	www.google.ba Bosna i Hercegovina	www.google.com.bd Bangladesh	www.google.be Belgium
www.google.bf Burkina Faso	www.google.bg България	www.google.com.bh Bahrain	www.google.bi Burundi	www.google.bj Bénin
www.google.com.bn Brunei	www.google.com.bo Bolivia	www.google.com.br Brasil	www.google.bs The Bahamas	www.google.co.bw Botswana
www.google.by Belarus	www.google.com.bz Belize	www.google.ca Canada	www.google.cd Rep. Dem. du Congo	www.google.cf Centrafrique
www.google.cg Rep. du Congo	www.google.ch Switzerland	www.google.ci Côte d'Ivoire	www.google.co.ck Cook Islands	www.google.cl Chile
www.google.cm Cameroon	www.google.cn China	www.google.com.co Colombia	www.google.co.cr Costa Rica	www.google.com.cu Cuba

Figure 6.1　Local domain Googles, where one is sent by default when located within that country. The graphic shows how Google globalized, or glocalized, in the sense of making its global product local.

Source: Google language tools, https://web.archive.org/web/20111118022541/http://www.google.com/language_tools. See also 'See results for a different country', https://support.google.com/websearch/answer/873?hl=en.

Apart from returning advertisements and legal context, local domain Googles also return 'local' results, and the question concerns how the local is epistemologically constituted by Google. Which types of sources are returned (by default as well as by special advanced settings)? In what sense are they local sources, or how to describe Google's sense of local? Thus, prior to being able to conduct social research with Google ('societal search'), one must interrogate the engine's definition of the local, or conduct medium research ('Google studies').

We start thus by examining the utility of Google's sense of the local. Does it enable the study of local (or national) concern? May one ultimately read societal tendencies or trends through search engine returns? These questions are posed so as to develop a new form of search engine critique as well as usage, where search becomes research, or the engine becomes more than an information, advertising and legal machine. Put differently, may one perform social research with Google, or is one always only studying Google?

In introducing this line of search engine (epistemological) critique and repurposing, it is instructive to discuss, briefly, how the search engine and its results are often held up to critical examination, before returning, in the main section, to the issues at hand when considering the engine as research machine as opposed to another type. Search engine critique, at least as presented here, could be of at least five varieties: the engine's results biases, cognitive effects, surveillance regime, hegemony as well as its invisible materiality. Each is briefly taken in turn, before the discussion moves on to how to perform search as research in the form of medium research ('Google studies') and social research ('societal search').

Search engine critique

Early investigations into engine result pages have been dominated by search engine bias studies, where the aim of the research is to uncover and explain the absence and presence of certain results, especially at the top of the returns, considered to be the most valuable space or 'real estate'. Early search engine critique focused on the ways in which search engines and other gateways to the web privilege certain information sources over others. 'Preferred placement' critique – which originated when AltaVista was the dominant search engine – concerns placing ads where 'editorial' content is meant to be, and obfuscating the crucial distinction (Rogers, 2000). Search engines, in another classic, idealistic critique, clash with the architecture of the internet as well as its design values, because they undermine 'the substantive vision of the web as an inclusive democratic space' (Introna and Nissenbaum, 2000: 181). From this perspective, differentiation between sources on the basis of ranking algorithms is interpreted as threatening the egalitarian, or democratizing, potential of the web.

Exclusion and deep burying

Search engines supposedly give rise to inequality of information in at least three ways: the exclusion of certain sources, the artificial boosting of others, and the naturalization of results that favour the rich and powerful. First, it is improbable for search engines to index the entire web. In their pioneering and often-cited articles in the late 1990s, computer scientists Lawrence and Giles investigated six search engines' web coverage. In finding it to be incomplete, they concluded that in fact there is a hidden or 'deep web' never visited by crawlers (Lawrence and Giles, 1998, 1999). The deep web thus became an object of study and fascination, as a subset out of reach and difficult to plumb. Second, search engine results may be biased because search engines are prone to manipulation. Since the early days, search engine optimizers and content producers have been attempting to rank well in search engines by trying to influence engine results, leading Google to issue webmaster guidelines but also to demarcate the web into neighbourhoods, some good and others spammy (Pringle et al., 1998). More recently there have been calls to audit algorithms to uncover not so much epistemological inequalities or advertising in disguise, but rather machine bias and discrimination, such as when African-American name searches trigger Google ads for background checks or when women receive ads for lower-paying jobs on Google's ad network (Sandvig et al., 2014; Datta et al., 2015). Third, search engines have a kind of favouritism built in where 'the rich and the powerful', as well as the web savvy, will dominate the top (Introna and Nissenbaum, 2000: 177; Hindman, 2008). Those sites receiving the most links (from sites which themselves receive many links) are boosted, as if organically, as the results produced by the algorithm are often described. When mention is made of how sources are buried by engines (through a lack of indexing, or by their measurable dearth of authority or influence), one may speak of engines' social effects.

Attention deficit

There is additionally critique about engines' cognitive effects, with the rise of what could be called Google-assisted intelligence. To the cultural critic, Nicholas Carr, we are witnessing the decline of 'contemplative man', and the coming of 'flickering man' (Carr, 2007). Through 'googling' during conversations but also with the intrusion of smartphones, social media and messaging apps, there has been a concomitant rise of what Linda Stone has called 'continuous partial attention' (Stone, 2008). Users are not only distracted but also displaced, owing to the maintenance of remote intimacy as well as ambient friend-following.

User studies also have found what could be termed engine attention effects, whereby fewer and fewer results pages are browsed. As FairSearch (2010: 1), the trade industry alliance, put it more starkly: 'Links below the fold receive less than 1% of users' attention', which also introduces language used by journalists as well as marketeers about the value of not only the top results but also the screen space prior to scrolling. The 'fold' once referred to broadsheet newspapers, folded, whereby those headlines and stories above the fold were most significantly placed. Nowadays it is the size of the real estate affected by the shrinking screen space of the smartphone, and the overpopulation of the top of engine returns with Google properties, that has been a cause for consternation (and industry complaints).

Surveillance vessel

There are further critiques of engines to be aware of, as they also bear upon the potential use of Google as research machine. One concerns the search engine as surveillance vessel, which collects, stores and acts upon user information, such as language and location. One's 'flecks', pieced together by the search engine, form a data body (or second self) that has agency, for information is readied and delivered to you on the basis of your profile (Critical Art Ensemble, 1998; Fuller, 2005). Search engines may be critiqued for filling out the data body through the collection and retention of one's search history, which, as the AOL release of users' rich search history data revealed, may be thought to contain a personal 'database of intentions' (Battelle, 2003). Perusing one's data dump, a download of everything Google has stored about you, has been likened to 'reading the diary I hadn't intended to keep' (Hanley, 2018).

Projects such as scroogle.org (now discontinued), TrackMeNot and Ruin My Search History are reactions to Google as data collection (and surveillance) vessel, where the former, once an interface atop Google, 'crumbled' cookies, blocked ads and Google properties, and saved no user history. The latter two, a Firefox extension and a webpage, camouflage user queries and mask one's history by sending random words, or noise, in an act of obfuscation (Brunton and Nissenbaum, 2011; Serhat, 2016). On a regulatory level, 'do not track' has been implemented as a feature in browsers (albeit disabled by default), requesting that the website loaded in the browser does not itself track the user's behaviour or allow a third party to do so, such as Google's Doubleclick trackers. From a research standpoint, checking the 'do not track' box in the browser's privacy settings could give the user a sense of which websites are complying, and which are ignoring the user's wishes – by noticing whether ads are still following you around the web, so to speak. DuckDuckGo, one search engine that does not track its users, once ran a billboard ad for a month in Google territory (San Francisco), marketing itself as a privacy enhancing technology (or PET), to use the standard term (see Figure 6.2).

Figure 6.2 DuckDuckGo's billboard advertisement in San Francisco, January 2011.
Picture credit: Gabriel Weinberg.

Googlization

A fourth, broader set of critiques centres on actual and conceptual monopolization, or the 'creep' of Google as well as Google's 'free business model' into more and more markets and more service areas (Rogers, 2009b). A glance at Google's list of products (which appears as a menu item in its flagship web search service) is telling (maps, places, news, shopping, travel, etc.), as is its market share across search markets, and the related decline of national search engines, with distinctively different algorithms than Google's, with relatively few exceptions such as Baidu in China, Naver in South Korea, Seznam in the Czech Republic, Yandex in Russia and Yahoo! in Japan. More conceptually, one could argue that Google's PageRank and subsequent algorithmic updates that have driven the engine towards personalization has led to algorithmic concentration, which is a variation of market, or media, concentration, describing the search engine company as both monolithic as well as hegemonic.

The term to surface summarizing this political-economy style critique is 'Googlization', put forward by library scientists concerned about the Google Books project, and its march (or creep) into the hallowed halls and shelves of the library (Vaidhyanathan, 2011). Here Google becomes mass media, with a model that strives to serve the greatest audience (with a quality level to match it), together with high barriers of entry for any competitors, given the size (and expense) of the infrastructure needed to compete against it. In an appeal for donations, Jimmy Wales, founder of Wikipedia, once opened by saying that 'Google might have close to a million servers' (Wikimedia, 2011). Wales was comparing the relative muscle of Google to Wikipedia's.

Rematerializing the cloud

The materiality of Google, once understudied, has become the subject of a variety of exposés, ranging from investigative reporting on negotiations between the company and city and state governments, artistic and ethnographic trips to data centres and works of art that show buildings scrubbed from Google maps (Burrington, 2014). To be sure, there is a vast technological infrastructure in the service of delivering fast engine results and seeding 'the cloud'. The infrastructures in turn compete for natural resources with the local population, farmers and others in what are dubbed 'water wars', for they require cooling (Gallucci, 2017). The materiality of the cloud is captured in Timo Arnal's (2014) artwork, *Internet Machine*, as well as in Trevor Paglan's (2016) *Deep Web Dive* where the artist swims to an undersea cable. Paglan's work is about surveillance, though it does point to the physicality of the cloud (and the lengths to which one must go to uncover it). In Arnal's work, the nondescript, often secret, data centre is actually entered (see Figure 6.3). After a series of security layers, the camera takes us down long corridors, laced with cables, and through doors to the server rooms that whirr with the sounds of fans. Apart from surprisingly high noise levels there are also temperature extremes; there are 'hot aisles' and cold ones (Levy, 2012). To keep the systems up there are massive diesel generators for back-up power, and steel containers of cooling water in case of calamity. It is remarkably emptied of people, with few signs of maintenance workers.

The cloud, the airy metaphor that deftly stands in for physical systems of cables, data centres, servers and electricity, is often illustrated with impressive numbers – the billions of searches served in milliseconds around the world and the number of bytes (zettabytes even) held 'up there', in what technology historians would call exemplary of the 'arithmetic sublime', whereby the reader stands in awe of its incomprehensible vastness, well beyond any human mathematical capacity. The term 'technological sublime' was coined to capture the statistical and other jaw-dropping descriptions of great technological displays such as the illuminations of city streets in the nineteenth century, when electricity and public lighting were introduced (Nye, 1994). Such thinking is often followed by what these numbers (and the awe) obscure: a sprawling political economy of resource extraction, low-wage work and data centre user capture, fuelling growth, such as when Apple OS nudges its users to save files onto iCloud rather than their own hard drive (Merritt, 2013).

Figure 6.3 Facebook data centre signage. 'Other companies don't put their names on their data centers.'
Source and picture credit: Lardinois, 2016.

The clouds of the likes of Amazon, Google, Apple and Facebook have now been brought down to earth through the materialist and environmental critique, one that has found a starting point for research in the lists of data centre locations as well as their resource consumption provided by the companies themselves in displays of corporate social responsibility. That is, for some years now the companies have issued reports not only on 'transparency' (related to requests from governments around the world to block content or identify users) but also on 'environmental responsibility' where in one of Apple's documents, for example, it is stated that in 2016 the company used 630 million gallons of water (up 10 per cent from the previous year's consumption owing to the data centres) (Apple, 2017). On back-ups, it also burned 261,580 gallons of diesel. The listing of such figures is couched less in the prose of technological wonderment than in the incremental progress towards a more sustainable pace.

Google studies or societal search?

The very idea that one may use Google as social research machine is not unusual, when one considers that the science built into its algorithms (and entire apparatus) is in the first instance a variation on citation analysis, adapted to the web (Brin and Page, 1998; Rieder, 2012; Marres, 2017). The difference between the engine as it was and as it grows, however, lies largely in a change in the engine's definition of 'relevance' (Van Couvering, 2007). Where once results were deemed to be the best match between document (page) and subject matter (query) (and ranked by influential inlink counts), increasingly that match has been made less on the basis of content than on other variables, too, such as user clicks, page freshness and domain age. Where it once had little or nothing to do with it, now relevance is in some sense user-driven, or perhaps consumer-driven, if one prefers to emphasize the commercialization of Google's results. More conceptually, search results are a product of our 'living within [Google's] lab', meaning that we as users are all a part of Google's experiments and beta-testing that previously would have been performed in-house, with user groups or with students spot checking results against a list of what would constitute desirable outcomes (Davies, 2015: 377). Results now are adjusted according to how they are actually used rather than arriving preconceived from the beautiful mind alone or tested in-house.

The delivery of relevant pages based on user feedback could be thought of as one means of determining hierarchies of sources and societal concerns. Or such is the question. What sorts of source hierarchies are revealed when studying engine results? Is one able to study societal concern, or is one always only studying Google? In the following the answer lies somewhere in the middle, given that (on the one hand) engine effects are not to be eliminated, but (on the other) may be identified as well as mitigated.

Figure 6.4   Visualization of google.com and google.cn results as technique for comparison.
Source: Langreiter, 2017.

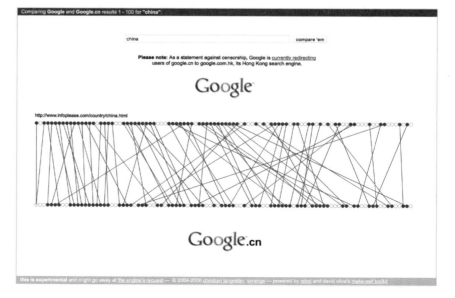

Medium research as Google studies

Below I begin by using the engine for medium research ('Google studies'), before determining how (and whether) it may be used for social research ('societal search'). The Google studies projects ultimately seek to pave the way for societal search.

The first ones concern the types of sites returned in local domain Googles (google.nl, google.be, google.de., google.fr and so forth, now accessible as 'regions' in the advanced settings), and invite questions concerning Google's definition or sense of the 'local'. What is local to Google? Here one is able to critique Google's capacity as research machine for cross-country analysis by showing the extent to which Google returns transnational, regional or some (other) combination of results in its local domain engines. One compares the results of the same query across multiple local domain Googles (see Figure 6.4).

This project is medium research in the sense that the analysis seeks to tease out a Google notion of the local. In this project one queries one ambiguous or underspecified term of relevance in multiple locations or local domains (Rogers, 2013b). The analysis in question queries [diversidad] (or diversity) first in three pertinent local domain Googles (Colombia,

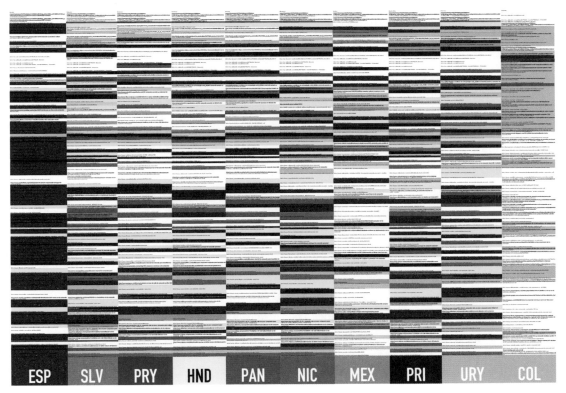

Figure 6.5 Locations of sources compared in local domain Googles in Spanish-speaking countries, where the majority are from Spain. Analysis by Natalia Sánchez Querubín and the Digital Methods Initiative, 2011.
Source: Rogers, 2013b.

Peru and Venezuela, all in the Amazon river basin) and subsequently across Spanish-speaking domains, finding that the vast majority of the results are sources in Spain, rather than from Latin America (see Figure 6.5). Spanish sources are identified not only by the country domain (.es), but also from the 'about us' information as well as the specificity of the Spanish language used on the pages.

In another exercise of this sort [Amazonia] (Amazon) is queried in Spanish-language local domain Googles, and the URLs returned per domain are compared. For Spain (google.es) the results originate largely in Spain. For all the other countries Google provides in each sources from Spain, and the remainder are Latin American results, nearly uniform for each country. It is as if there is a result set for Spain and another one for all of Latin America (see Figure 6.6). Google's local is national for Spain but transnational (and rather colonial) for Latin America, where Spanish sources retain authority. Here one may pursue search engine returns as one expression of the coloniality of knowledge (Grosfoguel, 2004).

Google studies with social research implications

In another comparative source origin project, ["human rights"] is queried in various local domain Googles (in the respective local languages), asking whether the results return local or non-local pages. This undertaking is again medium research, or Google studies, but the implications begin to fall into the realm of social research or societal search. That is, taking the query into account, one also may ask which countries have well-developed content providers for human rights issues, and which rely on non-local, perhaps even establishment sources. The case study explores the distinctiveness of local results across local domain Googles, with the additional consideration of the type of query made, human rights, which to some is a universal as opposed to local or regional issue, as in the first sample project.

Where are the returned information sources based? The aim is to retrieve the location of the information sources outputted per local domain Google engine. The location of a website may be thought of in a number of ways, including country code top-level domain (ccTLD), registration (site owner's geographical location) and/or host (geographical location where a website is stored) (Sottimano, 2013). In this project location is gleaned from the address of the website's registrant (through the contact address on the website and/or its 'whois' information, when available). 'Local' sources are defined as those registered in the country of the local domain Google (e.g., for the results provided by google.com.eg, the source, anhri.net, is considered 'local' because it is registered in Cairo, Egypt).

After the term ["human rights"] is queried in the local language, the top ten information sources are captured and geolocated, and the results visualized on a geographical map (see Figure 6.7). Remarkably, nearly half of the local domain Googles have no local results in the top ten sources returned. When comparing the number of local sources, the uneven distribution across national webs becomes apparent. The countries with the most local sources are European, some North American, South American and Asian countries.

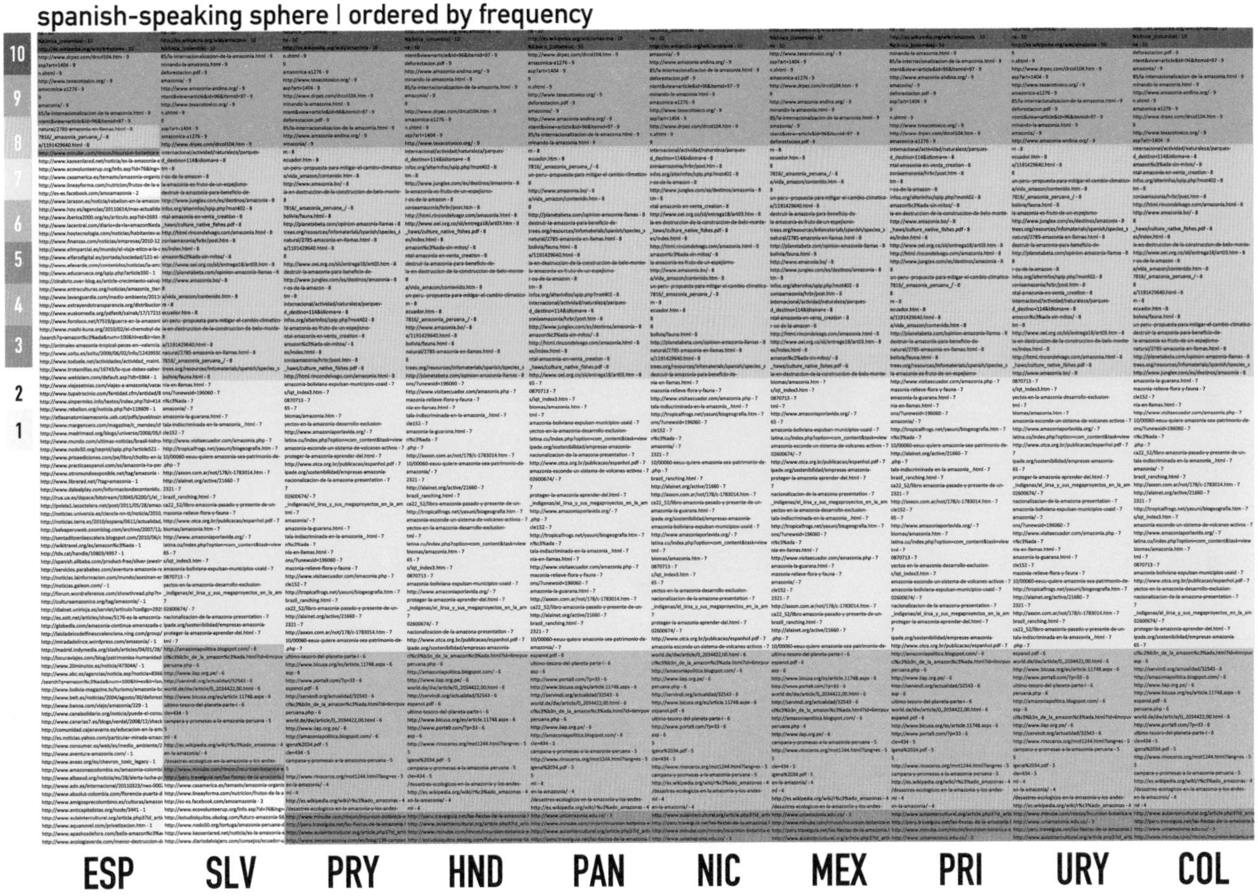

spanish-speaking sphere | ordered by frequency

Figure 6.6 URLs compared across local domain Googles in Spanish-speaking countries; colours indicate the number of local domain Googles in which a set of results appear. Analysis by Natalia Sánchez Querubin, Diana Mesa and the Digital Methods Initiative, 2011.

Source: Rogers, 2013b.

Most countries in the top ranks have location-specific languages. African and Middle Eastern countries are found towards the bottom of the list.

The most prominent information source across 121 national Googles, queried in 43 languages, is un.org, with 80 of the local domain Googles returning un.org as one of the top ten results (see Figure 6.7). In the Arab-speaking Middle East and northern Africa (MENA), local

Map generated from the issuegeographer by the Digital Methods Initiative, Amsterdam

Local and International Information Sources
Human Rights Sources According to Local Domain Googles

About this map | Digitalmethods.net

Findings

(Default to Global)   (Regional Hubs)

The issue of human rights is articulated differently depending on where, and in what language, one searches. The map displays the sources returned for the query 'Human Rights' in over 50 languages and in 135 national and regional Google search engines.

Analysis_ Erik borra, Chris Castiglione, Martin Fuez, Carolyn Gerlitz, Michael Stevenson, Marijn de Vries Hoogerwerf and Esther Weltevrede. Design_Marieke van Dijk. Digital Methods Summer'09

121 Google-language combi

Select a url from the Google countries it was in the top 10

www.un.org (80)
www.ohchr.org (53)
www.hrw.org (43)
en.wikipedia.org (31)
www.hrweb.org (30)
es.wikipedia.org (19)
www.monografias.com (19)
www.derechos.net (17)
www.asil.org (12)
anhri.net (11)
www.unhchr.ch (11)
plato.stanford.edu (11)

Currently seeing all countries their top 10 human rights res

Mouseovers and clicks in the click Deselect All to enable th

Figure 6.7   Bordered sources: local and international information sources. Graphic by Esther Weltevrede and Erik Borra, Digital Methods Initiative, Amsterdam, 2009.

sources (with the exception of anhri.net) are virtually absent (see Figure 6.8). The shared sources are primarily USA-based, and also include the Brazilian NGO, huquqalinsan.com. Half of the sources returned in the Arab-speaking countries are identical; in the 11 national Googles, un.org, arabhumanrights.org, hrw.org, ar.wikipedia.org and anhri.net appear at the top. On a number of the MENA Googles, we found local results on the second page.

Figure 6.8 Bordered sources: where are the human rights information sources from Arab-speaking countries based? Graphic by Esther Weltevrede, Digital Methods Initiative, Amsterdam, 2009.

Societal search with Google studies artefacts

This project is principally societal research as we are looking to Google to provide a ranked list of societal concerns per local domain Google. Are there distinctive or similar rights that reach the top in Finland, the Netherlands, France, Italy, Switzerland, Germany, Austria, Sweden, Russia, Japan, Canada, the United Kingdom, Australia, Philippines, Ivory Coast and other countries?

The first step is to query the term [rights] in the local languages in the local domain Googles, e.g., [õigused] in google.ee, [direitos] in google.pt, etc. One may use a VPN to be located in the country or local Google domain in question, or use the region setting in advance search. The second step is to read and interpret the results and make lists of the top ten distinctive rights types, leaving them in the order that Google provided.

As noted above, the query design takes advantage of Google as research machine, and particularly its strength in dealing with ambiguous queries such as [rights] rather than its other strength of massive (fresh) site indexing, which is behind a second set of societal search projects below. With respect to its original strength, as Brin and Page (1998: 9) phrase it, 'the benefits of PageRank are the greatest for underspecified queries'. Discrete or less ambiguous keywords would decrease the salubrious algorithmic effects.

SWEDEN	FINLAND	ESTONIA	LATVIA	UNITED KINGDOM	NETHERLANDS	BELGIUM (Flemish)	BELGIUM (French)
human rights	children's rights	citizen's rights	animal rights	human rights	works council rights	human rights	human rights
patients' rights	everyman's right (freedom to roam)	children's rights	human rights	author's rights	air passengers' rights	disability rights	internet rights
children's rights	animal rights	environmental rights	air passengers' rights	digital rights	children's rights	cyclists' rights	youth rights
air passengers' rights	consumer rights	air passengers' rights	pension rights for non-citizens	minorities' rights	human rights	volunteers' rights	citizen's rights
creator's rights	women's rights	author's rights	immigrants' rights	citizen's rights	minorities' rights	air passengers' rights	intellectual property rights
equal rights	air passengers' rights	patients' rights	copyright	employment rights	prostitutes' rights	works council rights	patients' rights
citizen's rights	renter's rights	property rights	children's rights	publicity rights	taxpayers' rights	children's rights	women's rights
women's rights	patients' rights	landowners' rights	social rights	abortion rights	youth rights	job applicant's rights	children's rights
right of collective bargaining	youth rights	workers' rights	teachers' rights	photographers' rights	islam and women's rights	immigrants' rights	workers' rights
food rights	right to education in native sign language	sexual and health rights	consumer rights	children's rights	author's rights	patients' rights	the right to defend yourself in court

Figure 6.9   The nationality of issues: rights types (excerpt). Digital Methods Initiative, Amsterdam, 2009. *Source*: Rogers et al., 2009a.

When reading and interpreting the results, there are editorial decisions to be taken with respect to Google artefacts. Since the effort is to mitigate them (for societal search) rather than to highlight them (for Google studies), artefacts, however fascinating, may be removed.

For example, Wikipedia is a top result or nearly so for most local domain Google queries. One could make a separate project out of the differences in rights types across Wikipedia language versions, as is the effort in cross-cultural Wikipedia studies (in the next chapter). Another Google artefact is the result R.I.G.H.T.S. (rightsforartists.com) in google.com. It is a Google artefact in the sense that it highlights how Google relies on certain 'signals' to boost websites in the rankings (Dean, 2016). Among other indicators of how Google boosts sites, the word 'rights' is part of the URL, and R.I.G.H.T.S. is in the page header.

In the findings, rendered as labelled icons, countries could be said to have diverging hierarchies of concerns per (Google) country (see Figure 6.9). For example, everyman's rights in Finland, prostitutes' rights in the Netherlands, computer programmers' rights in Japan and the right to oblivion in Italy (the right to have personal data deleted) are unique to the respective countries. The order of appearance per country invariably differs.

Given the focus on cultural distinctiveness, it should be noted that the specific issue language per country is retained, rather than grouped as equivalents. Thus, LGBT rights in the United States and homosexual rights in Hong Kong are not considered the same. Indeed, one could make a small sub-study of the terms (and thus inclusiveness) across the local domain Googles for these particular rights as well as others.

In all, the short case study starting with the underspecified query, [rights], has found distinctiveness between rights types and rights hierarchies across the local domain Googles. One could consider techniques to harden these findings, such as returning to the idea of engaging in cross-cultural Wikipedia studies as well as other means of grounding the findings online. It is also a thought piece for discussing rights types cross-culturally.

Google studies and societal search combined: Source distance and partisanship detection

Google, as related above, creates hierarchies of credibility through returning ranked sources for a query. When the query is substantive, such as ["climate change"], sources at the top are given the privilege of providing information on the matter of concern, while others lower down are less likely to be read. Here the question concerns the distance from the top that partisan sites appear, giving voice to a particular side or position. The case in question is the climate change issue. Partisanship concerns giving voice, or a platform on its website, to climate change sceptics. Which sites mention the sceptics, and quote and represent their viewpoints? Are they close to the top of the engine returns for the query ["climate change"]? Source distance is medium research for it asks whether the web via Google (or Google in particular) gives the sceptics top-ranked space.

Indeed, in the first instance, it could be said that we are studying Google. Query Google and consider whether the engine's ranking procedures place sceptic-friendly websites towards the top of the climate change space.

It is a two-step query design (see sample project below). First, query ["climate change"] and save the results. Subsequently, keeping the results in the order they appeared, query each individual result for names of climate change sceptics, through [site:] queries, or the use of the advanced setting 'search one site'. Visualize where the sceptics appear in the top results (see Figure 6.10). (Such work also may be performed with the Lippmannian Device, also discussed below.) The sceptics are represented in a few sites returned (in the first 50 or so) but not at the very top. Put differently, in the journalistic convention both sides of the story are represented, but in the climate change space provided by Google the sceptics' presence is relatively scant, it was found.

When considering the results anew, however, it also could be said that we are undertaking social research as we are considering the presence of sceptics in the climate change source space more generally, and we are identifying specific sources where they are present. Without considering positive or negative mentions, one is studying the 'impact' of the sceptics – whether their overall presence is felt. One is also able to evaluate sources according to sceptic mentions. After closer reading, one notes there are sceptic-friendly 'science' websites as well as sceptic-funders. Another website type where sceptics appear is a watchdog site, with critical mentions of the sceptics. There are also those that do not name sceptics, providing no mentions. Through sceptic presence and absence source evaluation and characterization are performed.

Figure 6.10   Top climate change sources on the web, according to Google Web Search, resized according to the quantity of mentions of a climate change sceptic. Output of the Lippmannian Device and Tag Cloud Generator, Digital Methods Initiative, Amsterdam.
Source: Rogers, 2013b.

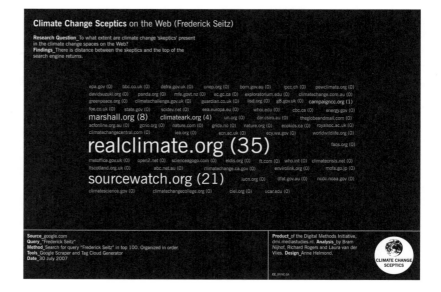

Conclusions: From Google critique to repurposing Google results

Above the question was posed concerning the capacity of Google to serve as a research machine, despite becoming a consumer information appliance (as well as a national advertising and legal machine) over the past two decades. Google is still a research machine in how it allows for foraging through online information as its creators envisioned in their seminal paper (Brin and Page, 1998). In the search engine critique that has since arisen, it also has evolved into a hegemon (market-wise), 'googlizing' industries and public resources (such as libraries and art institutions). It has purportedly had cognitive impacts (as illustrated by the coinage of 'flickering man'). Rather than an equalizer, it boosts both through its original algorithmic innovations as well as its subsequent tweaks the rich and now the popular. As an advertising company, Google also has been described as a front-page real estate hog, populating search engine results pages with its own properties, as well as a surveillance machine, inviting privacy-enhancing technologies that mask and obfuscate users as well as competitors as DuckDuckGo that trade on privacy. Google also captures users, nudging one to stay logged in, so disentangling oneself from the device has become burdensome.

But because Google recursively collects a user's data and recommends URLs on the basis of its 'knowledge' of the user, a researcher could consider avoiding obfuscation techniques such as 'track me not' or others (Howe et al., 2011), as they would potentially sully the engine results (garbage out, garbage in). Another approach would be having few traces available in the first place.

By installing a separate instance of a browser (such as Firefox) as a 'research browser', the researcher prepares a clean slate, free of cookies and other engine entanglements such as history and preferences. If one has a Google account, disable customized results, an option in one's web history. ('Do not track' could be enabled.) If one does not have a Google account, the Google cookies should be removed and not allowed to be set. The slate is cleaner (rather than completely refreshed) because Google by default serves localized results zoomed in to a city or similar. In the advanced settings, change the setting to a region (where there is a country drop-down list to choose from). Now results should be rather depersonalized.

Once a browser is so prepared, the work to undertake medium and social research commences. As indicated, medium research concerns engine effects on sources (including their placement in returns), whereas social research is conceived of as source evaluation with the aid of the engine.

To be clear, here we are turning the tables on Google, seeking to use it as a research machine – making social studies via or on top of engines – rather than being used by it as a subject of surveillance and targeted advertising. As you work, be aware that researching with Google requires vigilance, for the engine is continually striving to know you, and customize the results.

PROJECT 8

Determine the impact of climate change sceptics using search engine results

RESEARCH GOAL To show the impact of climate change sceptics through their quantity of hits and their distance from the top of search engine results in a set of sources on climate change (e.g., the top 100 Google returns for the query ["climate change"]).

1   Make a list of climate change sceptics. There is a variety of sources that provide lists of the names of climate change sceptics, as well as the organizations that sponsor them. One may triangulate expert lists or make a list based on an associative query snowballing, as explained in the Issuecrawler chapter. One may also make a list on the basis of the keynote speakers and/or attendees of climate change sceptics conferences (e.g., hosted by the Heartland Institute).

The following list of climate change sceptics is derived from triangulating mentions of the names of sceptics by Source Watch, *Mother Jones* magazine and the sociologists, Aaron McCright and Riley Dunlap (Rogers, 2013b).

List of sceptics (as well as organizations that support sceptics)

Persons

- S. Fred Singer
- Robert Balling
- Sallie Baliunas
- Patrick Michaels
- Richard Lindzen
- Steven Milloy
- Timothy Ball
- Paul Driessen
- Willie Soon
- Sherwood B. Idso
- Frederick Seitz

Sceptical organizations

- American Enterprise Institute
- American Legislative Exchange Council
- Committee for a Constructive Tomorrow
- Competitive Enterprise Institute

- Frontiers of Freedom
- Heartland Institute
- Marshall Institute
- Science and Public Policy Institute

Such a list may be used during the analysis of the results (e.g., when noting the affiliation or partisanship of a source with (many) mentions of the sceptics). Are sceptics predominantly mentioned by the sceptical organizations, or also by other organizations? Or do watchdogs mention the sceptics most significantly? The question also may be whether there are other organizations that mention sceptics apart from sceptical organizations and watchdogs, indicating more widespread uptake. One also could consider undertaking such research across countries (or local domain Googles).

2   To facilitate the work, the Google Scraper may be used. One also may undertake the work manually by querying each term in each site; for example, in Google, query [site:www.epa. gov "Willie Soon"]. For the automated approach using the Google Scraper, first download and install the DMI toolbar, which is a Firefox extension. Install and use a separate instance of Firefox as a 'research browser'. In Firefox, choose preferences > privacy & security, then uncheck 'Block popup windows'. Switch off search history personalization in Google's preferences, log out of Google and enable 'do not track' in the browser settings.

3   Set Google preferences to return 100 results. Query ["climate change"] in google.com. (The list of sceptics provided above is principally American and not necessarily current, so one may wish to curate the list anew if researching another cultural space, though one also could study the globalization of climate change scepticism by compiling a current American list.)

4   Select and copy top 100 Google results. That is, on the Google results page, select all results (avoid the sponsored results), right-click and use 'view selection source' (in Firefox) and then copy the highlighted text. One may also use the Link Ripper (https://tools.digitalmethods.net/ beta/linkRipper/), and input the Google results page.

5   Paste that text into the Harvester, a separate tool at http://tools.digitalmethods.net/beta/ harvestUrls/ Choose as output 'exclude URLs from Google and YouTube', 'only return hosts' and 'only return uniques', meaning unique hosts will be returned and later queried (e.g., http:// www.epa.gov, rather than https://www3.epa.gov/climatechange//kids/index.html).

6   Select and copy the results into the top box of the Google Scraper.

7   In the bottom box of the Google Scraper, enter the keywords (i.e., a list of climate change sceptics), one per line. Place the names in quotation marks.

8   Select the number of desired results (1–100). Use a larger number of results if there is an expectation that most sources mention the keyword, and a lower number if seeking only presence or absence of the mention of the sceptic per source. Name the output file and press Scrape Google (or Scrape Search Results on the Search Engine Scraper, with Google selected).

9   Keep the Google Scraper window open, and wait until the scrape is completed (i.e., until the output file is available). If a pop-up window appears, type in the captcha and close the pop-up window, and the Scraper will resume.

10   View the results as a source cloud. View multiple sources and single issue for a source cloud of each sceptic. View multiple sources and multiple issues for a source cloud of all sceptics.
11   View visualization for source distance or partisanship. Choose 'order of input in Google Scraper' to view how close to the top of the Google results the sceptic or sceptics resonate (source distance). Choose cloud output 'ordered by size' for a hierarchy of sources mentioning one or more sceptics, with those sources mentioning one or more sceptics the most at the top (impact and partisanship research).

In the case of the climate change sceptics listed above, it was found that there is distance between the sceptics and the top of the search engine returns (see Figure 6.10). Note that few sceptics appear on the websites of the top ten results in Google. When they do appear, their resonance is not particularly resounding.

One may evaluate sources according to the frequency with which each mentions the sceptics. There are sceptic-friendly sites, and less sceptic-friendly sites. From the visualization one is able to see the sceptic-friendly sources, such as realclimate.org and, to a lesser extent, climatescience.gov. Sourcewatch also is prominent, albeit as a progressive watchdog group 'exposing' the sceptics.

Remarkably, news sites, generally speaking, do not mention the climate change sceptics by name. While news watchers and listeners may have the impression that 'uncertainty' in the climate change 'debate' continues in a general sense (as opposed to, say, in more specific, scientific sub-discussions), 'uncertainty' appears to be discussed without resort to the well-known, or identified, sceptics.

With respect to the implications of the findings, one question concerns the extent to which the web stages climate change as a controversy *vis-à-vis* other media spaces, such as the news. Here the web is understood as a search-based medium, and controversy as the relative penetration of the sceptics in the climate change search results space. A comparison between the sceptics' resonance on the web and in the news could be a next step.

Video tutorial

For Project 8 on source distance, watch the video on how to operate the Google Scraper.

•   The Search Engine Scraper and Lippmannian Device (13' 28"), https://www.youtube.com/watch?v=hIPTrTM53ho

Tool

'Google Scraper', digitalmethods.net. Available at https://wiki.digitalmethods.net/Dmi/ToolGoogleScraper

Google studies with the Google Scraper and societal search with the Lippmannian Device

There is a series of further assignment options, where we are researching how (and for whom) Google works, or societal trends with Google. One option (set out in considerable detail below) compares the results pages of local domain Googles, so as to provide an understanding of Google's sense of the local and discuss the implications of that understanding. In the second option, one employs the engine to output hierarchies of societal (or organizational) concern, following one of the Lippmannian Device research protocols below.

Before choosing one of the options, consider whether you wish to study the medium, some combination of the medium and societal trends, or societal trends. Generally, medium research here is considered to be diagnosing how Google works, for example, by typing [http] into the search bar in order to see how Google ranks URLs generally, or by searching for the same keywords over and again so as to study the effects of personalization on results. Techniques are described for studying Google's sense of the local, comparative source origin, and societal search (with Google artefacts considered). Doing medium studies of Google would be teasing out Google's sense of the local. A combination of medium studies and social research would be to diagnose how Google works and consider the societal implications such as which types sources are privileged, and which ones buried. Finally, studying societal trends refers to relying on Google's rankings either through substantive, underspecified queries such as [rights] or by working with the Lippmannian Device to identify how close to the top are the sceptics in the climate change space, or the global human rights agenda (to name two specific examples).

PROJECT 9

Investigate Google's sense of 'the local'

RESEARCH GOAL To ascertain Google's sense of the local by comparing the results of pages of local domain Googles (otherwise known as Google 'regions').

1   Query design. With respect to choice of term, choose a discrete term, and substantiate your choice (e.g., an unambiguous or underspecified query term). Use an unambiguous term such as [Amazonia] for the question of which sources dominate the results across Latin American countries (i.e., Google regions). Use an underspecified term such as [rights] for the question of which rights are dear per country (i.e., Google region).

2   Language. Apart from dictionaries, there are at least three options to translate a term between languages. Use languages that are available to you or your group, use Google Translate, or use 'languages' in the left-side column of Wikipedia articles.

3   Selection of Google regions to be queried. For the [Amazonia] query, the Google regions may be countries that are in the Amazon river basin, or Latin American countries more broadly. For the [rights] query, the sources may be varied and numerous. Consider building in comparison or contrast into your Google region selection, such as all former Soviet countries (where some are now in the European Union). Unless you use a research browser, and specific (re)search settings, Google will auto-detect your location, and privilege city-level results.

4   Query the term in local language(s) per Google region. Use Google advanced search, setting language and region.

5   Saving results. Set your preferences to the number of returns you wish to save. In your browser, choose File > Save as > html, and name your file using a naming convention such as BE_rechten_50_1DEC2019, where BE is the Belgian Google region, [rechten] the query, 50 the results count and finally the date of the query, with the month indicated in letters in order to avoid confusion between US and western European date formatting conventions.

6   Analysing search engine results pages: source origin and categorization.

    a   There are multiple techniques for locating the 'origin' of a source: country domain (ccTLD), 'whois' information of the site registrant, and the contact information located on the websites. The location of the host (which may be local or far-flung) can be derived with the geoIP tool on tools.digitalmethods.net or another such tool. For the [Amazonia] query, the origins of the sources constitute the analytical question concerning Google's sense of the local.

    b   Categorization – keyword specificity and A/B schemes. For the [rights] query, the specific rights privileged per country are of interest, such as the 'right to roam' in Finland. Here it is important to retain specificity and resist the urge to group similar rights under umbrella terms. For the [Amazonia] query, one could consider employing an A/B scheme (presence or absence; programme or anti-programme), such as the presence of extractive industries in the top ten results per country.

    c   Categorization – source types in the results. For the [Amazonia] query, one may be interested in the presence of non-governmental or more specifically environmental sources in the results per country, or of non-Latin American results. One may glean source types from the top-level and second-level domains. See Wikipedia's articles on 'Top-level domain' and 'Second-level domain' for country-specific ones. For a finer-grained sense of the source type, peruse the 'about' page. One may pose critical questions of the dominance of one source type over another, inquiring into which sites have the privilege of being top sources, and providing information. For example, a ["climate change"] query may be dominated by intergovernmental sites, governmental agencies, NGOs and news outlets, while academic sources may be largely absent.

For finer-grained categorizations, consider using the 'other' category for items that do not fit the scheme, rather than 'neutral' which itself could be efforts made by actors (see the query design chapter).

7   Visualizing the findings. For the [Amazonia] query, a spreadsheet has Latin American countries as columns and source origin countries as rows. The 'visualization' is a colour-coded spreadsheet. For the [rights] query, per country (i.e., Google region), there is a list of rights types that have been artfully rendered as icons. One may consider using the triangulation tool, which takes lists of items as inputs and outputs commonalities and uniques.

The tag cloud generator at tools.digitalmethods.net provides means to visualize hierarchies, as does Wordle. If using Wordle, consider outputting all words horizontally and ordering them by frequency.

One also may consider populating a world map.

8   Drawing conclusions. Note that there are generally three discussions: medium research, some combination of medium and societal research, and societal research only, so to speak. For medium research, one is critiquing Google's sense of the local. If one chooses the combination of medium and societal research, the discussion could concern the extent to which Google is a globalizing or localizing machine, and the related issue of whether it may be used as a research machine, under what conditions and to what ends. If one is undertaking societal research, the capacity of Google to render countries' significant rights types becomes meaningful.

Video tutorials

For Project 9, there is a series of videos on how to transform Google into a research machine, set up a query, localize the outputs of a query and compare multiple results.

* 'The Research Browser' (1' 35"), https://www.youtube.com/watch?v=bj65Xr9GkJM
* 'Google Research Settings' (3' 48"), https://www.youtube.com/watch?v=Zk5Q_3g86qM
* 'Comparing Lists with the Triangulation Tool' (2' 54"), https://www.youtube.com/watch?v=jg9Uz-KcuuOE
* 'Localizing Web Sources' (4' 08"), https://www.youtube.com/watch?v=lyNMDUSBd9s

Consider watching a more general tutorial on analysing engine results in three ways:

* 'Analysing Engine Results: Organization Types, Hierarchies of Concern, Political Leanings' (3' 50"), https://www.youtube.com/watch?v=MsnSJPXpFno

Tools

Search Engine Scraper (and Google Scraper), digitalmethods.net. Available at https://wiki.digitalmethods.net/Dmi/ToolGoogleScraper

Harvester, digitalmethods.net. Available at https://wiki.digitalmethods.net/Dmi/ToolHarvester

Triangulation, digitalmethods.net. Available at https://wiki.digitalmethods.net/Dmi/ToolTriangulation

Resources

Google Translate, google.com. Available at http://translate.google.com/

'Top 500 Sites on the Web by Country,' alexa.com. Available at http://www.alexa.com/topsites/countries

PROJECT 10

Map and interpret bias with the Lippmannian Device

RESEARCH GOAL Determine source partisanship (side-taking) as well as its distribution of concern

The Google Scraper, when used principally for societal search, is also referred to as the Lippmannian Device. There are two overall use cases for the Lippmannian Device: source partisanship and source distribution of concern. For source partisanship, the question concerns the detection of side-taking by a particular source through its mentioning or failure to mention particular issue language. Above it was noted that particular organizations mentioned the climate change sceptics while others averred. For research on the distribution of concern one is often given a list of issues that a particular organization engages in, advocates for, or otherwise 'does'. The question is whether particular organizations show attention to particular issues (over other issues) through frequency of mentions on their websites. Here one relies on Google's second strength (massive, presentist site indexing) and renders a distribution of attention to a set of issues.

Lippmannian Device?

As a term the Lippmannian Device refers to a piece of equipment for mapping and interpreting bias, or, as indicated, it may be employed to gain a rough sense of a source's partisanship and distribution of concerns. It is named after Walter Lippmann, the American journalism scholar who in his *Public Opinion* book of 1922, and particularly in his sequel to it of 1927, *The Phantom Public*, called for a coarse means of showing actor partisanship:

The problem is to locate by clear and coarse objective tests the actor in a controversy who is most worthy of public support. (Lippmann, 1927: 120)

The signs are relevant when they reveal by coarse, simple and objective tests which side in a controversy upholds a workable social rule, or which is attacking an unworkable rule, or which proposes a promising new rule. By following such signs the public might know where to align itself. In such an alignment it does not … pass judgment on the intrinsic merits. (Lippmann, 1927, 120)

The device does not answer all of Lippmann's calls, though it seeks to begin with them by addressing a seminal Lippmannian sense (partisanship) as well as an extended one (distribution of partisanship). It also advances the calls by Lippmann, in an attempt to enrich the partisanship notion with the idea of distribution of concern on the part of actors. They may have a list of campaigns or issues they are working on, but which garner more returns? The Lippmannian device queries Google, in a two-step process, and makes the results available in in issue or source clouds (as well as in a spreadsheet).

Lippmannian Device project: Source clouds for the display of partisanship

The Lippmannian Device may be used to create source clouds that reveal partisanship towards a particular issue. With the tool, one may query a list of sources for one particular issue, or for a set of issues (keywords). Which source mentions 'security fence', which 'apartheid wall' and which neither (for the barrier between Israel and the Palestinian territories)? Source clouds display sources, each resized according to the number of mentions of a particular issue, according to Google.

Here is an example of employing the Lippmannian Device to study the 'synthetic biology' issue. Craig Venter has been considered a somewhat polarizing figure in the issue space, given that the science in his work often serves commercial interests and the (best-known) work itself is often construed as 'patenting life' (Glasner and Rothman, 2017). Thus we will ask which actors appear sympathetic to Craig Venter in the synthetic biology space.

Automated method

1   Set Google preferences to return 100 results. Query ["synthetic biology"] in Google.
2   Select and copy the top 100 Google results. That is, on the Google results page, select all results (avoid the sponsored results), right-click and use 'view selection source' (in Firefox) and then copy the highlighted text.
3   Paste that text into the Harvester, a separate tool. Choose as output 'exclude URLs from Google and YouTube', 'only return hosts' and 'only return uniques' – meaning unique hosts will be returned and later queried (e.g., http://www.synbioproject.org, not http://www.synbioproject.org/topics/synbio101/).
4   Select and copy the results into the top box of the Lippmannian Device.
5   In the bottom box of the Lippmannian Device, enter the keyword [Venter] or, for greater specificity, ["Craig Venter"].
6   Select the number of desired results (1–1000). Use a larger number of results if there is an expectation that most sources mention the keyword. Name the output file and press Scrape Google.
7   Keep the Scraper browser window open and wait until the scrape is completed (i.e., until the output file is available). If a pop-up window appears, type in the captcha and close the pop-up window, and the Scraper will resume.
8   View the source cloud results – multiple sources and single issue.
9   View different orderings. Choose cloud output 'ordered by size' for a hierarchy of sources mentioning Venter, with those sources mentioning Venter the most at the top (see Figure 6.11).

Manual method

1   Query Google for ["synthetic biology"]. Save results. Commit each host in the results to a row in a spreadsheet.
2   Query each individual result in the top 100 for "Craig Venter". Use 'site' queries: [site:http://www.synbioproject.org "Craig Venter"]. For each host queried, place actual and optionally estimated result count in spreadsheet.

3 Show the quantity of mentions of Craig Venter in top sources on synthetic biology with a source cloud. Resize sources (e.g., synbioproject.org) according to the number of mentions.

You may wish to consider normalizing the findings on the basis of the overall sizes of the websites.

Figure 6.11 Craig Venter's presence in the Synthetic Biology issue space, March 2008. Top sources on "synthetic biology" according to a Google query, with number of mentions of Venter per source. Source cloud ordered by frequency of mentions. Output by the Lippmannian Device, Digital Methods Initiative, Amsterdam.

nature.com (200) ncbi.nlm.nih.gov (200) nytimes.com (200) sciencemag.org (200) genome.org (200) biomedcentral.com (200) jcvi.org (191) berkeley.edu (191) etcgroup.org (126) connotea.org (104) physorg.com (80) lbl.gov (67) lse.ac.uk (63) rachel.org (53) sciencedaily.com (45) springer.com (38) boingboing.net (34) sciam.com (33) innovationwatch.com (28) economist.com (21) embl.org (14) sciencefriday.com (12) parliament.uk (11) bio.davidson.edu (10) bbsrc.ac.uk (9) foresight.org (8) springerlink.com (7) commondreams.org (7) paraschopra.com (7) eetimes.com (6) labtechnologist.com (5) selectbiosciences.com (4) lewrockwell.com (3) nestconference.com (1) esf.org (1) eecs.mit.edu (0) jbioleng.org (0) qb3.org (0) ietdl.org (0)

Lippmannian Device project: Issue clouds for concern distribution

The Lippmannian Device can also be used to create issue clouds that can reveal varying levels of concern by one or more sources. With the tool, one may query one or multiple sources for a set of issues or keywords. For example, Greenpeace International lists several issues for which it campaigns. Are there particular ones that are granted more attention (and perhaps resources)? Issue clouds display the campaign issues, each resized according to the number of mentions on the website (according to Google).

Another case in question are the issues listed by an NGO, Public Knowledge, dedicated to digital rights. Having copied and pasted their issues into the Lippmannian Device, and querying via Google publicknowledge.org for each issue separately, one may gain a sense of a distribution of concern. Here the next step may be to ground the findings with the actor itself and/or compare them to a larger agenda of the (digital rights) field.

1 Extract issues for the NGO by finding and copying its issue list. Public Knowledge's issue list is at http://www.publicknowledge.org/issues.

Copy and paste the issue list to bottom box of the Lippmannian Device, one issue per line, placing quotation marks around multiple-worded issues. An issue such as "Digital Millennium Copyright Act (DMCA)" could be inputted as follows:

"Digital Millennium Copyright Act" OR DMCA.

"700 MHz Spectrum Auction" OR "Spectrum Auction"

"Anti-Counterfeiting Trade Agreement"

"Broadband"

"Broadband Stimulus"

"Broadcast Flag"

"Comcast Complaint"

"Copyright"

"National Broadband Plan"

"Network Neutrality"

"Open Access to Research"

"Opening the White Space"

"Orphan Works"

"Patent Reform"

"Selectable Output Control"

"Text Message Petition"

"Trademark"

"WiFi Municipal Services"

"WIPO Broadcasters Treaty"

2   Place Public Knowledge's URL in the top box of the Lippmannian Device, http://www.
     publicknowledge.org.

3   Select the number of desired results (1–1000). Use a larger number of results if there is an
     expectation that the source mentions the issues in great quantity. For the public knowledge
     case, the setting 1000 results is entered. Name the output file (e.g., publicknowledge_
     issues_1DEC2019), and press Scrape Google.

4   Keep the Scraper browser window open, and wait until the scrape is completed (i.e., until the
     output file is available). If a pop-up window appears, type in the captcha and close the pop-up
     window, and the Scraper will resume.

5   View the issue cloud results. View issues per source. Choose cloud output 'ordered by size' for
     Public Knowledge's issue hierarchy (see Figure 6.12).

Video tutorials

For Project 10, there are videos on how to extract URLs from a web page and how to operate the
Lippmannian Device.

* 'Extracting URLs from a Web Page via the URL Harvester' (1' 25"), https://www.youtube.com/
  watch?v=kzaq9DXfO_g
* The Search Engine Scraper and Lippmannian Device (13' 28"), https://www.youtube.com/
  watch?v=hIPTrTM53ho

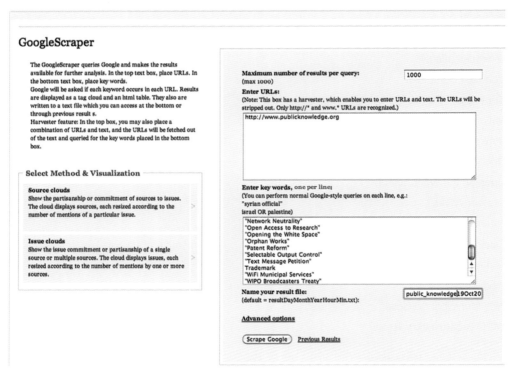

Figure 6.12 The making of Public Knowledge's concern distribution. Input of publicknowledge.org and its issues into Lippmannian Device. Output rendered as word cloud, showing the lower six issues on Public Knowledge's issue list, ranked according to number of mentions of its website according to Google site search, 2 October 2009. Output by the Lippmannian Device, Digital Methods Initiative, Amsterdam.

Tool

Lippmannian Device, digitalmethods.net. Available at https://wiki.digitalmethods.net/Dmi/ToolLippmannianDevice

SEVEN

CULTURAL POINTS OF VIEW
Comparing Wikipedia language versions

The counter-intuitive consideration of Wikipedia as source for cultural particularism

Wikipedia as cultural reference

The chapter is dedicated to the study of Wikipedia as cultural reference. On the face of it, such an approach to Wikipedia appears counter-intuitive, or even a category mistake, as Wikipedia is meant to be an online equivalent to and extension of an encyclopedia, with particular principles and standards that would prevent articles from being particularistic or parochial. One is not meant to read an encyclopedia, even one with distinctive language versions, for cultural points of view. Wikipedia articles follow core principles that would remove any perspectives or points of view that are not construed as neutral. The articles also are meant to be universal, or 'global', in their outlook. For example, the instructive 'globalize' template, similar to the scores of other banners placed on articles that are deemed to require editing work, points up the kind of view that Wikipedia articles should attain, and would err when they do not: 'The examples and perspectives in this article may not represent a worldwide view' (see Figure 7.1). In other words, articles should be drained of (national) cultural perspective, and arguably over time would have any perspective contained therein smoothed over, whereupon the template would be removed.

Figure 7.1 'Template:Globalize', Wikipedia, https://en.wikipedia.org/w/index.php?title=Template: Globalize&oldid=827245282.

Moreover, articles should season, even mellow, eventually becoming emblematic 'featured articles' that, apart from being 'well-written', 'comprehensive', 'well-researched', and 'neutral', are also 'stable', meaning that they are not subject to edit wars or dispute (Wikipedia Contributors, 2018b). As Jimmy Wales, the founder, put it during a fundraising drive: 'one person writes something, somebody improves it a little, and it keeps getting better, over time' (Wikimedia, 2010).

Generally, Wikipedia articles follow principles that seek to prevent specific viewpoints and bias and stabilize. They should have a neutral point of view, 'representing fairly, proportionately, and as far as possible without bias, all significant views that have been published by reliable sources' (Wikipedia Contributors, 2018c). They should be verifiable, with references made in the articles to reliable sources, often with outlinks. The verifiability principle means that articles are anchored by recognized knowledge. Wikipedia's third core principle is that the articles should contain no original research, however much it may be factual. One should be able to look up, outside of Wikipedia, the subject matter and contents of articles.

Counter-intuitively, then, this chapter discusses the specificity of Wikipedia language versions, such as quantities of unique articles, distinctive editing cultures as well as software projects that identify and highlight incompatibilities (so to speak) between them. The differences between the Bosnian, Serbian and Dutch language versions of articles on Srebrenica serve as a case study for the study of Wikipedia as 'cultural reference'; mention is also made of the differences between the German and Polish Auschwitz articles. The overall purpose of comparative Wikipedia language article analysis is to tease out cultural difference (both manually and with comparison tools), and ultimately account for it.

Wikipedia as reference work

In order to contextualize the very idea of Wikipedia as cultural reference, it is of interest to discuss the online encyclopedia as reference more generally, and how it has been the subject of empirical study of its contents. It should be mentioned at the outset that Wikipedians have set up a project on the encyclopedia's so-called systemic bias, which is described as Western in terms of both the distribution of quality and sheer volume of articles (Wikipedia Contributors, 2018d; Livingstone, 2010; Graham, 2011; Hargittai and Shaw, 2015). The main empirical work (and to an extent the critique of Wikipedia) follows from certain qualities of the online encyclopedia, all of which capture the improbability of the project *in toto* upon first inspection.

One is that Wikipedia is authored by 'amateurs' (or volunteers), who 'work' gratis, pointing up the significance of the empowerment of everyday web users as 'editors', who previously were shut out of content contribution by so-called old media gatekeepers (Baker, 2008; Reagle, 2008). While the work could be considered volunteering, it also makes Wikipedia more and more valuable (e.g., for attracting donations and building an endowment),

ERRORS IDENTIFIED: ENCYCLOPAEDIA BRITANNICA

Agent Orange

1. A very minor error is that Agent Orange is considered by the Vietnamese to be the cause of the diseases listed in the second paragraph from the 1970s to the present, not just from the 1970s to the '90s.
2. The entry should include the statement that other mixtures containing dioxin were also sprayed, including Agents Purple, Pink and Green, albeit in lesser amounts.

Aldol

1. The aldol REACTION is not the same as the aldol CONDENSATION.
2. Sodium hydroxide is by no means the only base to be used in the aldol and acid catalysed aldol reactions also occur (usually with concomitant loss of water).
3. The reaction steps in the second reaction sequence should be equilibria up to the dehydration step.
4. In particular, there is no mention of the acid catalysed process and scant mention of related reactions

Archimedes Principle
Reviewer: Prof. Timothy J. Pedley, G. I. Taylor Professor of Fluid Dynamics, University of Cambridge, UK.

1. In the fourth sentence the word 'floating' is used to mean 'at rest' and does not necessarily mean that in common parlance.
2. The very last sentence is true only for an object at rest; when a body is moving there are pressure forces, as well as viscous stresses, associated with the motion.

Australopithecus africanus

1. Dart did not find the fossil. It was brought to him by others.

Bethe, Hans

1. It should say that Bethe was dismissed from his post in Germany in 1933 because his mother was Jewish.

Cambrian Explosion

1. "Numerically dominant" [and in passing note this is not defined: species? individuals?] forms in the Cambrian are arthropods and sponges; neither phylum "became extinct".

ERRORS IDENTIFIED: WIKIPEDIA

Agent Orange

1. This entry implies that it was the herbicides that are problematic, which is not the case. It was dioxin, a byproduct of manufacture of 2,4,5-T that is of concern. Dioxin is persistent in the environment and in the human body, whereas the herbicides are not. In addition, there was a significant amount of dioxin in Agents Purple, Pink and Green, all of which contained 2, 4, 5 - T as well. However, we have less information on these compounds and they were used in lesser quantities.
2. The entry is on the verge of bias, at least. By use of the word "disputedly" in the second sentence there is at least an implication that the evidence of harm to exposed persons is in question. That is not the case, and the World Health Organization has identified dioxin as a "known human carcinogen", and other organizations such as the US National Academy of Sciences has documented harmful effects to US Air Force personnel.

Aldol

1. The mechanisms of base and acid catalysed aldol reactions should have every step as an equilibrium process
2. The acid catalysed process should include the dehydration step, which occurs spontaneously under acid conditions and, being effectively irreversible, pulls the equilibrium through to product.
3. The statement that LDA is avoided at all possible as it is difficult to handle is rubbish. Organic chemists routinely use this reagent – which they either make as required or use commercially available material.

Archimedes Principle
Reviewer: Prof. Timothy J. Pedley, G. I. Taylor Professor of Fluid Dynamics, University of Cambridge, UK.

1. In the section on acceleration and energy, which discusses how a body moves when it is not neutrally buoyant, it is rightly stated that the acceleration of a body experiencing a non-zero net force is not the same as in a vacuum, because some of the surrounding fluid has to be accelerated as well. However, it is implied that the mass of fluid that has to be added to that of the body, in using Newton's Law to calculate the acceleration, is equal to the mass of fluid displaced. This is not in general true - for example, the added mass for an immersed sphere is half the mass of fluid displaced.
2. The entry is rather imprecise. In line 3, for example, the object is said to "float" if the buoyancy exceeds the weight, so here "float" must mean "rise" and not "stay at the same level", which is probably not what was intended because the word has the other meaning, in the second paragraph of the section on "Density".

Figure 7.2 Errors identified in the same entries in Wikipedia and *Encyclopaedia Britannica*, 2005.
Source: Giles, 2005.

thereby opening up the online encyclopedia to critique as accruing value from free labour (Terranova, 2003). The value 'gifted' to users, however, could be said to be much greater than that gained by Wikipedia or its foundation.

While edited by volunteers, Wikipedia is surprisingly encyclopedia-like, not only in form but also in accuracy (see Figure 7.2). The major debate concerning the quality of Wikipedia compared to *Encyclopaedia Britannica* (and other reference works) has been the source of repeated scrutiny, not only in the famous article published in the journal, *Nature*, where it was found (and trumpeted in headlines) that Wikipedia is nearly as accurate as *Britannica* (Giles, 2005). It also has been the subject of subsequent analysis and follow-up work by information and library scientists, where most found that Wikipedia was actually far less accurate (and far more prone to glaring errors) than *Britannica*, *Encarta*, the *Dictionary of American History* and the *American National Biography Online*, to name certain of the sources for the comparative analysis (Rosenzweig, 2006; Rector, 2008).

Figure 7.3 Featured articles in English-language Wikipedia collected, laid out, printed and bound.
Source: Matthews, 2009.

Figure 7.4 The publishing project, The Iraq War: A Historiography of Wikipedia Changelogs, 2006–2009.
Source: Bridle, 2010.

Of course, Wikipedia is much larger in scope than the other reference works, and uneven in quality, with certain subject matters (such as contemporary events) enjoying far greater coverage and editor attention than others, additionally leading to thoughts of Wikipedia, instead of the newspapers, as authors of the proverbial first draft of history (Halavais and Lackaff, 2008). Moreover, articles in Wikipedia are always only versions, making the encyclopedia alone among its kind in its unfinished state. It also allows for pulling back the curtains to view the occasionally unruly discussions and debate on talk pages per article. Its unfinished state and rough-hewn origins did not stop Bertelsmann from publishing selections (featured articles) from the German Wikipedia as an encyclopedia in print

(Bertelsmann Lexikon Institut, 2008)! There also have been art projects that have done the same, for example, printing out all the edits that have been made to a particular article, on the Iraq war, in an effort to introduce materials for history-writing (see Figures 7.3 and 7.4), or striving (on multiple occasions) to print out the entire English-language Wikipedia, whose size at 7500 volumes proved insurmountable (Mandiberg, 2015). An ever-evolving and debated store of knowledge online is perhaps resistant to print culture.

The quality of Wikipedia

Print by reputable publisher may be one imprimatur of quality, but what is the source of Wikipedia's? Mention was made above of the core principles: neutral point of view, verifiability and no original research. On top of the principles, scholars are studying the relationship between the bureaucracy that is Wikipedia's consensus-building process, and the quality of articles, normally taking 'featured articles' as examples of such (Mesgari et al., 2015). Quality articles edited by power editors may be more likely to become featured articles, and thus quality may be attributed to a particular type of editor work (Butler et al., 2008).

Quality is additionally the outcome of Wikipedia's other editors – the bots. Without them the online encyclopedia could fall prey to spam, like certain comment spaces without moderators that finally were closed down. For quality control, there is also collaboration between the human editors and other non-human tenders such as alert software (Niederer and van Dijck, 2010). Indeed, in the 'Heavy Metal Umlaut' screencast documentary by Jon Udell (discussed in the website history chapter), he appears astonished by the agility of Wikipedians, catching (and correcting) vandalism just minutes after the defacement of an article has taken place (2005). One could argue that the bots and alert software keep not just the vandals, but also the experimenters, at bay, those researchers as well as Wikipedia nay-sayers making changes to a Wikipedia article, or creating a new fictional one, and subsequently waiting for something to happen (Chesney, 2006; Magnus, 2008). This other strand of work that seeks to understand the quality of Wikipedia, together with the so-called vigilance of the crowd, has been performed through article tampering that was 'caught' by the bots or by individual editors (Halavais, 2004; Read, 2006). In the experiments that also took into account the automated monitoring of reverts and other signs of flame wars and malicious editing (choosing to insert errors more randomly than in a pattern), it was found that some but not all of the errors were corrected. Often errors are the product of non-scholarly 'sneaky vandalism' (Tran et al., 2015), and the question concerns whether to rely on vigilant Wikipedians (with bots and software assistants) or develop more stringent thresholds to editing. Higher thresholds to entry, however, may remove the charm of volunteer work, especially when Wikipedia editing activity faces decline.

Research has been undertaken in reaction to findings that there is only a tiny ratio of editors to users in crowdsourced, substantive platforms, which became known as the myth of user-generated content (Swartz, 2006). As mentioned above, there is also work on the decline in the number of editors in Wikipedia, where the debate concerns the question of natural maturation versus overzealous regulation by Wikipedians, often summarized by the term 'deletionism' (Silverman, 2013). In this decline narrative faced by Wikipedia, heavy-handed editorial culture (and the busy work of writing edit summaries after editing) is exacerbated by the algorithmic toolbase (Halfaker et al., 2013). The boldness (without recklessness) Wikipedia recommends for its editors is met with automated pushback. Increasing mobile access to Wikipedia has been pointed out as adding to the decline, for mobile users edit much less than those of the desktop (Brown, 2015). Wikipedia co-founder, Jimmy Wales, often remarked (in the early days) that the dedicated community is relatively small, at just over 500 members. Beyond the small community there are also editors who do not register with the system. The anonymous editors and the edits they make were the subjects of the Wikiscanner tool, developed by Virgil Griffith at the California Institute of Technology. Anonymous editors may be 'outed', leading to scandals, as collected by Griffith himself. Among the better known (at least in the Netherlands) is the 'royal edit', where a computer in the Dutch royal household apparently was found to have made an edit to Princess Mabel's entry, whereby the information she gave about her past relations with a drug kingpin (Klaas Bruinsma) to the Dutch vetting authorities was changed from 'incomplete and false' to 'incomplete', thus excising the word 'false'. It is indicative of what Udell called the 'abnormally vigilant' Wikipedia community that the edit was reverted quickly after it was made, never since to reappear. That part of the story is rarely told.

Perhaps the most infamous edit was not anonymous. In his own article, Jimmy Wales edited out Larry Sanger as co-founder of Wikipedia. The editing of a Wikipedia article by its subject or by a representative of its subject matter has been critiqued as publicity management rather than encyclopedic editorial care, however much the subject may be closer to the material and thus both more informed as well as passionate about it (Aula, 2010). Thus quality (rather unexpectedly) may be gained, at least occasionally, from what is otherwise known as publicity management, though tools such as the Wikiscanner would remain a check against boosterism.

Wikipedia's relationship to Google

Quality also lies in how articles are sourced, and continuing traffic to Wikipedia articles where the 'many eyes' may spot errors and indeed become editors themselves. How is the knowledge sourced that appears in Wikipedia, including the outlinks? Wikipedians often refer to Google as a source to check for a subject's prior art. So, if it is not returned in Google results, it may not be considered as published. Wikipedia thus could be said to ground knowledge claims in the online, or at least routinely seek evidence for them there. That Wikipedians look up subject matters in Google (to confirm their existence) is one of the relationships between the search engine and the online encyclopedia.

Figure 7.5 The relationship between Wikipedia and Google by leftintherain, home-made picture thumbnail, rendering gunkglumb's Urban Dictionary definition of Wikipedia from 2005, https://www.urbandictionary. com/define.php?term=wikipedia&page=6
Source: Leftintherain, 2011.

The other, more prominent interrelation concerns the regular appearance of Wikipedia articles (their links and description text) at the top of Google results pages for substantive (or information) queries (see Figure 7.5) (Vaidhyanathan, 2011). The placement of Wikipedia at the top of Google results pages prompted the president of *Encyclopaedia Britannica*, Jorge Cauz, to call Google and Wikipedia's relationship 'symbiotic' (Carr, 2009). At the time of writing, the query for [encyclopedia] returns Encyclopedia.com as the top result at google.com, with Wikipedia second and Britannica third. Encyclopedia.com appears to be a Google artefact (discussed in the search as research chapter) in the sense of the proper name matching the query as opposed to being more renowned than Wikipedia and Britannica.

For years Wikipedia has hovered around fifth in the top global website rankings, according to Alexa. One may attribute widespread usage of Wikipedia in part to the top position regularly achieved in Google results, however much one may desire to peruse Wikipedia's hit logs to confirm such a supposition (Zachte, 2015). To Alexa (2018), Wikipedia receives a disproportionate amount of traffic from search, compared to others at the top (nearly 60%, compared to 13% for YouTube and 7% for Facebook). Wikipedia ranks highly in Google results pages (perhaps better than any other website) for informational queries, rather than for transactional or navigational ones, as a number of industry studies have found. Search engine optimization (SEO) and online marketing researchers have regularly lamented that Wikipedia does not appear to optimize its webpages for search, yet still comes out on top. Responding to an early study that found that over 95% of Wikipedia (English-language) articles are in Google's top ten search results (for a query related to the title of the article), one SEO developer wrote a Firefox search plug-in that removes Wikipedia from Google results pages (Googlecache, 2007; Critchlow, 2007). It is a form of critical commentary concerning the 'symbiotic relationship' between Wikipedia and Google, but also perhaps of interest for actual use to those who monitor search engine results (and tire of Wikipedia's steady appearance). It also could be employed to remove a Google artefact.

The roles reversed in the relationship between Wikipedia and Google, however, with the introduction of Google's knowledge graph in 2014–2015, and its outputs on search engine results pages. The text boxes or 'knowledge panels' appearing alongside so-called organic results (from substantive queries such as "Leonardo da Vinci") contain short descriptions taken from Wikipedia articles as well as other scraped sources. The use of Wikipedia material for Google's purposes has had its side effects – for Wikipedia. A Google user looking for a capsule summary of the medieval Italian polymath may be satisfied enough with the Google knowledge panel so as to not click through to the Wikipedia page. Wikipedia's traffic is thus affected by having had its content cherry-picked, at least according to an observation made in 2015, which appeared to point to a traffic decline on Wikipedia since the introduction of the knowledge panels (see Figure 7.6).

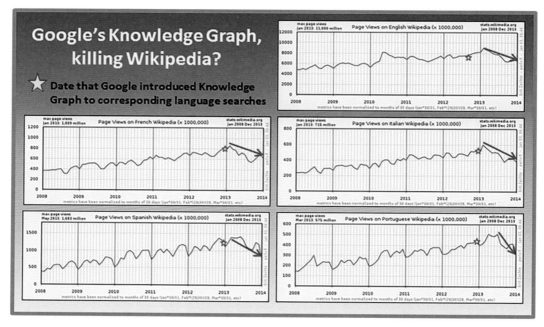

Figure 7.6   The apparent impact of Google info boxes (knowledge graph panels) on Wikipedia traffic.
Source: Kohs, 2014.

Studying culture with Wikipedia

National Wikipedias

At the time of writing the English Wikipedia has nearly 7000 disputed articles. These are neutral point of view (NPOV) disagreements (often having resulted in edit wars) about wide-ranging topics. That there are so many *ongoing* disputed articles is an indication of the difficulty of attaining a 'stable' state so that disputed articles might eventually become 'featured'. Wikipedia administrative culture – including the manner in which disputes are resolved – is an object of study in itself as is how Wikipedians stigmergically and routinely achieve decent quality (Elliott, 2016; Loveland and Reagle, 2013; Jemielniak, 2014). Here the culture of Wikipedia, including the distinctive social manner in which Finnish Wikipedians may resolve disputes and other issues compared to the Japanese, is one means of considering cross-cultural study with Wikipedia. In the event, the Finnish have no NPOV disputes (as a study reported), and the Japanese tend to make little use of the talk pages to resolve disputes (Nemoto and Gloor, 2011). As another case in point, featured article approval processes differ between Arabic and English Wikipedia communities, with the former far less formal than the latter (Stvilia et al., 2009).

Wikipedia as socio-cultural data

Another approach to studying societal and cultural specificity with (and on) Wikipedia is to consider its articles as sources of data, especially the hit logs and editing history. Taking the presuppositions of Google Flu Trends (discussed in the query design chapter) as their points of departure, Wikipedia data-driven monitoring devices for seasonal flu fluctuations have been demoed (McIver and Brownstein, 2014; Generous et al. 2014; Bardak and Tan, 2015). To chart the incidence of flu, studies use Wikipedia flu article hit logs (rather than, for example, page editing history or talk page activity). Other researchers expanded the log data of articles under scrutiny to include gastroenteritis, bronchiolitis, chickenpox and asthma, finding a significant relationship between page views and emergency department visits (Vilain et al., 2017). Other Wikipedia data show cultural priorities, such as the geolocations of the editors of particular articles, where the question may be which countries edit which articles with great fervour. Here the study concerns less Wikipedian platform culture (as above) than national and regional cultures. Why do certain African Wikipedians tend to edit the English-language Wikipedia far more than other specific language versions closer to home (Graham et al., 2014)? Why does the Japanese Wikipedia have far more anonymous editors than other Wikipedia language versions (Lih, 2009)?

Apart from article activity as indicator of cultural specificity, the meta-substance of Wikipedia articles (such as article titles per language) is also the source of data. Wikipedia article titles have served as keywords for censorship research in China (the Weibo study) and have been queried in Google to check Wikipedia page rankings, as mentioned above. In both instances Wikipedia's breadth of topics is made use of. Indeed, researchers have described Wikipedia as 'a giant multilingual database of concepts' (Milne and Witten, 2013).

Wikipedia and cultural difference

In a fourth approach to studying culture with Wikipedia one considers substantive differences across Wikipedia language versions (Gallagher and Savage, 2013). The basis for studying cultural differences and their implications has been well laid. As has been found, certain Wikipedias (e.g., the Arabic and the Korean) have substantial quantities of articles unique to themselves (Stvilia et al., 2009). Thus, it should not be expected that there is universality, however much certain Wikipedia language versions may have their specificity 'suffer' from translation from the English or another dominant language (Warncke-Wang et al. 2012). The Korean has a higher percentage of articles translated from English than the Arabic. Cross-cultural comparison is best served through organically written articles, whereupon the contents are of interest, rather than Wikipedia's administration, article activity or keyword availability. Across Wikipedia language versions, the accounts of historical events may differ. In another set of studies, the particular cuisines covered per Wikipedia show certain cross-cultural appreciations and lacks thereof (Gieck et al., 2016; Laufer et al. 2015).

Studying societal controversies with Wikipedia

In a fifth approach, treated briefly, the question of controversial articles is less a prompt for ethnographic Wikipedia work (why the Finnish do not appear to have NPOV disputes) but rather concerns which subject matters (and specific claims or findings) are disputed societally. A variety of projects take up the question of detecting and following controversiality in single articles, in the 'same' article across Wikipedia language versions as well as in ecologies of related articles, where, for example, a controversy in one piece migrates (or forks) to another article. Contropedia, as the software project is called, places a layer on an article showing which wikilinked passages have been most controversial over time (Weltevrede and Borra, 2016). Another project, 'the most controversial topics in Wikipedia', the interactive tool once featured in *Wired* magazine, ranks controversies per country, and also aggregates them by categories where, for example, the most controversial category in Spanish is sports which elicits no controversy in the Arabic (see Table 7.1).

Wikipedia language version comparison projects

The approach taken here for the comparative study of Wikipedia language versions is relatively straightforward. The comparisons are based on a form of content analysis which focuses on basic elements that comprise an article: its title, authors (or editors), table of contents, images and references (McMillan, 2000). Added are two further elements that are more medium-specific: the location of the anonymous editors (based on IP address), and a reading of the discussion pages that are behind the articles. Left out (but not forgotten) are other similarly specific elements of interest in the study of Wikipedia articles, such as the activity of software robots (bots), which are often highly active editors both across an entire language version of Wikipedia and of a single article (Geiger, 2011). Another medium-specific object is not emphasized but remains on offer. The special study of templates such as the 'globalize' one discussed at the outset may be undertaken when making comparative study of articles; these templates also appear when comparing the images from a series of the 'same' articles across language versions, as discussed below. Thus, the opportunity for template study is built into a tool for cross-article image comparison.

Table 7.1 Most controversial articles in select Wikipedia language versions. Italicized titles are translated for the sake of comparison. Source: Yasseri et al., 2014.

en	de	fr	es	cs
George W. Bush	Croatia	Ségolène Royal	Chile	Homosexuality
Anarchism	Scientology	Unidentified flying object	Club América	Psychotronics
Muhammad	9/11 conspiracy theories	Jehovah's Witnesses	Opus Dei	Telepathy
LWWEe	*Fraternities*	Jesus	Athletic Bilbao	Communism
Global warming	Homeopathy	Sigmund Freud	Andrés Manuel López Obrador	Homophobia
Circumcision	Adolf Hitler	September 11 attacks	Newell's Old Boys	Jesus
United States	Jesus	Muhammad al-Durrah incident	FC Barcelona	Moravia
Jesus	Hugo Chávez	Islamophobia	Homeopathy	Sexual orientation change efforts
Race and intelligence	Minimum wage	God in Christianity	Augusto Pinochet	Ross Hedvíček
Christianity	Rudolf Steiner	Nuclear power debate	Alianza Lima	Israel

hu	ro	ar	fa	he
Gypsy Crime	FC Universitatea Craiova	Ash'ari	Báb	Chabad
Atheism	Mircea Badea	*Ali bin Talal al Jahani*	Fatimah	Chabad messianism
Hungarian radical right	Disney Channel (Romania)	Muhammad	Mahmoud Ahmadinejad	2006 Lebanon War
Viktor Orbán	Legionnaires' rebellion & Bucharest pogrom	Ali	People's Mujahedin of Iran	B'Tselem
Hungarian Guard Movement	Lugoj	Egypt	Criticism of the Quran	Benjamin Netanyahu
Ferenc Gyurcsány's speech in May 2006	Vladimir Tismăneanu	Syria	Tabriz	*Jewish settlement in Hebron*
The Mortimer case	Craiova	Sunni Islam	Ali Khamenei	Daphni Leef
Hungarian Farright	Romania	Wahhabi	Ruhollah Khomeini	Gaza War
Jobbik	Traian Băsescu	Yasser Al-Habib	Massoud Rajavi	Beitar Jerusalem F.C.
Polgár Tamás	Romanian Orthodox Church	Arab people	Muhammad	Ariel Sharon

Srebrenica in the Serbian, Bosnian and Dutch Wikipedias

In a comparative study of Wikipedia language versions, one goal is to extract and place side by side significant differences. The first case in question concerns the Serbian, Bosnian and

Dutch Wikipedia articles about the events of July 1995 in Srebrenica, so as to learn about the specific cultural points points of view (if any) of each (Rogers and Sendijarevic, 2012; Rogers, 2013b). Thousands of Bosniaks were killed by Bosnian-Serb forces in the 'safe haven' of Srebrenica where Dutchbat, the Dutch UN battalion, was stationed.

The three language versions, in other words, are chosen for the significance of the countries during what is known as the Srebrenica massacre, Srebrenica genocide or the fall of Srebrenica, as the Serbian, Bosnian and Dutch Wikipedia versions respectively refer to it in the title of the articles. As a starting point, not only the titles of the article but a particularly salient fact appearing in each are compared (see Table 7.2). Through the comparison of the victim counts, it is observed that the Serbian and Dutch versions tend to round down, and the Bosnian lists the higher figure only. There are also differences in the articles not only substantively but also in terms of illustration and reference, where the images and sources are often unique. The most significant unique image, included in the Bosnian article, is the gravestone of a 13-year-old boy. It provides support for the genocide designation in the article title, for he is not of fighting age. The Dutch and Bosnian versions contain neither that term in the title nor the image. Moreover, the only reference shared (from a comparison of the links at the base of the articles) is un.org; the sources otherwise tend to be national, which should not be a surprise, given the distinctive languages. One could argue (or at least consider) that the article differences may stem from the distinctive sources anchoring the articles, and sourcing cultures deciding which ones to choose. To that end the talk pages ('behind' the Wikipedia articles) are open for browsing, for there are discussions about how to handle new information that has come to light and choose sources to reference. When studying sourcing decisions, one may pinpoint specific moments in the timeline of an event, or annual commemorations of events. Every year in July Srebrenica article editing activity has increased.

Table 7.2 Wikipedia articles on same subject compared across Wikipedia language versions, 20 December 2010. Comparison of article titles and victim counts.

Wikipedia language version	Name of Srebrenica article	Number of Bosniak victims
Dutch (Nederlands)	Fall of Srebrenica	7000–8000
Bosnian (Bosanski)	Srebrenica Genocide	8000
Serbian (Srpski)	Srebrenica Massacre	6000–8000

Through a comparison of the Wikipedia language versions, one may make findings about the extent to which Wikipedia articles express not so much a neutral as a cultural or national point of view. Alternatively, one may seek to view the neutral and the national points of view as mutually reconcilable, by asking, neutral for whom? The specificity of one Wikipedia language version's account over another may be framed as divergent collective memories, where two sets of editors arrive at accounts of events that are neutral to them, so to speak. One also could argue that the debates in the talk pages together with the discussions about the choice of sources, images and other information provide the scholar with material to describe the 'circumstances under which counter-memory becomes collective memory' (Whitlinger, 2011).

Auschwitz in the Polish and German Wikipedias

A second case study takes up how Auschwitz is described in Wikipedia (Bielka et al., 2017). In particular, it inquires into the unique aspects of the German, Polish and Portuguese articles on Auschwitz. There is occasion to make such a comparison. US President Obama (in 2012) and others have referred to Auschwitz as the 'Polish death camps', presumably using a possessive adjective referring to place rather than complicity. Associating them with the Polish rather than with the Nazis was not only offensive to the Poles (and others) but also prompted observers (including the Polish foreign minister) to call Obama ill-informed and incompetent and his statement as anathema to the struggle against denialism (Dharapak, 2012). In the event, there is extensive discussion of the notion of 'Polish death camps' in the Polish version of the article, whereas no such discussion exists in the German or Portuguese. It is the most significant finding by far in the overall comparison, but another smaller observation concerns how Auschwitz has become so synonymous with the concentration camp that the article names in both the Portuguese and even the Polish (where the city is located) are just Auschwitz or Auschwitz-Birkenau rather than having camp in the title. The German article bears concentration camp (or KZ in German) in its title, and also redirects from Auschwitz.

Conclusions: Cross-cultural article comparison

Wikipedia articles, whether they have achieved some measure of quality through feature article status or maturity, may be considered neutral, yet have a national or cultural point of view, teased out through comparison with other articles of the same subject matter, as exemplified in the cases of Srebrenica (comparing Dutch, Bosnian and Serbian versions) and Auschwitz (comparing Polish, German and Portuguese). Omnipedia (from Northwestern University) as well as Manypedia (from the University of Trento) are computer science projects (and computational achievements) that derive compatibility or similarity scores between articles (see Figure 7.7; see also Hecht and Gergle, 2010; Bao et al., 2012; Massa and Scrinzi, 2011). They are useful for spotting differences from which one may subsequently make an account (e.g., on 'Polish death camps') which presumably would be flagged by the software, should it be able to handle the language translation.

There are also relatively simple digital methods tools that may be used to compare the articles, including the Wikipedia TOC Scraper, Wikipedia Cross-Lingual Image Analysis and Wikipedia Edits Scraper and IP Localizer. The TOC Scraper extracts the tables of contents from the inputted articles for comparison at a glance, where one may note (for example) if the articles contain a controversy or criticism section in one language version, but not in another. The brevity of TOC Scraper is advantageous when relying on online translation tools.

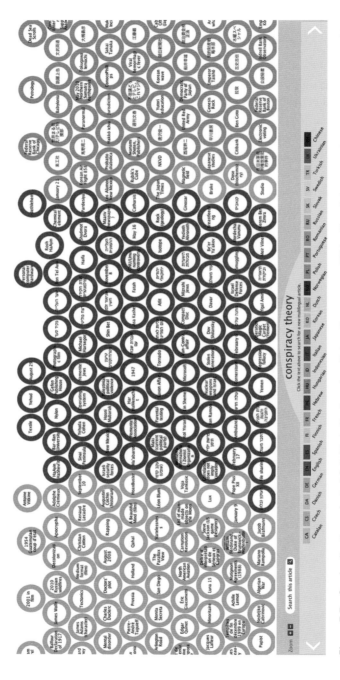

Figure 7.7 Omnipedia, the project of CollabLab, Northwestern University, compares Wikipedia articles across language versions, http://omnipedia.northwestern.edu.

The Wikipedia Cross-Lingual Image Analysis extracts and places in a grid the images of the respective articles for comparison. The tool enabled the ready discovery of the image of the 13-year-old boy's gravestone in the Bosnian version of the Srebrenica article, and its absence in the Dutch and Serbian ones. The Wikipedia Edits Scraper and IP Localizer extracts the anonymous edits and geolocates the place from where the edits were made, allowing findings such as whether the Serbian Wikipedia article on Srebrenica is largely edited from within Serbia only, and the Dutch one within the Netherlands. (Only anonymous edits are geolocated; it would be telling to know the location of the non-anonymous edits, too, but that information, even if logged, is not available.) One other piece of software, the Triangulation tool, allows for the comparison of the references in the articles, where it was found (as mentioned above) that the Dutch, Bosnian and Serbian articles share hardly any sources. Taken together these techniques enable the identification of discrepancy and specificity among the articles in question that enable more in-depth study and close reading.

PROJECT 11

Compare the 'same' article across Wikipedia language versions

RESEARCH GOAL To undertake comparative analysis of the 'same' Wikipedia article across different language versions.

Wikipedia, as a top website both in terms of traffic and placement atop Google results, is deserving of study, however much it may be considered counter-intuitive to study it as a cultural reference rather than as a reference work like an encyclopedia, where questions revolve around accuracy and quality. Here we consider the difference between the same article across Wikipedia language versions, including how the Wikipedia articles have evolved over time, inquiring into whether they converge (one point of view across all Wikipedia language versions) or diverge (cultural particularism).

1   Choice of article and language versions. Choose a subject matter that is shared across two or more Wikipedia language versions. Note that the same articles in other languages are often linked from one Wikipedia version to another in the sidebar on the left-hand side of the article, under languages. You need not be restricted to the other language version linked from the article, as there may be similar articles.

   a   Consider choosing an article where the two or more language Wikipedia versions share its subject matter significantly, as in the Auschwitz case related above, or are likely to have varying views on the same subject matter, such as gay (or LGBT) rights. To begin, note the distinctive titles of what may be considered the same article.

   b   Consider choosing languages which are associated with a particular country or culture, as opposed to many countries and cultures. English, for example, is spoken in many countries and may thus not be a good indication of a cultural point of view, however much there is a discussion about its particular 'American' biases (and Wikipedia articles about that). Consider that different language Wikipedias may have particular user and information cultures too (e.g., that there are relatively few disputes on the Finnish). Shared language versions, however, can be places where different cultural perspectives are in evidence in the edit history and talk pages, such as in the English-language article on the 'Srebrenica Massacre', where, for example, both Serbian and Bosnian editors have been active (and certain ones banned).

   c   Articles may have been translated from one language to another, often originating in the English-language Wikipedia. These are less organic (or *sui generis*), and perhaps should be avoided, unless one wishes to compare the original English-language version with the current reworked article, demonstrating those differences. Additionally, analysing the most recent English-language version compared to the most recent, once translated language version may show distinctive variation worthy of analytical treatment.

2   Comparative analysis. There are generally two approaches to comparative Wikipedia analysis, both resulting from the online encyclopedia's affordances (or 'research affordances'): networked content analysis and medium-specific features analysis. The one is concerned more with the substance of the articles, and the other with the bureaucracy or apparatus behind the articles.

   a   Networked content generally, refers to how the content in Wikipedia is both interlinked or tethered to other content and held together by the network of humans and non-humans (bots) that keep the content in good shape. Without them spam build-up and other deleterious effects would turn Wikipedia into gobbledygook. More specifically, it concerns the content fields in the Wikipedia database, so to speak, such as title, table of contents, images, references and info-boxes.

   b   Medium-specific features refer to (among other elements) the editing history and the talk pages behind articles. They also include the 'templates' or those banners indicating that the article is featured, disputed, locked, up for deletion, etc.

3   Networked content analysis. Compare the title, tables of contents, images, references, and info-boxes. What is shared and what is unique? Develop an account of the specificity of a Wikipedia language version.

To compare tables of contents, there is the Wikipedia TOC Scraper. For comparative image analysis, there is the Wikipedia Cross-lingual Image Analysis tool. Lay out tables of contents and images in side-by-side pages or columns, so as to enable comparison. Organize the items to show presence/absence. For comparative reference analysis, consider employing the link ripper as well as the triangulation tools. Note that not all references are always hyperlinked. Truncate URLs of references to hosts to enable source-level comparison; retain long URLs for article-level scrutiny.

4   Medium-specific features analysis. Consider an analysis of (power) editors, anonymous editors as well as templates regarding the style of editing or bureaucratic culture of a Wikipedia language version *vis-à-vis* another. More specifically, take note of how Wikipedia's core policies and guidelines are deployed. NPOV does not mean that there cannot be different perspectives in a page, but that the perspectives should be written from a third person standpoint (balanced, neutral and verifiable). Apart from NPOV, other policies may be referenced. Consult the talk pages to analyse how editors back up their claims.

Each Wikipedia article has a revision history page. On that page, note the external tools which can come in helpful: revision history statistics, contributors, etc. One may make a comparative analysis of the editors using the history stats of each of the articles under study.

For anonymous editor analysis, consider using the tool, Wikipedia Edits Scraper and IP Localizer. It can be used to extract all edits from a particular Wikipedia page and to geolocate the anonymous edits. Here one may begin to perform an analysis of the 'places of edits', inquiring into the amount and specific type of content anonymous editors edit together with their locations.

5   Interpretation. Refrain from cultural clichés, and instead describe, in a comparative framework, the substantive viewpoints (for networked content analysis) or styles (for medium-specific features analysis).

6   Citing Wikipedia. When citing a Wikipedia page, use the permanent link pointing to the exact revision of the page, available in the sidebar of the Wikipedia article.

Video tutorials

For the project, watch 'Analysing Wikipedia Articles through the Front-End' for an overall introduction to comparing the 'same' article across different Wikipedia language versions. For more specific techniques, watch the 'Cross-lingual Image Analysis' video to learn how to extract and compare images across two or more Wikipedia articles, and the 'Triangulation tool' video to compare the references listed on two or more Wikipedia articles. For those undertaking talk page and revision history analysis, see the Wikipedia 'Back-End' tutorial.

- 'Analysing Wikipedia Articles through the Front-End' (14' 21"), https://www.youtube.com/watch?v=wc1GdGpv5QE
- 'Wikipedia Cross-lingual Image Analysis Tool' (2' 16"), https://www.youtube.com/watch?v=L49fFd_O8ZA
- 'Wikipedia2geo Tool (Wikipedia Edits and Scraper and IP Localizer)' (1' 37"), https://www.youtube.com/watch?v=Pd51MaRUhzM
- 'Comparing Lists (Triangulation tool)' (2' 54"), https://www.youtube.com/watch?v=jg9UzKcuuOE
- 'Analysing Wikipedia Articles through the Back-End' (10' 37"), https://www.youtube.com/watch?v=tY7E8sXCAWw

EIGHT

PLATFORM STUDIES
Twitter as story-telling machine

*Debanalizing tweets (three ways), rather than
debunking Twitter's role in the revolution*

The 'platform'

'Platform studies' could be said to inquire into the (research) uses of a certain class of online software, exemplified by Twitter, Facebook, Instagram, YouTube and others. Platforms, roughly, are online services that host and deliver user-created content, or, in Tarleton Gillespie's (2010: 350) terms, are 'content-hosting intermediaries'. In introducing platform studies, Gillespie relates why it is worthwhile to study the evolution of the usage of the term 'platform', together with its understanding, by both social media companies and users. Initially, the platform could be understood as a software code base that roots an ecosystem of products, such as Apple's OS, Microsoft Windows and Google Android. The 'computing platform' article in Wikipedia defines it as 'simply … a place to launch software' (Wikipedia Contributors, 2014). The term's deployment by social media companies also may be attributed to its other meanings and connotations. A platform is a raised plateau or surface where people may stand or things may be placed; the political platform derives from this first dictionary meaning – a stage where politicians would stand – and is also a manifesto or set of positions of a political party, known, too, as a plank, which refers to the wooden boards from which the stage is built. Platforms, then, provide an opportunity to launch one's ideas, and dress up and present oneself. Especially in his follow-up blog posting on the same theme, Gillespie (2017) notes that the definition that emphasizes software is no longer *au courant*. The platform has become a space where users can have their say, build fan bases, and settle into niches of interest to advertisers. Even more importantly for the business side, the term also connotes a mere channel, like a telephone line, where people speak freely without editorial interference. '"Platform" suggests an impartial between-ness' (Gillespie, 2017). If they are only conduits rather than publishers, platforms are not considered (mass) media companies, and thus their content would not be regulated under laws that protect the public interest, such as striving for diversity of viewpoint and preventing concentration of power in single sources, situations enjoyed by such market leaders as Google (for search), Facebook (for social) and Instagram (photo-sharing). Following Latour (2005b), platforms could be called 'mediators' (rather than intermediaries), for they transform the material the user enters rather than merely transmitting it (Grusin, 2015).

Walled garden and platformization critique

For both enclosed content spaces and proprietary software environments, however, platform connotes 'walled garden', where access, publishing and content rights are limited (Dekker and Wolfsberger, 2009). Critiques of walled gardens follow from the constraints put on users, developers as well as researchers. Facebook's content is described as 'trapped' behind password (and privacy) protections and unable to be directly linked to, crawled, archived or indexed (McCown and Nelson, 2009). Log in to continue, or create an account, as Facebook's interface reads, when a user is unregistered or logged out, and wishes to browse the content. Until recently, users tired of Facebook could only deactivate rather than delete their accounts, which led Dutch artists to create the so-called 'Web 2.0 Suicide Machine' that provided an automated means to witness the slow deletion of one's Facebook-led social life (Langelaar, 2012). (Facebook threatened legal action until the artists removed the little Facebook Connect 'f', or social button, from the Machine's interface.) Since then Facebook has made account deletion and the capacity 'to be forgotten' more manageable.

It has been argued that Facebook not only encircles or walls in its users, their friends and the content they produce. In a double logic, Facebook also makes the open web 'platform-ready' (Helmond, 2016). Logging into a website via Facebook places web users into Facebook's database. In doing so it allows the social media company to track users and ultimately categorize them for advertisers (see Figure 8.1). In all, 'platformization' is a data capturing ploy that strives to integrate the web into Facebook and vice versa. Much like Googlization was once used, platformization also could be applied to how the web is being transformed by social media (Vaidhyanathan, 2011; Thielmann et al., 2012).

Unlike mere channels or conduits, platforms are involved in decisions about publishing, and there are human editors taking decisions about content fitness. Facebook has (outsourced) low-wage content moderators and volunteer fact-checkers (Riesewieck and Block, 2018). Overexposure to online vitriol and indecent content led a Berlin-based company that cleans Facebook content to issue a statement that it has appropriate mental health services in place for its employees to turn to (Krause and Grassegger, 2016). Google once had students look over search engine results, via http://eval.google.com, to see whether they seem to make sense (Van Ess, 2005). Twitter has a 'trust and safety' team, looking out for abusive trolls.

Figure 8.1 'Taxonomy of humans according to Twitter'.
Source: Lavigne, 2017.

Other platforms control content, too. Apps made by developers to be sold in the App Store are vetted by Apple. Politically and socially charged apps may be kept from the store; an app game where the user could throw a shoe at the then US President G.W. Bush was banned, as was one to bounce President Obama up and down in the Oval Office so as to pop balloons on the ceiling. 'Me so holy', where one may paste a selfie onto a Jesus-like figure (or other holy men), was pulled. A drug-peddling game (selling heroin and other substances across New York City) was kept from reaching users. Perhaps most famously, 'I am rich', which sold for a day for the maximum iTunes store price of $999.99, was also banned. An art work, it was described as having the sole purpose of demonstrating one's wealth by holding up the phone and showing onlookers a shimmering bauble (see Figure 8.2). They are humorous. But the theme that runs through the withdrawal decisions is presumed offensiveness, where Apple decides the fitness of the app for public consumption. (The 'I am rich' work by a German artist was seemingly construed as a scam.)

The 'walled garden' was originally put forward as a term for hardware, where without a common standard one would be locked into using only one company's products (Arthur, 1989; Pon et al., 2014). It also applies to interlocking hardware and software ecologies. As a case in point, iPhones need 'jail-breaking' to run unapproved apps, including a series of operating system 'tweaks' that allow custom modding, such as removing bloatware (unneeded software that comes pre-installed with phones) or installing homescreens with enhanced functionality such as weather tracking.

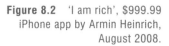

Figure 8.2   'I am rich', $999.99 iPhone app by Armin Heinrich, August 2008.

Platforms and research restrictions

More to the point here is critique of walled gardens with respect to researcher use of platform data (Lomborg and Bechmann, 2014). Over the past decade or so, platforms have 'updated' their terms of service so as to disallow more and more data on them being scraped, stored, redistributed or repurposed. Since a brief attempt at a web search API (or data access point in 2010), Google has not allowed its search engine to be queried outside of its search bar, its search engine results stored or derivative works made of them. Facebook's terms of service (and its API) were once more open, too. It allowed one to study one's own friends, and their friends, making the social networking platform a site for 'tastes and ties' research; a researcher could delve into whether friends have similar profile preferences, for example, making them into cliques, a question sometimes put by social network analysis. Access to such data was shut down with Facebook's 2.0 version of its API (in 2015), whereupon only pages (and groups) could be studied, not friends and profile information, or their actions such as likes, shares, comments, shared comments and later reactions (Hogan, 2014; Rieder, 2015a).

Instagram shuttered its data interface for researchers (in 2016) and had those who had built tools upon it 'reapply' for access, often without success (Rieder, 2016). The ability to query for hashtags as well as geo-coordinates (for 'selfie city' research, for example, or hashtag publics) was thereby thwarted (Tifentale and Manovich, 2015; Bruns and Burgess, 2015). Unauthorized workarounds or enlisting the services of a media monitoring company would be some means to regain researcher access.

In the wake of the Cambridge Analytica scandal, where university researchers harvested Facebook profile data for the purposes of performing a psyops campaign, Facebook also had researchers reapply for access to its Pages API (Bruns et al., 2018; Rogers, 2018). At the time of writing access had not been granted, leaving data extraction software applications (such as Netvizz and Netlytic) in limbo (Rieder, 2018).

Twitter, which has been called the last of the Web 2.0 applications (for its openness to external, live data collection to make 'mash-ups'), changed its terms of service as it became a publicly traded company (in 2011), making the exporting of tweets and shared tweet collections in violation of them (Burgess, 2016). It was one of those moments when one's work is scuppered by a new version of software. A researcher at Harvard's Berkmann Center noted that Twitter is not 'considering the myriad number of PhD students who basically just lost their work, or the researchers that were close to saying something meaningful and now have no way to do it' (Watters, 2011). In the event, one is able to share tweet ID numbers (rather than the tweets themselves), which then allows another researcher to recompile a tweet collection from them, effectuating sharing. Among other effects, recompiling allows deleted, suspended and withheld tweets – three interesting categories for analysis – to be filtered out of any newly reconstructed collection, in keeping with Twitter's rules.

Collections of such tweets exist for research purposes. Politicians' deleted tweets are captured by the Politwoops project by the Dutch Open State Foundation (and the Sunlight Foundation in the USA), where one may study scandals prompted by impetuous and salacious tweeting. Twitter once cut its access to these foundations' data-collecting, before agreeing that politicians' tweets are matters of public record rather than violations of 'Twitter Rules' on user's expectation of privacy. Twitter's annual 'transparency report', in part a product of that debate, provides facts and figures concerning withheld tweets, where for example in 2016 Turkey and France had the most tweets withheld, 2232 and 1334 respectively, though the actual number of blocked tweets appears to be much higher, at least for Turkey, raising questions about the transparency reporting practices (Tanash et al., 2015). As researchers did for Turkey, one could conceivably take stock of tweets withheld from one country by doing the capturing in another country. Suspended accounts (such as the wave of them that hit the 'alt-right' in the USA in 2016 and 2017) are emptied of previous tweets, making them inaccessible to researchers. One such case, @nero, Milo Yiannopoulos's Twitter account, has no trace left on Twitter.com. Independent archiving services (such as tweetsave.com) may have the tweets, where one could study what constitutes behaviour worthy of suspension, to whom it applies and how the standards may have changed over time.

Twitter as stored object, and its research ethics

Prior to becoming a corporation traded on the stock exchange and selling data to researchers including historical tweets (through Gnip), Twitter appeared particularly open to researcher access. In the halcyon days of Web 2.0, data mash-ups were common, such as placing Twitter's trending topics on a Google Map. Such a spirit of 2.0 openness, together with the significance of Twitter as data set, are expressed in the announcement, around the same time, of its donation of almost every tweet ever tweeted to the Library of Congress for scholarly usage (Raymond, 2010a). Twitter provides a 'historical record of communication, news reporting, and social trends', as well as a prism to study events such as the 'US presidential elections in 2008 and the green revolution in Iran in 2009' (Raymond, 2010b). Therein lies the presumed scholarly value: news, trends and event analysis together with communication studies.

Twitter, Inc. described its agreement with the Library in another blog post, together with the limits placed on studying the most recent tweets: 'It should be noted that there are some specifics regarding this arrangement. Only after a six-month delay can the Tweets be used for internal library use, for non-commercial research, public display by the library itself, and preservation' (Stone, 2010).

As the Library described it, 'bona fide researchers' would have access, and deleted tweets are not included, thereby respecting user intent (Raymond, 2010a, 2010b). (Old tweets deleted from Twitter but already archived in the Library presumably would live on, however.)

Some years on, however, the Library has not been able to provide access to it, even after fielding hundreds of written requests from researchers (Osterberg, 2013; McGill, 2016). The Twitter archive has become data too big for the Library to handle beyond sheer preservation (Zimmer, 2015). By January 2018 the Library announced it would no longer preserve Twitter's entire volume but would curate selective events and themes, 'similar to our collections of web sites', which could mark a return, in the web archiving tradition, to disasters, (presidential) transitions and elections (Osterberg, 2017). The Library has the first 12 years of tweets (the text) stored.

One could envisage a new media platform with an interface onto a so-called data firehose and API for researcher access to tweets (as Gnip or Texifter provide), but working with the Library's Twitter collection promises to become more cumbersome than that. 'Currently, executing a single search of just the fixed 2006–2010 archive on the Library's systems could take 24 hours' (Osterberg, 2013).

What are some of the concerns about working with stored tweets? In an analysis of the discussions around the Twitter archive, Michael Zimmer argues that the Library is not taking into account users' expectations of privacy, raising the larger question of whether it is ethical to store tweets (not to mention mine and analyse them) without user consent. Are they publications (to be cited)? Michael Beurskens (2013) has argued that since the users do not hold copyright on their tweets there is no legal case to cite tweets or attribute them to an author, though there may be a normative and scholarly case to be made. Or are tweets utterances in a larger sea of clamour not intended to be captured, stored (and analysed)? If it is too unwieldy to ask users to grant permission, could they at least be given the means to opt out (as is the case with websites in the Internet Archive)? In a spirited debate in the comment space of a Zimmer blog posting, Zimmer (2010b) writes: '[J]ust because they are public doesn't mean the intent was to allow them to be automatically archived [and] processed. That's the issue regarding whether additional consent is necessary.'

In another article, Zimmer found that the vast majority of researchers using Twitter data do not consider the ethics of user data collection and analysis (Zimmer and Proferes, 2014). There appears to be an overriding assumption that the 'data are already public' and that users have agreed to Twitter's terms of service, granting researchers licence: 'The fact that users grant Twitter a license to use their tweets (which is necessary for the service to work) means nothing in terms of whether it is ethical for researchers to systematically follow and harvest public tweet streams' (Zimmer, 2010b).

Interpreting Twitter's terms of service for researchers

Should users expect that their tweets are analysed by researchers? Like other social media companies, Twitter generally seeks to follow a 'transparency and choice approach' to privacy, where the user is told how the tweets are disseminated and (re)used and is offered forms of protection in software settings (Nissenbaum, 2011). The approach is laid out in its policies. Twitter has terms of service, a privacy policy, more general policies on use and abuse as well as developer terms that include sections on 'user protection' and privacy expectations. Emphasizing the publicness and extensive reach of the service, each provides descriptions (sometimes graphic ones) about what users should expect when they tweet.

In the terms of service, one grants Twitter the licence 'to make your content available to the rest of the world and to let others do the same' (Twitter, 2017a). Here there is an emphasis on wide-ranging reach as well as reuse. In the privacy policy, the emphasis on reuse is expressed as an admonition that one's data is being mined:

> Twitter broadly and instantly disseminates your public information to a wide
> range of users, customers, and services, including search engines, developers,
> and publishers that integrate Twitter content into their services, and organiza-
> tions such as universities, public health agencies, and market research firms that
> analyze the information for trends and insights. When you share information
> or content like photos, videos, and links via the Services, you should think care-
> fully about what you are making public. (Twitter, 2017b)

Twitter thus explicitly states that university researchers are to make use of one's tweets. Once the warnings have been given, the more general policies put the onus on users to protect their privacy by protecting tweets (as well as modifying and deleting them). One also may create a 'verified' account to guard against impersonation, though the cachet implied by a verified account (and exploited by political actors on the far right, for example) later gave Twitter pause, and in early 2018 that service was suspended.

Developers, finally, are asked to respect user intentions and 'partner' with Twitter by not retaining deleted, withheld, suspended as well as modified tweets (where, for example, the geo-coordinates have been removed). Twitter also is explicit about disallowing certain types of mining and analysis, especially those that aim 'to target, segment, or profile individuals based on health (including pregnancy), negative financial status or condition, political affiliation or beliefs, racial or ethnic origin, religious or philosophical affiliation or beliefs, sex life or sexual orientation, trade union membership...' (Twitter, 2017c). Twitter is targeting work (presumably including research) that segments and profiles groups.

There is another section in the developer terms of service that relates to remote event-following (which is discussed as an analytical strategy below) that is addressed to governmental researchers. Twitter should not be used by states to surveil or monitor protesters, demonstrators and such, it reads. Twitter thereby provides some legal cover for (university and other) researchers to mine and analyse data, at the same time restricting some types of use. Indeed, the most specific scenarios of data use are contained in the developer documentation, including the suggestion that one can be 'grouped' among protesters at a demonstration, and sorted into a category such as climate change sceptics (Pearce, 2018). Such a label may be difficult to shed; users also may not know that they have been profiled.

An additional issue for ethics and privacy researchers is that people do not read the terms of service, as evidenced by their online behaviour. When Twitter users do not modify their behaviour, but rather just post away, it appears they have not read the terms of service, have no reasonable expectation of being mined and analysed, or think it is futile. 'If people expect to be monitored, if they anticipate that their recorded views will be shared with particular third parties for money or favors, they are likely to be more watchful, circumspect, or uncooperative' (Nissenbaum, 2011: 45).

Whenever users expect to be surveilled or monitored, they presumably will change their behaviour, as was the case during the Iran election crisis when it was rumoured that repressive state authorities were checking user locations; all people employing the #iranelection hashtag were subsequently asked to change their Twitter location to Tehran. Here one may study not just chilling effects (and self-censorship) but also media tactics. How are users affected by surveillance? Does surveillance kill content and info-sharing?

Before moving on to strategies of tweet collection-making and analysis, it is worth pointing out the first comment made by a web user to the Library of Congress's FAQs that questions the research value of Twitter generally and historical tweets particularly. He wrote: 'It's critical that future generations know what flavor burrito I had for lunch' (Raymond, 2010b). Thus summarizes the idea of the banality of Twitter (Farhi, 2009). It also has been the object of sampling analysis, one of which found that 40% of tweets are 'pointless babble' (Pear Analytics, 2009). The marketing research described pointless babble as the '"I am eating a sandwich now" tweets' (Pear Analytics, 2009: 3). The question to be posed of its study, then, is how to debanalize Twitter (Rogers, 2013a). Or, more specifically, what kinds of techniques and heuristics may be put to use to make sense of Twitter data, and to what scholarly ends? Previously, the presumed scholarly value (of the Twitter archive) is said to lie in the analysis of news, trends and events, together with communication studies.

To those ends, the research undertakings below follow from taking the digital objects given by the device (hashtags, @mentions, retweets, shortened URLs), and thinking how to repurpose them for social research, which could be seen as the digital methods approach. It asks how to make a tweet collection, and how to analyse the tweets so as to debanalize Twitter. It thereby takes advantage of Twitter as news or event-following medium rather than its earlier moniker as the what-I-had-for-lunch device. It also turns Twitter into an issue space, where publics organize and compete to establish what is at stake.

Twitter as urban lifestyle tool for ambient friend-following

Created by Jack Dorsey and partners in San Francisco in 2006, Twitter arguably began as an American urban youth lifestyle tool, meant as a means to provide status updates on friends' whereabouts (see Figure 8.3). The Twitter user would answer the question, 'What are you doing?' It is a tool for people out and about town, adding what is sometimes referred to as 'ambient intimacy', and what Dorsey described as 'the physical sensation that you're buzzing your friend's pocket' (O'Reilly and Milstein, 2009; Sarno, 2009a). In 2006 and 2007 Dorsey maintained a Flickr account, where he posted photographs of his urbanite life and times, including his 'twttr sketch', which he annotated with an origins story, including his work at a start-up dispatch company in Oakland for courier, taxi and emergency services (Dorsey, 2006). In the two-part interview Dorsey gave for the *Los Angeles Times*, he notes how he borrowed the short messaging service (SMS) format, which has the constraint of 160 characters, before the message is split in two parts (Sarno, 2009a). The original 140 characters allowed in a tweet (later doubled) left 20 characters for username and other metadata needs. The URL stat.us (in Dorsey's original sketch) comes from the period when ccTLD name hacks like del. icio.us were *en vogue*, and twttr (a five-character code in keeping with messaging protocol) is also notably a Web 2.0-like name like flickr, thereby dating the application.

Often also originally associated with (and used at) events, Twitter outputs the real-time, and it is fleeting, not only in its continually updated interface, but also in the number of days of tweets stored for searchers of Twitter's API (perhaps 10). In a sense, it makes new media more ephemeral than the web. Dorsey said:

> I don't go back in time. You're kind of as good as your last update. That's what you're currently thinking or doing, or your current approach towards life. If that really interests me, I go to that person's profile page and read back a little bit. But in terms of my timeline, I'm just not obsessive about going all the way back in time and catching every single message that people have updated about. It's only relevant in the now, unless I'm fascinated by it. (Sarno, 2009b)

Figure 8.3   Original 'twttr sketch'
by Jack Dorsey.
Source: Dorsey, 2006.

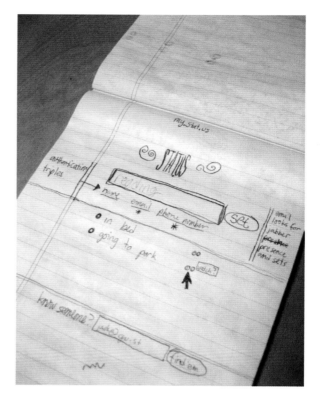

In 2009 Twitter changed the question it posed to its users from 'What are you doing?' to 'What's happening?', perhaps parlaying and translating Twitter's success at events, but also thereby creating a market for Twitter data from the once banal to the newsworthy. Indeed, why tweet? Is it to make news, gain followers, be retweeted or 'liked'? Is it to pad one's metrics? And who is one tweeting for? Is one treating one's audience as a fan base (Marwick and boyd, 2011)? Populist politicians such as Geert Wilders in the Netherlands and Donald Trump in the USA follow nearly no one, but rather treat Twitter as a broadcast medium for large throngs of fans and supporters (or supporters as fans).

The research affordances of Twitter's natively digital objects

Apart from studies of phatic communication and 'remote intimacy' of Dorsey's Twitter (2006), researchers have approached it as more than a real-time personal status update machine (for young urbanites) (Miller, 2008; Marwick and boyd, 2011; Papacharissi, 2012). Many of Twitter's research affordances owe to their natively digital objects, which are in part user innovations (Bruns, 2012; see Figure 8.4). The hashtag groups tweets by topic, the retweet indicates pass-along value and the @reply and @mention are threads and references.

Thus, through analyses of hashtags, Twitter is said to organize urgency and information flows such as around disasters and other events. One may study hashtag publics and explore the claim that they are 'fleeting' rather than stable (Rambukkana 2015; Bruns et al., 2016). Concentrating on RTs (a button for which is built into the Twitter interface), they can be made to give an account of the unfolding of events, as discussed below (Rogers et al., 2009b). Here the question is the extent to which it may be employed for 'remote event analysis', and how these accounts would hold up to other first drafts of history, such as in newspapers and in Wikipedia articles (Bruns and Weller, 2016). By focusing on the @replies, Twitter may be analysed as a conversation-maker, where one may explore the extent to which there is dialogue, or broadcasting, on Twitter (Honeycutt and Herring, 2009; boyd et al., 2010). In considering @mentions, one also may pinpoint (and critique) dominant voice, as in who is being mentioned the most in a tweet collection, compiled to capture a certain issue space such as global health and development, where for example the Gates Foundation may be the actor most mentioned. Here the question may revolve around the extent to which these voices are driving the agenda and organizing urgency and symbolic power for some issues (and care strategies) rather than others (Couldry, 2001, 2012; Chouliaraki, 2013).

Figure 8.4 Chris Messina, Twitter user and Twitter hashtag inventor in 2007.
Source: Parker, 2011. Photo credit: Kris Cheng.

Tweet collection studies and critical analytics

Tweet collection-making generally follows from hashtag and keyword queries, though one can also query a user's account (Geert Wilders' or Donald Trump's historical tweets), or one or more @mentions (who mentions the alt-right?).

For the sake of robustness, it may be advisable to undertake a two-step query design. Having explored the (hashtag and keyword) language in an issue or event space (through Google or in Twitter itself), make an initial tweet collection through a search, and perform hashtag frequency or co-hashtag analysis with the results, which in the latter case is a list ranked by frequency of those hashtags that occur together in the tweets in your collection. Add newly discovered, significant hashtags to the query, and launch the search again. This second query, in the two-step process, is the one that results in the tweet collection under study.

With such tools as DMI-TCAT, there is often a battery of analytical modules to be explored (Borra and Rieder, 2014). The critical analytics strategy put forward here is only one means to study a tweet collection, and it is especially geared towards the critical study of social issues and their publics through relatively simple techniques (Rogers, 2018a). A second analytical strategy, for event-following or 'remote event analysis', follows below.

Among the critical analytics to study an issue space are dominant voice, concern, commitment, positioning as well as alignment. Dominant voice, as mentioned, is a list of those @mentions that appear in an issue space. Ranked by frequency (and by frequent co-occurrence) it provides a sense of whose voice resonates (or is referenced) the most. (Vocality, contrariwise, is a measure of who tweets with the greatest frequency in an issue space.) Hashtags are often embedded issues (as well as campaigns and events), so concern, as an analytic measure, is a list of hashtags most used. Co-hashtag lists may be employed to study the twinning of concerns, and issue hybridization, for example, #rivers and #humanrights (see Figure 8.5). Commitment is the persistent appearance of users and issues in a space and is measured over time. There is a module in DMI-TCAT called the 'associational profiler' that provides associations between hashtags overtime (Marres, 2015). The technique could be employed for users as well as for users together with hashtags and/or keywords. Do particular NGOs move in and out of issue spaces depending on their newsworthiness, or do they remain engaged? Positioning is the use of specific keywords rather than others. Do I choose to use the term 'blood diamonds' (thereby taking a stand with activists) or 'conflict diamonds' (lining up with industry)? Alignment, finally, means those actors using the same issue language. Who else uses #apartheidwall (the official Palestinian term), and who else #securityfence (the official Israeli term for the barrier between Israel and the Palestinian territories)?

Twitter revolutions and other claims to be debunked (and empirically tested)

Twitter has often been dubbed a micro-blogging platform, but it may be characterized as a medium in a variety of ways. On Twitter users may follow other users, meaning that, like

GEAG @GEAG_India · Jun 24 ⌄
#Rivers get **#HumanRights** :They can sue to protect themselves bit.ly/2rFps0j
@indiawater @guardian @intlrivers @Indian_Rivers

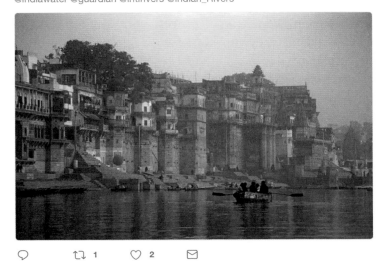

○   ⊔ 1   ♡ 2   ✉

Figure 8.5 Issue hybridization of rivers and human rights. Tweet containing multiple, issue-oriented hashtags, a reference as well as authoritative @mentions.

other social media platforms, one could view and study Twitter as a social network (Java, 2007; Huberman et al., 2009). If one studies the trending topics (a front-page interface item and metric on Twitter), one finds that they often concern news items, thus making Twitter a rebroadcaster (Kwak et al., 2010). As mentioned above, one may also study how populist politicians and others (with many followers, but who follow few to none) use the medium primarily for broadcasting. Do these together constitute an echo chamber, filter bubble or even culture war, or are there distinctive anomalies that would force those concepts to be stretched or rendered less usable? A larger question (for media research) concerns how to characterize the medium for specific user groups deemed worthy of research, despite Twitter's terms of use. How to describe the distinctive concerns of the new right? Who do they @mention, which hashtags do they use, and which sources do they reference? How to characterize their media tactics and communication strategy?

There is another strand of research which may be called Twitter impact studies. For example, one undertakes analysis of how tweets organize awareness, and measure, or enunciate, word on the streets and word of mouth (Jansen et al., 2009). Possibly the best-known ideas about Twitter impacts came into existence around the Iran elections of June 2009, where the term 'Twitter revolution' was coined (Berman, 2009). In its disambiguation page, Wikipedia notes that the term may be used in connection with a series of 'spring' and 'colour' uprisings: the Moldovan civil disturbances of 2009 as well as the Tunisian and Egyptian revolutions of 2011, otherwise known as part of the Arab Spring (Wikipedia Contributors, 2018a). It also could refer to Euromaidan, the Ukrainian uprising of 2013. Here one often strives to research the 'role' of Twitter (and other social media) in such events (Zuckerman, 2011; Srinivasan, 2014). Such a study of the role or part played by

Twitter often begins by challenging the idea of technology as revolutionary or central to social change. In one such undertaking, the researchers debunked the claim of Twitter as vital in the Iran election crisis (Burns and Eltham, 2009). In a turn of events similar to those described by Evgeny Morozov in *The Net Delusion* (2011), Burns and Eltham (2009: 306) write: 'Iranian Twitter users did not take counter-deception measures to deal with the Basij, who then used Twitter to identify, locate and in some cases kill Iranian protestors.' Rather than revolutionary, Twitter becomes the inverse. It is the authoritarian regime's tool to quell the disturbance.

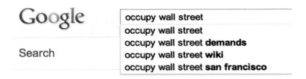

Figure 8.6　Occupy Wall Street, Google suggested searches, google.com, 2 December 2011.

The subject of Iran government-sponsored infiltrators was discussed (retweeted) in the #iranelection Twitter subsphere in June 2009, where users were asked to change their location to Tehran, so that everyone appeared to be there physically, as mentioned above. The introduction of noise became a media tactic. These manoeuvrings and their implications are some of the means by which a movement or network, and especially resistance, may be studied through hashtag analysis (Lindgren and Lundström, 2011; Poell and Borra, 2012). To what extent is the hashtag issue space tactical as well as substantively distinctive? What kind of an account of events does it provide? One may evaluate hashtag accounts of what is transpiring on the ground by contrasting them with the story told of the same events in the news or on Wikipedia, thereby inquiring into the features of the various first drafts of history, as mentioned above.

In the Occupy Wall Street protests in major Western cities in the autumn of 2011 and beyond, a variety of media accounts claimed that the protestors had no demands, until one list was made, and became the subject of debate among the OccupyWallSt.org collective (OccupyWallStreet, 2011). Occupy Wall Street demands also have been a top suggested search in Google (see Figure 8.6). Media accounts often serve as starting points for exercises that both critique the typical news frames (protest prompts violence) and provide alternative accounts (protest is substantive). The research question concerns the kind of account of Occupy Wall Street organized by its hashtags as well as its related hashtags *vis-à-vis* that in the news. Does it compete with or provide a corrective to dominant media accounts? Does it tell a compelling story of what is happening in the parks and on the grounds where tents have been raised (and torn down)? These are at least a few ways in which one may employ Twitter as a research tool, and at the same time debanalize it.

Debanalizing the medium, or Twitter as story-telling machine

In work completed in 2009 when Twitter emerged as a medium for remote event analysis (and debunking revolutions), the question concerned how to repurpose the output of Twitter so as to create a compelling account of what was happening on the streets and in social media (Rogers et al., 2009b). Entitled 'For the ppl of Iran: #iranelection RT', the piece followed the methods of the medium in so far as hashtags organize subject matters, and RTs point to significant content. The top three retweeted tweets per day (for some 20 days) were captured, and placed in chronological order, inverting the reverse chronological order of Twitter (and blogging software more generally). As mentioned, Twitter's reverse chronological order (though later combined with algorithmic hierarchy) is one reason to call it a blogging platform, with the term 'micro-blogging' referring to the meagre amount of characters per post. With the remote event analysis technique, the overall story of the 20 days of the Iran election crisis is recounted (see Figure 8.7):

> The crisis unfolds on Twitter with the discovery of the value of the #iranelection hashtag, and tweeters both in and outside Iran begin using the tag to mark all tweets about the events there. Mousavi holds an emergency press conference. The voter turn-out is 80%. SMS is down; Mousavi's website and Facebook are blocked. Police are using pepper spray. Mousavi is under house arrest, and declares he is prepared for martyrdom. Neda is dead. There is a riot in Baharestan Square. First aid info is here. Bon Jovi sings "Stand by Me" in support. Ahmadinejad is confirmed the winner. Light a candle for the ppl of Iran. (Digital Methods Initiative, 2009)

Employing the same technique (with the addition of manual filtering by theme), sub-stories also were created around censorship, Neda, arrests, Internet and violence. For example, the censorship sub-story concerns internet filtering by the state, and efforts (and tips) to circumvent it. Note that the well-known blocking of the networks by the Iranian government unfolded in that event space on 13 June, and Twitter's announcement on 16 June to postpone scheduled system maintenance resonated, too.

The great Twitter revolution debate revisited

How did the great Twitter revolution debate unfold, and how may it be studied? Contemporaneous bloggers and writers in the intellectual press (*Dissent*, *Foreign Policy*, *New Yorker*, *Prospect* and others) deliberated over the extent to which a 'Twitter Revolution' took place in Iran in 2009 and elsewhere, especially the protests in Moldova that transpired just weeks prior to the events in Iran and provided the revolution theme with momentum. Put into circulation by the American blogger, Andrew Sullivan (2009), the notion elicited

Figure 8.7 For the ppl of Iran – #iranelection RT.

Source: Digital Methods Initiative, 2009.

rounds of debunking, where the platform's role was repeatedly cut down to size. Among the seemingly most damning critiques of the revolution thesis is that the Iranian regime blocked access to the internet and the mobile phone network (mentioned above), thus rendering Twitter locally useless, despite the urging of the US State Department to Twitter to postpone its maintenance so that it could be used by Iranians (Ostrow, 2009). Another critical point made (and often repeated across the articles) is that only 19,235 people in Iran were registered Twitter users at the time, a mere 0.027% of the national population (Sysomos, 2009). Thus, Twitter certainly would not have been used *en masse*, however much 20,000 users also could be construed as a considerable number compared to the handful of Moldovan Twitter users during its own Twitter revolution (Bennett, 2009). Iran's uprising, rather than organized on Twitter, was coordinated by word of mouth, and was not principally technology-driven, it is said. As Golnaz Esfandiari (2010) writes in *Foreign Policy*: 'Twitter was definitely not a major communications tool for activists on the ground in Iran.' More poignantly, using Twitter and other social media would make Iranians targets of the authoritarian regime.

The value of the internet for the authoritarian regime and/or for activists proved to be a point of contention in the debate. On that subject, Clay Shirky (2010) writes, '[T]he net value of social media has shifted the balance of power in the direction of Iran's citizens', while Evgeny Morozov (2010) rejoindered, '[D]espite all the political mobilization facilitated by social media, the Iranian government has not only survived, but has, in fact, become even more authoritarian'.

There are also many stories worth considering that have aided in the debunking of a Twitter revolution in Iran, questioning the platform's veracity and 'ground-truthing' capacity. Mousavi, the green opposition candidate, was said on Twitter to be under house arrest, a claim later disputed, making Twitter into a rumour mill and unreliable source (Mostaghim and Daragahi, 2009; Esfandiari, 2010). Indeed, Evgeny Morozov (2009: 11) likened Twitter to child's play: '[T]his new media eco-system is very much like the old game of "Telephone," in which errors steadily accumulate in the transmission process, and the final message has nothing in common with the original.' Here one may compare contemporaneous accounts with more settled ones that have stood the test of time.

Another larger point worthy of investigation is that there were few Twitter users on the ground in Tehran at the time (tweeting in Farsi), making Twitter into a something other than an eyewitness medium. Indeed, one of the more significant users tweeting about events on the ground was @oxfordgirl, residing in a village in the UK (Weaver, 2009; Esfandiari, 2010). How may one characterize the 'groundedness' of the users of the #iran-election hashtag? Here one may look at platforms used and inquire into desktop versus mobile use. Would a lack of groundedness damn the accounts of events? Does Twitter become an event commentary medium (another way of filling in 'event-following'), rather than one for witnessing?

Conclusions: From ambient friend-following to remote event analysis

Twitter's 'about' pages highlight the changing purposes of the platform. In 2006, Twitter was 'for staying in touch and keeping up with friends no matter where you are or what you're doing'; by 2017, Twitter was 'what's happening in the world and what people are talking about right now'. Twitter thereby has evolved from a local urban lifestyle tool (conceived for young San Francisco users) to an international news and event-following medium, at least in the renderings of the medium mission statements.

The research agenda has followed this transformation of Twitter from a banal 'what-I-had-for-lunch' medium to one purportedly and controversially having a hand in contemporary revolutions. As such, research also 'debanalized' Twitter. The techniques devised include taking advantage of the user-led research affordances of the platform, including the threading of topics by hashtag and the identification of significant content by retweet. Remaking Twitter into an analytical story-telling machine, with the capacity to chronicle events on the ground and in social media is one digital method described above. Another concerns techniques to monitor and analyse substantive spaces of particular user groups, be they activists, NGOs or new social movements and formations, such as Black Lives Matter and the alt-right. The critical analytics put forward are means to evaluate the substance of these spaces, inquiring into who dominates the discussion. Is the matter of concern fleeting? That is the critical point made of 'hashtag publics' who appear like a flash mob and dissipate just as quickly. Their commitment, or longevity of concern, is another critical analytic. The competition between hashtags, and hashtag publics, may be studied in the programme/anti-programme approach put forward in the query design chapter. The idea of Twitter as a platform primarily for 'status updates' of users 'in bed' or 'going to the beach' (as in the original Twttr sketch) has receded, and its vibrancy (and techniques to capture it) are put to the fore.

PROJECT 12

VIDEO 6 Twitter as
story-telling machine

Debunk the Twitter revolution (again)

RESEARCH GOAL To peruse the literature surrounding the great Twitter revolution debate of 2009–2010 (and beyond) and confirm, refute, modify or otherwise productively engage with the claims put forward.

To start, one would compile a catalogue of claims, and examine their robustness by analysing a tweet collection of the Iran election crisis, 10–30 June 2009, which includes some 650,000 tweets using the hashtag #iranelection. The hashtag is significant, for not only was it among Twitter's highest trending topics for the year, but it also was the object of scorn by analysts questioning users' blind faith in it: 'Western journalists who couldn't reach – or didn't bother reaching? – people on the ground in Iran simply scrolled through the English-language tweets post with tag #iranelection' (Esfandiari, 2010).

Data set

Tweets with hashtag #iranelection, 10–30 June 2009, http://rettiwt.digitalmethods.net/ (request login)

Data analyses available

Languages used (overall)

Platforms used (overall)

Platforms used per language

Tweets per user

Tweets per green_normal avatar

Tweets per day

Ranked list of retweets

Retweeted users (ranked @mentions)

Other hashtags used with #iranelection (co-hashtags)

URLs found in combination with #iranelection

Rumours (tweets containing the word)

Confirmed (tweets containing the word)

Sample project outcome

'For the ppl of Iran – #iranelection RT' (10' 00"), https://www.youtube.com/watch?v=_h2B2CA-btY

PROJECT 13

Debanalize Twitter by analysing a tweet collection for its substantive value

RESEARCH GOAL To debanalize Twitter by studying a tweet collection, constructed by queries for hashtags and keywords (issue spaces and/or events), user captures (populist politicians or other public figures and organizations), or social movements (networks as movements).

Twitter data

Twitter users send 140–280-character posts, or tweets, either from the web or through dedicated applications on computers, smartphones and tablets. Each tweet is linked to a user account, the source of the tweet, publishing date and contents, including markers with potential analytical value such as hashtags (#hashtag), @username, RT (identical tweet, or modified tweet), a (shortened) URL and/or a geotag. While only a small (but growing) percentage of tweets are geotagged with a latitude/longitude marker, location, if the focus of the research, could also be derived from a user's account information, the date of account creation, a profile image, the specific language they post in, the message text or the time zone. The demarcation of the Australian twitterverse, for example, benefited from the time zone (see Figure 8.8).

Hashtags are used to thread or tag communication around specific events, topics, issues, locales and so on. They also may organize a subculture or a political persuasion. Mention markers (@username) allow users to directly address or refer to another user. Retweet markers in early tweet collections (RT @username) or identical (and quoted) retweets in tweet collections since 2015, indicate that a message from another user is forwarded, presumably because it has 'pass-along value'. URLs, shortened with t.co or other services, point to sources. All these elements can be employed for 'remote event analysis', that is, to understand events on the ground, and their interplay with social media – including the effects of the platform (the practices it supports), its users and of course the content, however succinct. They also may be used to study issue (or subcultural) spaces with critical analytics, inquiring into dominant voice, concern, alignment and commitment. Consider a comparative approach, #blacklivesmatter (and related hashtags) together with #alllivesmatter, as these may be considered antagonistic hashtag publics, with a respective programme and anti-programme (as discussed in the query design chapter).

Issue space analysis with Twitter

The research considerations below follow from the kinds of Twitter studies discussed above: (a) social issues and trends, (b) news and events, (c) politicians' (and other individuals' or organizations') historical tweets and (d) social movements (networks as movements).

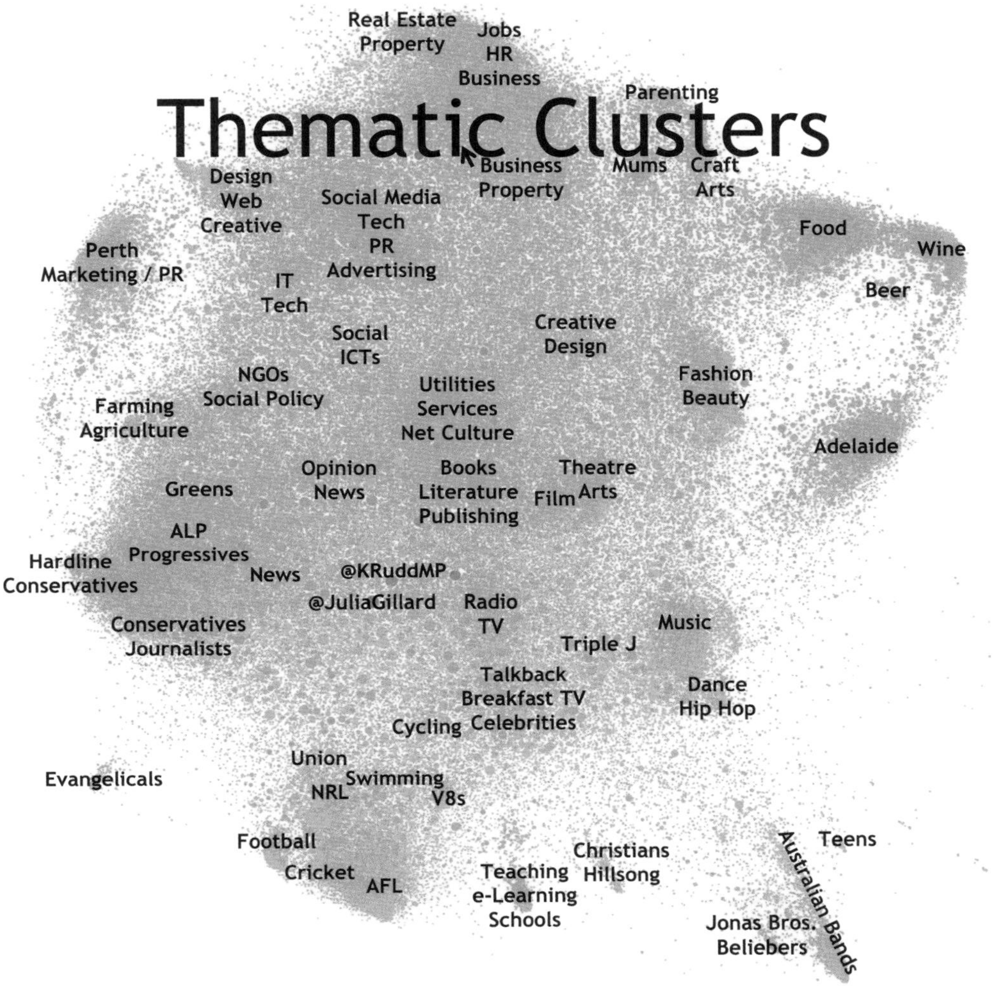

Figure 8.8 Australian Twittersphere, 2012.
Source: Sun, 2012.

Social issues and trends

Data collection: Make tweet collection of an issue space, or use existing one

Be advised that Twitter allows one to collect tweets going back in time about a week or so. Historical data sets of tweets are available on DMI-TCAT; for a list of collected data see https://tools. digitalmethods.net/beta/tcat/. Historical tweets also may be purchased from Twitter's subsidiary (Gnip), and cost estimates were available via Texifter, https://sifter.texifter.com, where one would estimage the size of historical tweet data, and (for example) develop critiques of data commodification.

For new data sets, one may consider performing a two-step query design for demarcation of an issue space.

1   First spend time with the issue by reading tweets in that space. One may search Twitter and/or Google for hashtags concerning the issue(s) in question. Note the hashtags and keywords used. Alternatively, compile a list of hashtags using the associative query snowball technique, discussed in the Issuecrawler chapter.

2   In DMI-TCAT or another tweet capture software application, query the list of hashtags and/or keywords, and build a tweet collection over the period of a few days (or, if time allows, a week or two). In DMI-TCAT the query assumes the form of both hashtags and keywords.

3   Perform hashtag and/or co-hashtag analysis, and list most frequently occurring or co-occurring hashtags by frequency.

4   Add newly discovered hashtags to original list and launch the query anew in DMI-TCAT or another tweet capture software application.

5   The results of the second query constitute the tweet collection. Unless useful, one may dispose of the results of the original query.

For existing data sets, query inside them by date range, hashtags, keywords and/or @usernames.

Issue space analysis: Critical analytics procedures

1   Concern – hashtag analysis – social issues as embedded in hashtags. Make a list of hashtags as well as co-hashtags ranked by frequency, in order to show hierarchies of concern.

2   Dominant voice – @mention analysis – who speaks and whose speech is referenced? For who speaks, one may count the @usernames tweeting most often in the issue space, introducing a metric concerning 'vocalism', or the exercise of voice. Dominant voice concerns which @usernames are mentioned the most. Interpreted differently, it also allows the identification of expertise. Make a list of @usernames mentioned, ranked by frequency. Note whether the dominant voices propagate the top concerns, thereby dominating the agenda.

3   Commitment – over-time analysis of persistence (repeated co-occurrence) of hashtags, users, or hashtags and users. Note which hashtags (and which co-hashtags) persist over time. Note whether there are certain users that persevere along with them. In DMI-TCAT, the 'associational profiler' performs a form of commitment analysis.

4   Positioning – competing keyword and hashtag deployment. #blacklivesmatter and #alllivesmatter (or #bluelivesmatter) may be considered programmes and anti-programmes in the overall issue space of (police) violence in America and elsewhere. Identify the hashtag competition, and consider scoping, substantive and media tactics analyses. Scoping refers to size and composition, substantive analysis to related hashtags as well as URL references, and media tactics to the tactical use of the space, such as by twinning issues, reverse hashtag use, and hashtag hijacking. Consider how one group frames another, thereby creating an outgroup.

5   Alignment – co-occurrence of users and hashtags. What other company does a hashtag keep? Which other hashtags does a user employ? Here one may analyse alliances and unlikely bedfellows.

Remote event analysis and news

Data collection: Make tweet collection of event space

1   Collect tweets as the event unfolds. As you learn about the event (spanning time with it), consider making multiple queries, and concatenating (or merging) tweet collections of the event.
2   An event space is often demarcated by sets of hashtags and keywords, and competing hashtags (and their publics) may emerge. Consider making a collection that encompasses the competition, so as to allow for an analysis of the different accounts of the 'same' event.

For example, the far-right march in Charlottesville, Virginia in August 2017 elicited hashtag reactions on Twitter, from #charlottesville to #thisisnotUS as well as #standwithcharlottesville and #defendcharlottesville. An array of far right or alt-right hashtags also galvanized the throng of demonstrators and their adherents such as #unitetheright. Which publics do these organize, do they 'dialogue', and how 'fleeting' or part of a larger history of action are they? Here one could engage with the literature on hashtag publics (Rambukkana, 2015; Bruns et al., 2016).

Event space: Remote event analysis

1   Story-telling – retweet analysis – most retweeted tweets per day tells story of an event as it unfolds.
2   Source-mentioning – URL analysis – shows content that is most referenced. Note the 'missing references', or what one may expect to be present but is absent. How mainstream or fringe is the collection of sources? Compare the sources referenced by two camps, or programmes and anti-programmes, showing commonalities and differences (see Figure 8.9).
3   First draft of history. With the help of a timeline, compare the story told by the space to the story told by the referenced sources, or other first drafts of history such as Wikipedia articles of the event (perhaps across different Wikipedia language versions, too).
4   Competing accounts of events. With the help of a timeline, compare the account of the event given by the hashtag to an account provided by dominant media sources. Demarcate dominant media sources by date range and characterization of type of news (e.g., top quality newspapers or top tabloids).

Politician broadcasting: Issue and 'target' analysis

Data collection: Capture one or more politicians' tweets.

One may capture public figures' tweets or those of an organization or institution. Optionally, one may capture all leading politicians' tweets prior to an upcoming election, perhaps together with the political parties' tweets. Consider capturing tweets from verified accounts. Note that Twitter has a limit to the amount of tweets that may be captured in total per account (going back in time).

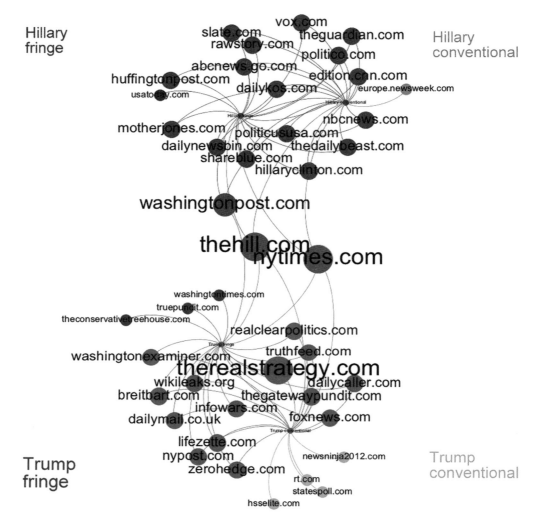

Figure 8.9   Shared and uniquely referenced sources by Hillary and Trump supporters, respectively, on Twitter, 2016.
Source: Bouma et al., 2017.

Politicians and other public figures as well as organizations often envisage the audience they are tweeting to (supporters and/or fan bases) rather than engaging in (direct) conversation and dialogue with other Twitter users. Whom do they target, and about which issues? Which sources do they reference (see also Figure 8.9)?

Here one may wish to explore a claim and fill it in substantively. For example, it has been claimed that Geert Wilders, the Dutch politician, is a leading figure in the 'new right'. How to characterize the 'new right's' issues? Are they primarily Islamophobic (or counter-jihadist), anti-establishment or another orientation? Here one would categorize (a subset of) Wilders' tweets.

Network as movement

On Twitter (and in other platforms) social movements are active such as Black Lives Matter and the alt-right. In order to chart the movement's concerns and tactics, one could first make a list of its leading figures, by reading contemporary news accounts, magazine and Wikipedia articles as well as otherwise spending time in the movement space online. Having made a list of the names of the leading figures (and looking up their Twitter accounts), one may query their @mentions. Who mentions these names? One charts the inner and outer rings of the movement (as network) by determining which users mention them all, mention all but one, mention all but two and so forth. Mentions of leading figures become links, and one can make a network diagram of the movement in ring form, from inner to outer. Analytical pathways include those discussed above, from critical analytics to issue as well as target analysis.

Tools

- DMI Twitter Capture and Analysis Toolset (DMI-TCAT). Available at https://github.com/digital-methodsinitiative/dmi-tcat. The DMI-TCAT tool should be installed on a server.

- Gephi. Available at https://gephi.org.

Video tutorials

For Project 13, see the TCAT overview video as well as one or the other Gephi tutorial, depending on the type of analysis to be undertaken (@mention or co-hashtag).

- 'DMI-TCAT: Overview of Analytical Modules' (25' 39"), https://www.youtube.com/watch?v=ex97eoorUeo
- 'Gephi Tutorial for Working with Twitter Mention Networks' (50' 10"), https://www.youtube.com/watch?v=snPR8CwPld0
- 'Combine and Analyse Co-Hashtag Networks (Instagram, Twitter, etc.) with Gephi' (17' 39"), vhttps://www.youtube.com/watch?v=ngqWjgZudeE

NINE

MEMES OR VIRALS
Identifying engaging content on Facebook

The history of the meme as object of study is
one of its gradual denaturalization

Dominant forms of platform content

Virals on YouTube, rants on blogs, tweet storms on Twitter, listicles and scrollytellings on news sites, long-form on Medium and fake news on Facebook – online content has forms that may be considered platform-specific. Or, at least, there are emergent genres associated with particular platforms. When considering Twitter, one would not think of a listicle, for example.

While one could make an argument for each of those cultural forms to be 'of the medium' and thus specifically digital culture, the meme stands out. As Limor Shifman (2014: 4) argues, it is often considered to be 'fundamental' to digital culture, facilitated by the circulatory architecture of the internet and more recently that of social media platforms. Where once the hyperlink (perhaps superseded by the like) and the website (challenged by the app) were considered the seminal web objects, now the meme is held up as of special interest, given that it is both a form of content, best known as the two-liner image macro, and invested with a power to spread in social media – aided by likes and shares, and the news feeds on which they algorithmically appear. In fact, memes have been found to be the most shared content on (particular) Facebook pages, which raises questions concerning the source and implications of their power (Renner 2017; see Figure 9.1).

With its origins in the biology of replication (and survival), and its association with virality as well as persuasive messaging (and advertising), the meme is of considerable conceptual and historical interest. It comes canned in the form of in-group aphorisms or 'small truths', making it a creative means by which to express as well as add to a collective viewpoint or sentiment. Perhaps what makes the study of memes most significant these days are their accompanying machines, which route and boost content both globally as well as through friend networks. Memes, either as image macros, lines of (well-formatted) text only or other (photoshopped or Imgur'd) content that contributes to an ecology, have become more pervasive with the rise of social media platforms. One question that may be put to platforms (such as Facebook) is the extent to which they are meme machines (rather than social network sites or another descriptor such as ad platform). Another is whether memes would do as well outside digital culture.

Figure 9.1   Most shared content from Breitbart Facebook page, 2016.
Source: Renner, 2017.

The study of memes in digital culture

There is arguably an evolution to the study of the meme over the past forty years from the biological to the cultural, to put it broadly. Since its coining in 1976 by Richard Dawkins, it is an object of study in digital culture that scholars have struggled with, largely because it first appeared as natural or naturalizing rather than human-made (see Figure 9.2). It could be argued that meme studies over the past decades could be read as efforts to denaturalize the meme, to rid it of its naturalness, or to shed it of its cultural equivalence to the gene.

The meme, whether in the scholarly or popular realm, continues to maintain a relationship with the biological, and in particular with the viral. It could be said that the meme's relationship with the viral lends it its mystifying quality, through its potential to infect and even zombify consumers, thereby bringing it in line with other manipulative techniques, often from the history of marketing such as subliminal advertising and priming. That is,

Figure 9.2 Book cover of Richard Dawkins's *The Selfish Gene* (1976), where in the final chapter he introduces the meme as cultural equivalent to the gene. Cover art: Desmond Morris.

these days one can study the meme itself as an intriguing object of online culture relevant across disciplines, but for the media field it also should be placed in the broad history of media manipulation, media manufacture, and influence campaigning.

The idea that the meme quietly or without our knowing is infecting us on the one hand or manipulating us with agendas on the other may owe partly to Douglas Rushkoff's (1994) work on media as virus, among others. The meme as such certainly has become an object of intense scrutiny since the US presidential elections of 2016 which also have been described as a 'meme war', where the question has been posed, did the US elect a meme (together with a president)? In posing such a question, one journalist described the revelations made just after the improbable presidential victory of 'meme magic' – another, mystifying means of describing its power:

> Trump's victory last week was the moment when something bubbling along the fringe for nearly two years hit the mainstream with the same intensity of a Facebook meme. His campaign has synthesized the most effective parts of Gamergate, men's rights activism, the tea party, the anti-EU movement … and distilled it into something that can reach the most number of eyeballs. Trump's victory is the moment the participants of a meme become aware that it's a meme. (Broderick, 2016)

Here the meme is much larger than an image macro or single cultural gene. It is wide-scale cultural production of interlinked and inter-textual materials by an array of subcultures, as the journalist listed. By making and circulating a home-made video – such as the infamous one of Trump's wrestling a CNN reporter – one contributes to the larger pool of subcultural production, adding materially to a sentiment. In the loop, the US president himself has retweeted on occasion such home-made videos, thereby accelerating further cultural production, whereby a spate of additional videos follows of a similar theme.

Meme as content collection and meme types

In her book that redefined the concept – away from Dawkins's original biological sense and distinctive from Rushkoff's viral – Limor Shifman (2014) calls the meme user-created derivatives (plural) of an original piece of content. The meme is thus *a collection of content*, which comes in a series of distinctive types. Shifman describes three, referring largely to YouTube content: user-generated, globalizing commercial and subcultural.

'User-generated' and aspirational luxury memes

'Charlie Bit My Finger' (the famous video) is of the user-generated variety, to use a term, like 'produser', that was coined to elevate the status of the maker from the 'amateur' to a DIY professional and could be employed to describe the meme-makers these days (Bruns, 2009). The finger-biting video is supposedly funny, but is somewhat pernicious, given the sneer Charlie imparts after the bite that perhaps explains its appeal, also in a trolling sense, which I return to. 'Gangnam Style', one of the most popular YouTube videos of all time, exemplifies the second type; it is globalizing commercial content (a professional music video that appeals across national markets and tastes) which invites 'riffing' and remixing. It also encapsulates another element that has found firm footing in digital culture – aspirational luxury, well-known in Instagram, where one seeks to show celebrity and fandom, albeit in this case without vanity metrics such as high follower counts and like numbers (Marwick, 2015; Abidin, 2016). In Shifman's sense, 'Gangnam Style' is the 'original piece of content' that invites derivatives, and also contributes to a larger content ecology that is both playful and standpoint-taking. As a case in point for the latter, 'my binders full of women exploded' (the 'Gangnam Style' image with one-liner) contributes to the meme surrounding (gendered) comments made by the then presidential candidate Mitt Romney in a 2012 debate with Barack Obama, the eventual winner of his second presidential term. Romney (the challenger in the televised debate) remarks about staffing equality that he 'went to a number of women's groups to help us find [qualified candidates] and they brought me binders full of women', a short quotation that is worthy of meme treatment. The photoshopped image (or, perhaps more accurately, Imgur'd image) of 'Gangnam Style' becomes content added to the pool. There is a Tumblr page with 'binders full of women' containing a series of serious homemade images protesting against women as binder-filler, contributing further to the meme. It is a collection that not only accumulates (one can add to the meme), but can also be curated by a moderator or administrator (on a Tumblr or Facebook page) (HeyVeronica, 2012).

In sum, as alluded to above, memes as media formats are often two-liners, if viewed as a standardized object made by online generators such as Imgur, originally made for the Reddit community, itself a rich source of memes. These pieces of software are image macro makers, with two text fields, inviting an opening and closing remark, above and below the image. They may include a hashtag, or an otherwise brief aphorism that summarizes a pithiness one can hold on to. These witticisms can be catchy, and even infectious. Often triggered by one-liners (binders full of women), memes then accumulate content (see Figure 9.3). The additive content itself may be worthy further 'meme treatment', thus making the meme more than a collection of derivatives of a single piece of content, to which I return in a discussion of the Trump meme.

Figure 9.3 'Gangnam Style' as original piece of content worthy of meme treatment. Example by Shifman, 2014.

Subcultural memes

The third meme type beyond user-generated and globalizing commercial (often with aspirational luxury) is the subcultural, and here examples are drawn from the meme war (mentioned above) as well as the specific meme culture surrounding the Trump campaign and thereafter. If one were to expand upon Shifman's definition, one could argue that the Trump meme is an additive collection, however much with multiple triggering pieces of content. These multiple catalysts may include campaign slogans such as 'drain the swamp' and 'make America great again' (including hashtagged and coded versions such as #maga3x for Trump's troll army), animosities expressed by the candidate towards individuals satirizing him (such as Alec Baldwin on the television programme *Saturday Night Live*) or providing critical coverage (such as CNN). The prompts for content creation may be similar to the Mitt Romney example of 'binders full of women', too. One such instance of a one-liner worthy of meme treatment is Hillary Clinton's 'basket of deplorables': 'to just be grossly generalistic, you could put half of Trump's supporters into what I call the basket of deplorables. Right? The racist, sexist, homophobic, xenophobic, islamophobic – you name it' (Holan, 2016).

Arguably troll feed, Trump's opponent's 'deplorables' remarks triggered memetic cultural production, with deplorables placed in hashtags and in the online aliases of trolls and other produsers. On the Inauguration Day in Washington, DC in January 2017 there was a DeploraBall, attended by internet trolls, finally meeting one another like in other virtual-to-real gatherings of the past more associated with the left and progressive culture, such as a Pariser Moveon meet-up and a Rheingold virtual community WELL party (Boyd, 2003; Rheingold, 1993). Now the right had productively appropriated the internet and were celebrating. At the ball were the makers and circulators of the materials that 'memed Trump into the presidency': the 'researchers, compilers and meme magicians', as one attendee put it, who came together to crowd-work through leaked emails from the Hillary campaign and turn them into amusing, spreadable product, such as the YouTube ditty, 'What difference does it make?', which remixes to music speech fragments from Clinton's and FBI director James Comey's public statements about her use of a private email server while in public office (Chace, 2017; Socialistmop, 2016). Another attendee remarked how Trump himself was the troll-in-chief, having baited fellow challengers like Marco Rubio with the name 'Little Marco'. Later he would call the North Korean leader 'Rocket Man' and, as the exchange between them became heated, 'Little Rocket Man'.

Trump meme collection

In one of the best-known additions to the Trump meme collection (retweeted by Donald Trump, Jr.), 'the deplorables' photoshopped image of Trump and his dark-clad band of followers includes the cartoon figure, Pepe the Frog, together with other codes that associate the Trump meme with the alt-right, the subcultural movement emanating from previous 'new right' formations such as the Tea Party and counter-jihadism (see Figure 9.4). It also attracts older strains of the extreme right online, like the Daily Stormer and the Daily Shoah, as well as anti-political correctness and anti-feminist provocateurs such as Milo Yiannopoulos, collectively known as the alt-lite.

The alt-right and the alt-lite – whether serious or ironic, actual neo-Nazis or 'Ironi-Nazis', as one analyst phrased it – are part of the participatory culture germinal to the Trump campaign, populating the meme incubators of 4Chan, 8Chan and Reddit that spilt over into Facebook, for example to God Emperor Trump, a page (with hundreds of thousands of likes) containing iconography of Trump as vainglorious leader in imperial period costume (often with Putin and other strongmen). Other themes that became part of the meme – now

Figure 9.4   The deplorables meme content, made after Hillary Clinton remark, adds Pepe the Frog and other alt-right figures to the poster of the movie *The Expendables 2*. Retweet by Donald Trump Jr.

Source: pic.twitter.com/IFD1hfC60w (account suspended).

defined as inter-textual subcultural content with multiple triggers and historical predecessors rather than as that birthed by one utterance – include Gamergate, fashwave, country ball, deus vult, cultural marxism, the manosphere as well as more hardline 'white culture' pursuits such as race realism and identitarianism, not to mention white supremicism (Nagle, 2017; Tuters, 2018). Facebook temporarily took down the God Emperor page, likely because it broke content decency guidelines, whereupon the page editor posted to the r/The_Donald subreddit, rallying for support, and demonstrating the links between the produsers of the platforms. He also wrote about Facebook's complicity in the Trump meme (a topic discussed below): 'Facebook realizes the alt right uses Facebook and memes to create a community and spread conservative ideas, and [by taking down the page] they are committing censorship' (fbGodEmperorTrump, 2016).

Followed in such online news sites as Buzzfeed, TechCrunch, ProPublica and the Daily Beast, the meme subcultures ultimately were reported on at length on the US nightly TV news (e.g., MSNBC), where Pepe the Frog in particular had his mainstream coming-out. In footage of one of Hillary's stump speeches, a heckler in the crowd responds to her usual 'basket of deplorables' comment with the cry, 'Pepe'; to the newscaster it was a moment of triumph for the alt-right, and hilarious (in a trolling sense) (Maddow, 2016). The newscaster subsequently shows muffled, undercover footage of a speech by Richard Spencer, a significant figure in the earlier extreme right circles, and argues that the movement (or subcultures that would later hit the streets as demonstrators in Charlottesville, South Carolina and elsewhere) deploys memes like the smug Pepe the Frog and rhetoric like 'free speech rally' to turn the tables on the supporters of liberal (or progressive) culture, often referred to as 'social justice warriors' or just #sjw. For the newscaster the discovery and explanation of Pepe the Frog as meme is undercover reporting (heckler in the crowd, Spencer on concealed camera), and as such gestures to memes as not only subculture but also having a hidden provenance as well as agenda in a Rushkoff sense. Pepe the Frog may seem innocuous but in fact represents and rallies the alt-right, and as such it is described as a flare or beacon, and one means by which to know that you are among kin. One yells out in the crowd 'Pepe', wears a hashtag T-shirt or otherwise shows codified knowledge of the followers by employing such terms as 'cuck', 'based', 'pede' and 'kek', a god that would bring magical chaos not so unlike that of a Trump presidency (Hine et al., 2017). Originating from the /pol/ (politically incorrect) board on 4Chan, there are collections being made of 'rare Pepes'; the Anti-Defamation League (as reported by the Southern Law Poverty Center) also has them in its Hate Symbols Database (Bergado, 2015; Morlin, 2016; see also Figure 9.5).

Figure 9.5 Pepes sourced from 4Chan's /pol/.
Source: Lynch, 2016.

Trolling culture

Pepe as heckle and (to its creator) irksome appropriation continues a tradition of memes associated with trolling culture. Like Pepe (from Matt Furie's 2005 cartoon *Boy's Club*), the seminal trolling meme, 'This is why we cannot have nice things', also has its origins in popular culture of decades ago; it references in a denigrating, class-oriented sense a household that cannot have valuable or expensive things because they will end up broken (see Figure 9.6). The meme also hints at Godwin's law, where all seemingly rational conversations online shall come to an end, because someone will reference Hitler. The conversation will always be ruined. In any such conversation it is also difficult to tell whether one is being serious, which is Poe's law, often referenced in connection with the trolling culture surrounding Gamergate as well as the Trump meme-makers. Together with starting futile, time-wasting arguments and inciting flame wars or indignant responses, 'seeming sincerity' as irony is a key characteristic of troll messaging more generally (Herring et al., 2002; Aikin, 2009). The stakes are high. Ashley Lynch, referenced above, often makes the point that there is no difference *in effect* between neo-Nazis and Ironi-Nazis, as she calls them, thereby elevating the threat posed by trolls beyond playing games (Lynch, 2016).

Figure 9.6   Arguecat. Seminal trolling meme, and title of Whitney Phillips's (2015) book on trolling.
Source: Knowyourmeme.com, 2018.

Trolling has developed together with various harassment and outing exploits (DDoS-ing, doxxing, etc.), some for the nihilistic impulse, and others for societal impact. Coleman (2011) notes how the (in)famous collective, Anonymous, fractured between those who were more interested in writing memes for memes' sake and those engaged in their weaponization. In recent years such so-called weaponized trolling has become especially prevalent in gamer culture, becoming well known across internet-related research during Gamergate, a wide-ranging conversation about misogyny, trolling, and gamers, sparked when a female game developer, striving to publish her game, *Depression Quest*, was repeatedly harassed (Foxman and Nieborg, 2016). Trolling is normally considered as a form of anti-social behaviour in online spaces especially prevalent in the 'bottom half of the web' and comment spaces, though during the meme war it became associated with a politics of division and culture warring, where for example Milo Yiannopoulos, a public figure in the alt-lite, was banned from Twitter after a tweeting harassment campaign that broke Twitter's rules (Reagle, 2015; Warzel, 2016). He also is a self-described troll and culture warrior, and his online booking agency (trollacademy.org) once described his mission (and his offered speaking services) as 'teach[ing] America how to effectively fight the culture war for the soul of western civilization' (Troll Academy, 2017).

Prior to its involvement in the new culture war (which is both historically contiguous with and at once larger than the Trump meme campaign), trolling has been described as the culture of griefing, and schadenfreude, where one takes pleasure in giving someone else grief. The term has a longer internet history, like a lurker, newbie and sockpuppet, all emerging from Usenet (Wilton, 2003). Both in myth and online, the troll resides under a bridge, as it were, waiting to pounce. The troll is engaged in identity play, deceiving others;

upon acting he displays 'sadistic glee at the distress of others' (Donath, 1999; Buckels et al., 2014: 101). Apart from the work of bored adolescents, trolling is described as an instantiation of deindividuation, where one becomes less of an individual in the sense of being able to relate and compare oneself to others or display empathy (Shachaf and Hara, 2010; Griffiths, 2014; Bishop, 2013). The psychological distance between the troll and the victims is said to be achieved through live action role-playing, or larping, as if in a fantasy costume game (Jones, 1986).

Trolling per platform

Scholars have discussed how media lend themselves to trolling, and the implications per medium (Phillips, 2015). Trolling thereby becomes a product (and also a policy critique) of platforms that enable it, often in the first instance through anonymity. Among the many cases, one *New York Times* reporter, repeatedly harassed on Twitter with anti-Semitic remarks and personalized imagery, left the medium that allows anonymity for Facebook, where trolls, he remarked, 'can't hide behind fakery to spread their hate' (Wemple, 2016). Wikipedia (where one can edit anonymously) has experience with trolling and defines it generally as a 'violation of the implicit rules of Internet social spaces' but also specifically as being continually engaged in flame wars, revert wars, point-of-view warrioring, vandalism and other acts that may be deciphered (Wikimedia Contributors, 2018). While the one-liner, 'don't feed the troll', is often repeated in some platforms as a guideline, in Wikipedia editors receive different instructions such as the strategy of 'slow reverts' (leaving inappropriate content by trolls up for a day or so) before changing it back again. This is a form of flame retardation.

Trolling is also a subfield of study within media literacy, thought to be an important part of the curriculum in secondary school and beyond (Livingstone, 2014). It is central in gender and media discussions of online safety. How to decode, decipher and interpret what is happening in media, and how to act when confronted by a troll? There is also the question of deprogramming trolls.

Meme history: Naturalization

Richard Dawkins coined the term 'meme' in 1976 (as mentioned), Douglas Rushkoff in 1994 associated the viral (and meme) with the internet, and in 2002 Daniel Dennett discussed the danger of the meme as viral. In this arc of history, memes are first biological and akin in their workings to genes, and subsequently borne by media and dangerous as viruses. To Dawkins, memes as genes spread by copying and there is a natural selection, where the catchier, the higher rate of survival. At an Oxford Union gathering in 2014 Dawkins himself explained that he put forward the meme quite innocently in service of his notion of the selfish gene, not as a significant conceptual development with a research agenda but rather to say that it is conceivable that a gene-like replication mechanism could take place in 'stuff' (like culture) other than DNA: there may be 'another kind of replicator on this planet that could be doing the same job as DNA; [there could be] a unit of cultural inheritance … that behaves like a gene in human culture' (Dawkins, 2014). Hence the meme. The idea of genetic reproduction would be like memetic copying, and Dawkins uses examples such as whistling a tune that someone hears and subsequently catches. He or she starts whistling the same tune, spreading it throughout the town. Dawkins mentions that the meme effect could take sway for a style of dress, an accent, a favourite word, a style of pottery, or for woodcarving, where he mentions how generations of work flow from master to apprentice, and more broadly through cultural transference and inheritance. (Susan Blackmore (1999), an adherent of Dawkins, mentions arches, emphasizing materialist rather than media memes.) There is a distinct possibility for natural selection in the sense that some tunes and carving styles abide, while others do not. Later in the discussion, however, Dawkins (2014) avers that in culture the 'mutation rate is too high'. In the event, if one queries Pepe the Frog in Google images one would note an exceedingly high mutation rate, so to speak, that is rather different from how genes replicate. Thus, media memes perhaps would be of another nature.

The media theorist, Douglas Rushkoff, some years later, introduces the relationship between the viral and culture as one that is principally about media. For Dawkins it is culture that bears the meme, whereas for Rushkoff it is media that is the carrier or medium of the memetic, and it does so virally. Which have a chance to survive? Those media forms that resemble media the most (the self-similar) are able to replicate and circulate; media that look like media abide. He thus speaks of the viral in terms of successful media formats such as memes.

The subtitle of his book, *Hidden Agendas in Popular Culture*, links the viral specifically to marketing, brands as well as politics, not to mention the long line of work in persuasive messaging. The messages or agendas can be hidden in memes, and go viral, as long as they are formatted in ways that allow them to look and act most like media. Here one is reminded of the image macros circulating on Facebook and hashtagged placards (#bringbackourgirls or #kony2012) on Tumblr.

The philosopher Daniel Dennett took it up further, as exemplified in his 'Dangerous Memes' TED talk in 2002 (with some 1.5 million views), when TED as a format was in its infancy. (Dennett was seated.) Because they 'infect minds', carry these powerful messages, and move people to defend them with their lives, memes can be dangerous. Dennett's memes are sets of ideas that have replaced our 'biological imperatives'. Freedom, justice, truth, communism, capitalism, Catholicism and Islam are master or grand narratives (terms he does not employ) people feel are of greater import than biological survival or replication. Here he also mentions the celibate Shakers as a case in point of those choosing religion over survival. (The secularist or atheist point of view is also germane to the context of the talk.) Memes remain cultural units, but here they are less innocuous than woodcarvings, catchy tunes and arches, and have impacts greater than wide circulation in media, like 'Gangnam Style' going viral on YouTube.

Meme history: Denaturalization

The history of the meme as an object of study is one where the meme was first brought into being as a natural phenomenon and subsequently and gradually became denaturalized, in two steps. The first is to make the distinction between the meme and the viral, which is precisely how Shifman commences when arguing that a meme is a group of items with commonalities in content, form and/or stance. They are created with awareness of one another, where there is an intentionality on the part of the user. One creates a derivative with knowledge of the other content with the intention of contributing to the content pool (or sharing with the subcultures). With the viral, contrariwise, the user is a mere host. But as a meme-maker the user has agency and the capacity to act. Her distinction is not so much between the biological and the cultural; rather the meme is to be distinguished from the viral because the former is a group effort and the latter is one specific item that circulates. It is similar to the difference between cross-media (same story) and transmedia (collection of items that together make up a story across media). As in transmedia, meme effects may even be considered along the lines of 'additive comprehension' or grasping more of the narrative as content is added (Jenkins, 2011).

The idea of virality in social media is quite specific, at least in the online marketing discourse. The viral is strategic content planting. The viral is also worthy of measure and metric-making. To Upworthy, to be viral is to have many shares per view and many clicks per share (see Figure 9.7). The meme, rather, is a content collection with contributors. The larger point, in sum, is that Shifman makes a distinction that in effect separates the meme from the biological and is no longer viral.

Figure 9.7 Virality definition by Upworthy, a company founded by Eli Pariser. *Source*: Upworthy, 2012.

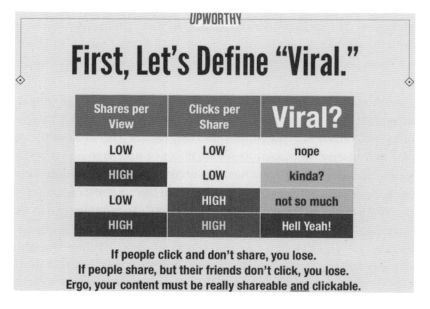

The end of the viral

The author who has taken the separation of meme from viral the farthest is Henry Jenkins (2009), with his notion of spreadable media, in a second step that denaturalizes and (perhaps overly) normalizes the meme as another product of 'participatory culture'. It is creative, cultural content production, or DIY culture (Ratto and Boller, 2014). He argues against the notion of the meme and the viral as the most important ideas behind shared content and content sharing, and instead prefers the spreadable. The meme becomes a form of spreadable media fashioned by participatory culture.

> 60% of American youth has created media and an increasing number circulates it. The story of King Arthur is one of passing through a folk process and arriving at a great literary work. Fan fiction, remixed into video, sampled into sound files, made into a meme that speaks to a political scene…. If it doesn't spread, it's dead. (Jenkins, 2014)

Like Lawrence Lessig (2004), Jenkins, describing participatory culture, argues that creativity itself comes from content sharing, derivative-making and content-additions (Jenkins et al., 2013). The users are contributing to the story, and also lending (qualitative) value to the content. It is an argument that originally spoke to copyleft, and to Creative Commons, whereby one should not lock down culture, but rather allow it to circulate in writable form. (It now could be said to speak to the Trump meme and the culture war.) Here the meme is but one content type in a much larger arena of creative content-making, or even critical making (Ratto, 2011). Rather than opening a discussion of cultural biology, and how we become infested by media content, pass it on and infect others (as Rushkoff might describe it), the point for Jenkins is that users make content on top of other content. Rather than hidden messaging, meme production is thereby subsumed under participatory culture.

In all, memes may be fundamental to contemporary digital culture, as Shifman has argued. Like Jenkins, she argues that the meme is distinctive from the viral, is a group of items that collectively and creatively are made with knowledge of one another, and share the same theme, story and even stance. They are triggered by an original piece of content, to which other content is added. Memes may become larger content ecologies with multiple catalysts. The maker space may be populated not only by popular culture contributors (fan fiction), but by another type of produser, the trolls.

Indeed, other fundamental aspects of digital culture these days could include trolling (griefing from gamer culture), once referring to disturbing and despoiling an online space for schadenfreude but more recently to produsers of participatory culture taking stances. Memes are also social content made to connect to others. As mentioned, the sociality of meme-making was exemplified in the DeploraBall, a meet-up party for trolls. Here is the reminder that the online is often a social, phatic space (of content-makers, exchanging one- or two-liners) rather than a debate or deliberative one, as previously envisaged.

Ontologizing memes

Above it is noted that memes are considered essential digital culture. It should be remarked that the essentials that have dominated digital culture have changed dramatically over time, often flipping over. Indeed, to peruse early editions of new media introductory text-books, one finds 'new media' described as essentially manipulable, networkable, dense, compressible, and earlier, digital, interactive, demassifying and virtual (Flew, 2005, 2008). If one were to ontologize memes for the study of new media these days, one might begin by noting that they are a particular type of means of expression – pithy and not so much unlike other shorter forms of expression that pack a punch such as aphorisms, slogans and bumper stickers. The meme is also a format, in which one can communicate, back and forth. It is a macro ready to be filled in that constrains the message space, focusing it. 'Contributive content' (which could be another manner of phrasing it) also may take the form of YouTube videos, such as remixes of speeches and other ditties. It also mobilizes publics or individuals. There are memes and counter-memes (Black Lives Matter vs All Lives Matter vs. Green Lives Matter – the Pepe the Frog version). 'I'm with her' and 'I'm with you' are slogans (and hashtags) formatted to mobilize publics and counter-publics in the 2016 US presidential election campaigns by Hillary Clinton and Donald Trump, respectively.

Finally, memes are new media formats that have machines. Tumblr is a platform that made memes into a part of the digital cultural machinery, or platform-specific content, where they became well known. It made more widespread placard culture, holding up signs, often with hashtags, such as #bringbackourgirls, referring to the 2014 kidnappings in Nigeria of schoolgirls, and #kony2012, the awareness-raising campaign (for a short documentary on the Ugandan war criminal) launched online. Increasingly Facebook, and Twitter (in a dif-ferent way), are considered meme machines, the one collecting them (on pages like a Tumblr) and spreading them in newsfeeds (on Facebook) and through hashtags and images (on Twitter). Memes thus become a format distinctive from rants, tweet storms, scrollytell-ings and listicles. On a webpage you may see a meme (with or without a hidden agenda to it) but you also may see 'nineteen things you should never do in Japan', a listicle compet-ing for attention alongside the image macro and the scrollytelling. Side by side in the same space, one could study these genres in parallel, and ask whether they are memetic, viral, purposive, and whether they add value as part of creative human culture.

The meme over the past forty years may have been denaturalized, and stripped gradually of its biological vitality, but it still has a special status, for it may be culturally infectious, catchy, and have pass-along value, as I discuss in a discussion of news and influence memes in Facebook. Indeed, it has been argued that users have agency, and are not merely hosts. Finally, memes are still studied as hidden messaging, manipulative and swaying the forma-tion of public opinion, however much they may address a particular subculture and filter bubble, shaping public opinion in niches, different from mass propaganda of old or grand narratives.

Implicating Facebook

Facebook, with its mass user base of 2 billion monthly users (including 200 million in the USA), is said to have played specific roles in the great meme war (and the broader culture war) by ideologically polarizing its users, abetting the preparation and circulation of fake news (especially right-wing content), and allowing a Russian influence campaign to take place on its platform (Broderick, 2016; Statistica, 2017). Where polarization is concerned, it has been implicated in the creation and amplification of filter bubbles, with the effect of drawing users increasingly towards the increased consumption of (ideologically) similar content, some of which of questionable provenance (Pariser, 2011). In its 'Blue Feed, Red Feed', the *Wall Street Journal* famously demonstrates the types of sources one would likely encounter on Facebook, given a particular political persuasion (Keegan, 2016). One's bent is gleaned from one's profile and other activity, and also offered to advertisers.

Figure 9.8   Meme (image macro) by Right Wing News. Highly ranked photo, with counter-jihadist sentiment.
Source: Right Wing News, September 2017.

Where fake news circulation is concerned, the top sites in the feeds (by fan count) are often partisan rather than mainstream news, and many could be construed as peddling in hyper-partisan claim-making such as Right Wing News, with some 3.5 million fans (see Figure 9.8). Right Wing News (which often posts memes) as well as Freedom Daily ('liked' on Facebook by Donald Trump) were part of an analysis that found, in a kind of fact-checking exercise of purported fake news, that in a week just prior to the election, a quarter of the stories qualified as such (Silverman, 2016). Freedom Daily, the most inaccurate according to the analysis, garnered the greatest engagement (sum of shares, reactions and comments), with stories such as President Obama calling for a world government during his final speech at the UN (see Figure 9.9). Facebook construes shares as the most signifi-cant engagement metric, for it lands a post on the news feed, and the greater the user engagement (e.g., liking, sharing and commenting), the higher these stories are positioned on the feed (Silverman, 2016). Accordingly, these features of the algorithms, together with their use, have pushed the most misleading stories to the top.

Figure 9.9 Freedom Daily's news
item, construed as misleading
and false in Buzzfeed analysis
(Silverman, 2016).

Source: Freedom Daily, 23 September
2016.

Thirdly, Facebook unwittingly facilitated a Russian influence campaign in the run-up to the US elections that contributed substantively to the culture war through Facebook page activism, ad buys as well as *kompromat*, or providing comprising material (e.g., the Hillary Clinton campaign emails hacked by Fancy Bear, the Russian group, and made available by WikiLeaks) (Franceschi-Bicchierai, 2016; Kramer and Higgins, 2017). Facebook hosted pages of Russian actors pretending to be American pro-Trump activists, such as Secured Borders, which, as the name indicates, propagated anti-immigration stances such as returning Mexicans resident in the USA (Kovalev, 2017) (see Figure 9.10). Facebook also released information concerning how Russian sources were the buyers of ads; the preferred means were 'dark posts', which refers to ads that are targeted to specific niche audiences but are otherwise not published on an advertiser's Facebook page. The sources, including the infamous Internet Research Agency (described as a Russian troll army), targeted segments of the US population on specific social issues (also known as wedge issues, meaning that they are divisive): 'from LGBT matters to race issues to immigration to gun rights' (Chen, 2015; Stamos, 2017). Here one question concerns whether these ads had clear provenance and ought to have been labelled as political ads, as would be required by regulation (Vaidhyanathan, 2017). Another is how engaging and spreadable they were, thereby contributing to the Trump meme and the overall culture war. Before Facebook removed (at least) six known Russian sources from its Crowdtangle platform (the Facebook pages Blacktivists, Heart of Texas, United Muslims of America, Being Patriotic, Secured Borders and LGBT United), one researcher managed to capture the page engagement data, and found they collectively had an 'organic reach' of hundreds of millions, meaning they were liked, shared, commented upon and otherwise reacted to by users on a mass scale (see Figures 9.11; see also Timberg, 2017).

Figure 9.10 Meme by Secured Borders, an activist organization with a Facebook page run by a Russian 'troll army'.
Source: Kovalev, 2017.

Advertising on Facebook and influence campaigning

At the time of the revelation of Russian ad buys on Facebook (as influence campaigning) more investigative tech reporting provides insight into the workings of Facebook advertising. When one wishes to advertise on Facebook, one types a keyword (e.g., immigration) and receives an audience size (about 34 million for that particular term in December 2016), upon which one decides to make a buy for that audience. Facebook has at least 50,000 interest or demographic categories for advertisers to search through; when choosing a category there are suggestions of adding other related ones, increasing audience size. An investigation by reporters in ProPublica's 'machine bias' series describes how Facebook advertising may be used to target particular groups in the culture war:

> [W]e logged into Facebook's automated ad system to see if 'Jew hater' was really an ad category. We found it, but discovered that the category – with only 2,274 people in it – was too small for Facebook to allow us to buy an ad pegged only to Jew haters. Facebook's automated system suggested 'Second Amendment' as an additional category that would boost our audience size to 119,000 people, presumably because its system had correlated gun enthusiasts with anti-Semites (Angwin et al., 2017).

Another analyst argues that the influence campaign not only supported a particular candidate (Trump) by using Facebook pages with wedge issue memes and targeted ad buys, but

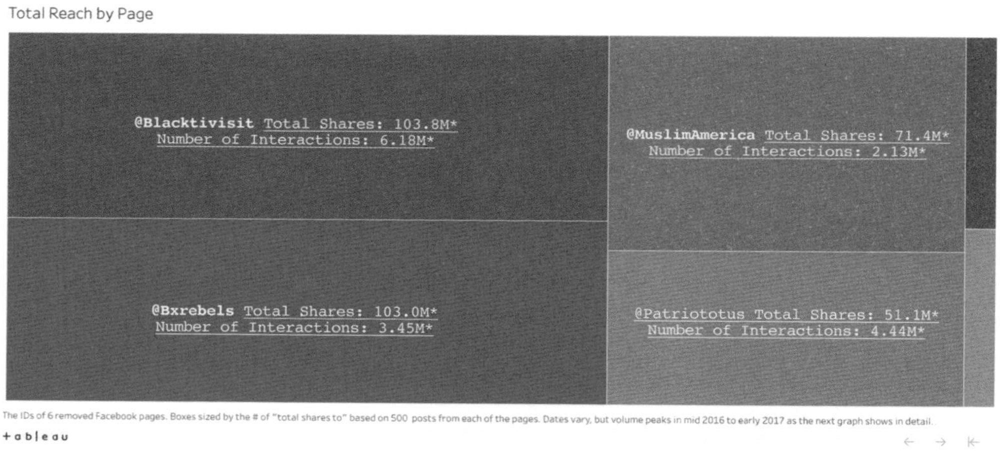

Total Reach by Page

@Blacktivisit Total Shares: 103.8M*
Number of Interactions: 6.18M*

@MuslimAmerica Total Shares: 71.4M*
Number of Interactions: 2.13M*

@Bxrebels Total Shares: 103.0M*
Number of Interactions: 3.45M*

@Patriototus Total Shares: 51.1M*
Number of Interactions: 4.44M*

The IDs of 6 removed Facebook pages. Boxes sized by the # of "total shares to" based on 500 posts from each of the pages. Dates vary, but volume peaks in mid 2016 to early 2017 as the next graph shows in detail.

+ableau

Figure 9.11   Shares and interactions scores of select Russian propaganda pages on Facebook. *Source*: Albright, 2017.

also by supplying US media with compromising materials on Hillary (the leaked emails), thereby successfully exporting Russian-style *kompromat*. Facebook (not to mention the web) allowed an opening into the US media system, once 'separate' from Russia's and its narratives, it is argued (Oates, 2017). Regarding the separation of media systems, in the 1990s 'cyberspace' once was thought to collapse them, but since the routine implementation of geolocation in the 2000s by web and platform services there are also geographical and linguistic lines drawn online. Even though it has country subdomains, Facebook, among other social media sites, arguably reglobalizes the web, or at least enables multiple languages and geographies in one space. Kompromat, or obtaining compromising materials and inserting them into the media system, allows for the sowing of doubt about an opponent. The insertion of them online likely was by Russian sources, but it is clear that Trump trolls (attending the DeploraBall) made political hay of the materials. A leaked email by Hillary's campaign manager, organizing vice presidential choices for her to consider into 'rough food groups' (African-Americans, Hispanic-Americans, women and rich people) became the material for a meme that was later produced by a troll, at least according to his online alias ('triggerbait') which manages to capture trolling motive: 'One of the meme magicians, this guy Triggerbait, turned that into a meme. Simple, just a picture of the food pyramid with little emojis of black people at the base, Hispanic people and women right above, rich people at the top' (Chace, 2017).

Conclusions: Facebook as meme machine and its study

Limor Shifman, author of an essential guide to memes in digital culture, has written, 'almost every major public event sprouts a stream of memes' (2014: 4). She also argues that memes and digital culture appear to be a 'marriage made in heaven' (2014: 5). Do memes tend to 'work' in digital culture (to paraphrase Rushkoff) better than other media (content) formats? Can Facebook be explored as meme machine, where memes work so well that they collectively provide an account of the event, as discussed by Shifman? Have they supplanted the 'iconic' image of mass media as a dominant media format of an event?

Shifman also has empirically examined memetic content (in her case, YouTube videos), and found common features: ordinary people, flawed masculinity, humour, simplicity, repetitiveness and whimsical content. On Facebook memes are often image macros, but also may be photoshopped (or Imgur'd) images with text or lines of text only that contribute to the ongoing story of an event, campaign, movement or another content cloud in the making. Memes, as 'contributive content', also may provide ongoing 'additive comprehension'. How would one describe Facebook's meme content features? How would one describe how memes fill in or add to a specific or competing comprehensions of events?

In sum, the idea of Facebook as meme machine rests on the spreadability of image macros on the platform. As has been found, memes are the most engaged-with content on particular pages, such as Breitbart News. Hyperpartisan pages such as Right Wing News regularly deploy memes, too, as a format of communication of standpoints.

Digital methods may be employed to study spreadability and the extent to which memes 'work' well in digital culture, compared (for example) to iconic images that have worked well in print and other media. Which content type is most engaged with on the platform?

One may capture 'most engaged-with' content on one or more Facebook pages manually or using Netvizz, a Facebook app, though other Facebook data capturing software may be deployed. The question concerns the extent to which memes are the most engaged-with content surrounding any event (broadly conceived), and whether, significantly, they dominate the event's interpretation online. Following Shifman's invitation, here one curates a set of event-related pages under study and identifies engaging content. The content may be a viral (single piece) or a collection (meme). One may also compare two Facebook pages for most engaged-with content and ask whether one page's content (and interpretation) has taken over the other's. It may be particularly pertinent in the case of influence campaigns, such as the ones run, Russian-style, on Facebook, where particular reasonable interpretations of events compete with other less reasonable ones.

VIDEO 7 Facebook as meme machine

PROJECT 14

Analyse the memetic content that animates a Facebook page

RESEARCH GOAL To determine whether memes dominate the Facebook content of an event. Do memes animate an event, taking over its interpretation?

Specifically, how much of the event-related content is memetic? Does it predominate, or is it in the minority? How significant are memes *vis-à-vis* other types of content? Do they tend to be the content that most animates? Apart from questions of scope, breadth and engagement, one may inquire into its relative importance in terms of the interpretation of the event.

To study an event, one may look at its dominant pages, such as 'We are all Khaled Said' for the Egyptian revolution of 2011. Alternatively, one may examine networks, movements, followers, sympathizers, supporters, and other loosely organized collections of publics in Facebook, and inquire into their engagement around an event. Among that which they like, share and comment upon, is that content primarily memetic?

The assignment is to examine one or more related Facebook pages, inquire into the extent of memetic content, together with its significance, determining whether the meme content provides a dominant interpretative version. Alternatively, one may create two sets of Facebook pages (e.g., supporters of competing candidates) and discuss the extent to which memes dominate and the type of narrative put forward.

Curate a collection of 'related pages', i.e., pages liked by other pages or pages people also like.

The procedure for curating a list of thematically related pages and determining 'most engaged-with content' is as follows:

1   Consider the theme to study before curating a list of Facebook pages related to it (e.g., right-wing groups in Europe or European migration crisis).
2   Query Google for site:facebook.com and theme. Make list of Facebook pages on a spreadsheet.
3   Query Facebook's graph search for the names found through Google (e.g., individual right-wing groups or individual migrant aid groups) or theme (e.g., European migration crisis), and place on spreadsheet.
4   Consider adding to the list 'pages liked by this page' and/or pages 'people also like'.
5   Triangulate or concatenate lists (use a threshold, e.g., top ten pages by like count).
6   Obtain Facebook page IDs for each page (e.g., https://findmyfbid.com).
7   Obtain 'most engaged-with content' scores of Facebook pages with Netvizz, Facepager or manually.
8   Optional. Undertake inter-liked page analysis and inquire into whether memes dominate one or more clusters of the network.

PROJECT 15

Investigate the role of Facebook memes during the 2016 US presidential election campaign

RESEARCH GOAL To determine whether memes dominated the 2016 US presidential campaign.

Pepe the Frog, #makeamericagreatagain (#maga), #basketofdeplorables, and #draintheswamp are just some of the signs and hashtags of a particular online network (with such actors as Breitbart News and Infowars) that created and circulated memes. The question concerns the extent to which these meme-makers became the dominant voices in the Trump campaign space online and animated it in comparison with other organized efforts (such as those by the Republican National Committee (RNC)). Here one stages a competition between the establishment and the upstart, if you will, by comparing each other's content over time, and their respective interpenetration.

One research strategy to explore the claim that the meme-makers became the dominant voice of the Trump campaign (and animated it compared to other efforts such as the RNC's) would entail the following:

1   On Facebook, compare the RNC page (facebook.com/GOP) with the Donald Trump page (facebook.com/DonaldTrump) for most engaged-with content over time, using Netvizz, Facepager or manually.

2   Array side-by-side and determine the extent to which Trump content, over the course of the campaign, began to overwrite or dominate RNC content (from his entrance in the race on 16 June 2015 to his election on 8 November 2016).

3   Determine the extent to which the Trump content is meme-like as well as oriented to the alt-right (in contrast to other orientations).

PROJECT 16

Investigate Russian influence on the 2016 US presidential election through Facebook

RESEARCH GOAL To establish the spread of memetic content from the Facebook pages of Russian influence campaigners.

The data from six Facebook pages, run by Russian influence campaigners and captured using the Crowdtangle software platform, have been made available online, via Tableau Public. The assignment is to explore the extent to which memetic content 'spread' compared to other content.

The Facebook pages (listed in order of engagement scores) – Blacktivists, Heart of Texas, United Muslims of America, Being Patriotic, Secured Borders and LGBT United – are now offline, but the text of the posts are still available in the Tableau Public database. One may strive to reconstruct whether the content that had the most engagement were memes. Note that the definition of a meme, as above, is more expansive than an image macro, and refers to additive content (Shifman) for the purposes additive comprehension (Jenkins), however much the actual format as well as its pithy presentation are of interest, too.

Data source: https://public.tableau.com/profile/d1gi#!/vizhome/FB4/TotalReachbyPage

PROJECT 17

Construct a history of a Facebook pages and its related meme use

RESEARCH GOAL To explore the rise (and fall) of meme culture within an event or issue space.

1   Choose a Facebook page, or curate a set of pages, concerning an event or a social issue.
2   From the beginning of the event or issue formation, create a timeline of the most engaged-with content.
3   Chart the meme's place in that timeline in a screencast. The 'timeline' could be a recorded downward (or sideward) scroll, or a recorded slide show where the narration concerns the content formats that emerge (and decline), and how these formats affect the story or account of what is happening.
4   Record the scrolling timeline or recorded slide show with screencast software or using webrecorder.io.

Tools

- Netvizz, https://apps.facebook.com/107036545989762/
- Webrecorder, http://webrecorder.io.

Note that the '.tsv' file (from Netvizz) that contains engagement values per post (quantities of likes, shares, etc.) stands for 'tab separated values', and may be opened in Excel or another spreadsheet software (such as Open Libre and Google Sheets).

Video tutorials

To work with Netvizz, the Facebook data extraction software, watch the 'downloading data' video (for most engaged-with content analysis) and Facebook Page Like Networks for inter-liked page analysis.

- 'Introduction to Netvizz 1.2+' (34' 24"), https://www.youtube.com/watch?v=3vkKPcN7V7Q
- 'Netvizz: Downloading Data and Producing a Macro View' (19' 39"), https://www.youtube.com/watch?v=jg9UzKcuuOE
- 'Facebook Page Like Networks with Netvizz and Gephi' (18' 41"), https://www.youtube.com/watch?v=mLOSLYNWmBA

TEN

CROSS-PLATFORM ANALYSIS
Co-linked, inter-liked and cross-hashtagged content

Overcoming API-led, single-platform studies
and the challenges of platform vernaculars

Digital methods before social media

Increasingly employed as an umbrella term for tool-based methods used in the digital humanities and e-social sciences, digital methods have as their point of departure a series of heuristics with respect to how to study online media (Rogers, 2013b). The first historicizes the web as an object of study, one that has undergone a transformation from a (virtual) site for the study of online culture specifically to a source of data about broader societal and cultural trends. Second, to extract the data one not only employs crawlers, scrapers, API logins and manual means, but also pays special attention to 'query design' and 'search as research' for creating tweet collections or sets of Facebook pages for social media analysis. To study those 'natively digital' source sets, digital methods learn from the methods of the medium (e.g., recommendation systems such as trending topics or newsfeeds). How may platform treatments of retweets and likes (for example) be repurposed for studying the unfolding of historical events (on Twitter), or the most engaged-with memes in a political campaign (on Facebook)? Digital methods, finally, consider the conditions of proof. When does it makes sense to ground the findings (e.g., about regional culinary preferences through geo-located engine queries and Instagram food photography)? When is 'online groundedness' less robust than mixed methods approaches?

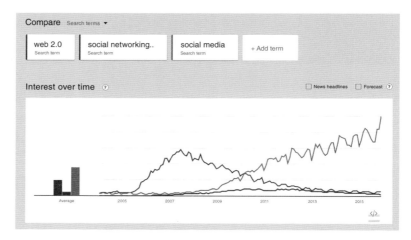

Figure 10.1 Comparison of search volume for [web 2.0], [social networking sites] and [social media], according to Google Trends, 19 November 2015.

One of the earliest digital methods maps the hyperlinking patterns between websites involved in the same social issue area so as to study the politics of association of actors from the purposively made as well as the missing links. The Issuecrawler, the software tool developed in the early 2000s for the so-called Web 1.0 era, provides a 'programmed method' for studying associations in issue networks online, or clutches of NGOs, funders, think tanks, academics as well as databases, widgets and other online objects, working on or serving a particular issue (Bruns, 2007; Rogers, 2010; Borra and Rieder, 2014). Once the links between actors have been found, one may begin to study association as well as the organization of networked publics (Latour, 2005b; Ito, 2008).

More recently, by calling for a move from 'so-called web 1.0 http or html approaches to 2.0 cross platform-based methods', Greg Elmer and Ganaele Langlois (2013: 45) argue that to study the web these days requires new methods that step past the hyperlink as the pre-eminent digital object tying it all together. They issue a much larger invitation to rethink the web more generally as an object of study, recognizing its increasing platformization, or the mass movement by web users to social media (Helmond, 2015). In the shift from an info-web (1.0) to a social web (2.0), recommendations are made through the participation of platform users rather than only by site webmasters (to use a throwback term). That is, recommendations, especially in the news feeds of platforms, follow from 'friends'' activity, such as 'liking' and 'sharing'. The content recommendations thereby distinguish themselves epistemologically from those derived from site owners or webmasters' linking to another webpage for referencing or other purposes. Following Tim O'Reilly, here the terms 'Web 1.0' and 'Web 2.0' have been used (or overused) to periodize not only the transition from the info-web to the social web, but also from the open web to the closed web or the walled gardens of platforms (O'Reilly, 2005; Dekker and Wolfsberger, 2009).

On the web's twenty-fifth anniversary in 2014, Tim Berners-Lee, who 'slowly, but steadily' has come to be known as its inventor, called for its 're-decentralization', breaking down new media concentration and near monopolies online working as walled gardens without the heretofore open spirit (Berners-Lee, 2014; Agar, 2001: 371). The web's 'appification' is analogous. Next to increased government internet censorship, mass surveillance and punitive copyright laws, Berners-Lee (2014) lists 'corporate walled gardens' or social media platforms as grave concerns related to the very future of the web and its mobile counterpart.

Digital methods after social media

Langlois and Elmer's point, however, implies that one should not only periodize and critique the dominant phases of the web, but also do the same for its methods of study. There are those digital methods that rely on hyperlinks, and thereby are in a sense still committed to an info-web, and those that have taken on board 'likes', 'shares' and other forms of valuation and currency (such as 'comments' and 'liked comments') on online platforms. Indeed, this analytical periodization is reflected in the much broader study of value online, reflected in the rise of the 'like economy' over the 'link economy' which itself supplanted the 'hit economy' (Gerlitz and Helmond, 2013). As a case in point, Google's Web Search once valued links higher than other signals (Hindman, 2008; Rieder, 2012). Through the rise of user clicks as a source adjudication measure, one could argue that Google Web Search, too, is valuing the social web over the document or semantic matching of the info-web (van Couvering, 2007). Metrification online, which starts with like counts and follower numbers and progresses towards Klout scores, similarly considers and makes rankings social. Thus, the new analytics, both Google's updated ones as well as Klout's, are oriented to a web gone social.

The notion of Web 2.0 (and the related idea of the social web) brought with it as its apparent forerunner Web 1.0 (with a more informational set of metaphors), but beyond the versioning rhetoric, Web 2.0 itself has been supplanted first by 'social network(ing) sites' and 'platforms' and later just by 'social media' (boyd and Ellison, 2007; Beer, 2008; Scholz, 2008; Allen, 2013; see Figure 10.1). The early distinction between social networking sites and social network sites, ushered in by boyd and Ellison, was normative as well as analytical. Social media users ought to have an interest in connecting with others online other than for the purposes of 'networking', which would suggest a kind of neoliberal activity of making sure that even one's social life (online) is productive. In a sense, the authors also anticipated the nuancing of social media into platform types, such as the ones for business (LinkedIn), family (Facebook) and professional doings (Twitter), though social media user practices in each remain diverse. Whether for networking or to connect with one's existing network, the analytical call made by boyd and Ellison seemed to be directed to the study of profiles and friends (together with friending).

The purposive use of the term 'platform', as Tarleton Gillespie (2010) has pointed out, could be viewed as particularly enticing for users to populate an otherwise empty database, thereby generating value for the companies. Platforms connote voice-giving infrastructure, where one can express one's viewpoints (political or otherwise), rise up, and make an online project of oneself. Polishing the profile, friending, uploading videos and photos, and liking, sharing and commenting become not only newly dominant forms of sociality, but also a kind of labour for a platform owned by others (Scholz, 2016). Cooperative, user-owned platforms would provide alternatives. Other critical calls for the analysis of Facebook have been made, certain of which have resulted in invitations to leave the platform, to liberate oneself or even to commit so-called Facebook suicide, which would allow you 'to meet your real neighbors', as suicidemachine.org's software project's slogan had it (Portwood-Stacer, 2013; Facebook Liberation Army, 2015; see Figure 10.2).

As Web 2.0 has given way to social network(ing) sites, platforms and, finally, social media, social media methods also have evolved. In particular, digital methods for social media analysis initially relied on social network analysis (the study of interlinked friends) as well as profiles and the presentation of self. For example, Netvizz, the Facebook data extraction software, originally was considered a tool to map one's own Facebook friend network (Rieder, 2013). The early digital methods work on social networking sites similarly studied friends and profiles. Dubbed 'postdemographics', this approach to studying profiles considered preferences and tastes as a starting point of analysis as opposed to gender, age, education and such (Rogers, 2009d). One study examined the interests of presidential candidates' MySpace 'friends'. Did Barack Obama's friends and John McCain's friends share the same favourite television shows, movies, heroes, and books, or was there a distinctive politics to media taste and consumption? For the most part, they did not share tastes, and thus TV shows and the other preferences could be considered to have politics of consumption (Rogers, 2013b). In the case of Netvizz friend-network mapping, as well as postdemographics, these methods could be called digital methods for social media 1.0, for they concerned themselves with profiles, friends and networking.

More recently, attention to social media in digital methods work has been directed towards events, disasters, elections and revolutions, first through the so-called 'Twitter revolution' surrounding the Iran election crisis (2009) and later the Arab Spring (2011–2012). Instead of starting with user profiles, friend networks or networking, such studies collect tweets containing one or more hashtags such as #iranelection (perhaps together with queried keywords), or focus on one particular Facebook page, such as We Are All Khaled Said (Gaffney, 2010; Lotan et al., 2011; Rieder et al., 2015).

The API and the ethics turn

Many of the more recent methods to analyse platforms rest upon and also derive from the individual APIs that Twitter, Facebook, Instagram, YouTube and others have to offer. As data are increasingly offered and delivered by polling one API, and no longer

Figure 10.2 (a) Facebook Liberation Army flyer, initiated in May 2015 by the Institute of Network Cultures and the Waag Society, Amsterdam, with franchiseable 'Facebook Farewell Party' as a principle awareness-raising format of action. (b) Facebook Liberation Army flyer, with its so-called directives, instructions and grievances.

Source: fla.waag.org.

screen-scraped or crawled from multiple websites (as in the days of the info-web), most work is a study of a page or multiple pages (and groups) on Facebook, or one concerning tweets containing one or more hashtags or keywords on Twitter. In social media analysis with digital methods, in other words, 'single-platform studies' have become the norm.

If there were a significant turning point towards single-platform studies steered by the API (rather than by scraping), it may have been the critique of a 2008 social network analysis of tastes and ties that used college students' Facebook data (Lewis et al., 2008b; Zimmer, 2010a; Marres and Weltevrede, 2013). It concerned a set of presumably anonymized users from a so-called renowned university in the northeastern United States. Not so unlike the effects of the release of AOL user search histories in 2006, its publishing prompted detective work to uncover the identities of the users, who turned out to be Harvard College students from the graduating class of 2009 (Zimmer, 2008). Michael Zimmer, both in the detective work and in the reflection upon the way forward for social media method, entitled his critique, 'But the data is already public', echoing one of the remarks of an author of the study. In giving rise to a sharper focus on ethics in web studies more generally, coinciding with a decline in scraping, Zimmer argued that in the Harvard study users' so-called contextual privacy was violated, for they not only did not give informed content, but also did not expect their publicly available data to be stored in a researcher's database and matched with their student housing data for even greater analytical scrutiny of their ties and tastes, the subject of the study (Nissenbaum, 2009). The actual data collection is described by the researchers as 'downloading' the profile and friend network data directly from Facebook, prior to the release of Facebook API 1.0 in 2010. In other words, the data were obtained or scraped in some non-API manner, albeit with permission from Facebook as well as Harvard for the project funded by the National Science Foundation and approved by the university's ethics review board. Ultimately, in the evolution of its API to version 2.0 (in 2014), Facebook would remove permissions to access friends' data such as ties and tastes (i.e., friends and likes, together with profiles), thereby making (sociometric) social network analysis like that performed in the Harvard study improbable, including even those of one's own network with all friends' privacy settings adhered to, as one did with Netvizz (Facebook, 2016). 'Internal' studies still may be performed, which Facebook data scientists also took advantage of with their 'emotional contagion' experiment (Kramer et al., 2014). The data science study (of some 700,000 users with a corpus of 3 million posts) analysed the risks associated with the Facebook news feed. Is user exposure to positive or negative posts psychologically risky (Meyer, 2015)? The study found that negative posts run the risk of 'emotional contagion'. In order to make the findings, Facebook selectively removed negative posts from users' news feeds. The ethics of the study were similarly questioned, for the users were unaware (and not informed) that their news feeds were being altered and their moods measured, however seemingly impractical and obtrusive it would be to gain such permission (Puschmann and Bozdag, 2014). Among the ethical issues raised, one concerned whether researchers can rely on the terms of service as cover for the otherwise lack of informed consent. Are users agreeing to being analysed for more than improvement of the site and services, as is usually stated?

It is worthwhile to recall from the AOL case that the 62-year-old search engine user told the *New York Times* that she never imagined that her queries would be made public, or that she would have to explain to anyone that her information-seeking about medical conditions was undertaken for her friends (Barbaro and Zeller, 2006). In joining a lawsuit brought against AOL at the Federal Trade Commission, the Electronic Frontier Foundation published highly personal and salacious query histories from unnamed individuals; another user's search engine query history was made into the mini-documentary, 'I Love Alaska: The Heartbreaking Search History of AOL User #711391', by the Dutch artists and filmmakers Lernert Engelberts and Sander Plug (2009), who were asked subsequently by the broadcasting company to seek out the identity of the woman, now intimately known. (Ultimately, they did not.) Neither the study of Harvard College's 2009 graduating class nor the emotional contagion study appears to have led to the subjects being identified and harmed through outing. It is also not straightforward to claim that informed consent would have been enough to preclude harm, given that the users may be unable to foresee the potential hazards of participation (van de Poel, 2009).

API-led hashtag and (liked) page studies

With the decline of scraping and the rise of issues surrounding human subject research in social media, the API-led studies (on events, disasters, elections, revolutions and social causes) rely increasingly on such content-organizing elements as the hashtag (for Twitter) and the (liked) page (for Facebook). Each is taken in turn, so as eventually to discuss with what limitations one may study them concurrently across platforms.

The Twitter hashtag, put forward by Chris Messina in 2007, was originally conceived as a means to set up 'channel tags', borrowing from similar practices in Internet Relay Chat (IRC). The proposal was to organize 'group-like activity' on Twitter that would be 'folksonomic', meaning user-generated rather than an editorial or taxonomic practice by the company or its syndicated partners, as in Snapchat's 'Stories' (Messina, 2007). Messina also proposed to provide a ranked list of the channel tags by activity (i.e., most active ones in the past 24 hours), showing on the interface where the activity is. This feature is similar to trending topics which Jack Dorsey, co-founder of Twitter, described a year later as 'what the world considers important in this moment' (Dorsey, 2008). With hashtags and trending topics, Twitter not only gained new functionality but also became a rather novel object of study for what could be termed both on-the-ground and 'remote event analysis'. As such, it thus distinguishes itself from Dorsey's original Twitter, created to provide what he called 'personal immediacy – seeing what's happening in my world right now' (Dorsey, 2008). Dorsey himself, in the interviews he gave for the *Los Angeles Times* after his temporary ouster as CEO, acknowledged the shift away from this more intimate Twitter, saying Twitter thrives on 'natural disasters, man-made disasters, events, conferences, presidential elections' (Sarno, 2009b). In the event, the study of Twitter as a space for ambient friend-following yielded, at least for a share of Twitter studies, to that of event-following, which is another way of distinguishing between digital methods for social media analysis 1.0 and 2.0 (Rogers, 2013a).

Not so unlike Google Trends that list the year's most sought keywords (with a geographical distribution), Twitter's initial cumulative list of the year's trending topics, published in 2009, provides a rationale for the attention granted to the study of the single hashtag for events. In the announcement made by the Twitter data scientist, Abdur Chowdhury (who incidentally was head of AOL Research when the search history data were released), one notes how serious content began to take a prominent place in a service once known primarily for its banality. In 2009 'Twitter users found the Iranian elections the most engaging topic of the year. The terms #iranelection, Iran and Tehran were all in the top 21 of Trending Topics, and #iranelection finished in a close second behind the regular weekly favourite #musicmonday' (Chowdhury, 2009). Some years later the universal list of trending topics became personalized according to whom one follows and one's geographical coordinates, however much one may change one's location and personalize trending topics exclusively by new location. In some sense the change from universal to personalized results (like Google Web Search's similar move in December 2009, which Eli Pariser (2011) relies upon for his notion the 'filter bubble') made trends more unassailable, for no longer could one call into question why a particular hashtag (like #occupywallstreet) was not trending when it perhaps should have been (Gillespie, 2012). Trending topics are in a sense now co-authored by the Twitter user, making them less compelling to study, at least as a cultural barometer. (The exception is trending topics that are location-based only.)

While the single hashtag, or more likely a combination of hashtags and keywords, remains a prominent starting point for making tweet collections to study events, disasters, elections, revolutions and social causes, as well as subcultures, movements, stock prices, celebrity awards and cities, researchers have widely expanded their repertoire for assembling them, first through techniques of capturing follower, reply and mention networks, and subsequently using the 1% random sample made available by Twitter, geotagged tweets and the Twitter ID number space in combination with time zones to identify national Twitter spheres (Crampton et al., 2013; Gerlitz and Rieder, 2013; Bruns et al., 2014).

Network analysis remains a preferred analytical technique in digital methods work, and as such it endures in the transition to method 2.0, but one somewhat novel strand of work worthy of mention here concerns Twitter content studies, discussed by way of a brief analytical tool description (Venturini, Baya Laffite et al., 2014; Kennedy and Hill, 2016).

The Twitter Capture and Analysis Tool and quanti-quali research

The Twitter Capture and Analysis Tool (TCAT) can be installed on one's own server to capture tweets for analysis (Borra and Rieder, 2014). Researchers thereby make individual tweet collections, instead of having one or more larger databases that are collaboratory-like repositories. Such archival fragmentation could not be avoided, because Twitter, once rather open, changed its terms of service upon becoming a publicly traded company, no longer allowing the sharing of tweet collections (Puschmann and Burgess, 2013). Thus, researchers must curate their own. The TCAT tool, installed on a server (with GitHub instructions), enables tweet collection-making (gathered from the streaming API) and provides a battery of network analyses: social graph by mentions, social graph by in_reply to status_id, co-hashtag, bipartite hashtag-user, bipartite hashtag-mention, bipartite hashtag-URL and bipartite hashtag-host. There are also modules, however, that direct attention towards forms of content analysis that are 'quanti-quali' and referred to as 'networked content analysis' (Niederer, 2016). By 'quanti-quali' is meant that a quantitative, winnowing analysis (not so unlike sampling or curating a collection) is performed so as to enable not only a 'computational hermeneutics' but also a thicker description (Mohr et al., 2015). Quanti-quali is preferred over the more usual quali-quanti moniker, owing to the order of the methodological steps (Venturini, Cordon and Cointet, 2014). Departing from a collection of 600,000 tweets gathered through a single hashtag, an example of such an approach is the #iranelection RT project, which sought to turn Twitter into a story-telling machine of events on the ground and in social media by ordering the top three retweeted tweets per day, and placing them in chronological order, as opposed to the reverse chronological order of Twitter (Rogers et al., 2009b). #iranelection RT relied on manual retweeting (where the user types RT in the tweet), whereas the TCAT module outputs, chronologically, 'identical tweet frequency', or narrowly defined 'native' retweets. Other forms of quanti-quali content analysis with a tweet collection are hashtag as well as URL frequency list-making to study hierarchies of concern and most referred-to content. It is the starting point for a form of content analysis that treats a hashtag as (for example) an embedded social cause or movement (#blacklivesmatter) and URLs as content for close reading. The (often fleeting) 'hashtag publics' mobilize around a social cause not only phatically (and affectively) but also with content (Bruns and Burgess, 2011, 2015; Papacharissi, 2015). Networked content analysis considers how and to what substantive ends the network filters stories, mobilizes particular media formats over others and circulates urgency (geographically), attracting bursty or sustained attention that may be measured. Techniques of studying social causes using hashtags in Twitter as well as Instagram are discussed below, including how to consider whether to downplay or embrace medium effects.

Positioning Facebook for cross-platform analysis

While, since June 2013, Facebook has included hashtags as proposed means of organizing 'public conversations', the straightforward 'cross-platform analysis' of Twitter and Facebook using the same hashtags is likely fraught. The study of Facebook 'content' relies far more on other activities, such as liking (or reacting), sharing and commenting, which is known as studying 'most engaged-with content'. For cross-platform work, the co-appearances of URLs (a.k.a. co-links) amplified perhaps by 'likes' (Facebook's as well as Twitter's hitherto favourites) may yield far more material for comparative resonance analysis.

From the beginning Facebook (unlike Friendster and MySpace before it) positioned itself as a social network site that would reflect one's own proper circle of friends and acquaint-ances, thereby challenging the idea that online friends should be considered 'friends' with quotation marks and thereby a problematic category worthy of special 'virtual' study. In a sense, such a friend designation could be interpreted as another mid-2000 marker of the end of cyberspace. Together with the demise of serendipitous (and aimless) surfing, the rise of national jurisdictions legislating (and censoring) the internet and the reassertion of local language (and local advertising) as organizing principles of browsing, Facebook also reor-dered the web, doing away with cyberspace in at least two senses. As AOL once did with its portal, Facebook sought to attract and keep users by making the web 'safe', first as a US college website offering registration only to on-campus users with an .edu email address, and then later as it expanded beyond the colleges by ID-ing users or otherwise thwarting practices of anonymization (Stutzman et al., 2013). This was an effort to prevent so-called 'fakesters', and thus distinguish itself from online platforms like MySpace, which were purportedly rife with lurkers and stalkers as well as publicized cases of sex offenders mas-querading as youngsters (boyd, 2013). Facebook's web was also clean, swept of visual clutter. In contrast to MySpace, it did not offer customization, skinning or 'pimping', so one's profile picture and the friend thumbnails would be set in a streamlined, blue interface without starry nights, unicorns and double rainbows surrounding the posts.

Facebook's safe and decluttered web brought a series of 'cyberspace' research practices down to earth as well, cleaning up or at least making seem uncouth such practices as scraping websites for data. For one, scraping social network sites for data became a (privacy and pro-prietary) concern and also a practice actively blocked by Facebook. Data would be served on Facebook's terms through its API (as mentioned above), and the politics and practices of APIs (more generally) would become objects of study (Bucher, 2013). In this case, terms-of-service-abiding, non-scraping data extraction tools would reside on Facebook itself as apps and require vetting and approval by the company. Be it through the developers' gateway or a tool on Facebook, one would log in, and the data available would respect one's own as well as the other users' privacy settings, eventually putting paid to the open-ended opportunities social network sites were thought to provide to social network research. With the API as point of access, Facebook as an object of study underwent a transition from the primacy of the profile and friends' networks (tastes and ties) to that of the page or group, and with it from the presentation of self to social causes (which I am using as a shorthand for events, disasters, elections, revolutions, and so forth). In a sense the company's acquisition, Instagram, could be said to have supplanted Facebook as the preferred object of study of the self through its ambassadorship of selfie culture, however much its initiator also would like the company to take the route of Twitter, at once debanalizing and becoming a news and event-following medium, too (Goel, 2015; Senft and Baym, 2015).

Figure 10.3   One rendition of the Facebook like button depicting a man's hand, thumbs up, with a single-button barrel cuff. Originally the like button was to be called the 'awesome' button. See Bosworth (2009). *Image source*: Wikipedia, 2015, https://upload.wikimedia.org/wikipedia/commons/1/13/Facebook_like_thumb.png.

If, with the API, Facebook analysis is steered towards the pages of social causes, 'liking' is no longer considered as frivolous, and like-based engagement analyses gain more weight (see Figure 10.3). As a case in point, liking a page with photos of brutal acts of violence requires the like button to be reappropriated, as Amnesty International (and other advocacy organizations) are wont to do by asking one not to take liking lightly (or communicate only phatically) but to see liking as an act of solidarity with a cause or support for a campaign (More recently, reaction buttons would allow more nuanced engagement, where 'angry' and 'sad' would often be combined, for example in the case of Syrian (Scuttari et al., 2017)). While it has been dismissed as a form of slacktivism (which requires little or no effort and has little or no effect), liking as a form of engagement has been studied more extensively, with scholars attributing to button clicking on Facebook distinctive forms of liking causes: '(1) socially responsible liking, (2) emotional liking, (3) informational liking, (3) social performative liking, (5) low-cost liking and 6) routine liking' (Brandtzaeg and Haugstveit, 2014: 258). In the event, low-cost liking would be especially slacktivist, though all forms of liking in the list also could be construed as a form of attention-granting with scant impact, as was once said of the 'CNN effect' when all the world's proverbial eyes are watching – but not acting (Robinson, 2002). The question of whether liking as a form of engagement substitutes for other forms, however, has been challenged, for social media activism, it is argued, aids in accumulating action and action potential (Christensen, 2011). It is also where the people are (online).

From single platform to cross-platform studies

Social movement, collective action and, more recently, 'connective action' researchers in particular have long called for multiple-platform, and multi-media, analysis (to use an older term). In an extensive study based on interviews, Sasha Costanza-Chock (2014), for one, has deemed the immigrant rights movement in the United States a form of 'transmedia organizing'. The organizing approach is a deliberate strategy, and each platform is approached and utilized separately for its own qualities and opportunities. Here one may recall the distinction made by Henry Jenkins (2006) between cross-media (the same story for all platforms) and transmedia (the story unfolds differently across platforms). Thus, social media, when used as a 'collapsed category', masks significant differences in 'affordances' (Costanza-Chock, 2014: 61–66). (I return to a similar problem concerning collapsed digital objects such as hashtags or likes across platforms with different user cultures.) If we are to follow Jenkins, as well as Costanza-Chock, a discussion of cross-platform analysis would be more aptly described as trans-platform analysis.

Researchers studying social causes on platforms have also called for 'uncollapsing' social media. Lance Bennett and Alexandra Segerberg, who coined the notion of 'connective action' as a counterpoint to collective action, argue that to understand the forces behind social change one should study those multiple platforms that allow for 'personalized public engagement', instead of choosing one platform and its API in advance of the analysis (Bennett and Segerberg, 2012). It is, in other words, an implicit critique of the single-platform studies (as collapsed social media studies) that rely solely on Twitter for one issue (e.g., Fukushima in Japan) or Facebook for another (e.g., the rise of right-wing populism), when one could have ample cause to study them across media. It is not only the siloing of APIs that prompts single-platform studies; as pointed out, the question of the comparability (and commensurability) of the 'same' objects across platforms (likes, hashtags) is at issue.

For multiple-platform (and transmedia) analysis *à la* Bennett and Segerberg it could be employed as an exploratory instrument at the outset of a study of a cause hyperlink analysis (with the Issuecrawler or Hyphe) could be employed at the outset of a study of a cause (on the web), in order to ascertain which websites (including blogs) and social media platforms are the focus of attention. In other words, hyperlink analysis could be construed as a Web 1.0 methodological starting point for multi-platform analysis. As described below, other 'interlinkings' (broadly conceived) may be studied, such as co-linked, inter-liked and cross-hashtagged content.

The 'cross' in cross-platform, and platform vernaculars

The purpose of the exercise here is to develop cross-platform methods, or digital methods for cross-platform studies, where one learns from medium methods and repurposes them for social and cultural research. It begins with a sensitivity to distinctive user cultures and subcultures, whereby hashtags and likes, digital objects used to organize and boost content (among other reasons), should not necessarily be treated as if they are employed equivalently across all platforms, even when present. For example, Instagram has inflated hashtag use compared to Twitter's, allowing up to 30 tags (and far more characters per photo caption post – 2,200 – than Twitter grants for a tweet). That is, users may copy and paste copious quantities of hashtags in Instagram posts (see Figure 10.4). Twitter (2016) recommends that one '[does not] #spam #with #hashtags. Don't over-tag a single Tweet. (Best practices recommend using no more than 2 hashtags per Tweet.)' While present, hashtags are under-utilized on Facebook.

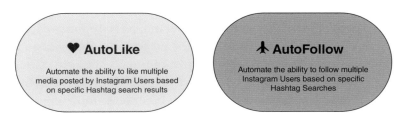

Figure 10.4   Sample of suggested tags to copy and paste as caption for an Instagram photo, in order to garner more likes and followers, as is claimed. Category of tags: 'most popular'.
Source: http://tagsforlikes.com, 25 May 2018.

Hashtags

A series of questions arises concerning the meaning of the term 'cross' in 'cross-platform analysis'. First, across which platforms are 'hashtags' worthy of study (Twitter, Instagram, Tumblr), which ones 'likes' (Facebook, Instagram, YouTube, Twitter, Pinterest), which ones 'retweets' or 'repins' (Twitter, Pinterest), which ones '@mentions' (Twitter), which ones 'links', including shortened URLs (not Instagram), and so forth (see Table 10.1)? The point is that platforms have similar affordances, such as like buttons and hashtags, but one should not necessarily collapse them by treating them equally across platforms. More specifically, if one were to perform cross-platform analysis of the same hashtags across multiple platforms, how would one build into the method the difference in vernacular hashtag use in Twitter and Instagram? Because of hashtag proliferation on Instagram, does one devalue or otherwise correct for hashtag abundance on the one platform while valuing it steadily on another? One could strive to identify cases of copy-and-pasting hashtag strings, and downplay their value, certainly if posts are being 'stuffed' with hashtags.

Hijacking

Second, certain platforms (and, perhaps more so, certain topics such as large media events on almost any platform) may indeed have user cultures and automation activity that routinely befoul posts as well as activity measures. Hashtag hijacking is a case in point, especially when one is studying an event or a social issue and encounters unrelated hashtags purposively inserted to attract attention and traffic, such as when spammers monitor trending hashtags and use them tactically to promote their wares. Hashtag junk may distract at least the researcher.

Bots

Third, while a more complex topic, bots and the activity traces they leave behind are often similarly considered worth special consideration during the analysis (Marres, 2015; see Figure 10.5). From a digital forensics point of view, bots that like and follow may have specific (network) signatures, for example they do not tend to be followed, or to be liked, meaning the bot often only has outlinks. For the purposes of this discussion, they may inflate activity in causes and such inflation may be considered artificial (though of course there are bots created for events and issues, too, and their activities are thereby purposive). Thus, manipulation as well as artificiality are additional (intriguing) complications in both single-platform and cross-platform analysis. Here bot detection becomes a substrand of study.

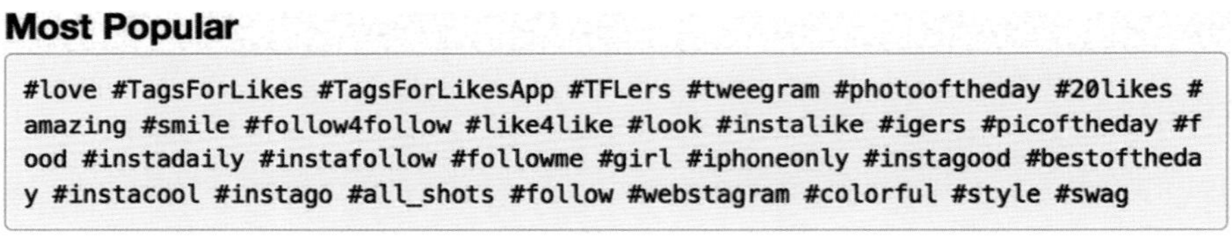

Most Popular

#love #TagsForLikes #TagsForLikesApp #TFLers #tweegram #photooftheday #20likes # amazing #smile #follow4follow #like4like #look #instalike #igers #picoftheday #f ood #instadaily #instafollow #followme #girl #iphoneonly #instagood #bestoftheda y #instacool #instago #all_shots #follow #webstagram #colorful #style #swag

Figure 10.5   Features of iFollowandLike, the Instagram bot, that takes the work out of liking and following through automation.
Source: Screenshot from iFollowandLike.com, 4 December 2015.

Device culture

Fourth, platforms have 'device cultures' that affect how one interprets the data from the API. That is, all platforms filter posts, showing particular content and letting other content slide downwards or off screen, so to speak (Eslami et al., 2015). Users thereby cannot 'like' all content equally. That which is liked may tend to be liked more often, and thus there may be power-law and long-tail effects that differ per platform. But we may not know how preferred posting affects activity measures. APIs will return like and share counts (for example) per post, but they do not let us know the extent to which all the content has been equally visible to those who would be able to like, share, comment, and so forth. And filtering styles and thus visibility effects differ per platform.

Above a series of questions has been posed concerning the limitations of comparing evaluations of content, recommended with the same type of button on different platforms, given that the platforms may have different user, spamming, bot and device cultures. How to nevertheless undertake cross-platform analysis? When studying recommendations and the content that rises, metrically, to the top of the platforms, it may be instructive to begin by examining briefly which digital objects are available in each of the platforms (as above and in Table 10.1) and subsequently inquire into how dominant devices (or in this case metrics such as Klout) handle these objects. Subsequently, it is asked, how to repurpose the metrics?

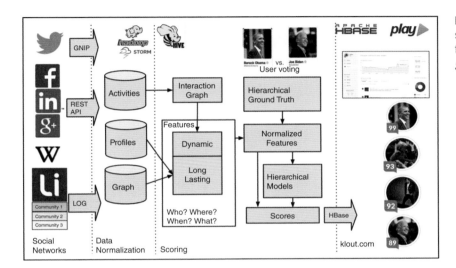

Figure 10.6 Klout scoring mechanism as flow chart.
Source: Rao et al., 2015.

Engagement (rather than influence) as cross-platform approach

Klout, as the term indicates, measures a user's 'clout', slang for influence, largely from data culled online, where the user is not only an individual but can be a magazine, institution, professional sports team, etc. Klout scores are measured on the basis of activity on Twitter, Facebook, YouTube, Google+, LinkedIn, Instagram, and Foursquare (Rao et al., 2015). It is an influence measure that takes into account particular appearance signals across the seven platforms (e.g., mentions on Twitter), and those mentions by highly influential user accounts grant more influence or clout to the user in question. It also grounds (and augments) the online appearance measures with 'offline factors' that take into account a user's 'real world influence' from Wikipedia as well as resonance in news articles (Rao et al., 2015: 3). Job titles, years of experience and similar from LinkedIn are also factored in. It is also a computationally intensive, big data undertaking and an aggregated form of cross-platform analysis.

If one were to learn from Klout for social research, one manner would be to shift the focus from power (measures of increases or decreases in one's influence) to matters of concern (increases or decreases in attention, including that from significant others) – be these to events, disasters, elections, revolutions, social causes, and so forth (see Figure 10.6). The

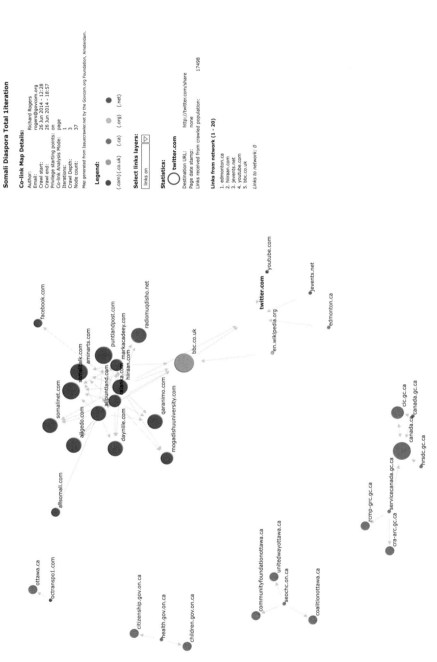

Somali Diaspora Total 1 iteration

Co-link Map Details:

Author:	Richard Rogers
Email:	rogers@govcom.org
Crawl start:	26 Jun 2014 - 12:28
Crawl end:	26 Jun 2014 - 18:57
Privilege starting points:	on
Co-link Analysis Mode:	page
Iterations:	1
Crawl Depth:	3
Node count:	37

Map generated from Issuecrawler.net by the Govcom.org Foundation, Amsterdam.

Legend:

● (.com) (.co.uk) ● (.ca) ● (.org) ● (.net)

Select links layers:

links on ▽

Statistics:

◯ **twitter.com**

Destination URL:	http://twitter.com/share
Page date stamp:	none
Links received from crawled population:	17498

Links from network (1 - 20)

1. edmonton.ca
2. hiiraan.com
3. jevents.net
4. youtube.com
5. bbc.co.uk

Links to network: 0

Figure 10.7 Issuecrawler map showing Twitter.com as significant node, albeit without showing individual, significant Twitter users.
Source: issuecrawler.net, June 2014.

shift in focus would be in keeping with how social media is often currently studied, as discussed above. That is, one could apply Klout's general procedure for counting user appearances and ask which causes are collectively significant across social media platforms, and which (key) actors, organizations and other users are linked to them, thereby granting them attention. Just as importantly, the attention granted to a cause by key actors, organizations and users may be neither undivided nor sustained. Such an observation would invite inquiries into partial attention as well as attention span, which together could begin to form a means to study engagement across social media.

When can so-called info-web methods based on the hyperlink still be applied to the study of the web and its platforms? By 'http or html approaches' to Web 1.0, I mean software like the Issuecrawler and other hyperlink analysis tools, which, generally speaking, crawl a seed list of websites, locate hyperlinks either between them or between them and beyond them, and map the interlinkings, showing unidirectional, bidirectional as well as the absence of linking between websites (see Figure 10.7). Problems arise. Through automated hyperlink analysis, the researcher may miss relationships between websites which are not captured by hyperlinks, such as sites mentioning each other in text without linking. One may also miss links between websites because servers are down, or JavaScript or other code impenetrable to crawlers is employed on one or more websites in the network. (Elmer and Langlois (2013) thus proposed to follow keywords across websites as well as platforms.)

Co-linked, inter-liked and cross-hashtagged content

As the info-web has evolved into a social web, hyperlink analysis generally captures links between pages or hosts on the web, but only links to social media platforms rather than from them. Social media is generally not crawl-able, and thus cannot be employed as seeds either at the outset or in a subsequent iteration (such as in an analysis with two degrees of separation). (Similarly, Google continually experiments with how its web search returns Twitter and Facebook content, although it still privileges web content.) These drawbacks have occasioned researchers to move in two directions at once: to develop crawlers and hyperlink analytical machines that pinpoint deep links between social media platforms and websites as well as within platforms (such as the Hyphe project mentioned in the issuecrawling chapter), and to consider new means to study relationships between platforms as well as between platforms and the web that do not rely on hyperlinks only. Joining in part with the call by Elmer and Langlois (2013), here the proposal would be to study content across the platforms (and the web): which content is co-linked, inter-liked and/or cross-hashtagged?

Table 10.1   Elements of cross-platform analysis

	Twitter	Facebook	Instagram
Query design	Hashtag(s), keyword(s), location(s), user(s)	Group(s), page(s)	Hashtag(s), location(s)
Data capture	In advance (for over-time data); on demand (for very recent data)	On demand (for over-time and recent data)	On demand (for over-time location data and recent hashtag data)
Platform user accounts (with primary actions)	user (follow)	user (friend, follow), group (join), page (like)	user (follow)
Content (media contents and digital objects)	tweet (text, photo, video, hashtag, @mention, URL, geotag)	post (text, video, photo, URL)	photo, video (hashtag, geotag)
Activities (resonance measures)	like (fav), retweet	like, reactions, comment, share	like, comment

Adapted from Rieder, 2015b.

Co-linked content is URLs (often shortened on social media) that are linked by two or more users, platform pages or webpages. Inter-liked content is content liked by users and pages across platforms. Cross-hashtagged content is content referred to by hashtags across platforms. As they are often embedded social issues (as well as events and slogans), the hashtags themselves could be considered the content.

We might ask, then, how to perform cross-platform analysis, and which platforms may be productively compared. When discussing the kind of research done with social media, even with the shift to the study of social causes over the self, it is worthwhile to point out that one may emphasize medium research, social research, or a combination of the two. For medium research, the question concerns how the platform affects the content, be it its presence or absence as well as its orderings. Additionally, specific cultures of use per platform, and (strategic) transmedia deployment, may inform the medium research, as discussed above. For social research, the question concerns the story the content tells, despite the platform effects. For a combination of medium and social research, the questions are combined: how does the platform affect the availability of content, and what stories do the content tell, given platform effects?

Conclusions: Digital methods for cross-platform analysis

In the call for methodological attention to the platformization of the web, Elmer and Langlois (2013) discuss how analyses based on the hyperlink do not embrace the analytical opportunities afforded by social media. Hyperlink analysis, and its tools such as the Issuecrawler, rely on an info-web (Web 1.0), where webmasters make recommendations by linking to another website (or non-recommendations through not making links, thereby showing lack of interest or affiliation). Focusing on links only misses the novel objects of Web 2.0, social networking sites, platforms and social media (as the social web has been called), such as the like, share and tweet. While Elmer and Langlois (2013) called for the analysis of the keyword over the hyperlink, but also perhaps over other social media objects, around the same time as their publication the API had arrived (Facebook's version 1.0 in 2010, Twitter's in 2006), and gradually became the preferred point of access to data over scraping, which the platforms actively sought to thwart. The API is of course controlled by the service in question, be it Twitter, Facebook or others, and steers research in ways more readily palpable perhaps than scraping, for the data available on the interface (that could be scraped) and through the developer's entry point may differ considerably. The ethics turn in web research, bound up with the rise of the social web and its publicly available, personal data, in turn has shaped the accessibility of certain data on the APIs such that Facebook no longer allows one to collect friends' 'tastes and ties', or likes, profile interests as well as friends. Such unavailability comes on the heels of a critique of a study of the same name that collected (or scraped, albeit with permission) Facebook profiles and friends' data from Harvard students and enriched it with their student housing information, without their knowledge. The Cambridge Analytica scandal prompted Facebook as well as other social media companies to further winnow data availability. Concomitant with the decline in the study of the self in social media analysis with digital methods (given the increasing dearth of available data through API restrictions) has been the rise in attention to events, disasters, elections, revolutions and social causes. Not only is it in evidence in Facebook research on (Arab Spring) pages (and to an extent groups), but also in Twitter (revolutions), where Jack Dorsey, its co-founder, signalled the shift in interviews in the *Los Angeles Times* in 2009, mentioning that Twitter did 'well' during events such as disasters, elections as well as conferences. Instagram, according to its founder Kevin Systrom, would like to follow the same trajectory, becoming a platform of substance and thereby for the study of events (Goel, 2015). The API, however, appears to have shaped social media studies beyond its selective availability of data. Rather, the APIs serve as silos for what I call 'single-platform studies', which are reflected in the tools discussed. Netvizz is for Facebook studies, TCAT for Twitter studies, the Instagram Scaper for Instagram, and so forth. (Researcher permissions were withdrawn in June 2016 on the Instagram Hashtag Explorer and Visual Tagnet Explorer, two Instagram API-based tools, though data may be captured through other means including scraping scripts, and manual extraction.) Unlike the Web 1.0 tools such as Issuecrawler, which find links between websites and between websites and platforms, the social web has not seen research tools developed for cross-platform analysis. Where to begin?

The purpose here is to develop techniques for multiple platform analysis that bear medium-sensitivity. Stock is taken of the objects that platforms share, whereupon cultures of use are taken into consideration. In other words, Twitter, Facebook and Instagram share the hashtag, however much on the one no more than two are recommended, on another it is rarely used and on the third it is used in overabundance. The cross-platform approaches that are ultimately described rely on hashtags for making collections of tweets (in Twitter) and posts (in Instagram), whereupon the media format (images, but also videos) common to the two is compared in the study of events. Another technique would be to compare user engagement of the same or similar content across the platforms, employing the platform-specific metrics.

PROJECT 18

Develop and execute a cross-platform analysis

RESEARCH GOAL To perform a cross-platform analysis on a chosen contemporary issue.

1   Choose a contemporary issue (revolution, disaster, election, social cause, and so forth) for cross-platform analysis. You may choose to follow an active or unfolding issue (an issue in motion, so to speak), or one from recent history (an issue from the past, where over-time analysis is desirable). Here you should consider which platforms provide over-time data (Facebook), and which do not without great effort (Twitter).

2   Design a query strategy. For social issues and causes, consider querying for a programme and an anti-programme (see the query design chapter). For example, in the 2015 US Supreme Court ruling for same-sex marriage the competing Twitter and Instagram hashtags reflected hashtag publics forming around a programme and an anti-programme, #lovewins and #jesuswins, respectively (see Figures 10.8 and 10.9). If hashtags are preferred, for an election, consider querying a set of candidates or parties, such as #Trump and #Hillary (perhaps together with additional hashtags as well as keywords). For a disaster (or tragedy), consider querying its name(s), for example, #MH17.

Figure 10.8   President Obama employs the #lovewins hashtag after US Supreme Court decision on same-sex marriage, Twitter, 26 June 2015.

3   Develop an analytical strategy. For social issues and causes, consider which programme or anti-programme is finding favour (including among whom and where). Does it have a set of networked publics and a particular geography? For an election, consider creating portrayals of the candidates via the associated issues, or comparing their relative resonance with current election polls. For a revolution, consider its momentum and durability (including the subjects that continue to matter and those that do not endure). For a disaster, consider how it is (continually) remembered or forgotten, and to what extent it has been and still is addressed

and by whom.

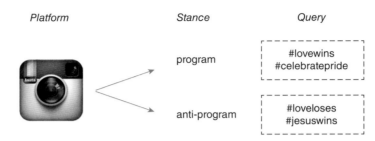

Figure 10.9   Instagram query design strategy for the study of the images (and its geographies) associated with the US Supreme Court ruling on same-sex marriage, 26 June 2015. Source: Baccarne et al., 2015.

4   Consider the configuration of use. It may be instructive for the analysis to look into how the platform is configured and set up by the initiator(s). Is it a group or a page, with or without moderation? Is it centrally organized or a collective effort? Are comments allowed? Does the user have a distinctive follower strategy?

5   Cross-platform analysis. Undertake the platform analysis, according to the query design strategy as well as the analytical strategy discussed above, across two or more platforms. For each platform consider engagement measures, such as the sum of likes (or reactions), shares, comments (Facebook), likes and retweets (Twitter) and likes and comments (Instagram). Which (media) content resonates on which platforms? Consider which content is shared across the platforms (co-linked, inter-liked and cross-hashtagged), and which is distinctive, thereby enabling both networked platform content analysis as well as medium-specific (or platform-specific) effects.

6   Discuss your findings with respect to medium research, social research or a combination of the two. Does a particular platform tend to host as well as order content in ways distinctive from other platforms? Are the accounts of the events distinctively different per platform or utterly familiar no matter the platform?

Cross-platform practicalities

In practice certain platforms lend themselves to comparison more artfully than others, given both the availability of objects such as the hashtag or geotag as well as roughly similar cultures of use. Through the vehicle of the hashtag, Twitter and Instagram (as well as Tumblr) are often the subject of cross-platform analysis. One queries the APIs with such tools as TCAT (for Twitter) as well as relatively simple Instagram and Tumblr hashtag explorers (or other means), creating collections of tweets and posts for further quantitative and qualitative analysis. Take, for example, certain significant events in the so-called migration crisis in Europe, one concerning the death of refugee children (Aylan Kurdi and his brother) and another the sexual assaults and rapes on New Year's Eve in Cologne (Geboers et al., 2016). For each case Twitter and Instagram are queried for hashtags (e.g., #aylan), whereupon tweet and post collections are made. For Twitter, one 'recipe' to sort through the contents of the collections would include the following:

a   Hashtag frequency counts ascertain the other hashtags that appear in the issue space. For the Cologne rape cases, the hashtag #einearmlänge is present, which was a trending topic referring to the remarks by the Cologne mayor that (as a solution) women should remain an 'arm's length away' from so-called strangers.

b   Mention frequency lists the usernames of those who tweet and who are mentioned so one notes which users may dominate a space.

c   Retweet frequency provides a ranked list of retweeted tweets, showing popular or significant content.

d   URL frequency is a ranked URL list showing popular or significant media (such as images and video). The most referenced media, especially images, become a focal point for a cross-platform analysis with Twitter.

For Instagram, hashtag frequency is undertaken together with image and video frequency analysis. (One is also able to query Instagram for geo-coordinates, which is not undertaken here.) Ultimately, the means of comparison are hashtag as well as image and video use, where the former suffers somewhat from hashtag stuffing in Instagram.

The question of platform effects is treated in the qualitative analysis, where in both the Aylan and the Cologne New Year's Eve cases the incidence of news photos was much greater in Twitter than in Instagram, where there were more derivatives, meaning annotated, photoshopped, cartoon-like or other DIY materials with (implied or explicit) user commentary (see Figure 10.10). Twitter thereby becomes a professional medium (with effects) and Instagram more a user-generated content medium, becoming a particular, user-led form of news-following platform to which its founder has been aspiring, as mentioned above. The Aylan case, however, appears to reduce this medium-specificity, because there is a relatively greater quantity of images that have been edited so as to come to grips with the tragedy of the drowned toddler.

Tools

Instagram

Instagram Scraper, https://wiki.digitalmethods.net/Dmi/ToolInstagramScraper

Twitter

DMI-TCAT (Twitter Capture and Analysis Tool), https://github.com/digitalmethodsinitiative/dmi-tcat/wiki

Video tutorial for TCAT, 'Overview of Analytical Modules', www.youtube.com/watch?v=ex97eoorUeo

Figure 10.10 Categorized Instagram photos concerning the Aylan Kurdi case, which symbolized the European migration crisis, 2015.

Source: Heine et al., 2016.

Figure 10.11 Categorized Twitter photos concerning the Cologne New Year's Eve sexual assault issue, which symbolized the Europe migration crisis, 2015–2016.

Source: Heine et al., 2016.

Facebook

Netvizz (Facebook Data Extraction Tool), https://apps.facebook.com/107036545989762/

Netvizz video tutorials:

'Introduction to Netvizz 1.2+', www.youtube.com/watch?v=3vkKPcN7V7Q

'Downloading Data and Producing a Macro View', www.youtube.com/watch?v=dfoYAPistYg

Tumblr

TumblrTool, https://wiki.digitalmethods.net/Dmi/ToolTumblr

Gephi-related

Gephi (The Open Graph Viz Software), https://gephi.org

'Gephi Tutorial for Working with Twitter Mention Networks', www.youtube.com/watch?v=snPR8CwPld0

'Combine and Analyse Co-Hashtag Networks (Instagram, Twitter, etc.) with Gephi', www.youtube.com/watch?v=ngqWjgZudeE

TRACKER ANALYSIS
Detection techniques for data journalism research

The study of 'telling data', or when snooping
is salutary for research

Digital forensics: Repurposing Google Analytics IDs

When an investigative journalist uncovered a covert network of Russian websites in July 2015 furnishing disinformation about Ukraine, not only did this revelation portend the state-sponsored influence campaigning prior to the 2016 US presidential elections. It also popularized a network discovery technique for data journalists and social researchers (Alexander, 2015). Which websites share the same Google Analytics ID (see Figure 11.1)? If the websites share the same ID, it follows that they are operated by the same registrant, be it an individual, organization or media group. The journalist, Lawrence Alexander, was prompted in his work by the lack of a source behind emaidan.com.ua, a website that appears to give information about the Euromaidan protests in 2013–2014 in Ukraine that ultimately forced out the pro-Russian Ukrainian president in favour of a pro-Western one. In search of the source, and 'intrigued by its anonymity', Alexander (2015) dug into the website code.

Viewing the source code of the webpage, he found a Google Analytics ID (see Figure 11.2), which he inserted into reverse look-up software that furnishes a list of other websites using the same ID. He found a (star-shaped) network of a single Google Analytics ID linked to eight other websites (in Figure 11.1 at the top), sharing a similar anti-Ukraine narrative. One of those websites also used an additional Google Analytics ID, which led to another cluster of related websites (in Figure 11.1 at the bottom to the right), also of similar political persuasion. Examining the whois records of several of these domains, he

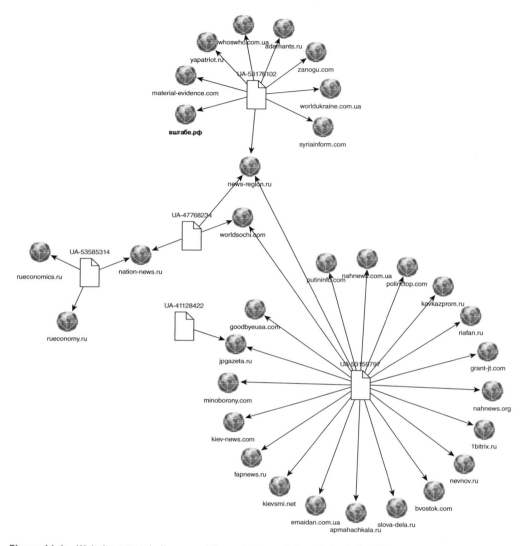

Figure 11.1   Website network discovered through (shared) Google Analytics IDs.
Source: Alexander, 2015.

found an associated email address, and subsequently a person's profile and photo on VKontakte, the Russian social networking site. The name of this person he then found on a leaked list of employees from the Internet Research Agency in St Petersburg, known as the workplace of the Russian government-sponsored 'troll army' (Chen, 2015; Toler, 2015). Drawing links between data points, Alexander put a name and face on a so-called Russian troll. He also humanized the troll somewhat, by pointing to his Pinterest hobby page, where there is posted a picture of Russian space achievements. The troll is a Cosmonaut space fan, too.

The Google Analytics ID

UA-866594-2

The prefix stands for Urchin Analytics. the web analytics service bought by Google in 2005

This autoincremented number is your Google Analytics account ID. Add or subtract one to see who signed up before and after you.

Your website profile number, incremented from1

Figure 11.2 Google Analytics ID, annotated. *Source*: Baio, 2011.

Employing so-called 'open source intelligence' tools as discovery techniques (and also digital methods in the sense of repurposing Google Analytics and reverse look-up software), Alexander and other journalists make and follow links in code, public records, databases, and leaks, piecing it all together for an account of 'who's behind' particular operations (Bazzell, 2016). 'Discovery' is an investigative or even digital forensics approach for journalistic mining and exposure, where one would identify and subsequently strive to contact the individual, organization or media group to interview them, and grant them an opportunity to account for their work. The dual accountings – the journalist's discovery and the discovered's explanation – constitute the story to be told. The purpose is to make things public, to wring out of the hairy code of websites the covert political work being undertaken, and to have this particular proof acknowledged (Latour, 2005a).

Google Analytics ID detective work has a lineage in the practice of unmasking anonymous online actors through exploits, or entry points to personally identifiable data that had not been foreseen by its creators. Mining Google Analytics IDs for network discovery and mapping is also a repurposing exercise, using the software in an unintended fashion for social research. The originator of the technique, Andy Baio, a journalist at *Wired* magazine, tells the story of an anonymous blogger posting highly offensive material, who had covered his tracks in the 'usual ways': 'hiding personal info in the domain record, using a different IP address from his other sites, and scrubbing any shared resources from his WordPress install' (Baio, 2011). Baio identified him because the blogger shared a Google Analytics ID with other websites he operated in full view. The cautionary tale about this discovery and unmasking technique concludes with Baio providing a safety guide for other anonymous bloggers *with a just cause*, such as those monitoring Mexican drug cartels, whose discovery could lead to danger or even loss of life. Here one also could test the robustness of the anonymity, and inform the journalists working undercover online of any vulnerabilities or potential exploits.

Discovering 'telling data' as research practice

Digital discovery concerns itself with code that leads to 'telling data'. On the websites represented in the Russian network diagram in Figure 11.1 there are digital objects, linked to data, concerning the websites' provenance. For example, on these websites a preponderance of Russian tracker and other objects is present: Yandex metrics, Yandex verification

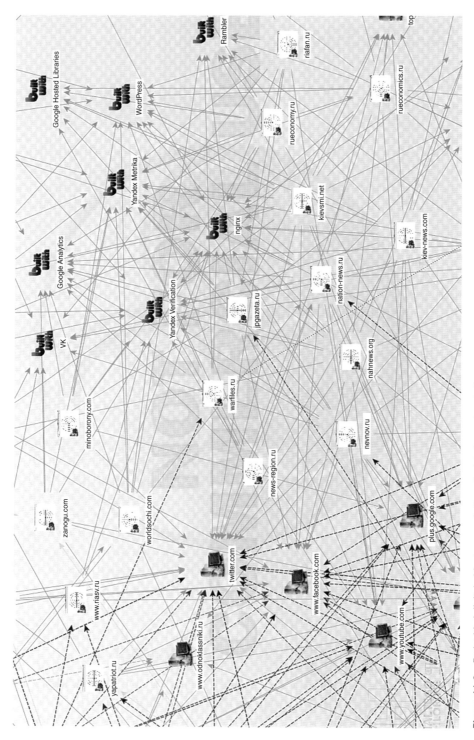

Figure 11.3 Embedded digital objects on websites, depicted as network diagram.

Source: Alexander, 2015.

software, Nginx servers as well as traces of components from Rambler and VKontakte (see Figure 10.3). Each may have registrants' information or clues that would lead one to the owner, and perhaps to his other properties, so that a more elaborate and telling network map can be fashioned, not so unlike those plotted by law enforcement agents tracing tax evasion or money laundering.

Metadata forensics

Apart from these components on the websites, there are other digital objects that are telling, including images. One may comb through the metadata of the websites' images by uploading them to software such as FotoForensics; it outputs the name of the image editing software (such as Photoshop) that created and modified each image, together with the precise version. In the event, a variety of the websites in the Russian network has images modified with the same version of the same software, indicating a single hand behind the editing.

Photo forensics also can furnish the name of the camera model and make that took a picture, together with the date and other so-called EXIF data, such as geolocation, or where the photo was taken, especially if snapped from a smartphone. Not all data is available per image. Indeed, it may have not been completely stored (as is often the case with .png files), but it also may have been purposively wiped.

Cloaking

Apart from discovery, a forensic research practice could begin to understand the extent to which the user has been cloaking himself. Active cloaking could be a strong indicator of covert activity. How many of these websites in the network have been wiped of production (image editing software traces), distribution (tracker code) and ownership traces (domain records)? Are they consistently cleansed of the same traces? Does the website owner cover up more traces than in the 'usual ways', for example, the default options of known, standard services available for making account information 'private'? Here one would notice the difference between professional covert activity and, say, a consumer who takes great care in shopping discreetly. As the web is securitized, more and more account information may be private by default or routinely made so.

One other website in the Russian network is worth mentioning, material-evidence.com, for it too was the source of investigative journalism a year earlier, as it bore signs of influence campaigning and anti-Ukrainian propaganda (Cush, 2014). It is the website that accompanies the photo exhibition 'Material Evidence – Chaos, Civil War, World Terror in the 21st Century', which has toured internationally in such cities as Berlin and New York. A journalist digging into the exhibition (and its website) found a cloaking practice in the physical media on display, too. The photos have no credits, and there are otherwise no names of photographers in sight. Moreover, on the website, the only contact information is the generic email address, truth@material-evidence.com. Here purposive anonymity lies in plain view on the exhibition walls as well as on the website interface.

The covert and the discreet

As touched upon above, it is worthwhile to put forward the distinction between studying and uncovering covert versus discreet, protective or preventive activity (Whitford and Prunckun, 2017). They all refer to having activities remain undisclosed, but each implies different motives, and draws from distinctive vocabularies – one more from intelligence, military or policing, and the others from activism, awareness-raising and consumer protection. Rather than covert activity, discretion could be behind trace-covering. Activists and some NGOs may wish to leave no footprint as a matter of standard working practice, given routine surveillance regimes and the prospects for data error, misuse, cross-use, leakage and breach. Something similar may be said for wary consumers actively opting out of behavioural targeting online. Having a 'do not track' option activated in one's browser and signing up one's telephone number on 'do not call' registries are measures designed for consumer protection against a range of practices from ads following users around the web to robocall intrusion and predatory lending. Another form of consumer media literacy would be to leave no traces so as to prevent being bullied, harassed, stalked, trolled or otherwise made to feel uncomfortable online. These behaviours may be contrasted with those in the Russian influence campaigning case (both online and in the exhibition), where the investigative journalists were not identifying acts of discretion, awareness-raising or consumer protection, but uncovering covert 'ops', and in making them public, seeking disclosure and accounting by those behind the activities.

Figure 11.4   Pepper-spraying cops of California (2011) and Istanbul (2013), memefied and rendered as multi-coloured, stencilled graffiti. Banksy-style stencil, 'Casually Butterfly Everything' posted on Reddit, *source*: GeneralLudd, 2011, and 'The more you press, the bigger it gets', *source*: Gruber, 2013.

From digital forensics to media theory critique

Studying covert and discreet activity online are of interest when seeking to make a discovery and have one's own account as well as the discovered one's made public. It also has the purpose of showing (and explaining) exposure, and the potential risks appertaining. Training courses and lists of pointers follow, as do larger studies undertaken to contribute to societal awareness-raising of exposure and media literacy.

Digital forensics, often deployed in the evidential arena and investigative reporting, may also be used for scholarly purposes. How to make use of 'forensic' camera data for social and media research? What can cookies and third-party elements make visible that challenges contemporary claims and enables research findings?

To begin with photo forensics, one may examine the data embedded in pictures found online, including significant ones made at major protest events, determine the cameras that took them, the software that edited them, and critique claims about the pervasiveness and impact of user-generated content and citizen journalism, including the distinctive narratives of events they make *vis-à-vis* those of more established news (Van Dijck, 2009; Wall, 2015). One also may make accounts of the 'editorial' (or co-authorial) practices of engines. Are crowds taking the significant pictures, and do engines and platforms serve predominantly crowd content? While social media and crowd platform users may be gate-watching (actively filtering mainstream media), might the engines be filtering out crowd content (Bruns and Highfield, 2015)?

The lady in red and other Gezi Park picture data

As a case in point, in 2013 protests took place in Gezi Park in Taksim Square, Istanbul, against a planned urban development project, which over the course of a few days became a larger anti-government protest camp, in the style of the Occupy movement. Police, dressed in riot gear and dispensing tear gas and pepper spray, sought to disperse the protesters so that the plans for the new shopping mall could proceed, and the bulldozers could resume their earth-moving. On the first day of Occupy Gezi (28 May), a woman in a red dress, carrying a tote bag, was pepper-sprayed by a policeman, and the image became both iconic and memefied, expanding on the theme (and meme) of the 'pepper spraying cop' from a Californian college protest two years earlier (Testa, 2013; see Figure 11.4). 'The lady in red' image spread in the (Western) news and online, reaching and maintaining the top of Google Image search results for ["Gezi"] for weeks. Variations on the image, both on hand-held banners and street graffiti as well as on websites and social media posts, captured the message of an increasingly authoritarian government (under the then Prime Minister, later President, Erdoğan) and bottom-up resistance (Toor, 2013). In an accompanying media crackdown, Turkish authorities chilled and fined the press (for reporting, among other things, the 3.5 million-strong protests), and delegitimized and eventually censored

Twitter for the crowdsourced stories and accounts available in the platform via such hashtags as #ayfagakalk ('stand up') (Tunc, 2013). The story of Gezi Park ('Twitter and Tear Gas') has been written through hybrid eyewitness and remote event analysis (Yaman, 2014; Tufekci, 2017), but one question remains concerning how the engines and platforms handled the content. Rather than discuss Twitter (Varnali and Gorgulu, 2015; Karkın et al., 2015), here the inquiry is about how Google Images portrayed the protest events of May to July 2013. Which images flowed to the top of the engine results for ["Gezi"], and whose were they? Do crowdsourced images dominate engine results? Whose story of the events of Gezi Park do they tell?

Crowdsourced and professional pictures in Google images

The question has to do with the crowd as source, and the engines' capacity to capture and portray it. The research weighs into accounts of the power of user-generated content and citizen journalism, and especially the relationship between top engine content and the pictures taken by the smartphone-carrying legion. It concerns the work of engines ranking and serving it over the duration of the protests. How to determine whether the significant accounts of the protests were from citizen media and 'of the crowd'? To what extent can camera data shed light on the origins of top engine content overtime?

In Google Images one may capture the most highly ranked images, day by day, using the date range in advanced settings, and note which particular images persist (and which fall from the ranks). One may also load the captured images into software that reads their (EXIF) metadata, showing the camera brands and the editing software (if any). Has it been taken with a Canon EOS and edited in Canon's Digital Photo Professional? Or has it been taken on an iPhone, and left unedited? The grade of camera and the use of editing software provide indications of professional photojournalist, citizen journalist and/or crowd contributions.

Having arrayed the top images outputted day to day on a timeline, to begin with, one could inquire into the engine's style of output. Is it raw, newsy, or more editorially curated? That is, are the top images fresh content, day to day, or do the same 'select' images abide? The analysis could draw upon Vilém Flusser's (2000) documentarist or visualist distinction of photographic work: the images may document events (stationary outlook) or visualize perspectives (distinct angle). Secondly, there is also the question of the provenance of those images that make it to the top. The highly returned images may be the product of professional journalism, prosumer citizen journalists or the crowd (however much that distinction may be productively blurred).

In the event, from the image data, it is found that the iconic image (of 'the lady in red') remains at the top as time goes by – not surpassed by the graffitied additions to its meme collection, incidentally (see Figure 11.5). Thus Google Images, unlike Facebook, would not deserve the moniker of meme machine, but rather of editorial engine. But the ascendant

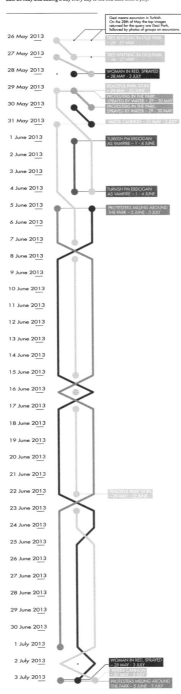

Figure 11.5 Timeline of top images on Google Image Search for the query, [Gezi], 26 May to 2 July 2013, with 'the lady in red' image moving in and out of the top slot, followed by 'the water cannon', both police reaction images (protest and violence).

Source: De Amicis et al., 2013.

content is also not of the day, in an event-following, news sense; it is rather iconic, a one-time, special visual angle. Here the image search engine appears to play the role of a magazine and of broadcast media, turning a particular image (or a small set of them) into iconic ones that then are repeated over time across the media landscape. The images also derive from the early days of the protests, and are thus also sticky, as if 'pinned' to the top, granting pride of place to the scoops, or early originality rewarded.

Camera brands and models that took the top pictures

What else is of interest from the camera data for our research purposes? With respect to the picture-takers, the top images that endure are from particular camera brands and models, such as a Canon EOS or Nikon D series (both professional grade, the latter retailing at €5000). At the top are not cheap pictures, so to speak; however, much lower down in the ranks (and by overall quantity) more economical, pocket-sized devices are well represented. Relating the price of the cameras that take the most visible pictures at crowded events to their placement in engines is a practice enabled by the availability of EXIF data as well as online price catalogues. More conventionally, one also can find, manually, the picture credits of the top three images: photographers at Reuters (lady in red) and the Associated Press (water cannon and green, peaceful sit-in) took the pictures. The overall point, though, concerns the dominance of types of coverage, and the extent to which the so-called 'flood of citizen content' and 'pop-up news ecologies' of protest camps and social media events are able to ascend, both in rankings as well as narrative (Wall and el Zahed, 2014; Aday et al. 2013). Ultimately, the more iconic but also violent protest images (police heavy-handedness covered in more established news) rise to the top and maintain their place, but the peaceful protest in the green park (an early crowd narrative) also endures, albeit lower down.

Tracker research and the politics of disclosure

When considering capturing and analysing cookies and other trackers embedded in websites, one may take on an investigative outlook as well as an academic one, examining conceptual claims, as above. To begin with, the journalistic story-driven exercises described here take advantage of the discoveries (to be made public) of trackers on certain websites: Jihadi websites that publish heinous acts and recruit extremists house Western ad-revenue software. In another discovery exercise, third-party trackers, serving data to corporate interests, reside on government websites. Extensions of such discovery work differentiate between tracker types on mainstream as well as junk or so-called fake news websites. As trackers proliferate, there is also the larger question of where on the web – a space increasingly undergoing platformization – the user is not watched. How to identify the trackerless web? Is it dying, or is there a particular vibrancy that may serve as an alternative space online?

Jihadi banner ads

With respect to the investigative outlook, a *Financial Times* headline read: 'Jihadi website with beheadings profited from Google ad platform' (Cookson, 2016). The strongly worded newspaper article pointed out that a jihadi recruitment site (with extremist content) had an AdSense account, serving clickable banners from other major Western firms (such as Citigroup, IBM and Microsoft), earning income for the website and the cause. The multinationals also received traffic and visibility in the jihadi online environment. Upon learning of the discovery and asked for an accounting of it, Google cancelled the AdSense account, and discussed how it violated its terms of service. The multinational advertisers, moreover, were unaware of their poignant placement, and also pledged vigilance going forward, lest their brands be damaged.

In the above case, one takes note of a jihadi website running an ad banner, discovers its use of Google AdSense and other off-the-shelf Western tracking and ad-generating software, and confronts Google (and the advertisers) with those facts. Such an undertaking could be less observational (the approach of noticing a single banner) and more forensic and systematic in a multiple-site inquiry; in a data journalism exercise, one could curate a longer list of jihadi websites, ranked perhaps by traffic and expertly categorized by well-known-ness and extremism. To determine whether the highest trafficked, best-known and most extreme jihadi websites are using Google Analytics (for example), one would pass the sites' code through software to extract trackers and other digital objects (see Figure 11.6). Expanding upon the above theme of jihadi use of Western software to generate revenue (and damage reputations), the outputs possibly could introduce the story of a more widespread use of Western software by nefarious actors, and even (known) negligence after earlier promises of policy change or vigilance. Financial news may couch the story in legality, corporate social responsibility and/or brand sensitivity, though allowing the use to persist presumably enables the monitoring of visitors to jihadi websites, too. One could perform a similar undertaking for porn websites, where in asking for an accounting the question of public image and taste may weigh more upon the firms than unbroken terms of service. In the event, it was found that specific trackers are behind that genre of website (such as DoublePimp), though Google, DoubleClick and Facebook Connect all make healthy appearances, too (Helmond et al., 2016).

Governmental cookies

One last example of the investigative outlook concerns institutional websites which would not be expected to place cookies and third-party trackers. What is a government website putting in my cookies folder? Indeed, over a decade ago students and I discovered that an EU website was setting a cookie, without any privacy policy listed on the site, or indication how the data would be used. When we notified the EU webmaster, we were thanked, with the addendum that they would look into the matter (and presumably stop setting a cookie

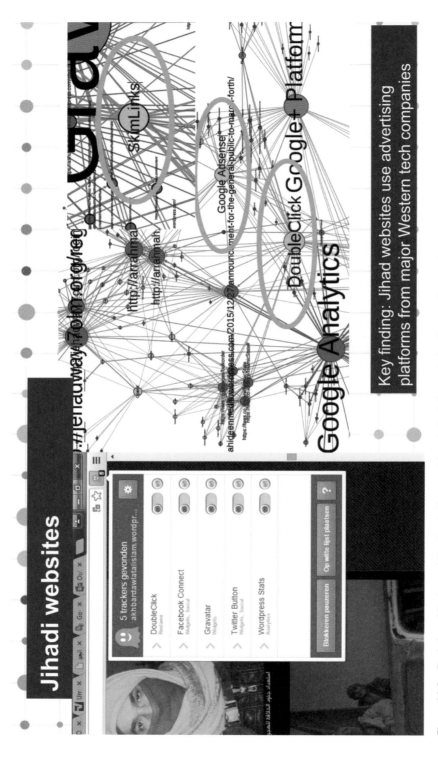

Figure 11.6 Depiction of findings of jihadi website use of Google Analytics and other Western firm trackers.

Source: Helmond et al., 2016.

until there was a policy, though we did not pursue the matter further). Some years later, cookies were no longer primarily considered aids for remembering user preferences and the lubricant for frictionless surfing (Elmer, 2003). They had become part of an ecosystem, together with so-called 'third-party elements', that enable the tracking of behaviour across the web (pulling data from users) as well as the customization of content and ads delivered (pushing content to users) (Gerlitz and Helmond, 2013).

Indeed, in the early 2010s, as the great cookie debate was under way in Europe that ultimately resulted in user consent notices popping up in one's browser, surveillance researcher Lonneke van der Velden took up the question of Dutch governmental cookie placement and especially the presence of third-party elements on government websites. She inquired not just into isolated incidents (like the single EU site we encountered without a privacy policy), but across the entire national governmental web landscape, some 1100 sites as listed in the registry (van der Velden, 2012). Over half of the active sites she found contained third-party elements, especially Google Analytics but also Facebook Connect and other ad and content delivery networks (see Figure 11.6). In all, the conclusion was that the governmental sites were not only playing their 'visible role as the main public service providers, but also contributing to the information economy by sharing (personal) data with major corporations' (van der Velden, 2014). The participation of the government in the tracking infrastructure was made visible. At the time of writing, overheid.nl and rijksoverheid.nl (the two main governmental portals) had been cleansed of trackers, but their other partner, ondernemer-splein.nl, is still running Google Analytics and related add-ins.

Tracking over time

Exposing (unknown or under-researched) entanglements of Western firms with repressive, extremist or otherwise dubious actors and milieux, and making them account for that consumption of corporate product, are examples of making things public with tracker forensics. The approach is not dissimilar, in spirit, to fingerprinting Western censorship and surveillance software in use by repressive regimes, as discussed in the internet censorship chapter. In the other example, public sector websites are serving commercial interests with site visitor data, a practice that ought to be worthy of exposure and accounting. Van der Velden (2012) kept a running account of the exposure research in the form of a 'third-party diary', making public her findings through research blog entries.

Beyond those cases deserving of investigation and public exposure, there are research use cases, too, that seek to make new claims or examine existing ones about the prevalence and implications of tracking online, over time. Has tracking increased over time, both in scope as well as in depth? Is more data being shared increasingly with third parties? One could examine the kinds of trackers and third-party elements in use on everyday news websites and compare that usage over time. What kind of trackers have been present on the *New York Times* from 1996 onwards, when the website was first archived (see Figure 11.7)?

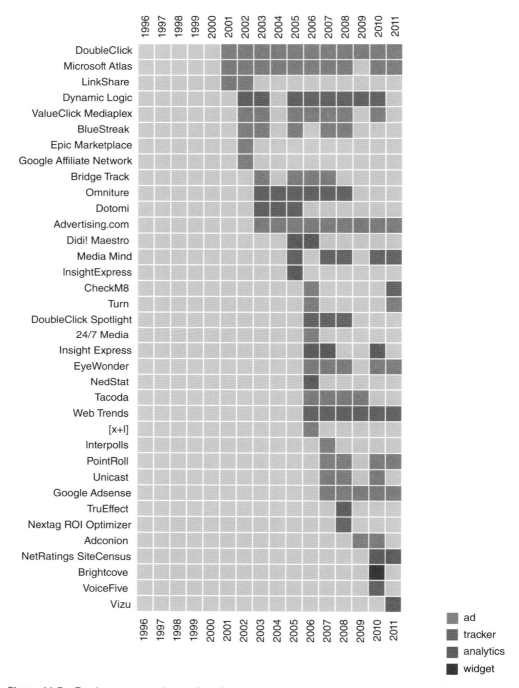

Figure 11.7 Tracker names and types found on nytimes.com over a 15-year period, indicating both a rise in overall tracking as well as specialized data sharing. Data from DMI's Tracker Tracker tool, Ghostery and the Wayback Machine of the Internet Archive.

Source: Helmond et al., 2012. See also: Helmond, 2017.

Have they become more invasive (extracting more and more data) and permissive (sharing more and more data with third parties)? Could one characterize the newspaper as comparatively more invasive and permissive than others, whether they are quality, tabloid or even 'fake news' sources? More poignantly for the newspaper perhaps, is the *New York Times* similar to a tabloid and to 'fake news' websites in its tracking? In order to undertake such work, one would extract the trackers and third-party elements from the archived versions of the newspaper at the Wayback Machine of the Internet Archive and use Ghostery's database (or another) to begin to gain an understanding of the trackers' characteristics that have been operating, and how they have changed over time. One would do the same for other newspapers.

Such techniques have been put into practice in the study of the 'techno-infrastructure' of fake news websites (Bounegru et al., 2017). It has been found that mainstream news sites are quite distinctive in their deployment of trackers compared to 'fake news' sites, where the former have engaged in more behavioural and customized tracking, and the latter in cheaper, off-the-shelf product (see Figure 11.8). In making such findings, one can begin to shed light on the user strategies of fake news websites *vis-à-vis* the mainstream. The one is for all takers, so to speak, and the other appears to be more personalized, following in the footsteps of online services that increasingly customize content (and behaviourally targeted advertising) to fit history and preferences.

The platformization of the web

A larger question concerns the rise of social media and engines, and the decline of the open (content) web through its platformization, most palpably in the spread of Facebook's login and tracking mechanisms, across website types from commercial to non-governmental and so forth (Roosendaal, 2012). Is the open web disappearing or under dire threat, as its inventor, Tim Berners-Lee, claimed on the anniversary of its twenty-fifth year? Even more broadly, along the same lines one could inquire into the normalization of tracking, where one's remit would be to seek the ever-shrinking web that remains tracker-free. Where to find websites not participating in the turn to monitoring? Are they in particular sectors, or in certain countries? Are they mainly lifeless websites, or do some still thrive without user data? Should they be curated and showcased in a critical art exhibition?

Anne Helmond (2015) has discussed platformization as the double logic of 'extending' platforms across the web and making websites 'platform-ready'. For a platformization project, it may be of interest to chart across websites the use of Facebook as login mechanism as well as the Facebook social buttons (as trackers) and map the larger ecosystem, examining at the same time that which is independent of it. One may consider a snapshot or a more longitudinal approach, checking for the creep of Facebook across the web, as Googlization scholars once spoke of Google's 'free' model, taking over such hallowed institutions as the library as well as highly competitive areas such as comparative shopping

DO MAINSTREAM MEDIA AND FAKE NEWS WEBSITES SHARE THE SAME TRACKER ECOLOGIES?

Scatterplot representing tracker usage on a series of fake news and mainstream media sites. While fake news sites and mainstream media sites share popular tracker services such as Google Adsense, DoubleClick and Google Analytics, mainstream media sites appears more mature and sophisticated in its use of trackers in terms of the number and diversity of trackers that it uses.

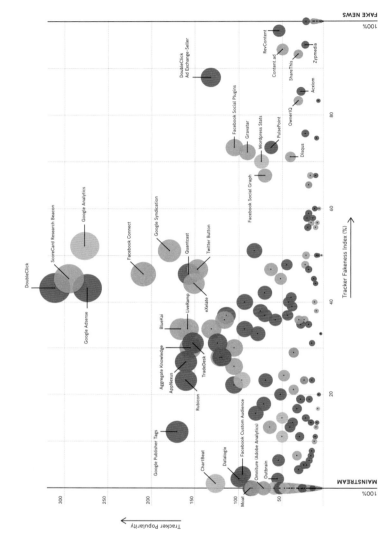

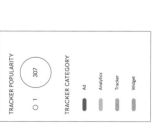

Figure 11.8 Comparison of trackers employed on mainstream and fake news websites.

Source: Bounegru et al., 2017.

websites (Vaidhyanathan, 2011). The latter ultimately resulted in an investigation by the European Union, and a multi-billion dollar fine being levied.

To study platformization one may use the Internet Archive's Wayback Machine, and capture segments of the web (or representative sets of parts of the web), using top-level and second-level domains, such as .com, .org and .gov, as well as particular countries and their second levels. Once some nominal (small-scale) commercial, non-governmental, governmental and national webs are curated, the URLs may be passed through the Tracker Tracker tool, and thus Ghostery's database, to gain a sense of the similarities and differences in tracking cultures. Thereupon the historical work may begin, collecting URLs from years past, and fetching them through Tracker Tracker. It should be noted that it appears that Ghostery's database is cumulative, and thus not unlike a virus collector's, which would maintain 'old' viruses as they likely still 'survive' on machines with outdated software. In Ghostery's case, historical trackers remain, and their signatures can be found on older webpages.

Where the network discovery stops (and starts again)

As indicated, the purpose of network discovery and other digital forensics techniques, often developed in the evidentiary arena, is to make visible and public certain sources that would rather remain undisclosed, as in the case of the Russian influence campaign mentioned at the outset. Embedded digital object mapping, such as with trackers and third-party elements, may be utilized for exposing ethically dubious commercial practices (use of Western advertising software by jihadi websites) as well as ill-advised governmental undertakings (such as the use of analytics software that passes citizen online activity to advertising companies). The outcomes of these discovery and exposure exercises are shown (where possible) to the influence campaigners, commercial companies and governmental agencies so that the disclosure accounts may be acknowledged and responded to. The dual accountings – made public – constitute the story.

It is worthwhile to point out that exposure techniques are misused, such as when trolls dox, or spread personally identifiable information to harass and otherwise victimize. With widespread use of search engines and social media platforms, exposure techniques are also becoming routinized, well beyond the work of trolls. In putting forth the notion of 'lateral surveillance' and 'peer-to-peer monitoring', Mark Andrejevich (2005) writes of the rise of online prying practices 'associated with marketing and law enforcement to gain information about friends, family members' and others. Indeed, users of social media not only keep up with friends, but also look up and look at people (Joinson, 2008). Platforms cooperate. In the early days of social networking sites, one's profile information often was available by default to friends only; over the years, concomitant with the development of granular privacy settings, more and more of one's self and content have been made public by default (boyd and Hargittai, 2010; McKeon, 2010). The settings may be well used, especially by the youthful and the skilled, but researchers nowadays still speak in terms of a 'privacy paradox', where there is great concern on the part of users but also vast self-exposure (Barnes, 2006; Kokolakis, 2017). Perhaps the more nuanced view of caring about privacy and still (over)sharing is the point made by Zeynep Tufekci (2008), who argued that youthful users are seeking to 'optimize' the relationship between 'disclosure and withdrawal'. There is also the idea that data may be public, but its (research) use would violate the 'contextual integrity' of the user, who does not consider the socializing space of the platform to be a site of surveillance or analysis (Nissenbaum, 2009; Werbin et al., 2017).

Conclusions: Salutary snooping

Rather than being driven by the routinization of sniffing around online (if you will) or by the 'open source intelligence techniques' themselves, the starting points for the media and social research projects discussed above are often claims made about phenomena related to new media (the power of the crowd and the spread of online surveillance), the under-researched (the depiction of an ongoing event in Google Images), or the seemingly novel (fake news websites). The repurposed natively digital objects, together with the extraction and reverse look-up software, become less tools for 'intelligence' work and more the jumping-off point for 'inventive methods', in that they have a 'variety and variability of [research] purposes' (Lury and Wakeford, 2012: 5). The extracted EXIF camera and editing software data may be able to shed light on 'crowd sources' of the dominant pictures in 'pop-up news ecologies' at major events. Cookies and trackers, when extracted from websites and categorized in the collection database (such as Ghostery's), can be made to show the pervasiveness and permissiveness of surveillance and personal data extraction. When the presence of trackers on archived websites is added, an over-time dimension enriches the research outcomes. Analytics and third-party elements on websites can be mapped in order to put on display commercial data infrastructures, including those of fake news websites.

Finally, mention was made above of what could be called the applied hacker ethics of writing a safety guide for anonymous bloggers doing undercover work, scanning for vulnerabilities and potential exploits and exposure, and quietly communicating the results. Thus, there are also forms of salutary snooping.

PROJECT 19

VIDEO 9 Data
journalism research

Carry out the protocols for network discovery, crowdsourced content, tracker comparison, or tracker-free web

RESEARCH GOAL To follow one of the four research protocols concerning network discovery, camera picture data, and tracker analysis, either in the contemporary moment or over time.

1   A network discovery and thematic characterization using Google Analytics and/or AdSense IDs.

    a   Curate list of 'suspect' websites, by which is meant that they are anonymous, or their source is underspecified or not well attributed.

    b   Identify Google AdSense and/or Google Analytics IDs on the websites and create a spreadsheet with the websites in one column and the IDs in two subsequent columns.

    c   Use the Table 2 Net software to transform the spreadsheet into network data.

    d   Import the network data file into Gephi (or other network analysis software) and visualize.

    e   Annotate (and narrate) the network, discussing the commonalities in its clusters and nodes.

2   An analysis of the 'crowdsourced' content of a major event, and the consideration of the extent to which the significant content (and the narrative it tells) is 'of the crowd'.

    a   Curate a set of images from an event, and look up each image's EXIF data, using EXIF data viewing software.

    b   Note the camera that has taken each picture and make a spreadsheet with at least the camera make and the picture name. You may wish to add a column for the editing software and version.

    c   Characterize cameras as professional, prosumer or consumer grade.

    d   Consider looking up retail prices of the cameras.

    e   In the analysis, demonstrate the extent to which the image content of the major event is 'user-generated' or professional. Consider hybrid categorizations such as prosumer or produser.

3   An analysis of the trackers on a set of sectoral or national websites, including on mainstream versus fake news sites:

    a   Curate a list of websites in one of two ways. Either the list is sectoral, for example, governmental, non-governmental, commercial, and educational sites. (Other categories may be added.) Or the list is national, sourced from Alexa or through another approach.

    b   Run the list through the Tracker Tracker tool. It outputs a .csv file as well as a .gexf file for Gephi.

c　Examine the results with the .csv file. Here one may be interested in the amount as well as types of trackers per URL, or URL type (e.g., governmental and non-governmental). Visualize the results using Gephi. The relationships of interest are between the URLs and the trackers, and the extent to which certain clusters emerge that indicate (sectoral and/or national) patterns.

4　An over-time analysis of the trackers on one or more (sets of) websites, with the optional consideration of whether there is a part of the web that is (relatively) tracker-free.

    a　Curate a list of websites as in 3 above.

    b　Retrieve Wayback Machine URLs (from archive.org) for each website from regular intervals in the past. Optionally, using the digital methods tool, Internet Archive Wayback Machine Network Per Year, retrieve the URLs of past versions of the websites, annually.

    c　Run the list of Wayback Machine URLs per website through the Tracker Tracker tool.

    d　Consider visualizing the number of trackers per website over time. Also of interest is the type of trackers over time per website.

Resources

- Firefox Lightbeam add-on (visualizes trackers on the websites visited).
- Ghostery add-on (provides information on the trackers on the websites visited).
- Tracker Tracker tool by the Digital Methods Initiative, https://wiki.digitalmethods.net/Dmi/ToolTrackerTracker.
- Video tutorial on the use of the Tracker Tracker tool, https://www.youtube.com/watch?v=UZpOrt-jkyno
- Google Analytics reverse look-up, https://www.tcpiputils.com/reverse-analytics/. The tool also provides reverse lookups for Google AdSense IDs.
- Gephi (the Open Graph Viz Software), https://gephi.org/.
- Table 2 Net software by Media Lab, Sciences-Po, http://tools.medialab.sciences-po.fr/table2net/

TWELVE

YOUTUBE TEARDOWN

Deconstructing YouTube recommendations, engine results and channel subscriptions

From the people's content to the vlogger's permanent update

Once considered a platform for you to 'broadcast yourself', as its original motto phrased it, over the years YouTube gradually transformed itself from an amateur content hub to a hosting site for music videos (and other more specific video genres), pirated content and, finally, for 'YouTubers' – online personalities and microcelebrities whose work is described as 'permanent updating' (Jerslev, 2018) (see Figure 12.1). These videographers are known as vloggers, or bloggers with video recorders, and are characterized as those who regularly post videos to their own YouTube 'channel'. Popular channel genres include video gamers (such as PewDiePie) who walkthrough and comment on games and gameplay, a culture that also has its 'own' platform in Twitch, and a live spectator sport called 'e-sports'. 'Unboxing' videos are also well watched (Marsh, 2016). Originating in the consumer electronics tech press (unboxing mobile phones) and extending to children's toys, the genre shares its lineage with 'product tear downs'. These are recordings of the dissembling of a gadget to lay bare its components. Tear down efforts pertain to the politics of knowledge. In reaction to undertakings by electronics companies to keep repair knowledge (and manuals) out of the public domain, iFixit, perhaps the most well-known teardown artists, routinely takes apart products and posts YouTube videos on how to fix them. They race to be the first to do so, thereby piling up views.

Figure 12.1 YouTube logo evolution, away from user-generated content, 2005 and 2018. The tagline, 'broadcast yourself', was removed in 2011.

Source: YouTube.com

YouTube is thus also a (competitive) 'how-to' site, with videos dedicated to fixing and making things, but also to preparedness. For example in 'how to pack for Rome in September', clothes and travel items are laid out and discussed. It has elements in common with 'what's in your bag?', a genre popularized by *The Verge* magazine, where the contents of one's bag are either unfurled (as in 'haul' videos showing one's purchases) or meticulously arrayed and photographed, not so unlike the haul of a drug or arms bust or even the reconstructed aftermath of a plane crash, where the retrieved parts are arrayed in a hangar. Like the video and computer game walkthroughs as well as unboxing videos, the unfurling and the arraying videos are forms of deconstruction and reconstruction.

How to begin to deconstruct YouTube? More recently, the deconstruction approach has been applied to platforms more generally, as in the 'Spotify Teardown' project (Johansson et al., 2019). Broadly speaking, deconstruction is a manner of reading or reinterpreting, whereby the text or object becomes more or different than it appears to be or functions as, through an examination of the assumptions behind it, or built into it. Platform scholars in the teardown mode have taken apart Spotify, the music streaming service, not only producing an alternative history and challenging the assumptions about its origins, controversially, as a system that originally contained pirated music files. They also 'looked inside' it by experimenting with its frontend and backend through scraping, network sniffing and starting a music label and uploading homespun songs. Each technical intervention both breaks down how the system works as well as for whom (with how much labour). For example, how do songs become 'discoverable' in the system, and what kind of toil is required for new artists to have their songs aired and liked? Notions such as 'relational labour' capture the work done to build and maintain an audience or fan base (Baym, 2018).

Figure 12.2 Youtube.com's (brief) origins as dating site, 28 April 2005.
Source: Wayback Machine of the Internet Archive, https://web.archive.org/web/20050428014715/http://www.youtube.com:80/

For YouTube, to begin a deep deconstruction, histories such as by Jean Burgess and Joshua Green aid researchers in contrasting how 'new media' were promoted to the public by the company and discussed in internal emails (2018). Owing to the copyright infringement lawsuit brought by Viacom against YouTube in 2006, the founders' early pitches to venture capitalists as well as other internal documents have been made public. In them it becomes clear that the social side of YouTube was emphasized over the content, or its contribution to 'participatory culture', or that the *new* in new media meant that one-time consumers would become producers of content in their own right (Jenkins et al., 2005). Contrariwise, YouTube was originally something of a dating site (see Figures 12.2 and 12.3); 'broadcasting yourself' was a means to attract attention from potential partners. Sharing content (or creating a content community) would build a user base, who would consume advertising and eventually might subscribe to 'premium content' (which YouTube now offers). Rather than idealistic, YouTube as a business model was a form of platform capitalism, whereby the 'intermediary' or 'aggregator' would fill its platform databases with any and all content (with the exception of violence and pornography) so long as it quickly grew ('scaled') its user base.

Figure 12.3 'Me at the zoo' by Jawed Karim. First YouTube video upload, 23 April 2005.
Source: https://en.wikipedia.org/wiki/Me_at_the_zoo

In an essay in the *Youtube Reader* (2009), Burgess and Green discuss the users and the evolving relationships between the commercial and non-commercial, and the professional and the amateur. In arguing that the commercial and non-commercial should not be seen in opposition to one another, the authors point out that YouTube grew its user base through both types of content and users. Professionally made content could be uploaded, and erstwhile amateurs or non-professionals may become professionals in their own right, raising themselves to the level of YouTubers, or influencers and micro-celebrities well known in the medium. The relationship between amateur and professional may be further complicated. Empirical studies at the time showed a shift in uploads from 'self-generated' content to videos of 'amalgamated' content that was originally professionally produced (Kruitbosch and Nack, 2008). On YouTube, remix joins prosumption, or consumer-produced content.

Studying YouTube commercialization

Commercialization, symbolically at least, may have begun with the first YouTube commercials. Actual 10-second spots were aired initially in 2007, though the commercialization of

YouTube has a variety of starting points for its study. Social Blade, the company that tracks user statistics on social media, has metrics for YouTube based on the two most basic statistics: channel subscriptions and video view counts. Those who run channels seek subscribers and views. Those with larger numbers are rewarded by YouTube with business tools that allow the tracking of copyright infringement or video reuse. When reaching the threshold of 100,000 subscribers (as of 2018), the channel owner has access to the 'content match' system, which shows whether one's own videos have been re-uploaded by another, and whether revenue has been earned by another through this 'freebooting.' (Snippets of 29 seconds or less appear to constitute 'fair use' for they are not currently 'matched'.) As mentioned, prior to this 'native' commercialization and copyright hunting toolkit, YouTube was the site of a copyright struggle over 'migrated' commercial content, when in 2006 and again in 2013, Viacom sued YouTube for copyright infringement of SpongeBob SquarePants and other video that appeared on the platform on a mass scale. The 'content matching' tools were originally developed as a result of those cases. Subsequently, these have been rolled out for premium, native users.

In reaction to YouTube's decision to provide business tools to only large channels, the YouTubers Union was founded, with demands including 'equal treatment for all' content creators (see Figure 12.4). For an understanding of how the system works (and for whom), it is instructive to read the claims and demands. There is a YouTube 'content department' that takes 'censoring' decisions. Bots do some of the dirty work. Small creators are

The Spark

Welcome to the official homepage of the YouTubers Union!

We are a community based movement that fights for the rights of YouTube Creators and Users. Our core demands are:

- *Monetize everyone - Bring back monetization for smaller channels.*
- *Disable the bots - At least verified partners have the right to speak to a real person if you plan to remove their channel.*
- *Transparent content decisions - Open up direct communication between the censors ("content department") and the Creators.*
- *Pay for the views - Stop using demonetized channels as "bait" to advertise monetized videos.*
- *Stop demonetization as a whole - If a video is in line with your rules, allow ads on an even scale.*
- *Equal treatment for all partners - Stop preferring some creators over others. No more "YouTube Preferred".*
- *Pay according to delivered value - Spread out the ad money over all YouTubers based on audience retention, not on ads next to the content.*
- *Clarify the rules - Bring out clear rules with clear examples about what is OK and what is a No-No.*

Everyone is welcome to join - we need you! No matter if you are PewDiePie or just a user.
You don't have to pay any money and you have zero obligations.
You can join us simply be becoming a member of our Facebook group and/or by joining our forum.

United We Stand!

Figure 12.4 Demands by the YouTubers Union.
Source: https://youtubersunion.org, 2018.

under-appreciated in the sense that they cannot receive ad revenue; Also, they do not have access to the content matching tools.

Another form of commercialization, more webby than platform-native, concerned YouTube video ideation. Which videos should one make in the first place? Which would attract viewers? Should they be to broadcast oneself (and one's pets), as the founders had it, and as vloggers would later perfect, achieving robust subscriber bases and annual incomes? Are there other ways to seed the platform? In the event, many videos also were made to match popular search engine queries. In what is termed 'demand media' or 'automated media', videos would be made to match popular search queries, and then optimized so that they would be found on top of the search engine query results (Roth, 2009; Napoli, 2014). A micro-industry (and so-called digital sweatshops) was born to create cheap videos for searchers, such as 'how to pack for Rome in September', as mentioned above. When coupled with advertising, videos optimized for search engines could result in high view counts and micro-payments adding up.

YouTube as user-generated, commercial and propaganda platform

Judging from its 'top videos' as well as the scholarship that has taken YouTube as its object of inquiry, the study of YouTube could be roughly characterized as beginning with the 'user-generated content' period (2005–2011), where questions revolved around both the deleterious 'cult of the amateur' and the mass consumption of poor taste and, conversely, the amateur's quasi-professionalization through the producerly use of professional grade equipment (Bird, 2011). *Time Magazine*'s 'You' as person of the year placed YouTube at the centre of the story of the rise of people's content: 'It's about the cosmic compendium of knowledge Wikipedia and the million-channel people's network YouTube and the online metropolis MySpace' (2006). These were the new halcyon days of the web, having recovered from the dot.com crash just a few years earlier, and buoyed by the coinage of the new term, web 2.0, or the web as platform. 'Participatory culture', the notion coined by Henry Jenkins and colleagues in 2005, described how software and online infrastructure (platforms) would enable creative expression and its sharing with others so it could be valued (2005). This is the rise of media creation and prod usage as an alternative to consumer culture, or mere spectatorship. Having dropped the tagline 'broadcast yourself' from its logo, from at least 2012 YouTube as a platform commercialized further, in the sense that the 'top' videos had become less amateur, as in 'Charlie bit my finger', and more polished, as in 'Gangnam Style' (see Figure 12.5). Scholarship indeed confirmed such a shift, while pointing out the great trove of amateur content (and produser material) still uploaded to the 'digital wunderkammer' (Gehl, 2009), and the complications of maintaining a dichotomy between commercial and non-commercial content, given the advent of the YouTuber, who builds subscribers, or a 'fan base', and generates advertising revenue, as discussed above.

Figure 12.5   Illustrated rendition
of 'Charlie bit my finger' video and
'Gangnam Style' by Psy.
Sources: Unknown and Wikipedia,
https://en.wikipedia.org/wiki/
File:Gangnam_Style_Official_Cover.png

In the most recent period, starting roughly around the US presidential elections of 2016 (but with deeper historical roots), YouTube has become a site known not only for its genres and rising commercialization (challenging or overtaking MTV as a premier music video site), but also for darker communities that consume YouTube content. ISIS propaganda videos, and exhortations by one of its founders, Abu Musab al-Zarqawi, have long been found on YouTube, and remained for years. Indeed, YouTube videos are a part of the media infrastructure of recruitment, which open intelligence and other researchers have documented (see Figure 12.6). While the platform made efforts to address the issue in the past, 2016 proved to be a turning point, as YouTube took steps (see also Figure 12.7). Among the initiatives, YouTube (with Facebook and Twitter) began sharing 'fingerprints' of extremist content in a joint effort to combat it. At YouTube, advertising controls, warning labels, 'trusted flaggers' as well as the 'redirect method' for users searching for extremist content (to counter-narratives) were introduced in 2017, as the platform engaged in curbing not only violence (as in the past) but also extremism (Counterextremism project, 2018).

Figure 12.6 Four stills from the YouTube video, 'You have made me cry, Oh Osama bin Laden. Paradise is yours, God willing'. Osama bin Laden speaks about the 9/11 martyrs. Posted 2 May, 2011.
Source: Memri, 2012.

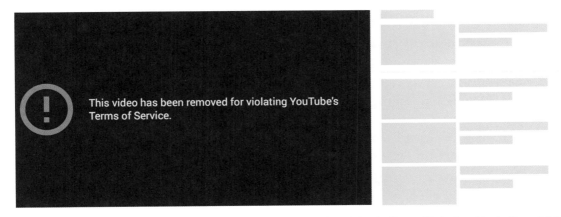

Figure 12.7 YouTube take down page (with empty related video template) for the Osama bin Laden video in Figure 12.6.
Source: https://www.YouTube.com/watch?v=8TLHtE-za1Y

YouTube deconstruction techniques

While not as extensive as the Spotify teardown methods of scraping, sniffing network data, and becoming an artist and populating the service with one's own songs, the experimental deconstruction of YouTube could entail the use of some digital methods described below, which aid gaining an insight into YouTube's workings. These approaches to studying YouTube as media (e.g., platform recommendations) are complemented by ones that employ YouTube data for insights into societal and cultural conditions. That is, one may also repurpose YouTube to undertake research into not just how but for whom the platform works (e.g., political operatives). The approaches relate to three modes of accessing YouTube: *watching* videos (and receiving recommendations for what's 'up next'), *querying* the search engine (and receiving ranked returns) and *subscribing* to channels (and receiving recommendations for 'related channels').

When watching YouTube, and studying it as a media platform, one may ask, which videos arrive next in the carousel? Do they remain on-topic, or even ever come to an end? Do they tend to be more popular (higher view counts), newer (fresher), more niched (thus privileging discoverability) or some combination?

In the second mode, querying, one can inquire not only into how the platform ranks, but the consequences of such rankings or source hierarchies per subject matter returned. Which videos have the privilege to arrive at the top for viewers of videos concerning the Syrian War? Are there news channels or perhaps micro-celebrities returned as 'authorities'? Here one captures the top results of multiple queries (on one date) or those of a single query (overtime). Are these results relatively consistent over time (Rieder et al., 2018)? Do particular sources persist at the top? Are there voices or points of view that dominate (at certain times)?

The third mode of watching (and eventually tearing down the system) is through channel subscriptions and their linkages. Channels may subscribe to other channels, thereby linking them to each other. They also may feature each other (see Figure 12.8). These linkages may be made into an object of study for relational, substantive mapping, locating pockets of thematic distinctiveness and their proximity to others. How far away are game walkthroughs from gamergate, and how far is that from the alt-right? Do they overlap?

Rather than a network approach, one also may retrieve the data from an individual channel, inquiring into the 'permanent updating' culture, and the regularity or rapidity in which one posts content. For health vloggers or others with a particular condition, one may follow the changes in vlogging patterns together with view counts as well as comments (Sanchez-Querubin et al., 2018).

With the above related techniques, larger questions and concerns may be addressed not only about the effects of recommender systems but the reach of 'algorithmic governmentality' (Rouvroy, 2013), which are platform exercises of power and order. Such a point of departure could be combined with the study of the platform as 'potential memory'

(Bowker, 2004) or 'active memory' (Chun, 2008). That is, at one time it picks out of its video storage particular items, but at another time could assemble a fresh set, refreshing memory of events and changing the order of things.

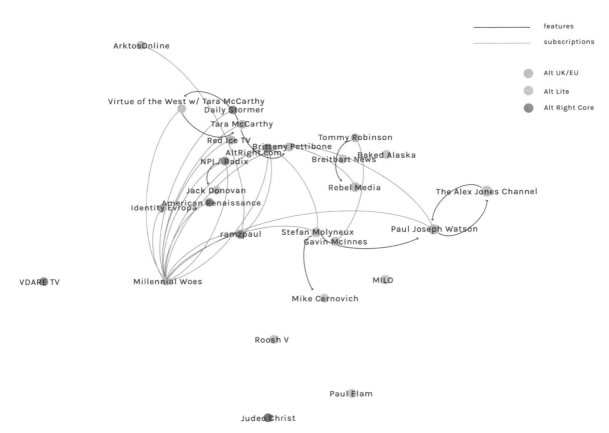

Figure 12.8   Alt-right subscription and feature networks.

Source: Alt-Right Open Intelligence Initiative, 2017.

VIDEO 10 YouTube teardown

PROJECT 20

'Tear down' YouTube's related videos, ranking culture, or channel and feature networks

RESEARCH GOAL To map and interpret YouTube's recommendations (related videos, ranked engine results and channel networks).

1   A network mapping of YouTube's related videos.

   a   Query design. First, choose one or more discrete terms. These may be unambiguous (or specified) queries, or alternatively, underspecified ones. Unambiguous queries (e.g., Barack Obama) would return video content associated with the former president, whereas underspecified queries (e.g., firearms) would return video content related to guns, but not a position on them (gun control or second amendment, in the US context).

   b   Analytical procedure. Using the YouTube data tools, video list module, query the term or terms, outputting results ranked according to 'relevance'. Optionally, consider an exercise in cultural comparison by comparing outputs of multiple Google region searches. One enters region codes for each search of the same keywords (or translated keywords).

   c   Visual output. Visualize results using the Rankflow tool.

   d   Interpretation of results. Identify and describe changes or differences in the top results either over time or at one time across queries (and/or, optionally, Google regions).

2   An analysis of YouTube's ranking culture through the study of its search engine results.

   a   Query design. First, choose one or more discrete terms. These may be unambiguous (or specified) queries, or alternatively, underspecified ones. Unambiguous queries (e.g., Barack Obama) would return video content associated with the former president, whereas underspecified queries (e.g., firearms) would return video content related to guns, but not a position on them (gun control or second amendment, in the US context).

   b   Analytical procedure. Using the YouTube data tools, video list module, query the term or terms, outputting results ranked according to 'relevance'. Optionally, consider an exercise in cultural comparison by comparing outputs of multiple Google region searches. One enters region codes for each search of the same keywords (or translated keywords).

   c   Visualize results using the Rankflow tool.

   d   Interpretation of results. Identify and describe changes or differences in the top results either over time or at one time across queries (and/or, optionally, Google regions).

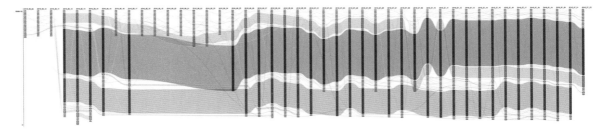

Figure 12.9 Related channels network, 2 degrees of separation, from Paul Joseph Watson, the alt-right figure and micro-celebrity. Gephi graph.
Source: Analysis by Bernhard Rieder.

3 An analysis of channel and/or feature networks on YouTube, and as an option a related channel network.

   a Query design. Choose one or more channels. These may be micro-celebrities, influencers, political operatives or actors in a social movement, among other types.

   b Analytical procedure. Using the YouTube data tools, channel network module, enter one or more channel IDs outputting results ranked according to 'relevance'.

   c Interpretation of results. Identify and describe clusters using the visual network analysis approach (discussed in the Issuecrawling chapter), where one concentrates in the first instance an analysis of the whole network (or panorama), identifying clusters and holes (the camps), together with their sizes and densities.

   d Optional. Related channel network. Using YouTube data tools, related channel network module, enter one or more channel IDs, and visualise with Gephi (see Figure 12.9).

Resources

- YouTube Data Tools, https://tools.digitalmethods.net/netvizz/youtube/
- Gephi, https://gephi.org/
- Rankflow, http://labs.polsys.net/tools/rankflow/
- Raw graphs, https://rawgraphs.io/
- Video tutorial on the use of YouTube Data Tools, https://www.youtube.com/watch?v=sbEr-TW2MzCY

THIRTEEN

SUMMARIZING DIGITAL METHODS

This chapter summarizes digital methods by first briefly resituating them in the computational or data studies turn in internet-related research. It touches on areas that have yet to be covered, such as geotagged web data. It finally extracts some of the highlights of digital methods theory and concept development together with specific contributions made to such undertakings as device studies for internet censorship research, single-site histories for web archive use, repurposing search engine usage, transforming Wikipedia into a cultural reference work, platform studies (particularly Twitter for remote event analysis and Facebook for most engaged-with content) and network discovery for data journalism research.

Computational turn

Beginning around 2007, there occurred what has been referred to retrospectively as a turn in internet-related research – be it called the computational or data studies turn. It recognized that the web is no longer studied as a space apart ('cyberspace') or bringing into being an offline society. Though the digital divide remains, there was no longer a call to study the 'virtual' separately. The web, rather, came to be studied as societal and cultural data sets. Two key articles in this regard – 'A twenty-first century science' by Duncan Watts (2007) and 'Computational social science' by David Lazer et al. (2009) – discussed how one could study societal condition and cultural preference with web data. Put differently, in heralding the 'end of the virtual', as I argued, the web became the source for more than the study of online culture only (Rogers, 2009a). As an initial example, web data were called upon to glean American regional culinary preference. Published in the *New York Times* the day before Thanksgiving in 2009, queries in the search engine of allrecipes.com allowed one to display, on a map, a geographical distribution of taste (Ericson and Cox, 2009). Queries for macaroni and cheese or corn casserole occurred with greater incidence in the old South and the corn belt, respectively, as cooks made their preparations for Thanksgiving. In a follow-up project, in 2014, a similar technique was used to display not overall culinary trends, but the most specific recipe query for a particular geographical area, showing 'unusually popular' ones per state such as pumpkin whoopie pie for New Hampshire and Maine and funeral potatoes in Utah (Upshot Staff, 2014).

Geolocation data for studying events and diasporic cultures

There are generally three geolocated data types. Apart from engine queries, there are Instagram postings where one may query the Instagram API for a city longitude/latitude as well a hashtag, as mentioned below. Another is the geolocated tweet. In a classic variation on the study of regional language differentiation, researchers explored *where* people tweeted 'pop', 'coke' and 'soda', the terms for soft drinks in the USA, and reaffirmed regional differentiation (soda in the Northeast and far Southwest, coke in the South and pop in the Midwest), albeit with some surprising term migrations.

There are two particular projects or techniques that I have referred to in the context of research using data that is linked to or derived with geolocation. Firstly, one is the study of events in a particular place using Google Images, where in the project discussed above we asked the question: could we use the engine to follow the events, visually, or will we only be studying Google? The research conducted on the Gezi Park demonstrations in Istanbul in 2013 found that Google Images, rather than an event-following media source (such as Twitter for 'remote event analysis'), is an iconic image producer. Indeed, the well-referenced (and memefied) image that emerged from the protests was that of 'the lady in red', capturing a woman being pepper-sprayed during the demonstrations. The analysis concerned the images of the demonstrations outputted by the engine across a 40-day period and found that the top ones were virtually the same, every day. Put differently, Google Images does not produce event chronology, but rather shows day after day the most iconic images in its search results. A second approach to the use of geolocation in research is with Facebook. To curate a list of Facebook pages, one may query Google, such as [site:-facebook.com Somali diaspora], and subsequently follow up with a query in Facebook's graph search, merging the two results sets. For a geolocated set of pages, one would query the local domain Googles, using the region setting in the advanced options, locating the diasporic pages in France, Belgium and other countries. We found that by using geolocated Facebook pages, one could compare diasporic activity per country, noting where they were more host land or homeland oriented, thus making findings about integration (Kok and Rogers, 2017).

In the remainder of this chapter, I would like to highlight both the concepts that have been developed together with methods and techniques for certain of the themes discussed above.

Source list-building techniques for internet censorship research

One of the great promises of a new politics that became attached to the internet in the early to mid-1990s was an online world without censorship. Part of the promise derived from the internet's architecture, and particularly two principles that appeared to have implications for civil liberties and human rights: packet switching and the end-to-end principle. Writing about civil liberties and the internet, theorists as well as cybergurus implied that packet switching meant messages would reroute around blockages and reassemble at their destination. The end-to-end principle suggested that the internet was content-neutral (a mediator or medium like the telephone) and would deliver the message no matter its politics. Some 25 years later, internet censorship, rather than thwarted by the architecture, is monitored actively in scores of countries. Traditionally, there are two key skills for conducting internet censorship monitoring and research, list-building (both URLs and keywords) and query design, where one fetches well-curated URL and/or keyword lists through the ISPs in the countries in question. Most list-building techniques are editorial, with a thematic approach. The thematic categories hark back to (and made active use of) the classic web directories of yesteryear such as Yahoo! and Dmoz. Nowadays, Wikipedia serves most readily as a supplier of lists (such as of human rights organizations), and tends to take an exhaustive, alphabetical approach (rather than one that is hierarchical, listing 'top sites' first). There are also new media techniques for building lists that are rather different from the editorial approaches. One such technique is crowdsourcing, a many eyes or hands approach, where the reporting of blocked URLs per country is solicited (via a browser add-on), as in the case of the Herdict project. Another is the 'device studies' approach, where one makes use of the outputs of multiple-country 'top source' lists, be they derived from relevance ranking (search engines), traffic (such as Alexa), advertising (per keyword per language), link sharing and content rating (such as Reddit or Balatarin in Iran), significant image boards, forums and so forth. Each has URLs deemed significant according to user clicks and recommendations, and could be harvested. It is the approach taken by greatfire.org which monitors Chinese internet censorship, and also taken in the digital methods work on demarcating and analysing the health of a national web. It was found that in Iran in 2012 much of the blogosphere was blocked, yet the content was still fresh, thereby providing an indication of active internet censorship circumvention (and diasporic interest) (Rogers et al., 2012). It also meant, at least in that particular moment in time, that censorship was not killing content.

One other technique developed in digital methods is dynamic URL sampling in which one enters an initial list of links (however well sourced) into the Issuecrawler or another crawling machine, and it finds additional URLs relevant to the seed set on the basis of hyperlink analysis, such as co-link analysis, meaning it adds to the initial list those URLs linked to by two or more seeds. For example, during the research into the blocking of Falun Gong websites in China, the curated seed list that was crawled resulted in a series of additional websites significantly related to original ones (though automated link analysis also outputs off-topic URLs that one may wish to remove). The research question concerned the effectiveness of Chinese internet censorship, and indeed it was found that China blocks all Falun Gong websites. In terms of the effectiveness as well as 'reach' of the censor, another case study concerned the United Arab Emirates, where we used proxies (servers located in the UAE) to explore blockages. Two rather different proxies (from two distinctive IP ranges) presented themselves, and as we fetched websites through them, we witnessed repeated blocking on the one, and porousness on the other. When we looked into it deeper we found out that one proxy was in Dubai, presumably used by the chosen few, while the other was the state telecom system in use by everyday people in the rest of the country. In this case, we found selective censorship, demographic disparity as well as class division, in a redefinition of a digital divide.

Finally, in a similar vain to the original internet architectural spirit of the mid-1990s, the web is still often considered a circulatory medium, in the sense that content is aggregated and repeated across multiple websites. One may ask, has content that has been blocked on one website found its way to an unblocked site, and thus still accessible? Would the circulatory medium allow for censorship circumvention in snippets? In the case of Pakistan, we found that content that has circulated from blocked websites is sparse (Rogers, 2009c). One observation made in this regard is that websites that are content repeaters would be considered spammy by Google, and therefore downgraded in search engine results in spite of their potential value as internet censorship circumvention vehicles.

The website as archived object for screencast documentaries

The website is oftentimes considered to be the seminal object of study for the web; it is what the television show is to television studies or the movie to film studies. It is seminal especially from the point of view of its contents, as traditionally the website's content is privileged over other elements such as ads when archived. If one were to undertake the study of websites from an infrastructural point of view, contrariwise, one could well inquire into how a site is designed first and foremost to be crawled and indexed (and found) rather than read. Much of its traffic remains non-human (from non-readers).

Owing to the dominance of the view of the web as content, the website's body text (together with some images and other contents) has been considered valuable and worth saving. Recall that the Library of Congress also privileged the preserving of the text of tweets rather than other fields in Twitter's archive.

Over the years a few specific approaches to saving the web or archiving websites have been developed. One insight concerning web archiving is that each approach (biographical, event-based, national and autobiographical) has implications for the kind of historical work that can be done; if websites are selected for saving with a particular approach in mind (e.g., the national), this lends itself to a history that can be written, such as official and national heritage stories (Rogers, 2018b). As a case in point, many countries do not have a national web archiving institution, leading to the loss of 'their' historical webs and resources for history-writing and other archival uses (such as copyright infringement cases).

The preservation of the historical web began otherwise. The Internet Archive sought to 'save everything' through a 'webby' crowdsourcing technique, facilitated by the Alexa tool-bar. Users would install the toolbar, and in exchange for information about the websites they visited, their surfing was logged, and the URLs, if not already archived, would be crawled by the Internet Archive. The proverbial crowd provided the URL lists and aided in the building of the archive. This was a cyberspace archive, borderless, though biased by the dominant users, their locations and the contents that interested them. The second type of web archiving tradition is called web sphere analysis, an approach for thematically related, time-bound events such as the US congressional and presidential elections. While preparing to make an elections collection, 9/11 struck, and an agile redirection of attention yielded the 9/11 collection, now housed at the Library of Congress. It also ushered in the tradition of event-based archiving of 'disasters and elections'. A third approach, alluded to above, is undertaken by national libraries, whose archival mandates imply the saving of 'the national', be it the public record and/or national heritage. An influential definition of what constitutes a relevant national website was deployed in Denmark and includes those sites from that specific top-level country domain; websites in that particular national language; websites about Danish heritage ('Danica'); and content concerning that country but published in any foreign language. National history-writing is thereby enabled. The event-based tradition also lives on in the national web archiving institutions, as in Denmark (but also elsewhere), where approximately two events per year are archived. While they can be international, in the main they are domestic. A final approach is the recent autobiographical or selfie history, where one must save one's own content, since it is behind a login, and APIs do not grant access to it, such as Facebook and Instagram accounts. Apart from combing through one's data dump, the approach that stands out is the recording of the evolution of a Facebook or Instagram account, enabled by webrecorder.io, developed by Rhizome on the occasion of the art project and feminist social media critique, 'Amalia Ulman: Excellences & Perfections'. This project is a commentary on especially young girls' use of social media, and Instagram in particular, and how (and at what cost) micro-celebrity-seeking and follower-count build-up are achieved.

Many archived web collections are underutilized (in the sense of not well cited), and much of the digital methods work has concerned itself with undarkening the archive and opening it up to scholarly use, through repurposing. One technique stands out, for it seeks to follow the research affordances of the Wayback Machine of the Internet Archive. The screencast documentary approach plays back the history of the webpage in the style of time-lapse photography. Narrated with a voiceover, the recording invites web, media or organizational (or 'digital') histories by focusing on significant interface changes. In one example of a media history, the *New York Times* as seen through the changes to its front page reverted from a distinctive new media 'cybertimes' back to a remediated newspaper over a twenty-year period. One other approach is noteworthy, for it too recognizes that the archived website is not only content but also code. By loading archived websites into a browser that has installed the Ghostery add-on, one is able to capture the trackers, cookies and third-party elements contained in the site, over time, thereby enabling the retelling of a history of tracking or surveillance of one or more websites (or website types). Has government been setting cookies in the past without privacy policies? Has tracking only increased over time, across much of the web (including the non-governmental parts)?

Google critique and repurposing

Among the terms one agrees to when querying Google is that it is executed through the Google interface's search bar, the results are not to be saved, and no derivative works are fashioned. There is a particular award-winning work of media art (Newsmap) that did precisely that for Google News, capturing and resizing the stories by amount of coverage, thereby providing a news attention economy critique and a means to study it, too. It also built in geography. Which news articles and news sections are gaining the most attention and where are they receiving that attention? In a sense it is both a study of Google News and of news, where in the case of the former it shows geographical source distributions (and Google News's blind spots), and in the latter which stories the sources are (not) covering per place. The Google Scraper and its alter ego, the Lippmannian Device, have the similar dual function of performing engine and web critique, and facilitating source analysis. The Google Scraper's original research purpose and approach is 'source distance', whereby one is studying how far from the top are particular actors or points of view, as organized and outputted by Google. How close to the top of the synthetic biology space is Craig Venter (described at the time of the query as desiring to patent life), or how far towards the top of the climate change space are the sceptics? In other words, one is asking the extent to which Google gives prominent placement (and voice) to particular actors over others and grants them the privilege to provide 'information' that is more likely to be viewed. These are inquiries into engine epistemologies, together with their consequences. The source distance approach also could be said to apply to the web, if the web is understood for the moment as search-based, where Google is the dominant engine. Thus, one would be studying medium or web epistemology, too. One would go about answering questions of web epistemology rather differently if one were to assume the medium is more 'social' than search-based, is organized predominantly by languages, or has geographical borders and vernaculars, like ru.net.

In its other guise, rather than critiquing the engine and the web, the Google Scraper repurposes Google for 'societal search'. In this version, referred to as the Lippmannian Device to emphasize the other, distinctive use case, it seeks to provide a 'coarse means' – as Lippmann (1927) phrased it – to show bias or partisanship. Here one seeks to take advantage of Google's workings, including its proclivity to output fresh, user-clicked sites (making it presentist and *ad populum*) as well as its capacity to index individual sites. Here the use cases for individual site study include concern or distributions thereof for particular issues. Of all of Greenpeace's campaigns, which ones are returned with what frequency by a

Google site search? One may expand the number of organizations of the site search to a curated list of human rights organizations, for example. Here the question concerns the current agenda. To gain a sense of it, one curates a list of human rights organizations (employing a list-building technique), visits each of the sites on the list, and extracts the issues on each webpage. At this point, one has a list of URLs and a list of keywords. One queries all the URLs for all the keywords, outputting an issue cloud, where each issue is resized according to how many human rights organizations list it as an issue. 'Estimated Google results' per issue provides a second indication of which issues are high on the agenda, and which are lower, where agenda in this case is a Google-assisted website collection search for human rights issue keywords.

Wikipedia as networked content for cross-cultural analysis

Wikipedia is oftentimes studied as a techno-knowledge project, placing it in a lineage with P. Otlet's Mundaneum, H.G. Wells's World Brain, V. Bush's Memex, T. Nelson's Xanadu, M. Hart's Project Gutenberg and even T. Berners-Lee's World Wide Web, among others. As an encyclopedia, it has been compared to *Encyclopaedia Britannica* and others for its accuracy, initially faring well in the facticity checks, and also in the contrasts; Wikipedia has breadth and timeliness. It is also studied as a piece of wiki software for (remote) collaboration; wiki technology has been overshadowed by Google Wave, which later become Google Docs. In Google's software, multiple people can edit and save the same document simultaneously, whereas even though a wiki enables multiple authorship, simultaneous editing results in edit conflicts. Wikipedia has also been considered a project of anonymous or collaborative authorship by 'Wikipedians', and one that reopens the debate surrounding the death of the author. With the rise of the author came a book that (with the help of critics) concentrates more on the author than on the contents (Barthes, 1967). Wikipedia also has been studied as an image burnishing or publicity management tool; many Wikipedia articles are authored by interested parties, prompting a debate about the effects of such partial editing on the quality of articles. Software projects, such as the Wikiscanner, have sought to out anonymous editors, and as such have succeeded in identifying particularly egregious cases of self-interest over accuracy. Wikipedia has also been studied as a well-functioning bureaucracy, achieving stigmergy. It also has a relationship with Google, where for years it benefited from being at the top of Google results for substantive queries (in one study some 95% of the time). More recently, following the introduction of Google's knowledge graph with its Hummingbird update in 2013, Wikipedia's relationship with Google's results changed. The knowledge graph displays thumbnail knowledge boxes (or panels) containing capsule summaries related to the particular query in Google's search engine results page. The panels contain summaries on the biography of an individual or an event that one searched for, for example, and the contents are borrowed from Wikipedia. Its introduction in various countries coincided with a decline in the amount of traffic to Wikipedia, generally, and specifically to Wikipedia via Google. Therefore, where Google once gave, it now takes away from Wikipedia.

Rather than regarding Wikipedia as a genealogical, epistemological, techno-authorial, bureaucratic or other object of study discussed above, with digital methods one is initially interested in taking stock of the natively digital objects embedded in Wikipedia and how its interface handles them. Wikipedia keeps its edit history, and the editors that made them, and when perusing a list of most active ones, bots are at the top. While they co-produce Wikipedia articles in numerous ways (e.g., interlinking), they also watch for vandalism. From a thought experiment (and an actual movie demo we made, where we turned off bot edits in an article), colleagues and I noted that turning off the bots would result in an unreadable encyclopedia, vandalized and rendered gobbledygook. 'Networked content' thereby became the term for considering how a network of bots holds together the content.

A second digital methods contribution again begins by looking at the interface and its objects and noting links to the 'same' article on other Wikipedia language versions (inter-wiki links). How to compare the articles? As other projects (such as Omnipedia and Manypedia) have discovered, the 'same' articles in different Wikipedia language versions may differ substantively. Tools may show the differences. For content comparison at a glance, there is a Wikipedia TOC Scraper. For image comparison, there is the Wikipedia Cross-Lingual Image Analysis tool. For comparing references in two or more Wikipedia articles across language versions, there is the Triangulation tool. Of course, one is able to perform such work without these scrapers, but they provide means to document and study the meanings behind the 'diff's', as the computational term has it to describe the differences between two files. The seminal project in this regard is that of Srebrenica articles on Wikipedia. Srebrenica is a historic site in Bosnia and Herzegovina that witnessed the massacre, the genocide or the fall of the city, as the Serbian, Bosnian and Dutch Wikipedia articles respectively entitle their articles on the events of July 1995, when 6000–8000, 8000, or 7000–8000 Bosniaks were killed (again depending on the same respective articles at the time of analysis). With this 'cross-cultural reference' approach one examines the various Wikipedia elements in an article, some of which are standard (title), and others are specific to Wikipedia such as anonymous editors, revision history, talk pages and templates. Indeed, the image capturing tool also grabs the templates, so one is able to see at a glance which issues (such as NPOV) articles may have.

Platform studies

There is an urgent realization that the open web is threatened by platformization. In this rendering social media become sticky sites that attract and arguably entrap users, locking them in (for their departure, even if desired, would have considerable cost to one's social life). As the web is depopulated of users and content migrates to social media, it is worth-while to take note of the new environment's publishing culture and vetting procedures. Social media platforms as well as OS systems on the smartphone are not considered as 'writerly' as the web for they 'moderate' content and 'approve' apps. Social media have been the object of critique precisely for the choice of the notion of 'platform', which in a computing sense means 'writable'. It also connotes content neutrality, but platforms rather police content. There are multiple examples that one could mention, but the stream of banned apps on Apple's App Store is one category. For example, in one banned app the user is a drug dealer, and in another one (Me So Holy) the user replaces the Messiah with her/his own selfie. Yet another banned app portrays then US President Obama on a trampoline in the Oval Office. Another banned app stands out for it is a work of art; the 'I am rich' app, a shiny bauble that one can open and show to others, has no other function than as a display of ostentation, and thus has been called a Veblen good. It sold for the maximum price allowed on the App Store at the time, $999.99, and was soon banned.

Among the social media platforms under study, Twitter, Facebook and Instagram stand out, however much what I would call 'secondary social media' are also of interest for the alter-natives they provide to the others in terms of research affordances. Twitter studies have held steady over the years, arguably because Twitter data are abundant and accessible, and can be put to use in a variety of research contexts, from marketing through to media and social research. In the context of academic research, a number of questions are often raised that could be placed in the web's 'good data' debate. For example, when making a tweet collection, does one obtain 'all' the tweets or not? In fact, this was one of the first contro-versies in Twitter studies when a Twitter researcher was quoted as saying that one has to work at Twitter in order to have access to all the tweets, as cited in the early 'big data' cri-tique (boyd and Crawford, 2012). Relatedly, it has been argued that researchers rarely clean Twitter data, meaning that most tweet collections and the studies based upon them have in their midst false positives and undisambiguated tweets. Twitter data are thus incomplete and messy (or even dirty). A third issue is that published Twitter studies rarely mention any ethical considerations in storing, analysing and publishing Twitter user data.

Debanalizing Twitter and studying engagement on Facebook

What is one studying when studying Twitter data? To begin, there have been at least three Twitters, beginning with the early 'What are you doing?' Twitter that was considered banal. One would study remote intimacy, ambient friend-following and, above all, phatic com-munication, for people were arguably 'only connecting' with each other rather than communicating substantively. The second Twitter arrived in 2009, with the new tagline, 'What's happening?' This is the event-following, newsworthy Twitter. It is also the revolu-tionary Twitter, the 140-character micro-blogging platform (which later doubled its character space size) that became associated with movement mobilization and aid pointers during the Iran election crisis and the Arab Spring. A more recent Twitter, the third, simply stated, 'Compose new tweet', as Twitter commodified (after the stock market capitalization) and sold more data for more generic research purposes. Twitter data were mobilized for celebrity award, election and stock market prediction. As these studies began to proliferate, questions arose about the demographics of users, and whether it could stand in for some measure of 'public opinion'. Or should it be considered a more elite, professional space? Most recently Twitter has returned to its most successful tagline, in the sense once related by Jack Dorsey, when discussing how Twitter 'does well at' events, elections and disasters. Indeed, digital methods have been developed to take advantage of Twitter II, or the 'What's happening?' Twitter. For 'remote event analysis' one may capture the top retweeted tweets per day and place them in chronological order (as opposed to the reverse chronological of a blog), so as to transform Twitter into a story-telling machine. Digital methods also have been developed for Twitter III, albeit for the study of issue spaces, or how issue professionals follow each other and contribute substantive tweets around global health and development, human rights and other issue spaces.

The three means to study Facebook described above – page playback (similar to a screencast documentary), inter-liked page analysis and most engaged-with content – are quite far afield from the social network analysis once heralded, and the postdemographics approach, where one studies the preferences and tastes of public figures' friends (such as Donald Trump's and Hillary Clinton's) and inquires into the extent to which they may actually be compatible, thereby allowing for a reinterpretation of the culture wars. Since an API 'update' by Facebook in 2015, tastes and ties research as well as the postdemographics variation have become less probable, given the end of that data stream as well as the inability to scrape the platform as an alternative means to collect the data. Facebook most recently has been one of the highest-profile staging areas for the fake news and Russian disinformation campaign debacle, where researchers have found high volumes of interactions of both hyperpartisan and Russian propaganda content, the most engaging of which were often memes. At least that is the empirical question put forward above, where Facebook is considered to be a meme machine, beyond its other guises as social networking site and ad-serving platform.

Network discovery for data journalism research

The tracker analysis method and project extends from the study of Russian information campaigning both around the US presidential election of 2016 and beyond. In identifying website code and using reverse look-up software, one seeks to discover 'networks' of disinformation purveyors and other questionable sources and interpret content dissemination strategies. The 'Russians' – often referring to the work of the Internet Research Agency but it also could be called a style – adapted their content strategy of stirring conflict with the West to fomenting it *within* the West.

Google Analytics and AdSense IDs have been used to map websites (and groups of websites) onto owners. The owners may be 'media groups', such as an entity that owns a variety of channels from lifestyle to hard news, and plants stories worthy of study in all of them. Other tracker work also was presented, especially of interest to (data) journalists, such as the existence of Google Analytics and other Western analytics software on websites authored by ISIS sympathizers and other terror-recruitment groupings

YouTube's ranking mechanisms

Finally, the erstwhile amateur video site has given way to commercialization as well as the rise of the 'native' YouTuber and micro-celebrity, although all three types of content-makers and their output continue to co-mingle in the massive repository. Popular instructional genres such as 'the walk-through', 'unboxing' as well as 'how to fix it' inform the 'tear down' approach put forward. There are at least three modes of watching in YouTube, via the related videos, search and channel subscriptions, each of which may be 'torn down' or its recommendations laid bare by capturing the outputs for further study. In the methods built into the YouTube data tools, the researcher is able to put on display 'relatedness', or the carousel of recommended videos 'up next', ranking cultures from YouTube's own engine results as well as the networks of channel subscriptions, including how YouTube relates channels to one another, and furnishes them as yet another form of suggestion. In each technique, the question of authority is measured, or who is privileged by the platform (and when). Here one undertakes both medium and social, asking whether native content providers (YouTubers or micro-celebrities) are becoming subject matter authorities given their standing on the platform.

REFERENCES

Abbate, Janet (2000) *Inventing the Internet*. Cambridge, MA: MIT Press.

Abidin, Crystal (2016) 'Visibility labour: Engaging with influencers' fashion brands and #OOTD advertorial campaigns on Instagram', *Media International Australia*, *161*(1): 86–100.

Ackland, Robert, O'Neil, Mathieu, Standish, Russell and Buchhorn, Markus (2006) *'VOSON: A web services approach for facilitating research into online networks'*, Paper presented at the Second International e-Social Science Conference, 28–30 June, Manchester, UK.

Ackland, Robert (2013) *Web Social Science*. London: Sage.

Aday, Sean, Farrell, Henry, Freelon, Deen, Lynch, Marc, Sides, John and Dewar, Michael (2013) 'Watching from afar: Media consumption patterns around the Arab Spring', *American Behavioral Scientist*, *57*(7): 899–919.

Agar, John (2001) 'Review of James Gillies and Robert Cailliau, *How the Web was Born*. Oxford: Oxford University Press, 2000', *British Journal for the History of Science*, *34*(3): 370–373.

Aikin, Scott F. (2009) 'Poe's Law, group polarization, and the epistemology of online religious discourse', *Social Science Research Network*, https://ssrn.com/abstract=1332169.

Akrich, Madeleine and Latour, Bruno (1992) 'The de-scription of technical objects', in Wiebe Bijker and John Law (eds), *Shaping Technology / Building Society: Studies in Sociotechnical Change*. Cambridge, MA: MIT Press, pp. 205–224.

Albright, Jonathan (2017) 'Itemized posts and historical engagement – 6 now-closed FB pages', *data set, Tableau public*, https://public.tableau.com/profile/d1gi#!/vizhome/FB4/TotalReachbyPage.

Alexa (2018) 'wikipedia.org Traffic Statistics', *Alexa.com*, https://www.alexa.com/siteinfo/wikipedia.org.

Alexander, Lawrence (2015) 'Open-Source information reveals pro-Kremlin web campaign', *Global Voices*, 13 July, https://globalvoices.org/2015/07/13/open-source-information-reveals-pro-kremlin-web-campaign/.

Alimardani, Mahsa (2014) 'Nearly 70% of young Iranians use illegal internet circumvention tools', *Global Voices*, 16 September, https://advox.globalvoices.org/2014/09/16/nearly-70-of-young-iranians-use-illegal-internet-circumvention-tools/.

Allen, Matthew (2013) 'What was Web 2.0? Versions as the dominant mode of internet history', *New Media & Society*, *15*(2): 260–275.

Alt-Right Open Intelligence Initiative (2017) *'Mapping the alt-right: The US Alternative Right across the Atlantic,'* Digital Methods Winter School, Amsterdam, https://digitalmethods.net/Dmi/AltRightOpenIntelligenceInitiative.

Andrejevic, Mark (2005) 'The work of watching one another: Lateral surveillance, risk, and governance', *Surveillance & Society*, *2*(4): 479–497.

Angwin, Julia, Varner, Madeleine and Tobin, Ariana (2017) 'Facebook enabled advertisers to reach "Jew Haters"', *ProPublica*, 14 September.

Apple (2017) 'Environmental responsibility report', Cupertino, CA: Apple, Inc.

Arnal, Timo (2014) 'Internet Machine', film, https://vimeo.com/95044197.

Arthur, W. Brian (1989) 'Competing technologies, increasing returns and lock-in by historical events', *Economic Journal*, *99*: 106–131.

Article 19 (2016) 'Tightening the net: Internet security and censorship in Iran. Part I: The National Internet Project', *report*, London: Article 19.

Aryan, Simurgh, Aryan, Homa and Halderman, J. Alex (2013) 'Internet censorship in Iran: A first look', *Proc. 3rd USENIX Workshop on Free and Open Communications on the Internet (FOCI '13)*, Washington, DC. Berkeley, CA: USENIX Association.

Aula, Pekka (2010) 'Social media, reputation risk and ambient publicity management', *Strategy & Leadership*, *38*(6): 43–49.

Babcock, William A. and Freivogel, William H. (2015) *The SAGE Guide to Key Issues in Mass Media Ethics and Law*. London: Sage.

Baccarne, Bastiaan, Briones, Angeles, Baack, Stefan, Maemura, Emily, Joceli, Janna, Zhou, Peiqing and Ferre, Humberto (2015) 'Does love win? The mechanics of memetics', Digital Methods Summer School 2015, https://wiki.digitalmethods.net/Dmi/SummerSchool2015DoesLoveWin.

Baio, Andy (2011) 'Think you can hide, anonymous blogger? Two words: Google Analytics', *Wired*, 15 November.

Baker, Nicholson (2008) 'The charms of Wikipedia', *New York Review of Books*, 20 March.

Bamman, David, O'Connor, Brendan and Smith, Noah A. (2012) 'Censorship and deletion practices in Chinese social media', *First Monday*, *17*(3).

Bao, Patti, Hecht, Brent, Carton, Samuel, Quaderi, Mahmood, Horn, Michael and Gergle, Darren (2012) 'Omnipedia: Bridging the Wikipedia Language Gap', *Proceedings of the SIGCHI Conference on Human Factors in Computing Systems*. New York: ACM Press, pp. 1075–1084.

Barbaro, Michael and Zeller Jr., Tom (2006) 'A face is exposed for AOL searcher no. 4417749', *New York Times*, A1.

Bardak, Batuhan and Tan, Mehmet (2015) 'Prediction of influenza outbreaks by integrating Wikipedia article access logs and Google flu trend data', *Proceedings of 2015 IEEE 15th International Conference on Bioinformatics and Bioengineering (BIBE)*, Washington, DC. Piscataway, NJ: IEEE.

Barnes, Susan B. (2006) 'A privacy paradox: Social networking in the United States', *First Monday*, *11*(9).

Barthes, Roland (1967) *The Death of the Author*, trans. A. Leavers. New York: Smith & Hill.

Bartlett, Jamie, Birdwell, Jonathan and Littler, Mark (2011) *The New Face of Digital Populism*. London: Demos.

Battelle, John (2003) 'The database of intentions', *John Battelle's Blog*, 13 November, http://battellemedia.com/archives/2003/11/the_database_of_intentions.php.

Baym, Nancy (2018) *Playing to the Crowd: Musicians, Audiences and the Intimate Work of Connection*. New York: New York University Press.

Bazzell, Michael (2016) *Open Source Intelligence Techniques: Resources for Searching and Analyzing Online Information*. North Charleston, SC: CreateSpace Independent Publishing Platform.

BBC Academy (2013) 'Israel and the Palestinians', in BBC Academy (ed.), *Journalism Subject Guide*. London: BBC. http://www.bbc.co.uk/academy/journalism/article/art20130702112133696.

Beer, David (2008) 'Social network(ing) sites…revisiting the story so far: A response to danah boyd and Nicole Ellison', *Journal of Computer-Mediated Communication*, 13(2): 516–529.

Ben-David, Anat (2016) 'What does the web remember of its deleted past? An archival reconstruction of the former Yugoslav top-level domain', *New Media & Society*, 18(7): 1103–1119.

Bennett, Daniel (2009) 'The myth of the Moldova Twitter revolution', *Frontline Club* blog, 8 April, https://www.frontlineclub.com/the_myth_of_the_moldova_twitter_revolution-2/.

Bennett, W. Lance and Segerberg, Alexandra (2012) 'The logic of connective action: Digital media and the personalization of contentious politics', *Information, Communication & Society*, 15(5): 739–768.

Bergado, Gabe (2015) 'The rare Pepe trade is booming on Craigslist', *The Daily Dot*, 10 September, https://www.dailydot.com/unclick/craigslist-rare-pepe/.

Berman, Ari (2009) 'Iran's Twitter revolution', The Notion blog, *The Nation*, 15 June, https://www.thenation.com/article/irans-twitter-revolution/.

Berners-Lee, Tim (2014) 'Tim Berners-Lee on the Web at 25: The past, present and future', *Wired*, 23 August.

Bertelsmann Lexikon Institut (2008) *Das Wikipedia Lexikon in einem Band*. Gütersloh: Mohn Media.

Beurskens, Michael (2013) 'Legal questions of Twitter research', in Katrin Weller, Axel Bruns, Jean Burgess, Merja Mahrt and Cornelius Puschmann (eds), *Twitter & Society*. New York: Peter Lang, pp. 123–133.

Bielka, Nathalie, Buhl, Helena and dos Santos, Monica (2017) 'Wikipedia as object of study: A cross-cultural research on the German, Polish and Portuguese versions of the Wikipedia article, "Auschwitz concentration camp"', course paper, University of Mannheim.

Bird, S. Elizabeth (2011) 'Are we all produsers now? Convergence and media audience practices', *Cultural Studies*, 25: 4–5, 502–516.

Bishop, Jonathan (2013) 'The effect of de-individuation of the Internet Troller on criminal procedure implementation: An interview with a hater', *International Journal of Cyber Criminology*, 7(1): 28–48.

Blackmore, Susan (1999) *The Meme Machine*. Oxford: Oxford University Press.

Bødker, Henrik and Brügger, Niels (2017) 'The shifting temporalities of online news: The *Guardian's* website from 1996 to 2015', *Journalism*, 7 February.

Borgman, Christine (2009) 'The digital future is now: A call to action for the humanities', *Digital Humanities Quarterly*, 3(4): 1–30.

Borra, Erik and Rieder, Bernhard (2014) 'Programmed method: Developing a toolset for capturing and analyzing tweets', *Aslib Journal of Information Management*, 66(3): 262–278.

Bosworth, Andrew (2009) 'What's the history of the awesome button (that eventually became the like button) on Facebook?', *Quora*, www.quora.com/Whats-the-history-of-the-Awesome-Button-that-eventually-became-the-Like-button-on-Facebook.

Bounegru, Liliana, Gray, Jonathan, Venturini, Tommaso and Mauri, Michele (2017) *A Field Guide to Fake News*. Amsterdam: Public Data Lab.

Bowker, Geoffrey (2005) *Memory Practices in the Sciences*. Cambridge, MA: MIT Press.

Boyd, Andrew (2003) 'The web rewires the movement', *The Nation*, 17 July.

boyd, danah (2013) 'White flight in networked publics? How race and class shaped American teen engagement with Myspace and Facebook', in Lisa Nakamura and Peter A. Chow-White (eds), *Race after the Internet*. New York: Routledge, pp. 203–222.

boyd, danah and Crawford, Kate (2012) 'Critical questions for big data', *Information, Communication & Society*, *15*(5): 662–679.

boyd, danah and Ellison, Nicole (2007) 'Social network sites: Definition, history and scholarship', *Journal of Computer-Mediated Communication*, *13*(1), article 1.

boyd, danah and Hargittai, Esther (2010) 'Facebook privacy settings: Who cares?' *First Monday*, *15*(8).

boyd, danah, Golder, Scott and Lotan, Gilad (2010) 'Tweet, tweet, retweet: Conversational aspects of retweeting on Twitter', *Proceedings of the 43rd Annual Hawaii International Conference on System Sciences*, Washington, DC. Los Alamitos, CA: IEEE Computer Society, pp. 1–10.

Boyle, James (1997) 'Foucault in cyberspace: Surveillance, sovereignty, and hardwired censors', *University of Cincinnati Law Review*, *66*: 177–255.

Brandtzaeg, Petter Bae and Haugstveit, IdaMaria (2014) 'Facebook likes: A study of liking practices for humanitarian causes', *International Journal of Web Based Communities*, *10*(3): 258–279.

Bridle, James (2010) 'On Wikipedia, cultural patrimony, and historiography', *Booktwo.org blog post*, 6 September, http://booktwo.org/notebook/wikipedia-historiography/.

Brin, Serge and Page, Larry (1998) 'The anatomy of a large-scale hypertextual web search engine', *Computer Networks and ISDN Systems*, *30*(1–7): 107–117.

Brock, André (2005) '"A belief in humanity is a belief in colored men": Using culture to span the digital divide', *Journal of Computer-Mediated Communication*, *11*(1), article 17.

Broderick, Ryan (2016) 'This is how Facebook is radicalising you', *Buzzfeed News*, 16 November.

Brown, Andrew (2015) 'Wikipedia editors are a dying breed. The reason? Mobile', *Guardian*, 25 June.

Brügger, Niels (2008) 'The archived website and website philology: A new type of historical document?' *Nordicom Review*, *29*(2): 151–171.

Brügger, Niels (2012) 'When the present web is later than the past: Web historiography, digital history and internet studies', *Historical Social Research*, *37*(4): 102–117.

Brügger, Niels (2015) 'A brief history of Facebook as a media text: The development of an empty structure', *First Monday*, *20*(5).

Bruns, Axel (2007) 'Methodologies for mapping the political blogosphere: An exploration using the IssueCrawler research tool', *First Monday*, *12*(5).

Bruns, Axel (2009) 'From prosumer to produser: Understanding user-led content creation', paper presented at Transforming Audiences, London, 3–4 September.

Bruns, Axel (2012) 'Ad Hoc innovation by users of social networks: The case of Twitter', ZSI Discussion Paper 16. Vienna: ZSI. https://www.zsi.at/object/publication/2186.

Bruns, Axel, Bechmann, Anja, Burgess, Jean, Chadwick, Andrew, Clark, Lynn Schofield, Dutton, William H., Ess, Charles M., Gruzd, Anatoliy, Halford, Susan, Hofmann, Jeanette, Howard, Phil, Jones, Steve, Katzenbach, Christian, Liang, Hai, Lewis, Seth C., Peng, Winson, Puschmann, Cornelius, Qui, Jack, Quinn, Kelly, Rogers, Richard, Rossi, Luca, Russel, Adrienne, Stromer-Galley, Jennifer, Van Dijck, José, Weller, Katrin, Westlund, Oscar, Zhu, Jonathan J.H. and Zimmer, Michael (2018) 'Facebook shuts the gate after the horse has bolted, and hurts real research in the process', *Internet Policy Review*, 25 April, https://policyreview.info/articles/news/facebook-shuts-gate-after-horse-has-bolted-and-hurts-real-research-process/786.

Bruns, Axel and Burgess, Jean (2011) 'The use of Twitter hashtags in the formation of ad hoc publics', *Proceedings of the 6th European Consortium for Political Research (ECPR) General Conference 2011*, University of Iceland, Reykjavik.

Bruns, Axel and Burgess, Jean (2015) 'Twitter hashtags from ad hoc to calculated publics', in Nathan Rambukkana (ed.), *Hashtag Publics: The Power and Politics of Discursive Networks*. New York: Peter Lang, pp. 13–28.

Bruns, Axel and Eltham, Ben (2009) 'Twitter free Iran: An evaluation of Twitter's role in public diplomacy and information operations in Iran's 2009 election crisis', *Communications Policy & Research Forum*, Sydney: University of Technology, pp. 298–310.

Bruns, Axel and Highfield, Tim (2015) 'From news blogs to news on Twitter: Gatewatching and collaborative news curation', in Stephen Coleman and Deen Freelon (eds), *Handbook of Digital Politics*. Cheltenham: Edward Elgar, pp. 325–339.

Bruns, Axel and Weller, Katrin (2016) 'Twitter as a first draft of the present: and the challenges of preserving it for the future', *Proceedings of WebSci16*. New York: ACM.

Bruns, Axel, Burgess, Jean and Highfield, Tim (2014) 'A "big data" approach to mapping the Australian twittersphere', in Paul Longley Arthur and Katherine Bode (eds), *Advancing Digital Humanities*. Basingstoke: Palgrave Macmillan, pp. 113–129.

Bruns, Axel, Moon, Brenda, Paul, Avijit and Münch, Felix (2016) 'Towards a typology of hashtag publics: A large-scale comparative study of user engagement across trending topics', *Communication Research and Practice*, 2(1): 20–46.

Brunton, Finn and Nissenbaum, Helen (2011) 'Vernacular resistance to data collection and analysis: A political theory of obfuscation', *First Monday*, 6(5).

Bucher, Taina (2013) 'Objects of intense feeling: The case of the Twitter API', *Computational Culture: A Journal of Software Studies*, 4.

Buckels, Erin E., Trapnell, Paul D. and Paulhus, Delroy L. (2014) 'Trolls just want to have fun', *Personality and Individual Differences*, 67: 97–102.

Burgess, Jean (2016) 'Twitter is the last of Web 2.0', personal communication, AoIR conference, Berlin, 5 October.

Burgess, Jean and Green, Joshua (2009) 'The entrepreneurial vlogger: Participatory culture beyond the professional–amateur divide', in Snickars, Pelle and Patrick Vonderau (eds), *The YouTube Reader*. Stockholm: National Library of Sweden, pp. 89–107.

Burgess, Jean and Green, Joshua (2018) *YouTube: Online Video and Participatory Culture*. Cambridge, UK: Polity Press.

Burrington, Ingrid (2014) 'The cloud is not the territory', Creativetime Reports, 20 May, http://creativetimereports.org/2014/05/20/ingrid-burrington-the-cloud-is-not-the-territory-wnv/.

Butler, Brian, Joyce, Elisabeth and Pike, Jacqueline (2008) 'Don't look now, but we've created a bureaucracy: The nature and roles of policies and rules in Wikipedia', *CHI'08: Proceedings of the SIGCHI Conference on Human Factors in Computing Systems*. New York: ACM, pp. 1101–1110.

Bychowski, Steve (2016) 'The Internet Archive Wayback Machine: A useful IP litigation tool, but is It admissible?' *Trademark and Copyright Law Blog*, 16 May, http://www.trademarkandcopyrightlawblog.com/2016/05/the-internet-archive-wayback-machine-a-useful-ip-litigation-tool-but-is-it-admissible/.

Callahan, Ewa S. and Herring, Susan C. (2011) 'Cultural bias in Wikipedia content on famous persons', *Journal of the American Society for Information Science and Technology*, 62(10): 1899–1915.

Campbell, Matthew T. (2003) 'Generic names for soft drinks by county, The Pop vs. Soda page', http://www.popvssoda.com/countystats/total-county.html.

Carr, Nicholas (2007) 'From contemplative man to flickering man', *Encyclopaedia Britannica* blog, 13 June, http://blogs.britannica.com/2007/06/from-contemplative-man-to-flickering-man/.

Carr, Nicholas (2009) 'All hail the information triumvirate!', Roughtype blog, 22 January, http://www.roughtype.com/archives/2009/01/all_hail_the_in.php.

Caucasian Causes (2009) 'Armenian bloggers confirm top websites blocked in Iran', Caucasian Causes blog, Yerevan: Caucasus Institute, http://www.caucasiancauses.com/2009/06/armenian-bloggers-confirm-top-websites-blocked-in-iran/.

Chace, Zoe (2017) 'Meme come true', Radio episode 608: The Revolution Starts at Noon. *This American Life*, Chicago: WBEZ, 20 January.

Chen, Adrian (2015) 'The Agency', *New York Times*, 2 June.

Chen, Edwin (2012) 'Soda vs. pop', blog posting, Edwin Chen's Blog, 6 July, http://blog.echen.me/2012/07/06/soda-vs-pop-with-twitter/.

Chesney, Thomas (2006) 'An empirical examination of Wikipedia's credibility', *First Monday*, 11(11).

Chouliaraki, Lilie (2013) *The Ironic Spectator: Solidarity in the Age of Post-humanitarianism*. Cambridge: Polity.

Chowdhury, Abdur (2009) 'Top Twitter Trends of 2009', Twitter blog, 15 December, https://blog.twitter.com/official/en_us/a/2009/top-twitter-trends-of-2009.html.

Christensen, Henrik Serup (2011) 'Political activities on the internet: Slacktivism or political participation by other means?' *First Monday*, 16(2).

Chikofsky, Elliot J. and Cross, James H. (1990) 'Reverse engineering and design recovery: A taxonomy', *IEEE Software 7*(1): 13–17.

Chun, Wendy Hui Kyong (2008) 'The enduring ephemeral, or the future is a memory', *Critical Inquiry*, *35*(1): 148–171.

Chun, Wendy Hui Kyong (2013) *Programmed Visions: Software and Memory*. Cambridge, MA: MIT Press.

Cohen, Daniel J. and Rosenzweig, Roy (2006) *Digital History: A Guide to Gathering, Preserving, and Presenting the Past on the Web*. Philadelphia: University of Pennsylvania Press.

Coleman, Gabriella (2011) 'Anonymous: From the lulz to collective action', The New Everyday, Future of the Book blog, 6 April, http://mediacommons.futureofthebook.org/tne/pieces/anonymous-lulz-collective-action.

Cookson, Robert (2016) 'Jihadi website with beheadings profited from Google ad platform', *Financial Times*, 17 May.

Costanza-Chock, Sasha (2014) *Out of the Shadows, Into the Streets! Transmedia Organizing and the Immigrant Rights Movement*. Cambridge, MA: MIT Press.

Couldry, Nick (2001) 'The hidden injuries of media power', *Journal of Consumer Culture*, *1*(2): 155–177.

Couldry, Nick (2012) *Media, Society, World: Social Theory and Digital Media Practice*. Cambridge: Polity.

Counter-extremism Project (2018) 'The eGLYPH Web Crawler: ISIS Content on Youtube', New York: Counter-extremism Project, https://www.counterextremism.com/sites/default/files/eGLYPH_web_crawler_white_paper_July_2018.pdf

Crampton, Jeremy W., Graham, Mark, Poorthuis, Ate, Shelton, Taylor, Stephens, Monica, Wilson, Matthew W. and Zook, Matthew (2013) 'Beyond the geotag: Situating "big data" and leveraging the potential of the geoweb', *Cartography and Geographic Information Science*, *40*(2): 130–139.

Critchlow, Will (2007) 'Search Google without Wikipedia – a Firefox search plugin', Distilled blog, 10 July, http://www.distilled.net/blog/seo/search-google-without-Wikipedia-a-firefox-search-plugin/.

Critical Art Ensemble (1998) *Flesh Machine: Cyborgs, Designer Babies, and New Eugenic Consciousness*. Brooklyn, NY: Autonomedia.

Currier, Cora and Marquis-Boire, Morgan (2015) 'A detailed look at Hacking Team's emails about its repressive clients', *The Intercept*, 7 July.

Cush, Andy (2014) 'Who's behind this shady, propagandistic Russian photo exhibition?', *Gawker*, 10 October.

Cutts, Matt (2005) 'How to write queries', blog post, *Matt Cutts: Gadgets, Google, and SEO*, 11 August, https://www.mattcutts.com/blog/writing-google-queries/.

Darnton, Robert (2014) *Censors at Work: How States Shaped Literature*. New York: W.W. Norton.

Datta, Amit, Tschantz, Michael Carl and Datta, Anupam (2015) 'Automated experiments on ad privacy settings', *Proceedings on Privacy Enhancing Technologies*, *2015*(1): 92–112.

Davenport, Coral (2017) 'With Trump in charge, climate change references purged from website', *New York Times*, 20 January.

Davies, William (2015) *The Happiness Industry: How Government and Big Business Sold Us Well Being*. London: Verso.

Dawkins, Richard (1976), *The Selfish Gene*. Oxford: Oxford University Press.

Dawkins, Richard (2014) 'Memes. Q&A at Oxford Union', Oxford University, 18 February, https://www.youtube.com/watch?v=4BVpEoQ4T2M

De Amicis, Giulia, De Gaetano, Carlo, Saulière, Saya, Bardelli, Federica, Rogers, Richard, Waardenburg, Thijs, den Tex, Emile, Kok, Saskia and Roginsky, Sandrine (2013) 'Gezi Park life: From trees to cops', Digital Methods Summer School 2013, 11 July, https://wiki.digitalmethods.net/pub/Dmi/GeziParkLife/PP_GreenpeaceProject_Final.pdf.

Dean, Brian (2016) 'Google's 200 ranking factors: The complete list', backlink.io, 5 November, http://backlinko.com/google-ranking-factors.

Dean, Jodi (1998) *Aliens in America: Conspiracy Cultures from Outerspace to Cyberspace*. Ithaca, NY: Cornell University Press.

Deibert, Ron and Rohozinski, Rafal (2010) 'Control and subversion in Russian cyberspace', in Ronald Deibert, John Palfrey, Rafal Rohozinski and Jonathan Zittrain (eds), *Access Controlled*. Cambridge, MA: MIT Press, pp. 15–34.

Dekker, Annet and Wolfsberger, Annette (2009) *Walled Garden*. Amsterdam: Virtual Platform.

Dennett, Daniel (2002) 'Dangerous memes', *TED Talk*, https://www.ted.com/talks/dan_dennett_on_dangerous_memes.

Dharapak, Charles (2012) 'White House: Obama misspoke by referring to "Polish death camp" while honoring Polish war hero', *Washington Post*, 29 May.

Digital Methods Initiative (2009) 'For the ppl of Iran – #iranelection RT', video installation, https://movies.issuecrawler.net/for_the_ppl_of_iran.html.

Dohmen, Joep (2007) 'Opkomst en ondergang van extreemrechtse sites', *NRC Handelsblad*, 25 August.

Donath, Judith S. (1999) 'Identity and deception in the virtual community', in Marc A. Smith and Peter Kollock (eds), *Communities in Cyberspace*. London: Routledge, pp. 29–59.

Dong, Fan (2012) 'Controlling the internet in China: The real story', *Convergence: The International Journal of Research into New Media Technologies*, *18*(4): 403–425.

Dorsey, Jack (2006) 'twttr sketch', image, *Flickr*, 24 March, https://www.flickr.com/photos/jackdorsey/182613360 (last accessed 25 April 2018).

Dorsey, Jack (2008) 'Twitter trends & a tip', Twitter blog, 5 September, https://blog.twitter.com/official/en_us/a/2008/twitter-trends-a-tip.html.

Dougherty, Meghan and Meyer, Eric T. (2014) 'Community, tools, and practices in web archiving: The state-of-the-art in relation to social science and humanities research needs', *Journal of the Association for Information Science and Technology*, *65*(11): 2195–2209.

Dougherty, Meghan, Meyer, Eric T., Madsen, Christine, van den Heuvel, Charles, Thomas, Arthur and Wyatt, Sally (2010) *Researcher Engagement with Web Archives: State of the Art*. London: JISC.

Elliott, Mark (2016) 'Stigmergic collaboration: A framework for understanding and designing', in Ulrike Cress, Johannes Moskaliuk and Heisawn Jeong (eds), *Mass Collaboration and Education*. Cham: Springer, pp. 65–84.

Elmer, Greg (2003) *Profiling Machines*. Cambridge, MA: MIT Press.

Elmer, Greg and Langlois, Ganaele (2013) 'Networked campaigns: Traffic tags and cross platform analysis on the web', *Information Polity*, *18*(1): 43–56.

Elmer-Dewitt, Philip (1993) 'First nation in cyberspace', *TIME International*, *49*, 6 December.

Eltgroth, Deborah R. (2009) 'Best evidence and the Wayback Machine: Toward a workable authentication standard for archived Internet evidence', *Fordham Law Review*, *78*(1): article 5.

Engelberts, Lernert and Plug, Sander (2009) 'I love Alaska: The heartbreaking search history of AOL user #711391', Minimovies documentary, Amsterdam: Submarine Channel.

Ericson, Matthew and Cox, Amanda (2009) 'What's cooking on Thanksgiving', *New York Times*, 26 November.

Esfandiari, Golnaz (2010) 'The Twitter devolution', *Foreign Policy*, 8 June.

Eslami, Motahhare,Rickman, Aimee, Vaccaro, Kristen, Aleyasen, Amirhossein, Vuong, Andy, Karahalios, Karrie, Hamilton, Kevin and Sandvig, Christian (2015) '"I always assumed that I wasn't really that close to [her]": Reasoning about invisible algorithms in news feeds', *CHI 2015, Crossings*, Seoul, South Korea. New York: ACM.

Facebook (2016) 'Facebook platform changelog', Facebook for Developers, webpage, https://developers.facebook.com/docs/apps/changelog.

Facebook Liberation Army (2015) *Directives*. Amsterdam: Waag Society, http://fla.waag.org/downloads/FLA-Infographic.pdf.

FairSearch, 2011. 'Fact Sheet', fairsearch.org.

Farhi, Paul (2009) 'The Twitter explosion', *American Journalism Review*, April/May, http://ajrarchive.org/article.asp?id=4756.

Farivar, Cyrus (2011) 'Iran's answer to Stuxnet', *MIT Technology Review*, 25 April.

fbGodEmperorTrump (2016) r/The_Donald/ subreddit comment, Reddit, https://www.reddit.com/r/The_Donald/comments/50y7sp/facebook_took_down_the_god_emperor_trump_page/.

Flew, Terry (2005) *New Media: An Introduction*. Oxford: Oxford University Press.

Flew, Terry (2008) *New Media: An Introduction*, 3rd edn. Oxford: Oxford University Press.

Floridi, Luciano, Kauffman, Sylvie, Kolucka-Zuk, Lidia, La Rue, Frank, Leutheusser-Schnarrenberger, Sabine, Piñar, José-Luis, Valcke, Peggy and Wales, Jimmy (2015) *'The Advisory Council to Google on the Right to be Forgotten'*, final report, *Mountain View*, CA: Google, 6 February.

Foucault, Michel (1970) *The Order of Things*. New York: Pantheon.

Flusser, Vilém (2000) *Towards a Philosophy of Photography*. London: Reaktion Books.

Foxman, Maxwell and Nieborg, David B. (2016) 'Between a rock and a hard place: Games coverage and its network of ambivalences', *Journal of Games Criticism*, *3*(1).

Franceschi-Bicchierai, Lorenzo (2016) 'How hackers broke into John Podesta and Colin Powell's Gmail accounts', *Motherboard*, 20 October.

Fuller, Matthew (2005) *Media Ecologies*. Cambridge, MA: MIT Press.

Gaffney, Devin (2010) '#iranElection: Quantifying online activism', *Proceedings of WebSci10*. New York: ACM.

Gallagher, Silvia Elena and Savage, Timothy (2013) 'Cross-cultural analysis in online community research: A literature review', *Computers in Human Behavior, 29*(3): 1028–1038.

Gallucci, Maria (2017) 'Google's data center raises the stakes in this state's "water wars"', *Mashable*, 23 April, http://mashable.com/2017/04/23/google-data-center-south-carolina-water-wars/.

Gazaryan, Karén (2013) 'Authenticity of archived websites: The need to lower the evidentiary hurdle is imminent', *Rutgers Computer and Technology Law Journal, 39*(2): 216–245.

Geboers, Marloes, Heine, Jan-Jaap, Hidding, Nienke, Wissel, Julia, van Zoggel, Marlie and Simons, Danny (2016) 'Engagement with tragedy in social media', Digital Methods Winter School 2016, Amsterdam, https://wiki.digitalmethods.net/Dmi/WinterSchool2016EngagementWithTragedySocialMedia.

Gehl, Robert (2009) 'YouTube as archive. Who will curate this digital Wunderkammer?' *International Journal of Cultural Studies, 12*(1): 43–60.

Geiger, R. Stuart (2011) 'The lives of bots', in Geert Lovink and Nate Tkacz (eds), *Critical Point of View: A Wikipedia Reader*. Amsterdam: Institute of Network Cultures, pp. 78–93.

GeneralLudd (2011) 'Casually butterfly everything', Reddit /r/pics, 22 November, https://www.reddit.com/r/pics/comments/mkvd1/casually_butterfly_everything/

Generous, Nicholas, Fairchild, Geoffrey, Deshpande, Alina, Del Valle, Sara Y. and Priedhorsky, Reid (2014) 'Global disease monitoring and forecasting with Wikipedia', *PLoS Computational Biology, 10*(11): e1003892.

Gerlitz, Carolin and Helmond, Anne (2013) 'The like economy: Social buttons and the data-intensive web', *New Media & Society, 15*(8): 1348–1365.

Gerlitz, Carolin and Rieder, Bernhard (2013) 'Mining one percent of Twitter: Collections, baselines, sampling', *M/C Journal, 16*(2).

Gibson, Angela (2016) 'URLs: Some practical advice', MLA Style Center, New York: Modern Language Association, 2 November, https://style.mla.org/2016/11/02/urls-some-practical-advice/.

Gieck, Robin, Kinnunen, Hanna-Mari, Li, Yuanyuan, Moghaddam, Mohsen, Pradel, Franziska, Gloor, Peter A., Paasivaara, Maria and Zylka, Matthäus P. (2016) 'Cultural differences in the understanding of history on Wikipedia', in Matthäus P. Zylka, Hauke Fuehres, Andrea Fronzetti Colladon and Peter A. Gloor (eds), *Designing Networks for Innovation and Improvisation. Springer Proceedings in Complexity*. Cham: Springer, pp. 3–12.

Giles, Jim (2005) 'Internet encyclopedias go head to head', *Nature, 438*: 900–901.

Gillespie, Tarleton (2010) 'The politics of platforms', *New Media & Society, 12*(3): 347–364.

Gillespie, Tarleton (2012) 'Can an algorithm be wrong?', *Limn*, 2.

Gillespie, Tarleton (2017) 'The platform metaphor, revisited', HIIG Science Blog, Berlin: Alexander von Humboldt Institute for Internet and Society, 24 August, https://www.hiig.de/en/blog/the-platform-metaphor-revisited/.

Ginsberg, Jeremy, Mohebbi, Matthew H., Patel, Rajan S., Brammer, Lynnette, Smolinski, Mark S. and Brilliant, Larry (2009) 'Detecting influenza epidemics using search engine query data', *Nature, 457*: 1012–1014.

Glasner, Peter and Rothman, Harry (2017) *Splicing Life? The New Genetics and Society*. London: Routledge.

Goel, Vindu (2015) 'Instagram to offer millions of current events photos', *New York Times*, 23 June.

Goggin, Gerard and McLelland, Mark (2017) 'Introduction: Global coordinates of internet histories', in Gerard Goggin and Mark McLelland (eds), *The Routledge Companion to Global Internet Histories*. New York: Routledge, pp. 1–19.

Googlecache (2007) '96.6% of Wikipedia pages rank in Google's top 10', Google Cache blog, 26 June, http://www.thegooglecache.com/white-hat-seo/966-of-Wikipedia-pages-rank-in-googles-top-10/.

Graham, Mark (2011) 'Mapping Wikipedia's augmentations of our planet', Mark Graham blog, http://www.zerogeography.net/2011/11/mapping-wikipedias-augmentations-of-our.html.

Graham, Mark, Hogan, Bernie, Straumann, Ralph K. and Medhat, Ahmed (2014) 'Uneven geographies of user-generated information: Patterns of increasing informational poverty', *Annals of the Association of American Geographers*, 104(4): 746–764.

Griffiths, Mark D. (2014) 'Adolescent trolling in online environments: A brief overview', *Education and Health*, 32(3): 85–87.

Grosfoguel, Ramán (2004) 'Race and ethnicity or racialized ethnicities? Identities within global coloniality', *Ethnicities*, 4(3): 315–336.

Gruber, Christiane (2013), 'The visual emergence of the Occupy Gezi movement, Part One: Oh Biber!' *Jadaliyya*, 6 July, http://www.jadaliyya.com/Details/28971/The-Visual-Emergence-of-the-Occupy-Gezi-Movement,-Part-One-Oh-Biber.

Grusin, Richard (2015) 'Radical mediation', *Critical Inquiry*, 42(1): 124–148.

Haas, Benjamin (2017) 'China moves to block internet VPNs from 2018', *Guardian*, 11 July.

Halavais, Alex (2004) 'The Isuzu Experiment', Alex Halavais:a thaumaturgical compendium blog, 29 August, http://alex.halavais.net/news/index.php?p=794.

Halavais, Alexander and Lackaff, Derek (2008) 'An analysis of topical coverage of Wikipedia', *Journal of Computer-Mediated Communication*, 13(2): 429–440.

Halfaker, Aaron, Geiger, R. Stuart, Morgan, Jonathan and Riedl, John (2013) 'The rise and decline of an open collaboration system: How Wikipedia's reaction to sudden popularity is killing it', *American Behavioral Scientist*, 57(5): 664–688.

Hargittai, Ester and Shaw, Aaron (2015) 'Mind the skills gap: The role of Internet know-how and gender in differentiated contributions to Wikipedia', *Information, Communication & Society*, 18(4): 424–442.

Hay, James and Couldry, Nick (2011) 'Rethinking convergence/culture: An introduction', *Cultural Studies*, 25(4/5): 473–486.

Hecht, Brent and Gergle, Darren (2010) 'The Tower of Babel meets Web 2.0: User-generated content and its applications in a multilingual context', *Proceedings of CHI '10*. New York: ACM Press, 291–300.

Heclo, Hugh (1978) 'Issue networks and the executive establishment', in Anthony King (ed.), *The New American Political System*. Washington, DC: American Enterprise Institute, pp. 87–124.

Heine, Jan-Jaap, Hidding, Nienke, Wissel, Julia, van Zoggel, Marlie, Simons, Danny and Geboers, Marloes (2016) 'Engagement of tragedy on social media: The visual language of Instagram and Twitter in two case studies', Digital Methods Winter School 2016, Amsterdam, https://wiki.digitalmethods.net/Dmi/WinterSchool2016EngagementWithTragedySocialMedia.

Helmond, Anne (2015) 'The platformization of the web: Making web data platform ready', *Social Media + Society*, 30 September.

Helmond, Anne (2016) 'The platformization of the web', PhD dissertation, University of Amsterdam.

Helmond, Anne (2017) 'Historical website ecology: Analyzing past states of the web using archived source code', In Niels Brügger (ed.), Web 25: Histories from the First 25 Years of the World Wide Web. New York: Peter Lang, pp. 139–155.

Helmond, Anne, Gerlitz, Carolin, van der Vlist, Fernando and Weltevrede, Esther (2016) 'AoIR 2016 Digital Methods Workshop – tracking the trackers', Slideshare.net, 5 October, https://www.slideshare.net/cgrltz/aoir-2016-digital-methods-workshop-tracking-the-trackers-66765013.

Helmond, Anne, Huurdeman, Hugo, Samar, Thaer, Steinfeld, Nili and van der Velden, Lonneke (2012) 'Traces of the trackers', Digital Methods Summer School 2012, 29 June, https://wiki.digitalmethods.net/Dmi/TracingTheTrackers.

Hermens, Eelke (2011) 'The New York Times – A web historiography', screencast documentary, Amsterdam: University of Amsterdam, https://vimeo.com/32319207.

Herring, Susan, Job-Sluder, Kirk, Scheckler, Rebecca and Barab, Sasha (2002) 'Searching for safety online: Managing "trolling" in a feminist forum', *The Information Society*, 18: 371–384.

HeyVeronica (2012), 'Binders full of women', Tumblr, http://bindersfullofwomen.tumblr.com.

Hindman, Matthew (2008) *The Myth of Digital Democracy*. Princeton, NJ: Princeton University Press.

Hine, Christine (ed.) (2005) *Virtual Methods: Issues in Social Research on the Internet*. Oxford: Berg.

Hine, Gabriel Emile, Onaolapo, Jeremiah, De Cristofaro, Emiliano, Kourtellis, Nicolas, Leontiadis, Ilias, Samaras, Riginos, Stringhini, Gianluca and Blackburn, Jeremy (2017) 'A Longitudinal Measurement Study of 4chan's Politically Incorrect Forum and its Effect on the Web', Proceedings of the 11th International AAAI Conference on Web and Social Media (ICWSM'17). New York: ACM.

Hobbs, Robert (2003) *Mark Lombardi: Global Networks*. New York: Independent Curators International.

Hockx-Yu, Helen (2014) 'Access and scholarly use of web archives', *Alexandria*, 25(1): 113–127.

Hogan, Bernie (2014) 'A comment on Fuchs' Social Media', Bernie Hogan blog, Oxford Internet Institute, 10 October, https://blogs.oii.ox.ac.uk/hogan/2014/10/10/a-comment-on-fuchs-social-media/.

Holan, Angie (2016) 'In context: Hillary Clinton and the "basket of deplorables"', Politifact, 11 September, http://www.politifact.com/truth-o-meter/article/2016/sep/11/context-hillary-clinton-basket-deplorables/.

Honeycutt, Courtenay and Herring, Susan C. (2009) 'Beyond microblogging: Conversation and collaboration via Twitter', *Proceedings of the Forty-Second Hawaii International Conference on System Sciences (HICSS-42)*. Los Alamitos, CA: IEEE Press, pp. 1–10.

Howe, Daniel C., Nissenbaum, Helen and Toubiana, Vincent (2011) 'Track me not', artware, http://cs.nyu.edu/trackmenot/

Howell, Beryl A. (2006) 'Proving web history: How to use the Internet Archive', *Journal of Internet Law*, 9(8): 3–9.

Huberman, Bernardo A., Romero, Daniel M. and Wu, Fang (2009) 'Social networks that matter: Twitter under the microscope', *First Monday*, *14*(1).

Internet Archive (2016) FAQ, San Francisco: Internet Archive, https://archive.org/about/faqs.php#265.

Introna, Lucas D. and Nissenbaum, Helen (2000) 'Shaping the web: Why the politics of search engines matters', *The Information Society*, *16*(3): 169–185.

Ito, Mizuko (2008) 'Introduction', in Kazys Varnelis (ed.), *Networked Publics*. Cambridge, MA: MIT Press, pp. 1–14.

Jacobsen, Grethe (2008) 'Web archiving: Issues and problems in collection building and access', *LIBER Quarterly*, *18*(3–4): 366–376.

Jacomy, Mathieu, Girard, Paul, Ooghe-Tabanou, Benjamin and Venturini, Tommaso (2016) 'Hyphe, a curation-oriented approach to web crawling for the social sciences', *Proceedings of the International AAAI Conference on Web and Social Media (ICWSM-16)*, Cologne, Germany.

Jacomy, Mathieu, Venturini, Tommaso, Heymann, Sebastien and Bastian, Mathieu (2014) 'ForceAtlas2, a continuous graph layout algorithm for handy network visualization designed for the Gephi software', *PLoS ONE 9*(6): e98679.

Jansen, Bernard J., Zhang, Mimi, Sobel, Kate and Chowdury, Abdur (2009) 'Twitter power: Tweets as electronic word of mouth', *Journal of the American Society for Information Science and Technology*, *60*(11): 2169–2188.

Java, Akshay, Song, Xiaodan, Finin, Tim and Tseng, Belle (2007) 'Why we Twitter: Understanding microblogging usage and communities', Joint 9th WEBKDD and 1st SNA-KDD Workshop '07, New York: ACM.

Jemielniak, Dariusz (2014) *Common Knowledge? An Ethnography of Wikipedia*. Palo Alto, CA: Stanford University Press.

Jenkins, Henry (2006) *Convergence Culture*. New York: New York University Press.

Jenkins, Henry (2009) *Confronting the Challenges of Participatory Culture*. Cambridge, MA: MIT Press.

Jenkins, Henry (2011) 'Transmedia 202: Further reflections', Henryjenkins.org blog, 1 August, http://henryjenkins.org/2011/08/defining_transmedia_further_re.html.

Jenkins, Henry (2014) 'Spreadable content makes the consumer king', interview, Pull Q Media, 20 January, https://www.youtube.com/watch?v=ZCKoLB1kUsY.

Jenkins, Henry, Ford, Sam and Green, Joshua (2013) *Spreadable Media*. New York: New York University Press.

Jenkins, Henry, Purushotma, Ravi, Clinton, Katie, Weigel, Margaret and Robison, Alice (2005) *Confronting the Challenges of Participatory Culture: Media Education for the*

21st Century, White Paper, Chicago: MacArthur Foundation, http://www. newmedialiteracies.org/wp-content/uploads/pdfs/NMLWhitePaper.pdf

Joinson, Adam (2008) 'Looking at, looking up or keeping up with people? Motives and use of Facebook', *CHI '08 Proceedings of the SIGCHI Conference on Human Factors in Computing System.* New York: ACM, pp. 1027–1036.

Jerslev, Anne (2016) 'In the time of the microcelebrity: Celebrification and the YouTuber Zoella', *International Journal of Communication, 10*: 5233–5251.

Johansson, Anna, Eriksson, Maria, Vonderau, Patrick, Snickars, Pelle and Fleischer, Rasmus (2019) *Spotify Teardown.* Cambridge, MA: MIT Press.

Jones, Tamara (1986) 'The great pretenders', *Washington Post*, 14 July, F01.

Kahn, Joseph (2006) 'So long, Dalai Lama: Google adapts to China', *New York Times*, 12 February.

Kao, Evelyn (2017) 'Making search results more local and relevant', Google blog, 27 October, https://www.blog.google/products/search/making-search-results-more-local-and-relevant/.

Karkın, Naci, Yavuz, Nilay, Parlak, İsmet and İkiz, Özlem Özdeşim (2015) 'Twitter use by politicians during social uprisings: An analysis of Gezi Park protests in Turkey', *dg.o '15: Proceedings of the 16th Annual International Conference on Digital Government Research*, New York: ACM, pp. 20–28.

Keegan, Jon (2016) 'Blue feed, red feed', *Wall Street Journal*, 18 May.

Kennedy, Helen and Hill, Rosemary Lucy (2016) 'The pleasure and pain of visualizing data in times of data power', *Television & New Media*, 7 September.

Klein, Martin, Van de Sompel, Herbert, Sanderson, Robert, Shankar, Harihar, Balakireva, Lyudmila, Zhou, Ke and Tobin, Richard (2014) 'Scholarly context not found: One in five articles suffers from reference rot', *PLoS ONE, 9*(12): e115253.

Knowyourmeme.com (2018) 'This is why we can't have nice things', meme entry, http://knowyourmeme.com/memes/this-is-why-we-cant-have-nice-things.

Kohs, Gregory (2014) 'Google's knowledge graph boxes: Killing Wikipedia?', wikipediocracy.com, 6 January, http://wikipediocracy.com/2014/01/06/googles-knowledge-graph-killing-wikipedia/.

Kok, Saskia and Rogers, Richard (2017) 'Rethinking migration in the digital age: Transglocalization and the Somali diaspora', *Global Networks, 17*(1): 23–46.

Kokolakis, Spyros (2017) 'Privacy attitudes and privacy behaviour: A review of current research on the privacy paradox phenomenon', *Computers & Security, 64*: 122–134.

Kovalev, Alexey (2017) 'Russia's infamous "troll factory" is now posing as a media empire', *Moscow Times*, 24 March.

Kramer, Adam D.I., Guillory, Jamie E. and Hancock, Jeffrey T. (2014) 'Experimental evidence of massive-scale emotional contagion through social networks', *Proceedings of the National Academy of Sciences of the USA*, 111(24): 8788–8790.

Kramer, Andrew E. and Higgins, Andrew (2017) 'In Ukraine, a malware expert who could blow the whistle on Russian hacking', *New York Times*, 17 August.

Krause, Till and Grassegger, Hannes (2016) 'Inside Facebook', *Süddeutsche Zeitung*, 15 December [in German].

Krebs, Valdis (2005) 'Social network analysis of the 9-11 terrorist network', webpage, Cleveland, OH: orgnet.com, http://www.orgnet.com/hijackers.html.

Kruitbosch, Gijs and Nack, Frank (2008) 'Broadcast yourself on YouTube – really?' HCC '08 Proceedings of the 3rd ACM international workshop on Human-centered computing, Vancouver, British Columbia, Canada, 31 October, pp.7–10.

Kücklich, Julien (2007) 'Homo deludens: Cheating as a methodological tool in digital games research', *Convergence: The International Journal of Research into New Media Technologies, 13*(4): 355–367.

Kurt, Serhat a.k.a. Hogg, Jon (2016) Ruin My Search History, software, http://ruinmysearchhistory.com/

Kwak, Haewoon, Lee, Changhyun, Park, Hosung and Moon, Sue (2010) 'What is Twitter, a social network or a news media?', *Proceedings of WWW 2010*. New York: ACM.

Langelaar, Walter (2012) 'Web 2.0 Suicide Machine', Presentation at Unlike Us #2: Understanding Social Media Monopolies and Their Alternatives, Network Cultures, Amsterdam, 9 March.

Langreiter, Christian (2017) 'Google.com and Google.cn results compared', *langreiter.com, 2004–2006*, http://www.langreiter.com/exec/google-vs-google.html.

Lardinois, Frederic (2016) 'A look inside Facebook's data center', *TechCrunch*, 13 July, https://techcrunch.com/gallery/a-look-inside-facebooks-data-center/.

Latour, Bruno (2005a) 'From realpolitik to dingpolitik or how to make things public', in Bruno Latour and Peter Weibel (eds), *Making Things Public: Atmospheres of Democracy*. Cambridge, MA: MIT Press, pp. 14–41.

Latour, Bruno (2005b) *Reassembling the Social*. New York: Oxford University Press.

Laufer, Paul, Wagner, Claudia, Flöck, Fabian and Strohmaier, Markus (2015) 'Mining cross-cultural relations from Wikipedia: A study of 31 European food cultures', *Proceedings of the ACM Web Science Conference WebSci '15*. New York: ACM, pp. 1–10.

Laursen, Cæcilie (2017) 'What is a data sprint? An inquiry into data sprints in practice in Copenhagen', Ethos Lab blog, 15 February, https://ethos.itu.dk/2017/02/15/caecilie-laursen/.

Lavigne, Sam (2017) 'Taxonomy of humans according to Twitter', *The New Inquiry*, 5 July.

Lawrence, Steve and Giles, C. Lee (1998) 'Searching the world wide web', *Science, 280*(5360): 98–100.

Lawrence, Steve and Giles, C. Lee (1999) 'Accessibility of information on the web', *Nature, 400*(6740): 107–109.

Lazer, David, Kennedy, Ryan, King, Gary and Vespignani, Alessandro (2014) 'The parable of Google Flu: Traps in big data', *Science, 343*(6176), 1203–1205.

Lazer, David, Pentland, Alex, Adamic, Lada, Aral, Sinan, Barabási, Albert-László, Brewer, Devon, Christakis, Nicholas, Contractor, Noshir, Fowler, James, Gutmann, Myron, Jebara, Tony, King, Gary, Macy, Michael, Roy, Deb and Van Alstyne, Marshall (2009) 'Computational social science', *Science, 323*(5915): 721–723.

Lee, Timothy B. (2013) 'Here's how Iran censors the Internet', *Washington Post*, 15 August.

Leftintherain (2011) 'Wikipedia is the new Google', image, Photobucket, http://media.photobucket.com/image/Wikipedia%20icon/leftintherain/google-Wikipedia.png?o=16.

Lessig, Lawrence (2004) *Free Culture*. New York: Penguin.

Levy, Steven (2012) 'Google throws open doors to its top-secret data center', *Wired*, 17 October.

Lewis, Kevin, Kaufman, Jason and Christakis, Nicholas (2008a) 'The taste for privacy: An analysis of college student privacy settings in an online social network', *Journal of Computer-Mediated Communication*, *14*(1): 79–100.

Lewis, Kevin, Kaufman, Jason, Gonzalez, Marco, Wimmer, Andreas and Christakis, Nicholas (2008b) 'Tastes, ties, and time: A new social network dataset using Facebook. com', *Social Networks*, *30*(4): 330–342.

Light, Ben (2017) 'Ashley Madison: Introduction to the walkthrough method', in Jeremy Wade Morris and Sarah Murray (eds), *Appified*. Ann Arbor: University of Michigan Press.

Lih, Andrew (2009) *The Wikipedia Revolution*. NewYork: Hyperion.

Lindgren, Simon and Lundström, Ragnar (2011) 'Pirate culture and hacktivist mobilization: The cultural and social protocols of #WikiLeaks on Twitter', *New Media & Society*, *13*(6): 999–1018.

Lippmann, Walter (1922) *Public Opinion*. New York: Macmillan.

Lippmann, Walter (1927) *The Phantom Public*. New York: Macmillan.

Livingstone, Randall M. (2010) 'Let's leave the bias to the mainstream media: A Wikipedia community fighting for information neutrality', *M/C Journal*, *13*(6).

Livingstone, Sonia (2014) 'Developing social media literacy: How children learn to interpret risky opportunities on social network sites', *Communications: The European Journal of Communication Research*, *39*(3): 283–303.

Livio, Maya, Mataly, Jules and Schuh, Mathias (2012) 'TheKnot.com – a website historiography', screencast documentary, Amsterdam: University of Amsterdam, https://www.youtube.com/watch?v=5cxVXJthETA.

Lomborg, Stine and Bechmann, Anja (2014) 'Using APIs for data collection on social media', *The Information Society*, *30*(4): 256–265.

Lotan, Gilad, Graeff, Erhardt, Ananny, Mike, Gaffney, Devin, Pearce, Ian and boyd, danah (2011) 'The revolutions were tweeted: Information flows during the 2011 Tunisian and Egyptian revolutions', *International Journal of Communication*, *5*: 1375–1405.

Loveland, Jeff and Reagle, Joseph (2013) 'Wikipedia and encyclopedic production', *New Media & Society*, *15*(8): 1294–1311.

Lury, Celia and Wakeford, Nina (2012) 'Introduction: A perpetual inventory', in Celia Lury and Nina Wakeford (eds), *Inventive Methods: The Happening of the Social*. London: Routledge, pp. 1–24.

Lynch, Ashley (2016) 'Gamers are still over (but they're not over Trump)', Extranewsfeed, 25 October, https://extranewsfeed.com/gamers-are-still-over-but-theyre-not-over-trump-807dde821512.

MacKinnon, Rebecca (2011) 'China's "Networked Authoritarianism"', *Journal of Democracy*, *22*(2).

Maddow, Rachel (2016) 'Media matters', MSNBC News, 25 September, https://www.youtube.com/watch?v=okoAQCoMYx8.

Magnus, P.D. (2008) 'Early response to false claims in Wikipedia', *First Monday*, *13*(9).

Mandiberg, Michael (2015) 'Print Wikipedia', art project, printwikipedia.com.

Manovich, Lev (2007) 'Cultural analytics: Analysis and visualization of large cultural data sets. A proposal from Software Studies Initiative', CALIT2, 30 September.

Marres, Noortje (2015) 'Why map issues? On controversy analysis as a digital method', *Science, Technology and Human Values*, 40(5): 655–686.

Marres, Noortje (2017) *Digital Sociology*. Cambridge: Polity.

Marres, Noortje (2018) 'Why we can't have our facts back', *Engaging Science, Technology, and Society*, 4: 423-443.

Marres, Noortje and Rogers, Richard (2008) 'Subsuming the ground: How local realities of the Ferghana Valley, the Narmada Dams and the BTC pipeline are put to use on the web', *Economy and Society*, 37(2): 251–281.

Marres, Noortje and Weltevrede, Esther (2013) 'Scraping the social? Issues in live social research', *Journal of Cultural Economy*, 6(3): 313–335.

Marsh, Jackie (2016) '"Unboxing" videos: Co-construction of the child as cyberflâneur', *Discourse: Studies in the Cultural Politics of Education*, 37(3): 369–380.

Marwick, Alice E. (2015) 'Instafame: Luxury selfies in the attention economy', *Public Culture*, 27(1): 137–160.

Marwick, Alice E. and boyd, danah (2011) 'I tweet honestly, I tweet passionately: Twitter users, context collapse, and the imagined audience', *New Media & Society*, 13(1): 114–133.

Masnick, Mike (2015) 'For 10 years everyone's been using "The Streisand effect" without paying; Now I'm going to start issuing takedowns', *Techdirt*, 8 January, https://www.techdirt.com/articles/20150107/13292829624/10-years-everyones-been-using-streisand-effect-without-paying-now-im-going-to-start-issuing-takedowns.shtml.

Massa, Paolo and Scrinzi, Federico (2011) 'Exploring linguistic points of view of Wikipedia', *Proceedings of the 7th International Symposium on Wikis and Open Collaboration*. New York: ACM, pp. 213–214.

Matthews, Rob (2009) 'Wikipedia, 5000 pages, fully printed', artwork, http://www.rob-matthews.com/index.php?/project/wikipedia/.

McCown, Frank and Nelson, Michael L. (2009) 'What happens when Facebook is gone?' *JCDL'09*. New York: ACM, pp. 251–254.

McGill, Andrew (2016) 'Can Twitter fit inside the Library of Congress?' *The Atlantic*, 4 August.

McIver, David J. and Brownstein, John S. (2014) 'Wikipedia usage estimates prevalence of influenza-like illness in the United States in near real-time', *PLoS Computational Biology*, 10(4): e1003581.

McKeon, Matt (2010) 'The evolution of privacy on Facebook', Mattmckeon.com, April, http://mattmckeon.com/facebook-privacy/.

McMillan, Sally J. (2000) 'The microscope and the moving target: The challenges of applying content analysis to the World Wide Web', *Journalism and Mass Communication Quarterly*. 77: 80–98.

Memri (2012) 'Special dispatch: The list of flagged videos', Middle East Media Research Institute, http://www.memri.org/publicdocs/youtube_flagging_9.11_list.pdf

Meng, Bingchun (2011) 'From steamed bun to grass mud horse: E gao as alternative political discourse on the Chinese Internet', *Global Media and Communication*, 7(1): 33–51.

Merritt, Harry C. (2013) 'Sharecropping in the Cloud', *Jacobin*, 7 November, https://jacobinmag.com/2013/11/sharecropping-in-the-cloud/.

Mesgari, Mostafa, Okoli, Chitu, Mehdi, Mohamad, Nielsen, Finn Årup and Lanamäki, Arto (2015) '"The sum of all human knowledge": A systematic review of scholarly research on the content of Wikipedia', *Journal of the Association for Information Science and Technology*. 66(2): 219–245.

Messina, Chris (2007) 'Groups for Twitter; or a proposal for Twitter tag channels', Factory Joe blog, 25 August, http://factoryjoe.com/blog/2007/08/25/groups-for-twitter-or-a-proposal-for-twitter-tag-channels/.

Meyer, Michelle N. (2015) 'Two cheers for corporate experimentation: The A/B illusion and the virtues of data-driven innovation', *Colorado Technology Law Journal*, 13(2): 273–332.

Michel, Jean-Baptiste, Shen, Yuan Kui, Aiden, Aviva P., Veres, Adrian, Gray, Matthew K., The Google Books Team, Pickett, Joseph P., Holberg, Dale, Clancy, Dan, Norvig, Peter, Orwant, Jon, Pinker, Steven, Nowak, Martin A. and Aiden, Erez Lieberman (2011) 'Quantitative analysis of culture using millions of digitized books', *Science*, 331(6014): 176–182.

Miller, Vincent (2008) 'New media, networking and phatic culture', *Convergence*, 14(4): 387–400.

Milligan, Ian (2016) 'Lost in the infinite archive: The promise and pitfalls of web archives', *International Journal of Humanities and Arts Computing*, 10(1): 78–94.

Milne, David and Witten, Ian H. (2013) 'An open-source toolkit for mining Wikipedia', *Artificial Intelligence*, 194: 222–239.

Mohr, John W., Wagner-Pacifici, Robin and Breiger, Ronald L. (2015) 'Toward a computational hermeneutics', *Big Data & Society*, 2(2).

Moretti, Franco (2005) *Graphs, Maps, Trees: Abstract Models for a Literary History*. London: Verso.

Morlin, Bill (2016), 'The Anti-Defamation League added the popular Pepe the Frog meme to its Hate on Display database', Hatewatch, Southern Law Poverty Center, https://www.splcenter.org/hatewatch/2016/09/28/pepe-joins-echoes-new-hate-symbols.

Morozov, Evgeny (2009) 'Iran: Downside to the "Twitter Revolution"', *Dissent*, 56(4): 10–14.

Morozov, Evgeny (2010) 'Why the internet is failing Iran's activists', *Prospect Magazine*, 166, 5 January.

Morozov, Evgeny (2011) *The Net Delusion: The Dark Side of Internet Freedom*. Philadelphia: Perseus.

Mostaghim, Ramin and Daragahi, Borzou (2009) 'Iran election anger boils; Ahmadinejad defends results', *Los Angeles Times*, 15 June.

Murphy, Jamie, Hashim, Noor Hazarina and O'Connor, Peter (2007) 'Take me back: Validating the Wayback Machine', *Journal of Computer-Mediated Communication*, 13(1): 60–75.

Nagle, Angela (2017) *Kill All Normies: Online Culture Wars from Tumblr and 4chan and the Alt-Right and Trump*. Winchester: Zero Books.

Napoli, Philip M. (2014) 'Automated media: An institutional theory perspective on algorithmic media production and consumption', *Communication Theory*, 24: 340–360.

Negroponte, Nicholas (1995) *Being Digital*. London: Hodder & Stoughton.

Nemoto, Keiichi and Gloor, Peter A. (2011) 'Analyzing cultural differences in collaborative innovation networks by analyzing editing behavior in different-language Wikipedias', *Procedia – Social and Behavioral Sciences*, 26: 180–190.

Niederer, Sabine (2016) *Networked Content Analysis: The Case of Climate Change*. PhD dissertation, University of Amsterdam.

Niederer, Sabine and van Dijck, José (2010) 'Wisdom of the crowd or technicity of content? Wikipedia as a socio-technical system', *New Media & Society*, *12*(8): 1368–1387.

Nissenbaum, Helen (2009) *Privacy in Context: Technology, Policy, and the Integrity of Social Life*. Stanford, CA: Stanford University Press.

Nissenbaum, Helen (2011) 'A contextual approach to privacy online', *Daedalus*, *140*(4): 32–48.

Noman, Helmi (2011) 'In the name of God: Faith-based internet censorship in majority Muslim countries', Open Net Initiative report, Toronto: Open Net Initiative, 1 August.

Nye, David E. (1994) *American Technological Sublime*. Cambridge, MA: MIT Press.

O'Reilly, Tim (2005) 'What is Web 2.0: Design patterns and business models for the next generation of software', blog post, Sebastopol, CA: O'Reilly Media, www.oreilly.com/pub/a/web2/archive/what-is-web-20.html.

O'Reilly, Tim and Milstein, Sarah (2009) *The Twitter Book*. Sebastopol, CA: O'Reilly Media.

Oates, Sarah (2017) 'Kompromat goes global? Assessing a Russian media tool in the United States', *Slavic Review*, *76*(S1): S57–S65.

OccupyWallStreet (2011) 'Forum Post: Proposed list of demands for Occupy Wall St movement!' 25 September, http://occupywallst.org/forum/proposed-list-of-demands-for-occupy-wall-st-moveme/.

Ooghe-Tabanou, Benjamin, Jacomy, Mathieu, Girard, Paul and Plique, Guillaume (2018) 'Hyperlink is not dead!', *WS.2 2018*, 3-5 October, Paris, France.

Open Net Initiative (2007) 'Google China search comparison', webpage, Toronto: Citizen Lab, http://opennet.net/google_china.

Open Net Initiative (2014) 'About filtering', webpage, Toronto: Citizen Lab, https://opennet.net/aboutfiltering.

Osterberg, Gayle (2013) 'Update on the Twitter archive at the Library of Congress', Library of Congress blog, 4 January, http://blogs.loc.gov/loc/2013/01/update-on-the-twitter-archive-at-the-library-of-congress/.

Osterberg, Gayle (2017) 'Update on the Twitter Archive at the Library of Congress', Library of Congress blog, 26 December, https://blogs.loc.gov/loc/2017/12/update-on-the-twitter-archive-at-the-library-of-congress-2/.

Ostrow, Adam (2009) 'Twitter reschedules maintenance around #IranElection controversy', *Mashable*, 15 June, https://mashable.com/2009/06/15/twitter-iran-election/.

Padgett, John F. and Ansell, Christopher K. (1993) 'Robust action and the rise of the Medici, 1400-1434', *American Journal of Sociology*, *98*(6): 1259–1319.

Paglan, Trevor (2016) 'Deep web dive: Behind the scenes', creators project, https://www.youtube.com/watch?v=h7guR5ei30Y.

Palfrey, John and Zittrain, Jonathan (2011) 'Better data for a better internet', *Science*. *334*(6060): 1210–1211.

Papacharissi, Zizi (2012) 'Without you, I'm nothing: Performances of the self on Twitter', *International Journal of Communication*, *6*: 1989–2006.

Papacharissi, Zizi (2015) *Affective Publics*. New York: Oxford University Press.

Pariser, Eli (2011) *The Filter Bubble*. New York: Penguin.

Parker, Ashley (2011) 'Twitter's secret handshake', *New York Times*, 10 June.

Pear Analytics (2009) 'Twitter study', San Antonio, TX: Pear Analytics, August.

Pearce, Warren (2018) 'Approach with care: Research within and beyond APIs', lecture, University of Southampton, 30 April, https://www.youtube.com/watch?v=DaIRdyMIzeA.

Phillips, Whitney (2015) *This Is Why We Can't Have Nice Things: Mapping the Relationship between Online Trolling and Mainstream Culture*. Cambridge, MA: MIT Press.

Poell, Thomes and Borra, Erik (2012) 'Twitter, YouTube, and Flickr as platforms of alternative journalism', *Journalism*, *13*(6): 695–713.

Pon, Bryan, Seppälä, Timo and Kenney, Martin (2014) 'Android and the demise of operating system-based power: Firm strategy and platform control in the post-PC world', *Telecommunications Policy*, *38*(11): 979–991.

Portwood-Stacer, Laura (2013) 'Media refusal and conspicuous non-consumption: The performative and political dimensions of Facebook abstention', *New Media & Society*, *15*(7): 1041–1057.

Pringle, Glen, Allison, Lloyd and Dowe, David L. (1998) 'What is a tall poppy among Web pages?', *Computer Networks and ISDN Systems*, *30*(1–7): 369–377.

Prodhan, Georgina and Lauer, Klaus (2016) 'Germans talk tough, fete Facebook's Zuckerberg', *Reuters*, 25 February.

Puschmann, Cornelius and Bozdag, Engin (2014) 'Staking out the unclear ethical terrain of online social experiments', *Internet Policy Review*, *3*(4).

Puschmann, Cornelius and Burgess, Jean (2013) 'The politics of Twitter data', in Katrin Weller, Axel Bruns, Jean Burgess, Merja Mahrt and Cornelius Puschmann (eds), *Twitter and Society*. New York: Peter Lang, pp. 43–54.

Raehsler, Lisa (2012) 'What people search for – most popular keywords', *Search Engine Watch*, 18 April.

Rambukkana, Nathan (2015) 'Hashtags as technosocial events', in Nathan Rambukkana (ed.), *Hashtag Publics: The Power and Politics of Discursive Networks*. New York: Peter Lang, pp. 1–10.

Rao, Adithya, Spasojevic, Nemanja, Li, Zhisheng and Dsouza, Trevor (2015) 'Klout score: Measuring influence across multiple social networks', *2015 IEEE International Big Data Conference – Workshop on Mining Big Data in Social Networks*. New York: ACM.

Ratto, Matt (2011) 'Critical making: Conceptual and material studies in technology and social life', *The Information Society*, *4*: 252–260.

Ratto, Matt and Boller, Megan (2014) 'Introduction', in Matt Ratto and Megan Boller (eds), *DIY Citizenship: Critical Making and Social Media*. Cambridge, MA: MIT Press, pp. 1–22.

Raymond, Matt (2010a) 'How tweet it is! Library acquires entire Twitter archive', Library of Congress blog, 14 April, https://blogs.loc.gov/loc/2010/04/how-tweet-it-is-library-acquires-entire-twitter-archive/

Raymond, Matt (2010b) 'The Library and Twitter: An FAQ', Library of Congress blog, 28 April, https://blogs.loc.gov/loc/2010/04/the-library-and-twitter-an-faq/.

Read, Brock (2006) 'Can Wikipedia ever make the grade?' *Chronicle of Higher Education*, *53*(10): A31.

Reagle, Joseph M. (2008) 'In good faith: Wikipedia and the pursuit of the universal encyclopedia', PhD dissertation, New York University.

Reagle, Joseph M. (2015) *Reading the Comments: Likers, Haters, and Manipulators*. Cambridge, MA: MIT Press.

Rector, Lucy Holman (2008) 'Comparison of Wikipedia and other encyclopedias for accuracy, breadth, and depth in historical articles', *Reference Service Review*, *36*(1): 7–22.

Renner, Nausicaa (2017) 'Memes trump articles on Breitbart's Facebook page', *Columbia Journalism Review*, 30 January.

Reporters without Borders (2013) 'Enemies of the Internet 2013. Special report: Surveillance', RSF report, Paris: RSF, http://surveillance.rsf.org/en/wp-content/uploads/sites/2/2013/03/enemies-of-the-internet_2013.pdf.

Reporters without Borders (2014) 'Saudi Arabia: Prime centre of content blocking', Enemies of the Internet series, Paris: RSF. 11 March, http://12mars.rsf.org/2014-en/2014/03/11/saudi-arabia/.

Reporters without Borders (2016a) 'Collateral freedom: thwarting censorship in 13 "Enemy of the Internet" countries', presentation, Paris: RSF, https://12mars.rsf.org/2016-en/presentation/.

Reporters without Borders (2016b) 'Iran creates "halal internet" to control online information', news report, Paris: RSF, 6 September, https://rsf.org/en/news/iran-creates-halal-internet-control-online-information.

Reporters without Borders (2017) 'The dubious but lucrative surveillance business', 12 March, Paris: RSF, https://rsf.org/en/reports/dubious-lucrative-surveillance-business.

Rheingold, Howard (1993) *The Virtual Community*. Reading, MA: Addison Wesley.

Rhizome (2014) 'Amalia Ulman: Excellences & Perfections', web project, New York: Rhizome, http://webenact.rhizome.org/excellences-and-perfections.

Rhoads, Christopher and Fassihi, Farnaz (2011) 'Iran vows to unplug Internet', *The Wall Street Journal*, 28 May.

Rieder, Bernhard (2012) 'What is PageRank? A historical and conceptual investigation of a recursive status index', *Computational Culture*, 2.

Rieder, Bernhard (2013) 'Studying Facebook via data extraction: The Netvizz application', *Proceedings of WebSci13*. New York: ACM Press.

Rieder, Bernhard (2015a) 'The end of Netvizz (?)', The Politics of Systems blog, 23 January, http://thepoliticsofsystems.net/2015/01/the-end-of-netvizz/.

Rieder, Bernhard (2015b) 'Social media data analysis', lecture delivered at the University of Amsterdam, December.

Rieder, Bernhard (2016) 'Closing APIs and the public scrutiny of very large online platforms', The Politics of Systems blog, 27 May, http://thepoliticsofsystems.net/2016/05/closing-apis-and-the-public-scrutiny-of-very-large-online-platforms/.

Rieder, Bernhard (2018) 'Facebook's app review and how independent research just got a lot harder', The Politics of Systems blog, 11 August, http://thepoliticsofsystems.net/2018/08/facebooks-app-review-and-how-independent-research-just-got-a-lot-harder/.

Rieder, Bernhard, Abdulla, Rasha, Poell, Thomas, Woltering, Robbert and Zack, Liesbeth (2015) 'Data critique and analytical opportunities for very large Facebook Pages: Lessons learned from exploring "We are all Khaled Said"', *Big Data & Society*, *2*(2).

Rieder, Bernhard, Matamoros-Fernández Ariadna and Coromina, Òscar (2018) 'From ranking algorithms to "ranking cultures": Investigating the modulation of visibility in YouTube search results', *Convergence: The International Journal of Research into New Media Technologies*, *24*(1): 50–68.

Riesewieck, Moritz and Block, Hans (2018) *The Cleaners*, documentary film, Cologne: Gebrueder Beetz Filmproduktion.

Robinson, Piers (2002) *The CNN Effect: The Myth of News, Foreign Policy and Intervention*. London: Routledge.

Rogers, Richard (2000) 'Introduction', in Richard Rogers (ed.), *Preferred Placement: Knowledge Politics on the Web*. Maastricht: Jan van Eyck Editions.

Rogers, Richard (2002) 'Towards a live social science on the web', *EASST Review*, *21*(3/4): 2–4.

Rogers, Richard (2009a) *The End of the Virtual: Digital Methods*. Amsterdam: Amsterdam University Press.

Rogers, Richard (2009b) 'The Googlization question, and the inculpable engine', in Felix Stalder and Konrad Becker (eds), *Deep Search: The Politics of Search Engines*. Edison, NJ: Transaction Publishers, pp. 173–184.

Rogers, Richard (2009c) 'The internet treats censorship as a malfunction and routes around it? A new media approach to the study of state internet censorship', in Jussi Parikka and Tony Sampson (eds), *The Spam Book: On Viruses, Porn, and other Anomalies from the Dark Side of Digital Culture*. Cresskill, NJ: Hampton Press, pp. 229–247.

Rogers, Richard (2009d) 'Post-demographic machines', in Annet Dekker and Annette Wolfsberger (eds), *Walled Garden*. Amsterdam: Virtual Platform, pp. 29–39.

Rogers, Richard (2010) 'Mapping public web space with the Issuecrawler', in Claire Brossard and Bernard Reber (eds), *Digital Cognitive Technologies: Epistemology and Knowledge Society*. Hoboken, NJ: Wiley, pp. 115–126.

Rogers, Richard (2013a) 'Debanalizing Twitter: The transformation of an object of study', *Proceedings of WebSci13*. New York: ACM.

Rogers, Richard (2013b) *Digital Methods*. Cambridge, MA: MIT Press.

Rogers, Richard (2013c) 'Right-wing formations in Europe and their counter-measures: An online mapping', Amsterdam: Govcom.org Foundation and the Digital Methods Initiative, May, https://wiki.digitalmethods.net/Dmi/RightWingPopulismStudy.

Rogers, Richard (2014) 'Political research in the digital age', *International Public Policy Review*, *8*(1): 73–87.

Rogers, Richard (2018a) 'Otherwise engaged: From vanity metrics to critical analytics', *International Journal of Communication*, *12*: 450–472.

Rogers, Richard (2018b) 'Periodizing web archiving: Biographical, event-based, national and autobiographical traditions', in Niels Brügger and Ian Milligan (eds), *SAGE Handbook of Web History*. London: Sage.

Rogers, Richard (2018c) 'Social media research after the fake news debacle', *Partecipazione e Conflitto*, *11*(2): 557-570.

Rogers, Richard and Ben-David, Anat (2010) 'Coming to terms: A conflict analysis of the usage, in official and unofficial sources, of "security fence", "apartheid wall", and other terms for the structure between Israel and the Palestinian Territories', *Media, Conflict & War*, 2(3): 202–229.

Rogers, Richard and Govcom.org (2008) 'Google and the politics of tabs', screencast documentary, Amsterdam: Govcom.org, https://movies.digitalmethods.net/google.html.

Rogers, Richard, Jansen, Fieke, Stevenson, Michael and Weltevrede, Esther (2009a) 'Mapping democracy', *Global Information Society Watch 2009*, Association for Progressive Communications and Hivos.

Rogers, Richard and Sendijarevic, Emina (2012) 'Neutral or national point of view? A comparison of Srebrenica articles across Wikipedia's language versions', paper presented at Wikipedia Academy 2012, Berlin, 29 June–1 July.

Rogers, Richard, Sanchez-Querubin, Natalia and Kil, Aleksandra (2016) *Issue Mapping for an Ageing Europe*. Amsterdam: Amsterdam University Press.

Rogers, Richard, Weltevrede, Esther, Borra, Erik, van Dijk, Marieke and the Digital Methods Initiative (2009b) 'For the ppl of Iran: #iranelection RT', in Gennaro Ascione, Cinta Massip and Josep Perello (eds), *Cultures of Change: Social Atoms and Electronic Lives*. Barcelona: Actar and Arts Santa Monica, pp. 112–115.

Rogers, Richard, Weltevrede, Esther, Niederer, Sabine and Borra, Erik (2012) 'National web studies: Mapping Iran online', Iran Media Program, Annenberg School for Communication, University of Pennsylvania.

Rogers, Richard, Weltevrede, Esther, Niederer, Sabine and Borra, Erik (2013) 'National web studies: The case of Iran online', in John Hartley, Axel Bruns and Jean Burgess (eds), *A Companion to New Media Dynamics*. Oxford: Blackwell, pp. 142–166.

Roosendaal, Arnold (2012) 'We are all connected to Facebook … by Facebook!' in Serge Gutwirth, Ronald Leenes, Paul De Hert and Yves Poullet (eds), *European Data Protection: In Good Health?* Dordrecht: Springer, pp. 3–19.

Rosenzweig, Roy (2003) 'Scarcity or abundance? Preserving the past in a digital era', *American Historical Review*, 108(3): 735–762.

Rosenzweig, Roy (2006) 'Can history be open source? Wikipedia and the future of the past', *Journal of American History*, 93(1): 117–146.

Roth, Daniel (2009) 'The answer factory: Demand media and the fast, disposable, and profitable as hell media model', *Wired*, 19 October, https://www.wired.com/2009/10/ff-demandmedia/

Rouvroy, Antoinette and Berns, Thomas (2013) 'Algorithmic governmentality and prospects of emancipation', *Réseaux*, 1(177): 163–196.

Ruan, Lotus, Knockel, Jeffrey and Crete-Nishihata, Masashi (2017) 'We (can't) Chat: "709 crackdown" discussions blocked on Weibo and WeChat', Citizen Lab report, University of Toronto: Citizen Lab.

Rushkoff, Douglas (1994) *Media Virus: Hidden Agendas in Popular Culture*. New York: Ballantine.

Russell, Edmund and Kane, Jennifer (2008) 'The missing link: Assessing the reliability of Internet citations in history journals', *Technology and Culture*, 49(2): 420–429.

Ryan, J. (2011) *A History of the Internet and the Digital Future*. London: Reaktion.

Sanchez-Querubin, Natalia, Couturier, Anna, Invernizzi, Michele, Jimenez, Carlos, Profeta, Giovanni and Werner, Nadine (2018) 'YouTube as an archive for the end of life', Digital Methods Summer School, Amsterdam, https://digitalmethods.net/Dmi/SummerSchool2018YouTubeArchiveEndOfLife

Sandvig, Christian, Hamilton, Kevin, Karahalios, Karrie and Langbort, Cedric (2014) 'Auditing Algorithms: Research Methods for Detecting Discrimination on Internet Platforms', paper presented at the 64th Annual Meeting of the International Communication Association, Seattle, WA.

Sarno, David (2009a) 'Twitter creator Jack Dorsey illuminates the site's founding document. Part I', *Los Angeles Times*, 18 February.

Sarno, David (2009b) 'Twitter creator Jack Dorsey illuminates the site's founding document. Part II', *Los Angeles Times*, 19 February.

Schneider, Steve and Foot, Kirsten (2004) 'The Web as an object of study', *New Media & Society*, *6*(1): 114–122.

Scholz, Trebor (2008) 'Market ideology and the myths of Web 2.0', *First Monday*, *13*(3).

Scholz, Trebor (2016) *Platform Cooperativism. Challenging the Corporate Sharing Economy.* New York: Rosa Luxemburg Stiftung.

Scuttari, Anna, Stolero, Nathan, Ridley, Arran, Teernstra, Livia, van de Wetering, Denise, Invernizzi, Michele and Geboers, Marloes (2017) 'Emotional Clicktivism: Facebook reactions and affective responses to visuals', Digital Methods Summer School 2017, https://wiki.digitalmethods.net/Dmi/EmotionalClicktivism.

Senft, Theresa and Nancy Baym (2015) 'What does the selfie say? Investigating a global phenomenon', *International Journal of Communication*, *9*: 1588–1606.

Shachaf, Pnina and Hara, Noriko (2010) 'Beyond vandalism: Wikipedia trolls', *Journal of Information Science*, *36*(3): 357–370.

Shelton, Taylor (2011) 'The (expanded) pop vs. soda debate', Floating Sheep blog, 3 October, http://www.floatingsheep.org/2011/10/expanded-pop-vs-soda-debate.html.

Shifman, Limor (2014) *Memes*. Cambridge, MA: MIT Press.

Shirky, Clay (2010) 'The Twitter Revolution: more than just a slogan', *Prospect Magazine*, *166*, 6 January.

Silverman, Craig (2016) 'Hyperpartisan Facebook pages are publishing false and misleading information at an alarming rate', *Buzzfeed News*, 20 October.

Silverman, Matt (2013) 'Wikipedia is losing editors, but why?', *Mashable*, 8 January, http://mashable.com/2013/01/08/wikipedia-losing-editors/.

Small Media (2017) 'Filterwatch: Iranian internet infrastructure and policy report. 2016 Year in review', Small Media report, London: Small Media.

Socialistmop (2016) 'Hillary Clinton & James Comey – What difference does it make?' YouTube video, 17 October, https://www.youtube.com/watch?v=WIARMMtUdZQ.

Sottimano, Dave (2013) 'Google ccTLDs and associated languages & codes reference sheet', distilled.net, 13 December, http://www.distilled.net/blog/uncategorized/google-cctlds-and-associated-languages-codes-reference-sheet/.

Srinivasan, Ramesh (2014) 'What Tahrir Square has done for social media: A 2012 snapshot in the struggle for political power in Egypt', *The Information Society*, 30(1), 71–80.

Stamos, Alex (2017) 'An update on information operations on Facebook', Facebook Newsroom, 6 September.

Statistica (2017) 'Number of Facebook users by age in the US as of January 2017', Hamburg: Statistica.

Stevenson, Michael (2016) 'Rethinking the participatory web: A history of HotWired's "new publishing paradigm," 1994–1997', *New Media & Society*, 18(7): 1331–1346.

Stone, Biz (2010) 'Tweet preservation', *Twitter Blog*, San Francisco: Twitter, Inc., 14 April, https://blog.twitter.com/2010/tweet-preservation.

Stone, Linda (2008) 'Continuous partial attention', Lindastone.net blog post, http://lindastone.net/qa/continuous-partial-attention/.

Stutzman, Fred, Ralph Gross and Alessandro Acquisti (2013) 'Silent listeners: The evolution of privacy and disclosure on Facebook', *Journal of Privacy and Confidentiality*, 4(2), article 2.

Stvilia, Besiki, Al-Faraj, Abdullah and Yi, Yong Jeong (2009) 'Issues of cross-contextual information quality evaluation: The case of Arabic, English, and Korean Wikipedias', *Library & Information Science Research*, 31(4): 232–239.

Sullivan, Andrew (2009) 'The revolution will be Twittered', *The Atlantic*, 13 June.

Sun, Max (2012) 'Twitterverse map shows what Australians are tweeting about', *The Advertiser*, 23 May, http://www.cci.edu.au/node/1358.

Sunstein, Cass (2001) *Republic.com*. Princeton, NJ: Princeton University Press.

Surowiecki, James (2004) *The Wisdom of Crowds*. New York: Doubleday.

Swartz, Aaron (2006) 'Who writes Wikipedia?' Raw Thoughts blog, 4 September, http://www.aaronsw.com/weblog/whowriteswikipedia/.

Sysomos (2009) 'A Look at Twitter in Iran', *Sysomos* blog, 21 June, https://blog.sysomos.com/2009/06/21/a-look-at-twitter-in-iran/.

Tanash, Rima S., Chen, Zhouhan, Thakur, Tanmay, Bronk, Chris, Subramanian, Devika and Wallach, Dan S. (2015) 'Known unknowns: An analysis of Twitter censorship in Turkey', *Proceedings of WPES'15*, New York: ACM.

Terranova, Tiziana (2003) 'Free labor: Producing culture for the digital economy', *Electronic Book Review*, 20 June.

Testa, Jessica (2013) 'How the "lady in red" became Turkey's most inspiring meme', *Buzzfeed News*, 4 June.

Thelwall, Mike, Vaughan, Liwen, and Björneborn, Lennart (2005) 'Webometrics', *Annual Review of Information Science and Technology*, 39, 81–135.

Thielmann, Tristan, van der Velden, Lonneke, Fischer, Florian and Vogler, Robert (2012) 'Dwelling in the Web: Towards a Googlization of Space', HIIG Discussion Paper Series No. 2012-03, Berlin: Alexander von Humboldt Institute for Internet and Society.

Tifentale, Alise and Manovich, Lev (2015) 'Selfiecity: Exploring photography and self-fashioning in social media', in David M. Berry and Michael Dieter (eds), *Postdigital Aesthetics*. Cham: Springer, pp. 109–122.

Timberg, Craig (2017) 'Russian propaganda may have been shared hundreds of millions of times, new research says', *Washington Post*, 5 October.

Time Magazine (2006) 'Person of the year: YOU', http://content.time.com/time/covers/0,16641,20061225,00.html

Toler, Aric (2015) 'Inside the Kremlin troll army machine: Templates, guidelines, and paid posts', *GlobalVoices*, 14 March, https://globalvoices.org/2015/03/14/russia-kremlin-troll-army-examples/.

Toor, Amar (2013) 'How a "lady in red" became the symbol of Turkey's unrest', *The Verge*, 7 June.

Tran, Khoi-Nguyen, Christen, Peter, Sanner, Scott and Xie, Lexing (2015) 'Context-aware detection of sneaky vandalism on Wikipedia across multiple languages', in Tru Cao, Ee-Peng Lim, Zhi-Hua Zhou, Tu-Bao Ho, David Cheung and Hiroshi Motoda (eds), *Advances in Knowledge Discovery and Data Mining*. Cham: Springer, pp. 380–391.

Troll Academy (2017), 'Home', Milo, Inc., https://www.trollacademy.org.

Tufekci, Zeynep (2008) 'Can you see me now? Audience and disclosure regulation in online social network sites', *Bulletin of Science, Technology & Society*, 28(1): 20–36.

Tufekci, Zeynep (2017) *Twitter and Tear Gas*. New Haven, CT: Yale University Press.

Tunc, Asli (2013) 'Turkish mainstream media's mask has finally slipped', *The Conversation*, 14 June, https://theconversation.com/turkish-mainstream-medias-mask-has-finally-slipped-15187.

Tuters, Marc (2018) 'Post-truth protest: How 4chan cooked-up the Pizzagate bullshit', *M/C Journal*, *21*(3).

Turow, Joseph (2006) *Niche Envy*. Cambridge, MA: MIT Press.

Twitter (2016) 'Using hashtags on Twitter', Help Center, San Francisco, CA: Twitter, Inc., https://support.twitter.com/articles/49309.

Twitter (2017a) 'Twitter terms of service', San Francisco: Twitter, Inc., 2 October, https://twitter.com/en/tos.

Twitter (2017b) 'Twitter privacy policy', San Francisco: Twitter, Inc., 18 June, https://twitter.com/en/privacy.

Twitter (2017c) 'Twitter developer agreement & policy', San Francisco: Twitter, Inc., 18 June, https://dev.twitter.com/overview/terms/agreement-and-policy

US Centers for Disease Control and Prevention (2014) 'CDC Announces Winner of the "Predict the Influenza Season Challenge"', press release, Washington, DC: US Center for Disease Control, 18 June, http://www.cdc.gov/flu/news/predict-flu-challenge-winner.htm.

Udell, Jon (2005) 'Heavy metal umlaut', screencast documentary, http://jonudell.net/udell/2005-01-22-heavy-metal-umlaut-the-movie.html.

Upshot Staff (2014) 'The Thanksgiving recipes googled in every state', *New York Times*, 25 November.

Upworthy (2012) 'How to make that one thing go viral', Slideshare.net, 3 December, https://www.slideshare.net/Upworthy/how-to-make-that-one-thing-go-viral-just-kidding/9.

Vaidhyanathan, Siva (2011) *The Googlization of Everything*. Berkeley, CA: University of California Press.

Vaidhyanathan, Siva (2017) 'Facebook wins, democracy loses', *New York Times*, 8 September.

Van Couvering, Elizabeth (2007) 'Is relevance relevant? Market, science, and war: Discourses of search engine quality', *Journal of Computer-Mediated Communication*, *12*(3), article 6.

Van Ess, Henk (2005) 'Google Secret Lab, Prelude', Henk van Ess's Search Engine Bistro, 1 June, http://www.searchbistro.com/index.php?/archives/19-Google-Secret-Lab,-Prelude.html.

Van de Poel, Ibo (2009) 'The introduction of nanotechnology as a societal experiment', in Simone Arnaldi, Andrea Lorenzet and Federica Russo (eds), *Technoscience in Progress: Managing the Uncertainty of Nanotechnology*. Amsterdam: IOS Press, pp. 129–142.

Van der Velden, Lonneke (2012) 'The third party diary', blog, http://thirdpartydiary.net/.

Van der Velden, Lonneke (2014), 'The third party diary: Tracking the trackers on Dutch governmental websites', *NECSUS. European Journal of Media Studies*, *3*(1): 195–217.

Van Dijck, José (2009) 'Users like you? Theorizing agency in user-generated content', *Media, Culture & Society*, *31*(1): 41–58.

Van Gilder Cooke, Sonia (2011) 'Europe's right wing: A nation-by-nation guide to political parties and extremist groups', *Time Magazine*, 29 July, http://content.time.com/time/specials/packages/article/0,28804,2085728_2085727_2085712,00.html.

Varnali, Kaan and Gorgulu, Vehbi (2015) 'A social influence perspective on expressive political participation in Twitter: The case of #OccupyGezi', *Information, Communication & Society*, *18*(1): 1–16.

Venturini, Tommaso, Baya Laffite, Nicolas, Cointet, Jean-Philippe, Gray, Ian, Zabban, Vinciane and De Pryck, Kari (2014) 'Three maps and three misunderstandings: A digital mapping of climate diplomacy', *Big Data & Society*, *1*(2).

Venturini, Tommaso, Bounegru, Liliana, Jacomy, Mathieu and Gray, Jonathan (2017) 'How to tell stories with networks', in Mirko Schaefer and Karin van Es (eds), *The Datafied Society*. Amsterdam: Amsterdam University Press, pp. 155–170.

Venturini, Tommaso, Cardon, Dominique and Cointet, Jean-Philippe (2014) 'Présentation – Méthodes digitales: Approches quali/quanti des données numériques', *Réseaux*, *188*(6): 9–21.

Venturini, Tommaso, Munk, Anders and Meunier, Axel (2018) 'Data Sprint: A public approach to digital research', in Celia Lury, Patricia T. Clough, Una Chung, Rachel Fensham, Sybille Lammes, Angela Last, Mike Michael and Emma Uprichard (eds), *Routledge Handbook of Interdisciplinary Research Methods*. London: Routledge.

Veronin, Michael A. (2002) 'Where are they now? A case study of health-related Web site attrition', *Journal of Medical Internet Research*, *4*(2): e10.

Vilain, Pascal, Larrieu, Sophie, Cossin, Sébastien, Caserio-Schönemann, Céline and Filleul, Laurent (2017) 'Wikipedia: A tool to monitor seasonal diseases trends?' *Online Journal of Public Health Informatics*, *9*(1): e52.

Wall, Melissa (2015) 'Citizen journalism: A retrospective on what we know, an agenda for what we don't', *Digital Journalism*, *3*(6): 797–813.

Wall, Melissa and el Zahed, Sahar (2014) 'Syrian citizen journalism: A pop-up news ecology in an authoritarian space', *Digital Journalism*, *3*(5): 720–736.

Warncke-Wang, Morten, Uduwage, Anuradha, Dong, Zhenhua and Riedl, John (2012) 'In search of the ur-Wikipedia: Universality, similarity, and translation in the Wikipedia inter-language link network', *WikiSym '12 Proceedings*, article 20, New York: ACM.

Warzel, Charlie (2013) 'How Iran uses Wikipedia to censor the internet', *BuzzFeed*, 12 November, https://www.buzzfeed.com/charliewarzel/how-iran-uses-wikipedia-to-censor-the-internet.

Warzel, Charlie (2016) 'Twitter permanently suspends conservative writer Milo Yiannopoulos', *Buzzfeed News*, 20 July.

Watts, Duncan J. (2007) 'A twenty-first century science', *Nature*, *445*: 489.

Watters, Audrey (2011) 'How recent changes to Twitter's terms of service might hurt academic research', ReadWriteWeb blog, 3 March, https://readwrite.com/2011/03/03/how_recent_changes_to_twitters_terms_of_service_mi/.

Weaver, Matthew (2009) 'Oxfordgirl vs Ahmadinejad: the Twitter user taking on the Iranian regime', *Guardian*, 18 September.

Webb, Eugene J., Campbell, Donald T., Schwartz, Richard D. and Sechrest, Lee (1966) *Unobtrusive Measures: Nonreactive Research in the Social Sciences*. Chicago: Rand McNally.

Weltevrede, Esther and Borra, Erik (2016) 'Platform affordances and data practices: The value of dispute on Wikipedia', *Big Data & Society*, *3*(1).

Wemple, Erik (2016) 'NYT editor Jonathan Weisman blasts Twitter over anti-Semitic trolling', *Washington Post*, 8 June.

Werbin, Kenneth C., Lipton, Mark and Bowman, Matthew J. (2017) 'The contextual integrity of the closet: Privacy, data mining and outing Facebook's algorithmic logics', *Queer Studies in Media & Popular Culture*, *2*(1): 29–47.

Whitford, Troy and Prunckun, Henry (2017) 'Discreet, not covert: Reflections on teaching intelligence analysis in a non-government setting', *Salus Journal*, *5*(1): 48–61.

Whitlinger, Claire (2011) 'From countermemory to collective memory: Acknowledging the "Mississippi Burning" murders', *Sociological Forum*, *30*(S1): 648–670.

Wikimedia (2010) 'An appeal from Wikipedia founder Jimmy Wales', Wikimedia, https://wikimediafoundation.org/wiki/Appeal17/en.

Wikimedia (2011) 'From Wikipedia founder Jimmy Wales', Wikimedia Foundation, https://wikimediafoundation.org/wiki/Keep_Wikipedia_Free.

Wikimedia Contributors (2018) 'What is a troll?', Wikimedia Meta-Wiki, https://meta.wikimedia.org/w/index.php?title=What_is_a_troll%3F&oldid=17543718.

Wikipedia Contributors (2014) 'Computing platform', Wikipedia, the Free Encyclopedia, article, 27 January, https://en.wikipedia.org/w/index.php?title=Computing_platform&oldid=592679632.

Wikipedia Contributors (2018a) 'Twitter revolution', Wikipedia, the Free Encyclopedia, article, 22 January, https://en.wikipedia.org/w/index.php?title=Twitter_Revolution&oldid=817942935.

Wikipedia Contributors (2018b) 'Wikipedia: Featured article criteria', Wikipedia, the Free Encyclopedia, article, 22 January, https://en.wikipedia.org/w/index.php?title=Wikipedia:Featured_article_criteria&oldid=766263132.

Wikipedia Contributors (2018c) 'Wikipedia: Neutral point of view', Wikipedia, the Free Encyclopedia, article, 22 January, https://en.wikipedia.org/w/index.php?title=Wikipedia:Neutral_point_of_view&oldid=820289964.

Wikipedia Contributors (2018d) 'Wikipedia: Systemic bias', Wikipedia, the Free Encyclopedia, article, 22 January, https://en.wikipedia.org/w/index.php?title=Wikipedia:Systemic_bias&oldid=821195348.

Williams, Raymond (1975) *Keywords: A Vocabulary of Culture and Society*. London: Fontana.

Wilton, Dave (2003) 'Word of the month: Usenet', Wordorigins.org, 1 June, http://www.wordorigins.org/index.php/site/comments/word_of_the_month_usenet/.

Woodruff, Andy (2011) 'Web cartography, or putting things on top of other things', andywoodruff.com, 9 June, http://andywoodruff.com/blog/web-cartography-or-putting-things-on-top-of-other-things/.

Woolgar, Steve (ed.) (2003) *Virtual Society? Technology, Cyberbole, Reality*. New York: Oxford University Press.

Wright, Joss (2014) 'Regional variation in Chinese internet filtering', *Information, Communication & Society*. *17*(1), 121–141.

Wright, Joss, de Souza, Tulio and Brown, Ian (2011) 'Fine-grained censorship mapping: Information sources, legality and ethics', *FOCI'11* (USENIX Security Symposium), San Francisco, 8 August.

Yaman, Alev (2014) *The Gezi Park Protests*. London: English PEN.

Yang, Fan (2016) 'Rethinking China's internet censorship: The practice of recoding and the politics of visibility', *New Media & Society*, *18*(7): 1364–1381.

Yasseri, Taha, Spoerri, Anselm, Graham, Mark and Kertész, János (2014) 'The most controversial topics in Wikipedia: A multilingual and geographical analysis', in Pnina Fichman and Noriko Hara (eds), *Global Wikipedia: International and Cross-Cultural Issues in Online Collaboration*. Lanham, MD: Rowman & Littlefield, pp. 25–48.

Ying, Miao and Yahyanejad, Mehdi (2017) 'Narrative documentation', *21:33*, 22 April, https://rhizome.org/editorial/2017/apr/21/seven-on-seven-2017/.

Zachte, Erik (2015) 'Wikimedia traffic analysis report – Google requests', Wikimedia Statistics, http://stats.wikimedia.org/wikimedia/squids/SquidReportGoogle.htm.

Zimmer, Michael (2008) 'More on the "anonymity" of the Facebook dataset – it's Harvard College', Michaelzimmer.org blog, 3 October, http://michaelzimmer.org/2008/10/03/moreon-the-anonymity-of-the-facebook-dataset-its-harvard-college/

Zimmer, Michael (2010a) 'But the data is already public: On the ethics of research in Facebook', *Ethics and Information Technology*, *12*(4): 313–325.

Zimmer, Michael (2010b) 'Is it ethical to harvest public Twitter accounts without consent?' *Michael Zimmer blog*, 12 February, http://www.michaelzimmer.org/2010/02/12/is-it-ethical-to-harvest-public-twitter-accounts-without-consent/.

Zimmer, Michael (2015) 'The Twitter Archive at the Library of Congress: Challenges for information practice and information policy', *First Monday*, *20*(7).

Zimmer, Michael and Proferes, Nicholas John (2014) 'A topology of Twitter research: Disciplines, methods, and ethics', *Aslib Journal of Information Management*, *66*(3): 250–261.

Zuckerman, Ethan (2011) 'The first Twitter revolution?', *Foreign Policy*, 15 January.

INDEX

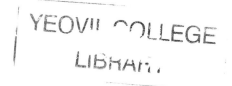